MODERN PREVENTION

Other books by Dr. Rosenfeld

The Complete Medical Exam
Second Opinion

MODERN PREVENTION

THE NEW MEDICINE

Isadore Rosenfeld, M.D.

BANTAM BOOKS

TORONTO · NEW YORK · LONDON · SYDNEY · AUCKLAND

MODERN PREVENTION

*A Bantam Book / in association with
Linden Press / September 1987*

PRINTING HISTORY

Linden Press edition published April 1986

*Metropolitan Height and Weight Tables courtesy of the
Metropolitan Life Insurance Company.*

Library of Congress Cataloging-in-Publication Data

Rosenfeld, Isadore.
  Modern prevention.

  Reprint. Originally published: New York : Linden
Press/Simon & Schuster, c1986.
  Includes index.
  1. Medicine, Preventive—Popular works. 2. Health.
I. Title. [DNLM: 1. Health Promotion—popular works.
2. Preventive Medicine—popular works. WA 108 R813m 1986a]
RA431.R84 1987   613   87-47557
ISBN 0-553-34460-9 (pbk.)

Published simultaneously in the United States and Canada

Bantam Books are published by Bantam Books, Inc. Its
*trademark, consisting of the words "Bantam Books" and the
portrayal of a rooster, is Registered in U.S. Patent and Trademark Office and in other countries. Marca Registrada. Bantam
Books, Inc., 666 Fifth Avenue, New York, New York 10103.*

PRINTED IN CANADA

WC   0 9 8 7 6 5 4 3 2 1

For my Camilla

Contents

MODERN PREVENTION

CHAPTER 1

Modern Prevention—The New Medicine

The best-kept medical secret of the eighties is that prevention works. It's the newest field in medicine—one in which the specialist is the patient, not the doctor. The diagnosis and treatment of diseases once they've set in are your doctor's job, but only *you* can prevent illness from occurring in the first place.

Artificial hearts, organ transplants, laser beams—these and other dramatic advances in medicine capture the imagination and make news headlines. As wonderful and important as they are, they are only stopgap measures in the fight for life. In following the saga of a patient with the heart of a baboon or an artificial cardiac device, it is easy to lose sight of the really important progress that has been made in the field of prevention. For there is a vast amount of new information that can help avoid, delay or reduce the risk of contracting those terrible afflictions for which there are still no cures.

Why Doctors Don't Talk

Despite this great potential for prevention, many practicing doctors are not doing enough to educate their patients to the facts.

There are several reasons for this inertia on the part of the medical profession. Doctors are basically disease-oriented. Your education is not their major concern. Then there is the matter of economics. An office visit usually commands a set fee regardless of whether the doctor spends five minutes with you or thirty. So an "in-depth" talking session is not cost-effective for him.* In the real world, his time is "better" spent doing something for which he is paid extra, like taking an electrocardiogram or a chest X ray, lancing a boil, performing blood tests, removing an eyelash from your eye—anything physical at all. But it has to be more than just talk.

If you have any doubt about doctors' priorities, try the following. Call a medical office and tell the receptionist you are feeling perfectly well, want to stay that way, but would like to see the doctor anyway to discuss "prevention." Five will get you ten that she will (a) turn you down flat with "I am sorry, the doctor is too busy," or (b) schedule you several weeks hence, and then cancel you at the last minute to make room for someone who "really needs the appointment."

It's Your Fault Too

Doctors' attitudes are not the only reason prevention takes a back seat in the scheme of things. Most patients are uncomfortable calling their doctors just for routine evaluation. They think it's more appropriate to wait until they're sick. I have known intelligent individuals who feel guilty, and even apologize, for having "wasted" my time after receiving a clean bill of health. "I'm so sorry, doctor. You could have been looking after someone with a problem."

There is also the matter of cost. Office visits for "no reason" are at least as expensive as when you're sick. In fact, they may cost more, because when you're well and the doctor has no specific diagnostic target, he may do test after test, just searching for "something." And that costs money.

Most people either can't afford to or are unwilling to spend money to discuss prevention, even when their doctor is prepared to do so. They often resent being charged just for "information." I remember one woman complaining to me about another doctor's fee. ("Imagine sending me a bill like that. All he did was talk with me. He didn't do

* Throughout this book, whenever I refer to "doctor," I mean "he or she." To make the text less clumsy, I will use the female designation in some chapters, the male in others.

anything!'') Finally, most insurance companies won't pay for just a "checkup." They will not reimburse you unless the doctor writes a diagnosis, any diagnosis, on the insurance form. You've got to be sick to collect what you spent; learning about prevention from your doctor in the course of a routine health-maintenance exam is apparently not worthy of any compensation!

Fun Today or Survival Tomorrow?

Some patients resent being "lectured" to and then charged for it—especially if they don't like what they've been told. Believe it or not, they prefer a more impersonal, technical relationship in which the necessary tests are done and medication prescribed. They'd rather not be nagged about diet, exercise, cholesterol levels, fitness, drinking and smoking. They feel they know it all, and will "behave" only when they're good and ready to do so. They don't need or want the doctor to keep scolding them—especially when it costs money.

At my barber's the other day, I overheard a "shave" telling a "haircut" about his recent medical visit. "This doctor is some kind of health nut. I went there just to have him check my blood pressure, and he started this long lecture about my weight, my diet and the stress I am under. That's not why I consulted him. All I wanted was to have my blood pressure read and for him to give me a pill. I was there for twenty-five minutes, instead of the five it should have taken —and he charged me for every second. Some of these doctors really take advantage of a guy." I suspect that what really bothered this man was not so much the charges but his guilt at not complying with the advice offered. Therein lies one of the problems with effective prevention. It may spoil today's "fun" in exchange for tomorrow's survival.

The Big Rip-off

Nature abhors a vacuum. Because doctors are not providing patients with enough solid, practical information about prevention, the public is looking for and finding it elsewhere—in mail-order advertisements, in magazines and on television talk shows. Unfortunately, the legitimate data are often lumped together with pitches for countless health fads, diets and longevity regimens, many of which are worthless, and some of which are dangerous. It's not always easy for the layman to distinguish between fact and fancy.

The net result, in my opinion, is a multibillion-dollar rip-off. For example, *Psychology Today,* a respected lay publication widely read in this country, revealed the results of a survey to which twenty-five thousand of its subscribers responded. Six percent were into herbal cures, 10 percent were on fasting or "imaging" regimens, and 11 percent were taking megavitamin "treatments"—all largely nonsensical nostrums. Advertisements everywhere challenge you with lines like "Want to be healthy and live a long life?" If you do (and who doesn't?), you're offered chelation, homeopathy, acupuncture, "clinical ecology," "stress reduction" or "nutritional therapy," the majority of which are either speculative and unproven or sheer quackery.

How Prevention Can Work

There is no reason for you to depend on any of the fad approaches. Following are some examples of how the new and tested knowledge in the field of prevention can work for you.

A forty-year-old woman was referred to me for diagnosis by a general practitioner in upstate New York. He was worried about her because she had been running a low-grade fever, on and off, for about three weeks. Interestingly enough, the patient denied feeling sick and was puzzled by all the fuss. Her appetite was good, she hadn't lost any weight, and she didn't have an ache or pain anywhere.

A physician can often tell simply by looking at a patient whether or not there is a real problem. At first glance, I was almost tempted to agree with this woman when she asked, "Don't you think my doctor is overreacting? All I've got is a stubborn virus that will go away in its own good time." And then she added, "Please, doctor, keep your tests to a minimum. I can't afford a fancy work-up."

However, as we reviewed her past medical history, she did remember (after I specifically asked) that when she was very young she frequently had "growing pains." Her knees and elbows would become swollen and hurt for weeks at a time. Yes, now that I mentioned it, she did recall that from time to time she had been told that she had a heart murmur. But her doctors were never concerned about it because they couldn't always hear it, and besides, she was generally so healthy and full of energy.

Three Cardinal Clues to One Diagnosis

In the course of my physical exam, there was a triad of ominous clues. (1) Her temperature was elevated to 101°; (2) she did indeed have a heart murmur; and (3) under the nails of two of her fingers I observed what looked like little wooden splinters. These findings added up to the diagnosis of subacute bacterial endocarditis (SBE)— infection of a heart valve, which is often fatal if untreated. (The "splinters" were actually tiny hemorrhages from very small blood vessels in the fingers and toes. We do not know why this bleeding occurs in SBE. But, remember, never coat the nails of your fingers and toes with polish when you go for a checkup. You may be concealing vital evidence.)

Just an Innocent Visit to the Dentist

Because I was almost certain that the murmur was due to a "bad" heart valve, I asked this patient a key question. "Have you been to a dentist recently?" (During almost any dental procedure, especially one in which the gums are made to bleed, otherwise harmless bacteria that are normally present in the mouth enter the bloodstream and lodge on one or more of the heart valves that happen to be diseased, usually by rheumatic fever. This does not happen to normal valves.)

"Yes, about two months ago, but only to have my teeth cleaned. There was no dental work done—no drilling or anything like that." As far as she was concerned, maintenance dentistry, in which the teeth are vigorously denuded of tartar, and the gums usually bleed, doesn't count as "dental work." She had also never told her dentist anything about a heart murmur.

The diagnosis of SBE was confirmed when streptococcus viridans, the bacterium responsible for most such cases, was found in the blood culture I had sent to the bacteriology lab. I arranged for the patient to enter the hospital, where she was given massive intravenous doses of antibiotics. Five weeks later she was discharged, completely cured. Had she not been treated (or had she contracted her SBE prior to 1945, before the availability of penicillin), she probably would have died. The infection might have gone on to destroy the affected valve, cause heart failure, or propagate tiny clots from the bacterial clumps on the valve cusps to seed other parts of the body, resulting in abscesses in such vital organs as the brain or kidneys.

A Little Prevention Goes a Long Way

This case of SBE is an excellent example of a serious, potentially fatal disease that still occurs thousands of times each year in this country, even though it is preventable. And prevention is so simple. It doesn't require a lifetime of dieting, or even giving up some bad but enjoyable habit. All one has to do is take the right antibiotic (usually penicillin or erythromycin) prophylactically when undergoing dental work, or any kind of surgery or "invasive testing" in which a diagnostic instrument is introduced into the body. This lady did not have that basic information, the lack of which nearly took her life, put her in the hospital for five weeks and cost almost $20,000. Of course, she now knows that she is vulnerable to SBE, and you may be sure she'll never let any dentist do anything in her mouth without also prescribing antibiotics.

A Cancer That Could Have Been Prevented

A previously healthy young man of twenty-four, single, a computer technologist, came to see me because he couldn't shake a dry cough that had been bothering him for the past few weeks. The very first question I ask anyone who has a persistent cough is "Do you smoke?"

He did not.

"Have you had any fever?"

"I don't think so, but I have no thermometer at home."

"Do you bring anything up when you cough?"

"Just a tiny amount of white phlegm, sometimes. Never any blood."

"Are you allergic?"

"No, sir, I'm not." Nor had he ever been exposed in his work to any toxic fumes or chemicals that might have injured his lungs. The only worrisome symptoms he volunteered, in addition to the cough, were some loss of appetite (he had dropped five or six pounds in the last month) and a slight gnawing pain low down in the left side of his abdomen. His bowel movements were regular and normal—as usual. He had no complaints about his sex life either, which he described as "great."

The Case of the Missing Testicle

When I listened to his chest with my stethoscope, his lungs sounded clear. I couldn't feel any lumps in his belly or anywhere else. But I did notice that his left testicle was missing from the scrotum—a phenomenon that occurs when the testicle sometimes fails to "descend" into the sac. Was this only an incidental finding or was it a vital clue? Had he known about it? Yes, but he had been told it was nothing to worry about, and that it would not affect his sex drive, performance or fertility.

Cannonballs in the Lungs

Although I had planned a systematic series of tests, we hit diagnostic pay dirt right off the bat with the chest X ray. There, to my dismay, were several little round shadows, the size of marbles, in both lungs. I had seen enough of these "cannonballs" over the years to know that they indicated cancer that had spread to the lungs from elsewhere in the body. But what was their source? The logical place to look was somewhere in the abdomen, since that was the only other area where this young man had any symptoms. So we sent him for an abdominal sonogram (in which sound waves are directed at the belly and the returning echoes identify any abnormal growths or fluid). The result? A mass, or growth, the size of a walnut, lying in the abdominal cavity. This was easily removed at surgery and analyzed.

The Importance of Getting into the Sac

What do you think it was? The missing testicle! It had remained in the abdomen all those years since birth, instead of descending into the scrotal sac where it belonged. And during that time, it had become cancerous. But since it was "undescended" and not on the outside where it could be examined with the fingers, its malignant transformation was not detected until it had spread to the lungs.

Although testicular cancer is not among the most common tumors overall, it is an important problem in young men. When a testis fails to descend, the likelihood of it becoming malignant is significantly increased. Why this is so is not clear. The higher temperature to which it is subject when it remains within the body cavity rather than moving down into the external scrotal sac may have something to do with it. In any event, what's important is the fact that when the absence of a testis is noted in an infant, there is a surgical timetable for its management that is crucial if one is to prevent cancer. That schedule is described in Chapter 23.

This particular story has a happy ending. Cancer is usually fatal by the time it has spread anywhere, especially to the lungs. But testicular tumors are different. Most of them can be cured by a combination of radiation and newer drugs (chemotherapy), even after they have traveled (metastasized) to other parts of the body. And that's what happened with this young man. But he could have been spared enormous pain and worry had his parents been aware of the simple cardinal rules of prevention demanded by his circumstance.

The Silent Killer—Also Preventable

Here's a classic example of how prevention might well have saved a life. Ted was a sixty-five-year-old film producer with a long history of high blood pressure. He refused any treatment to lower it because he felt so well, as many persons with hypertension do. He loved life and wanted to live it to its fullest, without side effects from medication. Then one day, several years after the diagnosis was made, he developed a hemorrhage deep inside his right eye, and lost its vision. Having learned his lesson the hard way, and terrified about becoming blind in the other eye, he now accepted the medication I prescribed.

Of Rhythms and Clots

All went well for three or four years. Then one day, in the course of a routine exam, I found his pulse to be abnormal. It was very irregular and rapid in a rhythm we call atrial fibrillation. Although this arrhythmia usually reflects some form of underlying heart disease (arteriosclerotic, valvular, hypertensive, or an overactive thyroid gland), it may also occur in otherwise normal individuals. Ted was unaware of his irregular heart rhythm as such patients often are. Atrial fibrillation usually requires treatment with two kinds of drugs —digitalis, to slow the heart rate, and an anticoagulant, to prevent a clot from forming in the fibrillating heart and traveling to some vital organ like the brain. I explained this to Ted, who, just as he had once refused to take pills for his elevated blood pressure, now also rejected the "blood thinner." He did not want the bother or responsibility of having his blood tested at regular intervals, which is necessary to make sure the anticoagulant dosage is correct. Also, he disliked "on principle" the idea of his blood being thinned.

I pleaded and cajoled. I even sent him excerpts from the medical literature documenting the importance of anticoagulants in atrial fibrillation. It was all to no avail. Finally, he put it to me very frankly. "Doctor, either you lay off pressuring me about anticoagulants or I won't come back." I wouldn't and he didn't. Four months later, he was admitted to a hospital in a coma, and he died within forty-eight hours. A large blood clot had suddenly made its way from his heart to a critical area of his brain. His death might well have been prevented had he simply taken one small anticoagulant tablet every morning.

The Bottom Line

As I mentioned at the very outset, the diagnosis and treatment of diseases are your doctor's main concerns. Prevention, learning what to do to *stay* healthy, is *your* responsibility. You must *think* prevention, *act* prevention and *know* all about prevention. No one can or will do that for you. Sure, as a cardiologist, I can treat your angina or send you for bypass surgery if you need it. But *you* must learn how to stop your arteries from clogging up in the first place. Almost any good orthopedist can fix your fractured hip, but *you* can prevent your bones from becoming brittle and breakable. Any neurologist can diagnose your stroke once you become paralyzed, but *you* now have access to the information that can prevent it from happening. A good surgeon can remove your cancerous breast, or bowel, or lung or thyroid. Only *you* can take those measures necessary to reduce the likelihood of these malignancies from developing.

If you take advantage and act on all the information available *right now,* you are virtually certain to enjoy a longer, healthier life. In the pages that follow, you will find most of what you need to know in order to do just that. You will learn not only how to thwart the major killers like heart disease and cancer, which shorten life, but also how to prevent such everyday medical problems as deafness, blindness, insomnia, seasickness, birth defects, kidney stones, osteoporosis and many others that impair its quality.

This book covers a wide spectrum of disorders that can be prevented in one way or another or modified—if you know the facts. Do not refer only to those in which you are particularly interested, or to which you think you are especially prone. Prevention, like life, is a continuum. Of course you should pay special attention to what you believe most applies to you, but I recommend you read straight through. The disease about which you know the *least* may one day threaten you most.

CHAPTER 2

Colds, Influenza and Pneumonia— All Common and Often Preventable

The common cold, flu and pneumonia represent a spectrum of upper-respiratory diseases responsible for much human misery. The most frequent forms of *pneumonia and the flu can be prevented*, and even a cold is more avoidable than most people think.

If you're like most Americans, you probably come down with a cold two or three times a year. Children may have as many as ten or twelve. As a result, the common cold is responsible for more visits to doctors in this country than any other malady. (Headache is number two.) Personally, I have found that my own patients are often too embarrassed to consult me for "just a cold." Most treat themselves with homespun or over-the-counter remedies, and feel better in a day or two. But if they run a fever for longer than two or three days, they begin to worry that they may really have the flu or even pneumonia and not just a simple cold. It's then that they come to see me.

Although the common cold contributes more than its share to mankind's malaise, it is not usually a serious medical event. During each siege, our noses either run or are stuffed up, we cough, spit, and sneeze, we ache all over, we've got no energy and we lose time from work or school; national productivity suffers in the billions of dollars annually. During each siege, we consume gallons of tea and fruit juice, megadoses of vitamin C (as a result of which Americans have the most expensive urine in the world), antihistamines by the score, pints of cough syrup, countless aspirins, and we wallow in used, soiled tissues. How is it, then, given all our medical and technical sophistication, which has made it possible to install human hearts, artificial hearts and baboon hearts, to exchange kidneys, knees, hips and shoulders, and even to make flaccid penises erect again with implants, that we cannot conquer the common cold virus? Why, having eradicated smallpox, controlled polio, developed vaccines to protect us against twenty-three different kinds of pneumonia, hepatitis B and influenza, is there still no prophylaxis against a cold? The answer is simple, even if the solution is not. It's because a cold may be due to any one of three hundred or more different viruses, and the number is constantly increasing due to their mutation. So even if we were able to make a single vaccine, it would not be effective against so many different and ever-changing agents.

Cold viruses gain access to the body through the mucous membrane (lining) of the eyes, nose and mouth. Whether or not they end up giving you symptoms depends on how many actually get in, and the state of your body's defenses or resistance if they do. Generally speaking, the ability to ward off a cold is determined in large part by the antibody level from previous "experience" with a particular virus. Antibodies, special proteins produced in response to viral infection, attack and destroy the invader. Over the years, the body comes to possess many such antibodies as a result of repeated challenges by several different cold viruses. That explains why the older you get, the fewer colds you have. Children are more vulnerable because they have not yet developed a sufficient number and variety of viral antibodies.

Despite the fact that researchers have not yet been able to make an anti-cold vaccine, there is one preventive agent of promise on the horizon—an antiviral substance called interferon. (Interferon may also prevent or modify hepatitis and herpes, as well as certain forms of cancer—breast, melanoma, lymphoma, leukemia.)

In a series of experiments in England, millions of cold viruses were instilled into the nostrils of healthy volunteers. Most of those who were pretreated with placebo developed colds, as expected. However, when cotton pledgets soaked in interferon were inserted in the nose, the cold never materialized. Since interferon can now be made abundantly and inexpensively, thanks to genetic engineering, it probably won't be long before we'll all be taking it in one form or another to prevent catching cold. At the moment, however, it is still experimental and available only under special circumstances. We've yet to decide over what period of time the interferon should be given, in what dosage and by what route. It's hardly feasible to have all of America going about its business with its collective nose filled with cotton pledgets resoaked in interferon solution every few hours.

For now, prevention of the common cold centers around common sense, and an understanding of how colds are transmitted.

"Take Two Tylenols and Call Me in the Morning"

Some time ago, one of my friends called to ask a very special favor. His three-year-old son was suffering from a very bad cold, coughing, all stuffed up and running a temperature of 102°. His wife had called their pediatrician, who assured her that children with colds often have high fevers and that her little boy's symptoms were all "par for the course." He prescribed lots of fluids, and for the fever and aches and pains, acetaminophen (Tylenol). He warned against using aspirin because of the suspicion that it may cause Reye's disease, a serious neurological disorder, when given to children with viral illnesses. "Call me in the morning if there is no improvement," he suggested.

"You mean you are not going to see my son for twenty-four hours even though he has a fever of one hundred and two degrees?" the mother asked incredulously.

"Yes, I'm sorry. But if you are very anxious about it, why don't you dress him warmly and bring him down to the office by car or taxi?"

Both parents were astonished and angry at this callous advice. "Are you actually suggesting, doctor, that I take this terribly sick child outdoors with a raging fever?"

"Only if it will make *you* feel any better to have him seen today," he replied. "I'd come to your house if I could, but I have an office full of kids with the very same symptoms. There is a lot of it going around these days."

The distraught mother hung up and prevailed upon her husband to call me. I responded out of friendship and not because I felt that I could improve on the pediatrician's recommendations.

When I arrived at their home, I found the child in bed, watching television, all stuffed up and coughing. His night table and bedclothes were littered with soiled tissues. Every few minutes, his mother or father would pick up a virus-laden Kleenex and use it for one more wipe. During the forty-five minutes I was there neither parent washed his or her hands, and from time to time they casually rubbed their eyes and noses. However, after *I* examined the child, I washed my hands thoroughly and never touched a used tissue.

The youngster recovered fully within thirty-six hours. I never caught cold at all. But both parents did! (They've also changed pediatricians three times in the last two years, all for the same reason— failure to respond to an "emergency.")

"Kiss Me but Don't Shake My Hand"

You may be surprised to learn that the most important route by which colds are transmitted is the hands. My friends caught their colds by contaminating their fingers with the virus-filled tissues with which they had repeatedly wiped their child's nose and mouth. Instead of throwing these tissues away after a single use, they economized and left them lying around for yet another blow. In so doing, they transferred the viral particles to their hands, and then to their eyes, noses or mouths. Of course, you don't have to be nursing someone to catch his or her cold. If the cold sufferer sneezes or wipes his nose, gets some of the infective mucus on his hands, then shakes yours, you will inoculate yourself with the virus when you rub your eyes or nose.

Patients often wonder why doctors don't catch cold more often than they do, given their frequent exposure. To some extent, it's because of the antibodies they've built up over the years. However, I think the fact that they wash their hands so frequently also has a great deal to do with it. You should too. Also, dispose of soiled tissues promptly and don't lend a used handkerchief to anyone. If someone in your home has a cold, ask him to use his own towels, dishes and utensils until he's over it. (Interestingly, a specially treated tissue that its makers claim can destroy the cold virus on contact is currently being tested. It is expected to be marketed under the trade name Avert. If it really works, it may go a long way toward reducing the spread of colds.)

In addition to hand transmission, the cold virus can, of course, infect you by the aerosol route. When the patient coughs or sneezes, the spray containing droplets of varying sizes travels for about six feet, after which the particles fall harmlessly to the ground. If you're standing close by while the virus is still airborne, you will inhale it. Larger droplets are more contagious than smaller ones, but they do not remain suspended in the air as long. But both can give you a whopping cold!

Here is the bottom line. Just sitting around for a couple of hours in the company of someone who has a cold is not likely to infect you unless he or she repeatedly coughs or sneezes directly into your face. Going to the theater during the "cold season" is not especially risky either. Practically speaking, you'd have to spend the better part of a day in really close contact with an infected individual in order to be at substantial risk of catching his or her cold. Touching hands, tissues, utensils and other contaminated objects constitutes a more important route of infection.

Fact, Myth and Speculation

Will vitamin C prevent the common cold? There is no doubt that most Americans believe it does. But the scientific community, with the exception of the persistent and indefatigable Dr. Linus Pauling, does not for the most part agree. Despite the official anti-vitamin-C position of "organized" medicine, almost every doctor I know, including myself, regularly takes it, and increases the dose at the earliest evidence of a cold. But I doubt that many of them consume the megadoses—20,000, 30,000 and even 40,000 units a day—recommended by Dr. Pauling. So he continues to insist that we have no right to dispute his claims about the efficacy of vitamin C since we are not using it in adequate doses. Although the hard evidence for vitamin C *preventing* the common cold is still in question, there are some studies suggesting that it actually does reduce the severity of symptoms once they have appeared.

I would like to be able to tell you that cigarette smokers are at greater risk for catching cold than are nonsmokers. This is apparently not so. But, before you light up again, you should know that when a smoker does come down with a cold, symptoms are apt to be more severe and last longer than they do in nonsmokers.

There is no evidence to suggest that any particular diet will prevent you from catching cold once you've been exposed. But what about chicken soup? I don't know of any statistics that indicate that Jews have fewer colds than do other ethnic groups, even though they consume the largest quantities of chicken soup on the advice of their collective grandmothers. Nevertheless, studies done in Miami and subsequently confirmed by researchers at the Mayo Clinic suggest that chicken soup does reduce the severity of symptoms. And it's apparently not just the hot vapor from the soup itself, because steam does not have the same effect. Although the mysterious beneficial ingredient has not yet been isolated, the Mount Sinai Medical Center in Miami is selling cans of its very own chicken soup in its gift shop. Rumor has it they may go national!

What about stress? There is no proof that being emotionally upset, or feeling very tired, will make you more vulnerable to catching cold. However, regular exercise may offer protection, probably by increasing blood flow (and therefore greater numbers of antibodies) to the lining of the nose and respiratory passages. And that's where the virus tries to gain entry. But in order to be protective, exercise must be *regular* and ongoing. A sudden workout after symptoms have set in isn't going to help. At that point, you need rest—not exercise.

Will you catch cold if you become wet and chilled? Surprisingly, the answer is no. The chill is a symptom, not a cause. By the time you've experienced it, you're already infected.

Once You've Caught a Cold

Should you take antibiotics for a simple cold? Will they prevent major complications? In most cases, again the answer is no, because antibiotics do not have antiviral activity. But the cold virus leaves the lining of the respiratory passages swollen, boggy and irritated, and more vulnerable to penetration by any bacteria in the area. Such bacterial "super-infection" is most likely to occur in children, who often develop ear trouble, and the elderly, in whom the consequences are pneumonia or bronchitis. Since antibiotics can kill bacteria, they are often prescribed to prevent such "secondary" infection. I recommend them if the cold hangs on for more than a week, or is accompanied by a fever of 101° for more than twenty-four hours. However, antibiotics may be more trouble than they're worth in a run-of-the-mill, uncomplicated, simple cold of short duration in young, healthy persons.

What can you realistically do to shorten the course of your cold, prevent its spread and minimize its complications? If at all possible, stay home for a day or two, especially if you're feeling poorly. This will at least reduce the chances of infecting someone else. If you're coughing and sneezing, wear a disposable mask when others are around.

I don't think it makes any difference whether you "feed" your cold or "starve" it. Eat if you're hungry and don't if you're not. But do drink plenty of fluids to help liquefy secretions. If your nose is stuffy or running, use over-the-counter nasal decongestants in spray form. They are more effective than the oral preparations. But be sure to check with your doctor before taking any of these products if you have high blood pressure, diabetes, thyroid trouble or some form of heart disease. Men with enlarged prostate glands may have trouble emptying their bladders as a result of the antihistamine present in many of these compounds. If you have a nagging cough, buy an over-the-counter preparation with dextromethorphan rather than codeine (the former is as effective and less constipating). You may use aspirin if you are an adult, but don't give it to children because of the possible association of aspirin with Reye's disease; for them, use acetaminophen (Tylenol or Datril). You should see your doctor if you spit up any blood, if your temperature stays above 101° for more than twenty-four hours, if the cold persists for more than seven days, if you develop pain in the chest on breathing or coughing, if your ears begin to hurt, if your throat gets very sore or if you have difficulty swallowing.

Finally, be philosophical and practical about it all. Exploit all your symptoms to your best advantage. If you know how to do it, you will generate lots of sympathy and tender, loving care. Breakfast in bed, a couple of days out of school or work, lots of time to read and relax, aren't all that bad, are they?

Preventing the Flu

Every September, without fail, patients begin calling my office to ask "Will there be a flu epidemic this year?" and "Should I be vaccinated?" My answer to the first question will be "Yes" or "No" (depending on the reports issued that year by the Centers for Disease Control). In response to "Should I be vaccinated?" I almost always say "Yes," because there's enough flu around for you to catch at all times, whether or not there is an epidemic. As a matter of fact, anywhere from ten thousand to twenty thousand people die from flu complications every year in the United States. When an epidemic does strike, that number climbs to almost forty thousand.

Influenza is a respiratory infection caused by any one of several viruses that are always "mutating," or changing (hence the constant need to identify the prevalent strain and modify the vaccine when necessary). The flu we usually encounter in this country is due to two major classes of virus—influenza A (the more common) and B. Both A and B viruses themselves consist of several strains, usually named after the area in which they were first recognized (Hong Kong, Russia, Bangkok, Philippines). The vaccines in use protect against both influenza A and B.

Clinically, flu resembles a bad cold, except that the fever is higher and the patient is sicker. Healthy young persons usually recover uneventfully, but "high-risk" individuals may develop serious complications, which can result in prolonged illness or even death.

Here are the latest "official" designations as to who is at special risk and should therefore be vaccinated: (1) Those with chronic heart and/or lung disease, diabetes, anemia, cancer under treatment (when resistance is apt to be low), kidney or liver trouble. (2) Anyone over sixty-five years of age. (3) Individuals working in the health-care field (that includes everyone from doctors to orderlies) who come in contact with patients to whom they can spread influenza or by whom they themselves can become infected. I also include pregnant women in their last trimester.

If the shot is good for high-risk individuals, why not just give it to everyone? The "authorities" offer two reasons. It costs too much, and what's more, the disease itself confers a more lasting and effective immunity than does the vaccine. So, according to them, if you are young, healthy, and so not likely to die from complications of the flu, and if your job would not be jeopardized by time lost from work, vaccination is not really necessary.

In my opinion, these are specious rationalizations. Widespread vaccination might save up to forty thousand lives per year. That's worth the cost, as far as I'm concerned. Also, recent statistical data indicate that the protection conferred by an influenza shot, even to the strong and healthy, results in less illness and fewer days lost from work. That may be why "officialdom" has relented, so that now *anyone* who wants the vaccine should have it, provided there is enough to first take care of those at high risk. Unfortunately, no more than 10 percent of all Americans, and a mere 20 percent of those at risk, are vaccinated each year. They are not offered it, or can't afford it, or refuse to accept it.

Can a Flu Shot Give You the Flu?

Let me tell you what happened to one of my patients a few years ago. Mrs. Jones, a sixty-eight-year-old woman, came for her annual checkup one October day. When we were through, I determined that she had two important problems—angina pectoris and chronic bronchitis, both mild. She was no longer smoking cigarettes, but she had for many years. I suggested that she be vaccinated because of her age, her heart trouble and her lung condition—all of which placed her in the high-risk category. But she balked. "Doctor, it may be good for most people, but I'd rather not have the shot. I don't mean to disagree with you and I hope you won't be angry, but I'd sooner take my chances getting the flu than be vaccinated. About three years ago, another doctor persuaded me to have the shot. The very next day I came down with the worst flu I've ever had. I swear that that vaccination gave it to me. So never again!"

She would not change her mind. She was convinced that the flu vaccine was dangerous and so she joined the ranks of the vulnerable majority of Americans who are unvaccinated and unprotected against influenza.

Mrs. Jones left the office with an appointment to see me again in three months when I would check on her angina and bronchitis. However, a couple of weeks later, she called to tell me she was very sick. She had had a "cold" for a couple of days, and had treated herself with the usual measures—aspirin, fluids and cough medicine.

But instead of improving within forty-eight hours, as she usually did, she had become progressively worse. Her temperature was now 102°, she ached all over, her cough was more troublesome and she had shaking chills every few hours.

Later that evening, I stopped by her apartment. My bedside examination left little doubt that Mrs. Jones not only had the flu but that it was complicated by pneumonia.

She had a rough time for the next few days while we plied her with antibiotics, amantadine (I'll tell you more about this agent later), cough medicine and aspirin. She finally recovered—somewhat weaker and, she admitted, a great deal wiser. Now, every September, she calls the office, not to ask about an impending epidemic, and whether or not to have a shot, but to find out when the new flu vaccine will be available.

The fact is the vaccine can *never* give you the flu, since it is made from the dead virus. Its only biological activity is to stimulate your resistance against the real thing. The experience with the swine flu back in 1976–77, when, at the exhortation of the government, 20 percent of all Americans were vaccinated against an epidemic that never happened, has left some individuals with a residual skepticism about all flu shots. At that time too, an uncommon neurological complication called the Guillain-Barré syndrome was observed in ten patients among every million vaccinated—an incidence of 0.001 percent. Unfortunately, that was enough to stigmatize flu vaccinations for years to come.

Complications from the modern vaccines, unlike the preparations used a few years ago, are minimal (except among the relatively few who happen to be allergic to chicken or eggs). There are two types of vaccine. One contains the whole virus; the other, split viral particles. The latter is better tolerated by the very young. Ask your pediatrician about it.

Most patients have no side effects whatsoever. Those who do are usually children or young adults who have never been exposed to either the flu or the vaccine, and whose bodies have little viral immunologic experience. These persons may complain of a minor local reaction in the arm and/or mild "constitutional" signs like a slight fever or achy joints—which rarely persist for longer than twenty-four hours. A couple of aspirin tablets will soon have them feeling fine again.

Sometimes, special precautions are called for when you get the vaccine, because it can affect liver function. When that happens, some commonly used drugs, like anticoagulants (blood thinners), certain anti-asthma agents, and various anti-cancer drugs, including interferon, normally broken down by the liver, can accumulate to toxic levels. This may be particularly hazardous in the case of anti-coagulants. So if you happen to be receiving medication for a chronic illness, remind your doctor about it *before* he gives you the shot.

Unless there has been a sudden and unexpected alteration (mutation) in the nature of the virus (something the U.S. Public Health Service is constantly monitoring very closely throughout the world), vaccination will confer anywhere from 70 to 90 percent protection against the prevalent strains of A and B—provided you've received it in time. This protection may last as long as two years, but you can't really be sure, so I advise a booster every fall. It takes two weeks for the vaccine to become effective.

Alternatives (and Extra Protection)

There is now available by prescription from your doctor an antiviral agent called amantadine (Symmetrel), which is both an effective addition and an alternative to the vaccine. (However, pregnant and nursing women should not use it.) If for some reason you'd rather not be vaccinated, amantadine will protect you against the flu, but only the A type. You must take it twice a day by mouth (100 mgs. per dose) for as long as you're at risk. But remember, don't miss a single day, especially in the midst of an epidemic. If you do, you'll be vulnerable.

Amantadine not only prevents the flu, it's also helpful in its treatment. It shortens the course of the disease and makes you feel better faster. But you must take it as soon as possible after the onset of symptoms. If you wait much longer than twenty-four hours, the drug loses some of its efficacy.

Given a choice between amantadine and vaccination, I recommend you get the shot. The drug may cause neurological symptoms (dizziness, drowsiness, changes in behavior and convulsions) as well as other complications, especially in older persons. The longer you take amantadine, the greater the likelihood of such toxicity. However, the incidence and severity of adverse reactions do not compare with the symptoms and risks of the flu itself.

If you did not receive your booster shot and awake one morning to learn there's a roaring flu epidemic in your community, get your flu shot right away. But start taking amantadine too. (The same advice applies if you had your booster shot more recently than two weeks ago.) The vaccination will protect you in two weeks, at which time you may stop the amantadine.

Rimantadine, a more recent version of amantadine, is now in its final testing stages. It is said to be at least as effective as amantadine, but with fewer side effects. Ask your doctor whether it is now available.

Just a word about antibiotic treatment. Unlike the common cold, flu is so likely to result in secondary bacterial infections such as bronchitis and pneumonia, especially in older persons, that most doctors, including myself, routinely prescribe prophylactic antibiotics to all patients with flu, regardless of age or other underlying disease.

Vidarabine (Vira-A), an antiviral preparation, when administered as an aerosol spray, shortens the duration of fever and other symptoms in both influenza A and B, as well as certain other viral respiratory diseases. It also renders you less contagious by reducing the number of viruses you cough up and spit out. Look for news of its final FDA approval.

Preventing Pneumonia

Pneumonia is an infection of the lung tissues. The bronchial tree (windpipe), carrying the oxygen we breathe, divides into progressively smaller branches that end up in the lungs. If an infection remains high up in the respiratory tree, you are said to have pharyngitis, laryngitis or bronchitis. If, however, it involves the lungs, you have pneumonia. Unless a bronchial infection is nipped in the bud, it can lead to pneumonia.

The earliest symptoms of pneumonia are usually an elevated temperature, pain in the chest on deep breathing or coughing (but not movement), a dry cough and general malaise. There may be shaking chills (depending on the degree of fever) and, later, expectoration of yellow, green or bloody sputum.

The diagnosis usually requires a chest X ray for confirmation but can often be made by careful examination of the lungs with a stethoscope.

Unlike the common cold and flu, which always result from viral infections, pneumonia can be caused by a variety of agents. These include many different viruses, bacteria, fungi and even parasites. Identifying the responsible organism requires sputum analysis.

There is one bacterium with many different strains, the pneumococcus, which is responsible for most cases of pneumonia in this country. Despite its response to antibiotics (it is usually very sensitive to penicillin), pneumococcal pneumonia still claims more than seventy-five thousand lives in the United States each year. Most deaths occur among the elderly, diabetics and those with chronic disease or impaired immunity. Younger, otherwise healthy persons, as a rule, recover quickly with appropriate treatment.

There is now a vaccine to prevent pneumococcal pneumonia. Its widespread use will no doubt result in significant reduction in the number of deaths from this disease. The first version of the vaccine, which became available in 1977, protected against fourteen different strains of pneumococcus. A product with fewer adverse reactions, and active against twenty-three bacterial forms, has more recently been developed. I recommend it to all my patients over fifty years of age, and to anyone who might become seriously ill or die should they come down with pneumonia. This includes not only the elderly and severe diabetics, but persons with lung trouble, heart disorders or who have had their spleens removed. *Remember, however, that you should get the pneumonia vaccine only once.* A second shot can result in serious adverse reactions. If you were injected with the earlier vaccine, do not accept the newer preparation at any time.

CHAPTER **3**

Hepatitis—Vaccines to the Rescue

There isn't a week that goes by without some worried patient calling to tell me he or she has been exposed to hepatitis and wants to know what to do about it. Despite the fact that hepatitis is so common, and some types are so serious (even potentially fatal), surprisingly few people understand what it is, when to worry about it (and when not to), the best way to treat it and—most importantly—how to prevent it.

Hepatitis—More Than One Disease

The word "hepatitis" is derived from "*hepar*," the Latin word for liver. The suffix "-itis" denotes inflammation or infection. So hepatitis refers to any process infecting or inflaming the liver. That broad definition encompasses many different causes, some of which are pretty exotic and not very common in this part of the world. For example, parasites and worms can invade the liver and give you hepatitis. Supposing you visit some area where hygiene is not as effective as the food is tasty, and you pick up amoebic dysentery. The organism usually remains in the bowel, but if undiagnosed and untreated, it can make its way to the liver, where it causes *amoebic hepatitis* or abscess formation.

Again, some medication you're taking—even a "harmless" one

that you can buy without a prescription, such as acetaminophen (Tylenol, Datril)—can occasionally hurt the liver and induce a *toxic hepatitis*. So can more powerful agents prescribed by your doctor. These include anesthetics like the halothanes, blood-pressure-lowering drugs (methyldopa, or Aldomet), and nonsteroidal anti-inflammatory drugs used as pain killers, like Clinoril or Dolobid. Other causes include various chemicals—for example, carbon tetrachloride, a solvent used in the home and in industry—and a variety of infections.

Hepatitis, regardless of its cause, usually results in fever, loss of appetite, fatigue, pain or discomfort in the right upper portion of the abdomen, and a yellowish discoloration of the skin and the whites of the eyes (jaundice). Whenever someone develops this constellation of symptoms, it's up to the doctor to determine the responsible agent. This usually requires a battery of blood tests, bacteriological, viral or other laboratory analyses, a sonogram or scan of the liver (to make sure the clinical picture is not due to cancer that has spread to that organ) and occasionally even a needle biopsy of the liver to study its tissue under the microscope. The time frame and the other associations in which the hepatitis occurred also help in making the diagnosis. If symptoms developed shortly after you received an anesthetic or started a new medication, or returned from abroad, attention will naturally be focused on the most likely offending agent. Hepatic injury by toxic industrial compounds can be prevented by following the posted precautions at the workplace. Injury due to drugs can also be acted upon. In this chapter, however, I want to focus on viral hepatitis, because it's the kind you and I are most likely to get, and can most easily prevent.

Three Kinds of Viral Hepatitis

There are several different viruses that can produce hepatitis, but the three most common ones in this part of the world are hepatitis A, B and non-A, non-B. These particular forms of hepatitis differ very much in severity, fatality rate and the likelihood of producing permanent liver damage or liver cancer. They are also spread, treated and prevented differently.

Of Raw Clams and Aphrodisiacs

Jane was a twenty-five-year-old woman who worked in a day-care center, looking after young children for several hours each day. One summer, she and her boy friend spent their two-week vacation together on the Maryland shore. They loved the beach and adored seafood. One day in late July they went clamming on Chesapeake Bay with great success. They brought the haul back to their bungalow and went at it with gusto, washing down clam after clam with lots of cold beer. It was a wonderful evening in every respect. An incidental observation they both made that night was that raw clams, like oysters, are indeed aphrodisiacs.

About three weeks later, near Labor Day, Jane began to feel a bit "off." She didn't seem to have her usual energy or appetite. She even lost her taste for cigarettes (she was a pack-and-a-half-a-day smoker). Ed, her boy friend, began to worry. He was sure all these symptoms—the fatigue, and particularly the nausea—added up to the conclusion that Jane was pregnant, thanks to his clam-enhanced passion that night on the beach three or four weeks earlier. But he didn't say a word about it. A couple of days later, when Jane began to ache in her joints, Ed was relieved. He remembered reading somewhere that pregnant women don't usually develop arthritis (he was correct, as far as rheumatoid arthritis is concerned). The possibility of pregnancy had never even occurred to Jane; she'd done everything right in that regard, passion or no.

When Ed too lost his appetite and began running a low-grade fever he completely abandoned the pregnancy diagnosis and assumed that both Jane and he had picked up a virus somewhere.

Some ten days later, Jane noticed that the whites of Ed's eyes were a little yellow. "It must be the lighting," he told her, "because yours are too." And with that, they went to bed, feeling unusually tired, even though it was only eight-thirty in the evening. The next morning, while shaving, Ed was shocked when he looked at himself in the mirror. He was jaundiced! Not only were the whites of his eyes yellow, but so was his skin. He also noted that his urine was a deep mahogany color, like strong tea. Jane and Ed called for an appointment to see me that afternoon.

It didn't take a genius to make the diagnosis. When two people who live together develop jaundice at the same time and both had eaten raw clams five or six weeks earlier, hepatitis A is almost certainly the cause.

When I examined them, in addition to their obvious yellow discoloration, their livers were enlarged. I could also feel their spleens, which one normally cannot do. I ran some liver-function tests and obtained blood samples to confirm the type of hepatitis. One of the analyses, the radioimmune assay, identified antibodies to the hepatitis A virus, but not to hepatitis B. That clinched the diagnosis.

I told Jane and Ed that they'd picked up hepatitis A from eating raw clams that had probably been contaminated by sewage, but that they'd both be fine. Jane asked if I was going to hospitalize them, and if not, how long they would be confined to bed at home. They were relieved when I told them that we don't usually admit patients with hepatitis A to hospital anymore, because the disease runs its course regardless of what we do; there is no specific treatment for it. Years ago, we used to put patients with hepatitis A to bed until their jaundice cleared and their liver-function tests were completely normal. We have since learned from experience that there is no advantage to such a conservative, cautious approach. We now permit resumption of physical activity as soon as liver-function tests begin to show improvement.

How long Ed and Jane remained in bed or at home was their decision. It would depend on how they felt. Whatever they were up to doing was permissible. What should they eat? Anything their hearts desired. Was there any specific food to be avoided? Absolutely not. Should they take vitamins? Only if it made them happy to do so. There is no evidence that vitamin supplements have any effect on the course of the disease. How long would they have to keep away from alcohol? I thought it was safe for them to begin to drink in moderation (no more than two ounces of liquor per day) when their liver-function tests began to return toward normal and the fever and malaise had passed. (Formerly, we advised patients with hepatitis to abstain from alcohol for months.) What were the long-term consequences of hepatitis A? Virtually none. I assured them the infection would clear up and that they would not develop chronic liver disease.

Jane asked when she might return to work, what with the children and all. My answer upset her. "I'd probably wait a week or two, although once the jaundice appears, you're no longer very contagious. You were *most* contagious during those first few weeks when you felt so poorly and didn't know why. So you'd better check to see if any of your children at the day-care center have hepatitis too."

The next day Jane phoned to tell me she'd learned that three youngsters in class had called in sick. I contacted their doctors, who confirmed that all three had hepatitis A. It was now too late to give the others in Jane's class gamma globulin, which, if administered within a few days of exposure to someone with hepatitis A, reduces the risk of the disease or at least modifies its severity. Gamma globulin is a protein that enhances the immune response, or resistance, to certain viral infections. Obtained from human blood, it is most effective when administered by intramuscular injection *before* exposure. I recommend it to anyone going to areas where the risk of infection by hepatitis A virus is increased.

Jane and Ed's story was typical for hepatitis A. This illness is caused by a virus that has actually been identified, which we call "A." Anyone affected by it develops specific antibodies that can be found in the blood. The job of these antibodies is to combat the viral invader. Hepatitis A may be so mild it is never even recognized. In fact, antibodies reflecting previous infection are present in almost half of all Americans, most of whom never knew when they had their hepatitis.

The A virus is harbored in the intestinal tract and is acquired by fecal contamination. It spreads like wildfire in crowded quarters—in schools, prisons, army camps, dorms—and day-care centers. Food purveyors who don't wash their hands transmit it. So do homosexuals who engage in oral-anal activities. But eating raw shellfish from water contaminated by sewage is probably the most common mode of infection. The keys to prevention are proper hygiene and some caution. For example, ask where the raw shellfish on your plate came from. Most health departments regulate its sale and distribution, and require identification of the waters from which it was taken. You have no such protection when you go clamming independently, such as Jane and Ed "enjoyed" doing. Nor can you tell whether the water from which the shellfish has been taken is sewage-contaminated just by looking at it or at the fish itself. The same holds true when you buy shellfish from local fishermen. Your best bet is to eat it only in licensed restaurants. Since the hepatitis A virus is transmitted in the stool, if you're a food handler, always wash your hands before serving food to anyone, either at your home or in a restaurant.

If you suspect that you've been exposed to hepatitis A, get a shot of gamma globulin as soon as you can. There is no vaccine yet available to prevent this disease.

If you do get hepatitis A, the worst that will happen is some jaundice, lack of appetite, perhaps a low-grade fever for several days and a decline in your energy level for a few weeks. As I indicated to Jane and Ed, it's a relatively benign disease. Virtually no one ever dies from it or even gets very sick. The chances of your liver becoming permanently damaged are remote. And once you come down with hepatitis A, you're probably immune to it for the rest of your life.

Hepatitis B—A Different Story

More than 200,000 people contract hepatitis B every year in the United States. This illness is an entirely different ball game from hepatitis A—in every respect. Although one person in four who is infected develops jaundice, 5 percent become so sick they need to be hospitalized. Ten percent of those who recover become carriers—a potential source of infection to others with whom they come in contact, especially newborn infants. Among these carriers, 25 percent later suffer from chronic hepatitis, 20 percent die of cirrhosis of the liver (serious scarring of that organ) and 5 percent die of liver cancer years later. So even though the majority of cases clear up completely, this is a disease you want to avoid at all costs. Happily, you can.

Hepatitis B is not only much more serious than is the A illness, it is also spread differently. For example, you do not get it primarily via the fecal-oral route, but from infected blood and blood products and, to a lesser extent, from body secretions like semen or saliva. The highest incidence of hepatitis B occurs among homosexual men, as a result of their oral-genital contact, during which they consume infected semen, as well as from oral-anal activity, which may result in their swallowing small amounts of blood from abrasions of the rectal lining.

Since the B virus is present in blood, drug abusers contract hepatitis by sharing needles with B carriers or patients. Doctors, nurses, dentists and other health-care workers who accidentally stick themselves with a contaminated needle are therefore also vulnerable. Patients receiving frequent transfusions—as, for example, those with kidney disease undergoing hemodialysis, or hemophiliacs—used to be at high risk, but are no longer, since we are now able to screen donor blood for the presence of the hepatitis B virus.

Now, the good news is that you can prevent this disease in almost 100 percent of cases by taking hepatitis B vaccine. If you fall into any of the above categories, get the vaccine now. You need do so only once. I took my shot two years ago and that's all I'll ever need. But you must get it *before* you're exposed.

I would have expected a rush on this vaccine as soon as it became available. Unfortunately, that was not the case early on. I think there were two reasons for this. First, hepatitis B vaccine remains very expensive. (It may cost anywhere from $60 to $100.) Second, and probably more importantly, was the fear of contracting AIDS from the vaccine, most of which was and still is made from the serum of patients infected with hepatitis B. Since this disease is common among homosexuals, who are also especially vulnerable to AIDS, the worry was that one might contract that dread illness from the hepatitis B vaccine.

There was never any evidence that this was so. I suppose it was theoretically possible that since the AIDS virus is a retro virus, which may not make its presence known for years, one could not be absolutely sure that there was no risk from receiving this vaccine. But these fears are no longer justified. All donor blood must now be analyzed for evidence of AIDS antibodies, thus virtually eliminating the risk of receiving an infected specimen. Furthermore, hepatitis B vaccine will soon be made not from human donor blood but from a product obtained from recombinant DNA techniques. So there is now no reason for not accepting the vaccine.

If you haven't been vaccinated, and think you may have been exposed (for example, if you're a lab technician and you pricked your finger with a needle while drawing blood), get the vaccine immediately and, at the same time, ask your doctor for a shot of specific hepatitis B immune globulin (that's not the same as the gamma globulin we use against hepatitis A). These interventions may reduce the risk and severity of the disease should you contract it.

Until quite recently, the above would have been all you needed to know about who is vulnerable to hepatitis B and how best to be protected against it. However, another high-risk category has recently been identified—the newborn. There are some one million carriers of hepatitis B in this country alone. These are individuals who can spread the disease but who are not necessarily sick with it themselves. The ethnic groups in which carriers are most likely to be found are Asiatics, South Americans, Alaskans, and persons coming from Africa and islands in the Pacific and the Caribbean. Among these individuals who emigrated to the United States the carrier incidence is about 20 percent. But they are not alone. Drug users, women working in the health related field—nurses, doctors, technicians—in fact anyone in regular contact with hepatitis B patients is a potential carrier. When one such person gives birth, her infected blood can transmit hepatitis B to the fetus. This is not immediately apparent, but serious problems develop as the child grows older. Nine times out of ten, he or she becomes a lifetime carrier, thus perpetuating a cycle of disease from generation to generation. And as many as one-third of these children develop cancer of the liver or cirrhosis later in life.

How can all this be prevented? First, every pregnant woman in a high-risk group should have her blood tested for hepatitis B surface antigen, present in all carriers. If it is found, the infant should be given the hepatitis vaccine and hepatitis B immune globulin at birth. The former is administered again months later and assures immunity over the long term. The latter, made from the serum of patients who have recovered from hepatitis B, contains antibodies that confer immediate protection. This combination of shots is 85 percent effective.

My own feeling is that *every* pregnant woman should be tested for the hepatitis B surface antigen. After all, they are routinely checked for syphilis—and hepatitis B is forty to fifty times as common!

Once you develop the symptoms of hepatitis B, no one can predict whether your illness will be benign, chronic or lethal. Nor is there any specific treatment for it. Bed rest, diet, steroids, vitamins—none of these apparently makes a difference. Avoid alcohol in the acute stage, when you're feeling lousy. A few weeks later you may begin to drink in moderation if you're on the road to recovery.

Non-A, Non-B—The Third Kind of Viral Hepatitis

Hepatitis A is not contracted from blood. Even though hepatitis B is primarily transmitted via blood, the risks of your getting it from a transfusion these days are small because donor blood can now be screened for the presence of this virus. So if it's neither A nor B, what is the virus responsible for the continuing high incidence of hepatitis after transfusion? Quite logically, we call the third virus non-A, non-B.

The non-A, non-B virus, like that causing hepatitis B, is spread for the most part via blood. The trouble is that, unlike the hepatitis B virus, we are not yet able to screen blood for its presence. Non-A, non-B accounts for 90 percent of the hepatitis we see after transfusions, as well as for about 25 percent of all cases of hepatitis. There are 100,000 or more cases of non-A, non-B hepatitis each year in the United States. Like hepatitis B, non-A, non-B is potentially serious. It has been estimated that anyone receiving five or more units of blood—no matter for what reason—has a 10 percent chance of developing this form of hepatitis. The non-A, non-B infection carries with it the same risk of chronic liver disease and death as does hepatitis B.

What can one do to reduce the risk of such infection? The first rule is never to have a blood transfusion unless it is absolutely necessary. In my experience, if you need only 1 to 2 units of blood, you probably don't need any. Sometimes, of course, there is no alternative to transfusion. Patients who suffer massive hemorrhage from some injury, or from a bleeding ulcer, or during heart surgery may need 5, 10 or 20 units. They should not be denied whatever blood is required. But I always insist that my patients first be given gamma globulin. It's not foolproof, but I believe that it reduces somewhat the risk and/ or severity of non-A, non-B infection. Here's some additional good advice. If you can foresee that you will need a surgical procedure that may require additional blood, donate your own blood in advance over a period of weeks and have it stored for your future use (autologous transfusion).

The good news about non-A, non-B hepatitis is that two different laboratories, working independently, have announced the discovery and isolation of a virus that may be responsible for the infection. If any of this proves to be true, then within a few years we may be able to identify all contaminated blood. What's more, as with hepatitis B, a vaccine may also become available.

CHAPTER 4

Senility, Alzheimer's Disease and Who's President of the United States

Would you be insulted if I were to ask you whether you know your address, the year, the month, the day of the week—and the name of the President of the United States? You'd probably think I was kidding around. Yet these very questions are posed, in all seriousness, countless times every day, as doctors examine previously normal persons who have become demented.

The symptoms of dementia are familiar ones. A patient will call to tell me, "Doctor, I hang up the phone after a thirty-minute conversation with my mother. An hour or so later she calls to ask why she hasn't heard from me lately." Or, "Dad doesn't seem to understand things anymore. We were watching television the other day when they showed a close-up of some starving, emaciated children in Ethiopia. He found it very funny, couldn't stop laughing." Or, "Mother used to be active, involved and interested in everything and everyone around her. Now she's apathetic, withdrawn, confused, afraid of strangers and afraid to go out alone. She no longer cares about her appearance, has become unkempt. She doesn't know where she is or why. She often doesn't recognize familiar people, places and things. She can't concentrate and it's impossible really to communicate with her anymore."

Whenever such symptoms develop, the first thought that comes to mind these days is Alzheimer's disease. (We used to call it "senility.") They are typical of the "organic brain syndrome," in which the brain is not functioning normally in an *intellectual* sense. The term is therefore reserved for those persons in whom only thought, memory and behavior are impaired. Someone who is paralyzed after a stroke, but who thinks clearly, remembers well and acts appropriately is not said to have an organic brain syndrome, even though a portion of the brain is actually damaged.

Alzheimer's disease is an enormous national problem. It is more common than cancer of the lung, occurs ten times more frequently than multiple sclerosis and a hundred times more often than amyotrophic lateral sclerosis (popularly known as "Lou Gehrig's disease").

One person in twenty over the age of sixty-five is "demented," while one in ten has some form of intellectual impairment. Since eleven percent of Americans are now sixty-five years of age or older and 600,000 more reach that age every year, by 2000 A.D., the "elderly" will comprise 25 percent of our population. That's going to add up to an awful lot of demented individuals!

I decided to write this chapter on Alzheimer's disease even though it cannot now be prevented, cured or even treated. I have done so in order to emphasize that much of what we think is Alzheimer's is actually some other condition, which, unlike Alzheimer's, frequently *can* be treated, cured, prevented or reversed.

The statistics on this matter are shocking. At autopsy, which is the final "court of appeal" as far as diagnosis is concerned, fully 50 percent of patients believed to have had Alzheimer's disease while alive were in fact found to have some other reason for their symptoms. For example, 25 percent had had several small strokes, none of which were recognized during life. Had they been, therapy might have helped prevent the development or progression of the behavior disorder. Twenty percent died of other conditions, such as brain tumors or brain injury, some of which might have been corrected surgically. Frequently, no physical abnormalities whatsoever were found to account for the behavioral abnormalities, suggesting that the underlying cause may have been depression, an adverse drug effect, malnutrition or a *treatable* nonneurological disease. So before you consign a parent, grandparent or other loved one to a nursing home because of incurable Alzheimer's disease, make sure that the diagnosis is correct.

There are at least fifty different conditions that can be and often are mistaken for Alzheimer's disease. Though I'll concentrate on some of the more common ones, I could fill an entire book with examples from my own experience of patients presenting with prima facie evidence for senile dementia who turned out to have some other disorder.

When Strokes Mimic Alzheimer's

Among the most important conditions confused with Alzheimer's is narrowing of the arteries that supply the brain (cerebral arteriosclerosis). As this process continues, less and less blood is delivered to that organ. When the diseased artery finally closes, the result is a stroke. The term "stroke" usually conjures up images of someone suddenly keeling over, paralyzed or lapsing into a coma and dying. Although it can happen that way, the event is more often much less dramatic. It may consist of nothing more than a transient headache, double vision or blurring, a few minutes of difficulty finding the right word, or a little weakness, numbness or tingling in an arm or a leg. A series of such "strokelets," each so minor it's barely recognized as such, can, over the years, result in enough brain damage to cause personality changes resembling and easily confused with Alzheimer's. Such disease is most likely to occur in individuals with high blood pressure (which accelerates the development of arteriosclerosis), in those who develop a specific heart-rhythm disturbance (atrial fibrillation), which can result in little clots leaving the heart, traveling to, lodging in and obstructing small cerebral blood vessels (cerebral embolism) and when plaques break off the large arteries (carotids) that supply the brain and block the smaller ones higher up. If the true cause is established in each of these circumstances, dementia can be rendered less likely to occur or even, in some cases, be prevented. For example, elevated blood pressure can be reduced; patients with atrial fibrillation can and should usually be anticoagulated, thus reducing the possibility of an embolism; carotid arteries narrowed by friable plaques can sometimes be surgically reamed out. In most cases, however, especially in the absence of symptoms, medical management with aspirin is effective.

Always Look for Brain Injury When Behavior Becomes Bizarre

Repeated head injuries, such as "punch-drunk" boxers incur, can also result in behavioral changes resembling Alzheimer's disease. In this particular instance, the correct diagnosis is really academic, since there is no way of undoing the brain damage. But an appreciation of the magnitude of the problem may at least lead to better regulation of boxing. The law now simply requires that any boxer who has been knocked down or out must have a CAT scan. Unless the scan is abnormal, he's allowed back in the ring. But brain damage can be present long before it is apparent on the scan.

Of course, you needn't be a boxer to hurt your brain. Even minor head injuries in older persons can result in blood clots under the skull and outside the brain (subdural hematoma). If large enough, they can exert pressure on the brain and damage it, producing all kinds of neurological problems—including some that mimic Alzheimer's. Such complications are almost always curable—when properly diagnosed.

If a careful work-up reveals that irreversible trauma to the brain is the cause of the behavioral abnormalities, it's important especially for the patient's family to *know* that Alzheimer's isn't the culprit. The risk of your eventually developing Alzheimer's is about 2 to 3 percent if there is no family history of the disorder, and rises to 8 percent when some blood relative (parent, sibling, aunt, uncle) has had it, particularly at an early age. And the more relatives you have with Alzheimer's, the greater the likelihood of your getting it.

Chronic alcoholics may present with symptoms indistinguishable from Alzheimer's disease. It's important to recognize this cause as well, since successful treatment of the alcoholic patient, as difficult as that may be, can sometimes prevent progression of symptoms.

In the roster of curable diseases that can be mistaken for Alzheimer's, one of the most common is malfunction of the thyroid gland —either underactivity (hypothyroidism) or, less commonly, overactivity (hyperthyroidism). The diagnosis at either extreme is harder to make later in life than it is in the young individual. I have seen several older patients who were slow, dull and apathetic because of low thyroid function, and who were originally suspected of having become "senile." A little thyroid supplement saved the day for them.

Any person, young or old, who develops behavioral changes must have a good neurological going-over. I have had patients at all ages, ranging from a child of four to a woman of seventy-four, who underwent personality changes as a result of brain tumors (usually in the frontal lobe, where intelligence originates). Removal of the tumor was followed by a return to normal behavior. While doctors are vigorous in their efforts to track down the cause of altered personality in young people, they are not nearly as aggressive as they should be in older persons.

When I was a medical student, one of my professors was constantly reminding our class to test for syphilis in every patient, "including your own grandmother." This still applies today, especially in someone with a personality disorder appearing late in life. Syphilis is a sexually transmitted disease that can silently affect the brain at the time of the original exposure. Behavioral symptoms may not appear for many years. This condition is referred to as GPI (general paresis of the insane). Because penicillin, which can cure early syphilis, has now been available for some forty years, we're seeing fewer patients with these delayed manifestations, but there is still a substantial number of them around. Unfortunately, by the time GPI has developed, there is nothing that can be done.

Another important reason to do a thorough neurological evaluation in the elderly with behavioral changes is to detect a condition called normal pressure hydrocephalus. In patients with this disorder, the fluid that normally circulates through and bathes the brain, and which is absorbed at the same rate at which it is produced, accumulates in the nervous system. As a result, cavities within the brain enlarge, compress the nerve tissues and ultimately affect brain function. This fairly common cause of altered personality in the aged is curable by surgery.

There are, in addition, many *nonneurological* conditions that afflict the elderly and have an impact on their behavior. Among the most important is faulty nutrition. Many older persons in this country suffer from malnutrition—for a host of reasons. These may be economic: senior citizens living on a fixed income, particularly in times of inflation, may not be able to afford a balanced diet. Their appetite may be impaired. They may eat too little or the wrong food because they are depressed or medicated, or because they live alone and find it too much effort to shop for or prepare tasty meals. There is also the matter of dentition: the loss of teeth and the inability to chew often render the diet inadequate. Nor are the elderly always able efficiently to absorb the food they do consume. As one gets older, there is decreased secretion of the digestive acids in the stomach. It also takes the stomach three times as long to empty its contents. Circulation within the intestinal tract may become arteriosclerotic, just as it does in the brain, the legs, the heart and the kidneys. When this occurs, there is decreased absorption and deficiency of important micronutrients and minerals. Whatever the reason, the end result is abnormal brain function.

In a recent study in the United States, older people living alone, some of whom had personality and behavioral abnormalities mistaken for Alzheimer's, demonstrated a measurable improvement in memory and other reactions after they were admitted to a nursing facility where the diet was balanced and the food attractively prepared. So if you have an elderly parent who has always been able to take care of himself or herself, but begins to show evidence of Alzheimer's, check very carefully into what he or she is actually eating.

Then there is the matter of medication. At the present time, persons over sixty-five years of age, who constitute only 11 percent of the American population, consume more than 25 percent of all the drugs prescribed in this country. Many of these are potentially toxic, especially when taken together. The diseases they are meant to improve may worsen if the patient fails to take the medication as directed, or takes too much of it. This phenomenon of "polypharmacy," the need for multiple medications, is particularly hazardous in the elderly. The drugs to watch out for, singly or in combination, are tranquilizers, antidepressants, sedatives, cardiac agents and medicines that lower blood pressure. Among the latter, the beta blockers are particularly important.

Some Cases in Point

James S. was fifty-four years old when his mother died of cancer of the breast. His father, Donald, eighty-one, was now living alone in the apartment he had shared with his wife. Jim asked Donald to move in with him and his family. His dad, though grateful for the offer, declined. He preferred his privacy. He was in relatively good health, had only recently sold his linen store, had enough money on which to live, and was fiercely proud and independent; so he decided to stay where he was. Jim kept in close touch with him and visited at least once every week or two with the grandchildren.

Everything seemed to be going just fine. Donald was apparently adjusting very well to living by himself. So that summer, Jim, his wife and children went on a month-long vacation to Europe. They knew Dad would be all right, because although most of his friends had either died or moved away to retirement communities, he was pretty resourceful.

When they returned, Jim called his father and suggested they all have brunch together at Tavern on the Green, a cheerful restaurant in Central Park in New York City. He expected an enthusiastic "Yes, of course. I'd love to see you all." Instead, it took all the persuasion Jim could muster to get his dad to join them. "I'm too tired, son. Let's make it another time. I think I'd prefer to rest this afternoon." But Jim wouldn't take no for an answer. He picked his father up at noon, and they drove to the restaurant together. Jim found him vague and uninterested. For example, he never inquired about their trip, whether or not the kids had enjoyed it, what plans Jim had for his law practice, or any of the other questions Donald would normally have asked. Also, for the first time ever, Donald was actually unkempt. He had a two-day stubble on his chin. There was a large egg stain on his tie, his shirt and suit were rumpled, and one of his socks was blue, the other brown. Jim did not comment about any of this to his dad. Neither did his wife or children.

The next day, he called his father's doctor. He asked whether Donald had been sick while the family was gone. "Not as far as I know," the doctor said. In fact, he hadn't heard from Donald in several weeks. "Maybe he's just tired. Why don't you see how it goes in the next little while and call me if you're really worried."

In the ensuing weeks, Jim was especially attentive to his father. He telephoned every day, visited at least once a week, but noted with great sadness that his dad was failing. He was also losing weight.

"What did you have for lunch today, Dad?"

"Oh, a TV chicken dinner and a can of soup, I think."

"Dad, were you out for a walk this afternoon? The weather was so beautiful."

"No, I just watched a little television and dozed off."

"Did you read the newspaper today? The economy seems in pretty good shape."

"Is it?"

And then the lethargy progressed to mild confusion. "I am happy to see you today, Jim, but I expected you on Sunday."

"But this is Sunday."

"Well, what do you know."

At this point, Jim decided it was time to consult the doctor again. He suggested that Jim bring his father to the office. When they arrived, the nurse drew blood for analyses, and the technician took a chest X ray and an electrocardiogram. The doctor then spent about five minutes talking with his patient. After the examination was concluded, he recommended to Jim that he look for a retirement home for his dad.

"Jim, he's now an old eighty-one. His mind isn't what it used to be. I honestly don't think he's able to take proper care of himself anymore. Once it starts, senility or Alzheimer's—and that's what your dad has—the course is all downhill. He's got enough money of his own so that you can at least find a decent facility for him."

It was a sad day for Jim when he went to discuss the matter with his father. However, it turned out to be less traumatic for both of them than he had expected. The old man wasn't in the least agitated or upset. He agreed readily to do whatever Jimmy thought best. It didn't much matter to him.

So they packed Dad's belongings. They didn't know what to do with all his personal effects—the photograph albums, coin collection, books and furniture. "Well, first things first," thought Jim. "Let's see how it goes at the nursing home. We can make arrangements for the apartment and its contents later on."

The facility was located in a rustic setting in Westchester County, a lovely suburb north of New York City. The rooms were cheerful and the grounds beautiful. Jim was pleased that his dad would be able to take long walks when the weather was good. But when Jim left, there were tears in his eyes; he couldn't help wondering where he himself would be thirty years from now.

Jim visited his father every two weeks. For the first few months he did not notice any real change. The staff doctor at the home assured him that Donald was comfortable and never complained about anything.

One day some three months later, Jim arrived for one of his regular visits but did not find his father in his usual chair in the TV room.

Nor was he in his own quarters. Jim asked the manager where his dad might be. "It's a lovely spring afternoon. He's probably out for a walk." Mildly surprised, Jim set forth to look for him. He finally found him sitting on a bench under a huge oak tree with a lovely-looking white-haired woman who reminded Jim of Helen Hayes. There they were, talking and laughing animatedly. In fact, they were practically holding hands! Dad was neatly dressed, hair combed, cleanly shaven and wearing for the first time the Chanel after-shave lotion Jim had given him when he had first entered the facility.

"Ah, there you are, son. Let me introduce Jennie. Would you believe we were neighbors in New York City for years? She even remembers seeing me shopping at Gristedes'. It's a small world. We've really gotten to know each other in the last little while. In fact, we thought it would be fun to take a weekend away from here and visit some of our old haunts together. My apartment's still there, isn't it?"

"Of course it is, Dad. When do you want to go? I'll drive you down."

"Nonsense, you've got enough to do. We'll hire a car, Jennie and I, and go ourselves."

And they did. The rest of the story is pretty straightforward. Donald and Jennie were married and moved out of the nursing home back to Donald's apartment, where they lived happily ever after. Donald's "senility" disappeared, because he had never been senile in the first place. He had simply become depressed after the death of his spouse, as do so many elderly persons.

There are several lessons to be learned from this one story. Depression often mimics senility and should be considered in virtually every case of bereavement. Its symptoms may go unrecognized, despite the fact that suicide is more common among the elderly than in any other age group. But it takes more than an electrocardiogram, chest X ray, blood tests and the cursory five minutes Donald's doctor spent with him to make the diagnosis of depression. Time, sensitivity and empathy on the part of the physician are what any patient needs, together with a careful psychiatric, neurological and general physical evaluation. Donald's story happened to have a happy ending. But there must be thousands like him who remain confined in nursing homes and who die there, depressed, not senile. Donald too might have spent the rest of his life in Westchester, with egg on his tie and urine stains on his trousers, if he hadn't met Jennie. But courtship is not the only remedy for depression, although I grant you it's the most pleasant. Psychotherapy and, perhaps even more important, antidepressant drugs are often extremely effective in treating emotional problems in this and every other age group. In any event, make Alzheimer's the last diagnosis, not the first.

A "Trivial" Head Injury

The second case highlights two other fairly common and reversible causes of "dementia." About fifteen years ago, the wife of one of my patients called me from Florida, where she and her husband were spending the winter. He was seventy-five years old, big in steel, very rich, and suddenly behaving very strangely. Aside from mild angina, he'd always been in pretty good shape. When I asked her to be more specific about what was wrong, she told me that Bruce "hasn't been himself" for the past two months. He was sleeping a lot more than usual, couldn't concentrate, didn't seem to remember his plans from one day to the next and occasionally even soiled himself. She also noticed a distinct mood change. Previously feisty and argumentative, he was now docile and submissive. She hadn't called me earlier because "I know there's nothing you can do about an aging brain."

I asked whether he had complained of headache. (A brain tumor must always be considered when behavior is altered.) No, he had not. Had there been any fever recently? (Infection may also cause malfunction of the brain.) Not as far as she knew. Had he been struck on the head or fallen in recent weeks or months? (A blood clot just under the skull, called a subdural hematoma, can press on the brain beneath it and cause behavioral changes.) No, she was not aware of a fall or any other injury. I didn't ask about nutritional deprivation because I knew from firsthand experience that Bruce and his wife had a superb chef whose talents they fully exploited. Had he complained of double vision, slurred speech, weakness of a hand or leg, numbness or tingling? (I wanted to make sure that Bruce hadn't had a stroke.) Well, he'd not had any visual problems, his strength appeared normal in all his limbs as far as she could tell, but yes, she had noted a change in his speech. It wasn't exactly slurred, but it did seem hesitant. "So," she asked after we had chatted for a few minutes, "what do you suggest I do?"

I had known Bruce too well for too long simply to accept the diagnosis of Alzheimer's disease, especially on the basis of a phone call. He needed a thorough evaluation. His wife thought that made sense, and so the following Sunday, she and Bruce returned to New York. I went over to their apartment to get a feel for the problem before launching into a full-scale work-up. I found things worse than I'd expected. This was a very different man from the one I had seen only six months earlier. He kept repeating himself, and it took him the longest time to complete a thought or sentence. He nevertheless was in the best of spirits, smiling and affable at all times.

The physical evaluation I performed at his home was not revealing. The simple neurological exam using the little hammer, tuning fork and pins was also normal. I arranged for his admission to a hospital for more sophisticated testing.

I ordered skull films first (this was in the days before the CAT scan and the magnetic resonance imaging machine). We hit it lucky and found the answer to Bruce's problem on this initial procedure. He had a large blood clot—a subdural hematoma—under his skull compressing his brain. He must have fallen or struck his head in some way, even though his wife was not aware of it.

The blood clot was removed by sucking it out through a small hole drilled on the outside of the skull. A few days later, Bruce was his old self again. No more Alzheimer's! I asked him whether he could now remember hitting his head in the recent past.

"Not really!"

"What do you mean, 'not really'? Did you or didn't you strike your head, Bruce?"

"Well, actually, now that I think of it, a few months ago I was in my bathroom. I bent down to pick something up off the floor. When I stood up, I knocked my head against Joan's wooden cosmetic shelf. Yes, of course, I remember it all very clearly. It didn't seem very important at the time. I didn't cut myself, and the blow didn't even give me a headache."

Well, that was what had done it. Even a trivial injury can result in a subdural hematoma in older people, whose blood vessels are fragile. Bleeding is followed by formation of a clot, which, if large enough, can cause a spectrum of neurological and behavioral changes.

That's not the end of the story, however. For three years after his discharge from the hospital, Bruce remained well and active in his business affairs. But then another complication developed. Although the angina pectoris which he'd had for years had remained under good control, his heart began to act up in other ways. He complained of a "thumping" in his chest, skipped beats and occasional dizziness. An electrocardiogram confirmed a cardiac rhythm disturbance, the kind that responds best to treatment with digitalis. I prescribed this drug in the usual dosage, and within seven or eight days Bruce's symptoms subsided. Some months later, his wife called. "He's acting funny," she said.

"Don't tell me he's knocked his head again."

"No, it's different this time. He's paranoid. He bought a gun, says it's loaded, and keeps it in our bedroom in case someone breaks in. The other night he was convinced there was a prowler in the living room, so at three A.M. he tore down the stairs, waving his pistol wildly. Thank goodness, there were no moving shadows. He'd have shot them up. And it's not only the gun that worries me. He's suspicious of everyone and everything. It's scary, and I'm afraid. At one point, he didn't even seem to know *me*."

I considered this an emergency. A disturbed, agitated, paranoid patient with a loaded gun is a potential killer. "Did all this develop suddenly?" I asked.

"No, it's been coming on for a few weeks, but it's definitely getting worse. I'm in a real dilemma. On the one hand, I'm afraid to leave him alone, and on the other I'm terrified to stay. But I can't seem to reach him. When I tell him he's overreacting or try to reason with him, he just looks at me and smiles knowingly. What shall I do? He's so totally irrational. It sounds like Alzheimer's disease, doesn't it?"

I visited with Bruce and confirmed his wife's observations. I went through the same questions I'd asked Joan the last time his behavior had changed. He was now completely paranoid and irrational. I could find no clues on physical examination. I then referred him to an excellent neurologist.

My colleague suggested a diagnosis that quite frankly had not occurred to me. "I'll bet this man is hallucinating and paranoid because of the digitalis he's taking for his cardiac arrhythmia." I must say that hearing about toxicity of a cardiac drug from a neurologist was not too good for my ego! And it seemed like a far-out possibility. In my more than thirty years of practice, I'd never witnessed a case of "insanity" from digitalis, although I had read about it from time to time. However, since all the other tests, which this time did include a CAT scan and an electroencephalogram (brain-wave recording), were normal, I agreed to replace the digitalis with another anti-ar-rhythmic drug. (Fortunately, there is more than one way to skin a cat in medicine.) I couldn't believe the results: within ten days Bruce was back to his normal self.

There is much to be learned from Bruce's experience. It empha-sizes once more the importance of putting Alzheimer's last on your diagnostic list whenever any patient, no matter how elderly, suddenly develops unexplained personality changes. There is no specific test to establish the diagnosis of Alzheimer's. We reach that conclusion only after we've excluded all others. In other words, it's a wastebas-ket diagnosis. Since Alzheimer's is neither treatable nor reversible at the present time, it's all the more critical that we look very hard for other possibilities that mimic it and may be manageable.

Alzheimer's is not due to or synonymous with the "aging pro-cess." As I so often tell my patients, age is not a disease. While it is true that vulnerability to certain conditions like arteriosclerosis and cancer increases as one gets older, these disorders merely accom-pany—but are not caused by—aging. Every symptom, every dis-ease, every complaint of any senior citizen has a root cause that can and should be determined as vigorously as we do in younger individ-uals. "Oh, it's just his [or her] age" is no longer an acceptable atti-tude.

So What *Is* Alzheimer's?

Thus far in this chapter, I have told you what Alzheimer's disease is not. A few words are in order about what it may be.

Alzheimer's is a progressive disease. For the first two or three years, the most obvious symptom is memory loss, characteristically only for recent events. Patients remember very clearly what hap-pened thirty or forty years earlier, but have little or no recollection about events in the last day, hour or even minute. As a result, they confabulate—that is, when they are embarrassed at not remembering something, they will make up a story to fit the facts. Impaired mem-ory is often followed by confusion, paranoia, suspicion and distrust of everyone—particularly strangers, but often even those they love most. Death usually occurs within ten years as these patients lose their ability to function. Their muscle strength diminishes; they become bedridden, literally waste away and finally die. We don't know why all this happens. At the moment, there is no treatment or prevention for these unfortunates. The doctor's greatest challenges are to provide comfort for the patient and support for the anguished family.

Even though there is no cure, you may find it interesting to read about the areas of current research in Alzheimer's disease.

When the brain of someone suffering from this disorder is examined after death, the cells in the cerebral cortex, where behavior, memory, personality and intelligence are determined, are found to be decreased in number. Under the microscope, we see what are called neural fibrillatory tangles—strands of brain tissue going every which way rather than in the usual orderly pathway. When this tissue is analyzed chemically, one finds a deficiency of those substances responsible for transmitting nervous impulses in the brain.

Researchers have tried to translate these observations into workable theories. For example, when we put some of this missing neurotransmitter (called acetylcholine) into a test tube and add an "anticholinergic" drug, the neurotransmitter is neutralized or destroyed. That may be what happens in the brain of the patient with Alzheimer's disease. Interestingly enough, we frequently prescribe anticholinergics in the daily practice of medicine. They are the antispasmodics your doctor gives you for painful spasms or cramps in your intestinal tract. When a normal person takes one of these drugs, a transient memory deficit is occasionally observed. This can be reversed by administering choline, derived from lecithin in the diet, and also by a drug called physostigmine. Some doctors, including me, are now hesitant to prescribe anticholinergics to elderly people. For the same reason, the health-food industry is promoting choline and lecithin supplements to prevent Alzheimer's disease. Scientists are now working with physostigmine in various dosages as a possible treatment. Although this area of research is promising, there is not enough evidence yet to warrant taking any of these substances. Many studies have been done in which behavior and memory have been measured before and after administering these chemicals. No significant differences have been noted. Still, the leads are being pursued.

Another theory proposed to explain Alzheimer's disease suggests that aluminum plays a role in its development. Aluminum is a neuro-toxin. It damages brain cells. When given to rats in large doses, it changes their behavior. More important, aluminum produces the same neural fibrillatory tangles in the rat brain that we see in the brains of humans with Alzheimer's disease. Perhaps most significant is the observation that the aluminum content of the brains of patients dying with Alzheimer's disease is ten to thirty times higher than in nondemented individuals. What's more, it's concentrated in the ab-normal-looking neural fibrillatory tangles. I know several scientists who are so taken with these observations that they personally avoid all contact with aluminum. They don't use antacids or skin deodor-ants that contain aluminum, and have even discarded their cooking utensils made of this metal. But before you stop treating your ulcer and change your antiperspirant, remember that this is still only a theory in its very earliest stages, and one that is by no means univer-sally accepted.

At the present time, we must pursue each and every lead which points to the possible prevention and treatment of Alzheimer's dis-ease. Until that time, it is important to focus on proper diagnosis, looking for the many remediable causes of dementia.

CHAPTER **5**

A High-Fiber Diet—The New Miracle Food

The truth is that most people really know, deep down, what they should do and eat in order to stay healthy. But that's not always easy, convenient or fun. So they constantly look for some painless, pleasant shortcut to prevention—of cancer, heart disease, aging or sexual decline. After all, why give up the cigarettes that keep you calm and thin? Why watch your weight when staying svelte means getting used to being a little hungry all the time? Why bother reducing your high blood pressure when you feel so well anyway, and when antihypertensive medications either keep you in the toilet all night or interfere with your sex life? Why waste valuable time exercising when it is so boring? Why follow a "prudent" low-fat, low-cholesterol diet when it means avoiding all the delicious gourmet foods you've grown to love? Instead, why not continue to enjoy life and just keep looking for the miracle formula, preferably a food or a pill, that will keep you healthy into old age?

Fiber—A Cinderella Story

How would you react to the news that there is a group of foods, not a drug, mind you, that many serious scientists say can actually delay or prevent the following seventeen common conditions? Hemorrhoids, constipation, colorectal cancer, arteriosclerosis, irritable bowel, diverticulosis, diabetes, gallstones, high cholesterol and tri-glycerides, appendicitis, hiatus hernia, varicose veins, obesity, dental cavities, gout, high blood pressure and osteoarthritis.

Count them. There are seventeen.

The food that allegedly does it all falls under the broad heading of "dietary fiber." Are the claims made for it justified? Should everyone be consuming a diet rich in fiber? What *is* such a diet? Is it safe to eat all you want or can too much harm you?

The first documented record of the possible beneficial effects of dietary fiber actually dates back to Hippocrates, who was aware of its laxative properties. Despite the present preoccupation with fiber, Americans paid no attention to it for years. On the contrary, we have been changing our food-processing techniques over the last century in order to eliminate it from our diet. After all, the reasoning has gone, why bother with fiber, which is nothing more than the indigestible remnants of the various plant foods we eat, left over after the gut has absorbed everything it needs. Why give a second thought to this residue, which provides no essential nutrients, vitamins or minerals, and whose destiny it is to be passed out of the body as waste. But in the 1960s, two researchers named Burkitt and Trowell noted that in the underdeveloped areas of the world the seventeen conditions listed above were much less common than in Western, developed lands. For example, in many parts of Africa and Asia, diverticulosis is virtually unknown. (This is a chronic disorder of the large bowel in which fingerlike projections, diverticula, develop in its wall, later become inflamed and can cause all kinds of trouble.) So are high blood pressure, cancer of the bowel, appendicitis, gallstones and arteriosclerotic heart disease. According to Burkitt, the really key factor in life-style that accounts for these differences between, let's say, a film producer living in Beverly Hills and a Masai native in the heart of Africa is what they eat. African natives consume a great deal of fiber. We do not. In fact, in the last hundred years, Americans have reduced their fiber intake by 80 percent, by cutting down on starches, other carbohydrates and wheat products like cereals, while at the same time greatly increasing consumption of refined sugar, white flour, red meat and fat. The African native eats very little of these products of "civilization," except when he moves from the bush to the city. And when he does, he becomes prone to our diseases. According to Burkitt and his associates, were we to adopt the diet of the African native, or at least of our forebears, we would substantially reduce the incidence of all seventeen disorders listed above.

How Fiber Works

Dietary fiber is made up of those components of plant-based foods that are resistant to the digestive enzymes in the gut. There are essentially two kinds of fiber, each with its own mode of action—the celluloses and hemicelluloses, and the gums and pectin. Despite the fact that the digestive process leaves them intact, these fibers are by no means inert or without biological effects. Indeed, they affect the intestinal tract in several very positive ways. The celluloses, for example, soak up water in the lower bowel, or colon, as they pass through it. The stool, into which they are incorporated, now becomes waterlogged and therefore heavier and softer. Pectin and the various gums, like guar, cause the stomach and small intestine to retain food for a longer time. The result is a more slowly and evenly digested sugar load. Here are some of the ways fiber, by virtue of these actions, specifically counters several common conditions:

- When you eat cellulose fiber, your stool leaves the bowel more easily and quickly. This prevents constipation. Many of our bulk laxatives, including the well-known Metamucil (derived from cereal bran), are made of cellulose.
- A high-fiber diet may prevent colon cancer since the bulkier stool moves along the large intestine so quickly that whatever it is that causes the cancer in the first place has less time to work its evil ways.
- The laxative effect of fiber also cuts down on the causes of hemorrhoids. There are fewer hard stools, less straining, and therefore decreased pressure on the rectal veins.
- Hiatus hernia may be prevented. This is a condition in which a portion of the upper stomach slips up into the chest due to a weakening of the diaphragm (the muscle that separates the abdomen from the chest). This causes symptoms of acid indigestion and gas. The more constipated you are, the harder you strain when you're evacuating, and the greater the pressure generated in the abdominal cavity. This elevates and weakens the diaphragm, making you more vulnerable to a hiatus hernia.
- The same mechanism of increased abdominal pressure due to consti-

pation probably contributes not only to hemorrhoids and hiatus hernia but to varicose veins in the legs as well.

- Bulky, soft stools, which move quickly down and out of the gut, also result in less pressure on the bowel wall, and so decrease the likelihood of diverticulosis, appendicitis and other bowel problems.
- Pectin and gums also reduce the risk of arteriosclerosis, bowel cancer and cholesterol gallstones—and do so in the following way. First, they bind the cholesterol you eat, which is then excreted in the stool instead of getting into your blood. Then they also combine with bile acids (made in the liver), which are rich in cholesterol. That drops the cholesterol level even further. Since most gallstones are made of cholesterol, the generally lower cholesterol blood levels resulting from the pectin and gums decrease the chance of gallstones forming. Finally, bile acids themselves have also been implicated in the causation of bowel cancer, so the less you have, as a result of their being bound by fiber, the better off you are.
- Pectin and gums acting on the stomach reduce the amount of sugar in the blood. In diabetics, this may decrease the requirements for insulin or anti-diabetic pills.
- The same mechanism that lowers blood sugar may reduce high blood pressure. Since there is less sugar absorbed, less insulin needs to be made by the body, and decreased insulin production appears to be associated with a drop in blood pressure.
- Osteoarthritis is improved as a result of the weight loss induced by fiber, since the affected joints are less stressed in thin persons than in those who are overweight.

Even though everything about fiber seems so logical, there are some doctors who are not convinced that it's all it's cracked up to be. Nevertheless, the relationship between fiber and cancer does have considerable support. In fact, the director of the National Cancer Institute has stated his opinion that were the intake of fiber in the American diet doubled to 30 grams per day there would be twenty thousand fewer deaths from colorectal cancer every year.

My own clinical experience with fiber has been good. It has prevented constipation in some very difficult situations—in pregnant women, the elderly, and in hospitalized persons, especially after a heart attack when we don't want them straining at stool. I have found it to work well in cases of diverticulosis and in many patients with inflammatory bowel disease (Crohn's, ulcerative colitis).

What's a High-Fiber Diet?

Try to take between 30 and 40 grams of fiber every day. What kind of diet is likely to provide that amount? One containing 100 percent whole-wheat flour instead of white flour, plenty of fresh fruit, raw or light cooked vegetables, and little if any refined sugar. You should also sprinkle miller's bran over your regular cereal or put it in tomato or orange juice. Start with a teaspoon and work your way up gradually to three tablespoons a day.

Four slices of whole-wheat bread per day, at 5 grams per slice, will give you more than twice the daily average intake of fiber in this country. A commercially available preparation called Fibermed is a tasty cookie containing 5 grams of the cellulose-type fiber. Many of my patients eat four or five of them a day, and love them. They work, they are convenient, and unlike most breakfast cereal, they don't require milk.

Since there are various kinds of fiber, each from different food sources and with varying modes of action, you should diversify your fiber source. For example, if you limit yourself just to bran (which contains mainly celluloses), you will benefit only from its effect on the lower bowel. But if you add the pectin and gums found in apples, oranges, bananas, peas, carrots, berries and potatoes, you will also lower your blood sugar and cholesterol.

In your enthusiasm for fiber, however, don't start with massive doses. (In fact, if you have any physical or organic problem involving your intestinal tract, don't start at all without first consulting with your doctor. In the unlikely and unfortunate event that you have some obstruction within the gut, the fiber may make it worse.)

Some years ago one of my patients, a health-food enthusiast of long standing, asked me whether she should add fiber to her diet. I was enthusiastic in my endorsement. She rushed out to the health-food store and returned home with bundles of whole-wheat bread, bottles of miller's bran, boxes of cereals, packages of nuts—and went at them with a vengeance. A week or so later, she came to see me— very displeased. "Doctor, let me tell you about your high-fiber diet. It may be good for the Africans, but it's awful for Americans! I followed it as you told me to, and all I've got is cramps, diarrhea and gas."

You may have the same problems if you launch into your new

high-fiber diet with the same enthusiasm. Bacteria in the lower bowel ferment the fiber and produce methane gas (the same gas that's given off by rotten eggs). People on high-fiber diets generally do have more gas than others, but in time, they usually accommodate to the fiber, and their symptoms, if any, are minimal. So start with small doses and gradually increase your intake to the optimal amount.

How do you know when you are taking enough fiber? When your stools are soft and pass easily and regularly. At that point, you needn't increase the dose.

A high-fiber diet is not necessarily risk-free. Because of the rapid transit time of the bowel contents, certain minerals and other nutrients (zinc, iron, magnesium and calcium) may be lost in the stool. When very large amounts of fiber are consumed by persons whose nutrition is poor to begin with, deficiencies in these minerals can occur. In fact, they are frequently observed in rural Africa, and among the elderly poor in this country.

I advise all my patients to educate their children to a high-fiber diet early in life (and incidentally, to one low in salt, sugar and fat). Add to that a commitment to regular physical exercise, avoidance of alcohol excess, abstinence from tobacco and "recreational" drugs, and you have laid the cornerstone of effective prevention against several important diseases.

CHAPTER **6**

Sleeping Problems—
Too Little, Too Much or Too Noisy

Insomnia—real, imagined or exaggerated—affects as many as fifty million people in this country. When one tallies up all the reasons for visits to a doctor, the common cold is number one, headaches are second and a sleeping problem is third.

Who is most apt to experience insomnia? Women more than men; also older persons and anyone with an obvious psychological or emotional problem. Surprisingly, the less education you have and the less money you earn, the more trouble you're likely to have getting a good night's sleep. This chapter contains some practical ways to improve the quality of your sleep, as well as the rest and satisfaction you can derive from it. (Incidentally, a good way to get lots of sleep is to try writing a chapter on insomnia.)

Strictly speaking, nobody suffers from insomnia, which is defined as total lack of sleep. What most people mean when they tell you "I don't sleep" is a relative inability to do so, characterized by any one of several different patterns. The most common form is the one in which you have trouble falling asleep, but once you do, you're out like a light for the rest of the night. Or you may doze off easily, but wake up a couple of hours later, and spend the rest of the night tossing and turning, sleeping for only short intervals. Some persons tell me they get to sleep with no problem, but awaken after only five or six hours—and don't feel that's enough.

The constellation of "insomnia" usually embraces a combination of these and other patterns. The elderly usually have a very special kind of sleep rhythm referred to as "polyphasic." Whereas most healthy individuals below the age of forty are active during the day and sleep only at night, older persons often feel drowsy during the day and nap frequently. As a result, they sleep less at night, and not very deeply.

We used to think that trouble sleeping at night was almost always due to excessive mental and physical stimulation at bedtime. We now know that's only part of the story. In at least one-third of persons with sleeping problems, the cause is psychological—the result of chronic stress during the day as well as at bedtime. Such individuals are usually depressed, and often suffer from other emotional disorders.

For many people the ability to fall asleep becomes an obsession. They remain awake trying too hard to fall asleep. The bedroom becomes the symbol not of sleep but of lack of sleep—the stimulus for a conditioned response. It's very much like what happened to Pavlov's dogs, whose keepers rang a bell at every feeding. After a while, when the food was withheld but the gong was struck, the dogs started salivating in the expectation of receiving their food. For these insomniacs, the bedroom itself is the "gong" of sleeplessness.

If the reason for your sleeping difficulty is not immediately apparent, bear in mind the possibility of stress. If you find that to be the case, you'll either have to learn how to cope with it or get help to do so. If you have worries, externalize them; that is, bring them out in the open, face them, discuss them and try to deal with them. Keeping things to yourself all day will end in their surfacing during the night when you should be sleeping.

Many cases of insomnia are due to drugs prescribed for the treatment of some chronic condition. A prime example is thyroid medication, too much of which will keep you awake for hours. Other agents that may interfere with sleep include most appetite suppressants; tricyclic antidepressants; medications containing phenylpropanolamine (PPA), available over the counter to promote weight loss or to relieve nasal congestion or other cold symptoms; or diuretics, which have you emptying your bladder at frequent intervals. Some patients tell me that the high-potency vitamins they take stimulate them to the point of insomnia. So if you have become a chronic insomniac and are on *any* medications over the long term, check with your doctor to see whether they may be the source of the problem.

Certain diseases may also interfere with sleep. Examples are enlargement of the prostate, which makes it necessary for the individual to void every hour or two during the night; the chronic pain of arthritis or cancer, or the shortness of breath due to disease of the heart or lungs.

Before You Retire

Keep out of your bedroom at night until you're sleepy; do not get into bed and wait for sleep. If you've been tossing and turning for thirty minutes, don't keep punishing yourself. Get up and leave the bedroom, relax in some other area of your home, wait until you are tired and then try again.

Bedtime should be determined not by the clock, but when drowsiness sets in. Don't ignore the desire to sleep by starting to work on some papers you brought home with you from the office. Just as continually ignoring the signal to evacuate your bowels until it is convenient can lead to chronic constipation, so will delaying sleep when your body is ready for it end up in insomnia.

Try to establish a regular sleep schedule. The body likes a routine. The most effective habit you can acquire—one that is apt to help your sleeping problem—is to get up at the same time every morning, every day of the week, regardless of when you went to bed. You should do that even if it means deliberately waking yourself after very little sleep. As tired and drowsy as you are, get up, get going and keep going until you're ready to sleep the following night. You'll find that if you can discipline yourself sufficiently to do this, you may very well resolve your sleep difficulties. If you're a poor sleeper, don't nap during the day. That will only perpetuate the cycle. The sleep you get when you should be awake is not the sleep you want or need.

You'd think from all the people you see sound asleep with books on their chests or snoring with the TV blaring that reading and watching TV at bedtime are ideal soporifics. Surprisingly, they're probably not, unless you've been tuned in to something quite boring or reading a dull text. A book or TV show that makes you laugh, interests you or stimulates you is not likely to be conducive to sleep. Also, don't work in bed. Leave your briefcase and its contents in another room. Worry, tension, deadlines, problems and decisions are not matters for the mattress.

Though you shouldn't have a heavy meal at bedtime, certain foods can help you sleep. That's because they contain L-tryptophan, an amino acid that triggers sleep by acting on the brain. Milk is rich in this substance, which explains how a glass of warm milk at bedtime became a popular insomnia remedy. Other foods with this amino acid are tuna, cottage cheese, soybeans, cashews, chicken, turkey and eggs. If you decide to have a snack rich in L-tryptophan, eat some carbohydrate or drink a glass of orange juice with it. This combination facilitates transmission of the tryptophan to the brain, where it is converted to a "neurotransmitter" responsible for drowsiness. One sure way to get all the L-tryptophan you need is to buy it at your health-food store. It comes in 500-mg. capsules or tablets and you'll need between three and six at bedtime to do the trick. It doesn't require a prescription. Although the Food and Drug Administration is not convinced that it works, I have been favorably impressed with it. But be careful. Some ophthalmologists believe L-tryptophan actually accelerates cataract formation. So if you're having any visual problems, check out the use of L-tryptophan with your eye doctor.

What about alcohol? A single glass of wine or one to two ounces of brandy at bedtime can help give you a good night's sleep. Larger amounts, however, usually have the reverse effect. A stiff drink or two may get you to sleep, but in a little while a withdrawal phenomenon sets in, waking you up. It also goes without saying that caffeine —in coffee, tea and many cola drinks—can interfere with sleep. It's perfectly all right to have caffeine in moderate amounts during the day, but after dinner, drink a decaffeinated beverage.

Cigarettes may also cause a problem. The nicotine in tobacco is a stimulant that may interfere with your falling asleep. The fire caused by a lighted cigarette will also surely keep you awake!

The world's literature would have us believe that there is nothing like sex for a good night's sleep—in someone's arms. That's certainly true for some people, perhaps even for most, but for others, the experience is too stimulating. Consider whether you might fall into this latter category. If so, you may find it more suitable to be an

"A.M.er" and have all your sex before breakfast and not before going to bed.

Exercise enthusiasts often like to work out in the bedroom, doing calisthenics or using a bicycle, treadmill or rowing machine just before retiring. They do so to burn up the calories they've eaten at dinner and to help them relax before sleep. The former is valid; the latter is not. I suggest you get your exercise during the day or at least a couple of hours before bedtime, and not when you're ready to go to sleep.

To wind down at night, try some deep breathing instead of a workout. This causes an accumulation of carbon dioxide in the blood, which may have a tranquilizing effect. This is how to do it: Take three very slow, deep breaths, exhaling fully after each. At the end of the third exhalation, pause without breathing for as long as possible. Repeat this cycle five to eight times, then breathe normally again. In many cases relaxation and sleep will come more easily.

Physical comfort is important to sound sleep. A room that's too cold because of air conditioning in the summer, or overheated and dry in the winter, will cause nasal crusting and insomnia. Keep the bedroom temperature between 64° and 66°. Make sure your bed is firm enough to support your shoulders and back, large enough for stretching and changing positions comfortably, and long enough so that your feet don't stick out uncovered and cold. Most bedding today utilizes the support characteristics of innersprings—steel coils in various counts, configurations and wire thicknesses. Layers of upholstery materials provide insulation and cushioning between the body and the coils. Bedding manufacturers design mattresses and foundations to work best when used together. The resilience, height and location of each spring is matched to the foundation. So placing a new mattress on an old foundation will reduce the life and performance of that mattress. Full-depth polyurethane-foam mattresses are an alternative to innersprings. Water-filled mattresses, when properly filled, may also be comfortable. But whatever bed you choose, the most important single consideration in purchasing a mattress is your comfort. Don't try to economize on the quality of your bedding. Also, lie down on the mattress right there in the showroom as they tell you to do in the TV ads. See if it's comfortable for you before you buy it. A recent report suggests that a fleecy wool pad between the mattress and the bottom sheet results in less tossing and turning.

(I'm sure the fact that this news comes from Australia has nothing to do with that country being the prime producer of wool.) I have found woolen blankets are more comfortable than synthetic covers, but I don't know of any statistical studies that confirm my impression.

Another way to induce sleep is to let your imagination wander—lie back and think of something pleasant to distract your mind from whatever anxious thoughts you may have. If you must worry, focus on a single problem rather than the many that are whirling around in your consciousness. It's easier to cope with just one difficulty than to face an overwhelming number.

Some of my patients are enthusiastic about biofeedback and progressive relaxation techniques as sleeping aids. Try to relax by loosening muscle tension in one area of the body at a time, while breathing slowly and rhythmically. A warm, but not hot, bath can be soothing and also induce drowsiness at bedtime by moving blood away from the brain and into the skin.

There is a variety of gimmicks and sleeping aids available to relieve tension and promote sleep. These include self-hypnosis recordings, and others which reproduce the sound of surf. "Masking" devices such as these are especially useful if your home is in a noisy area, downtown in a city, or near an airport or highway.

What about taking something to help you sleep? I've already mentioned L-tryptophan. If that doesn't work, try two aspirins at bedtime, unless of course there is some reason for you not to do so (asthma, a history of bleeding ulcer, or some other bleeding problem). You may think that any sleeping potion that doesn't require a prescription is perfectly safe and may be taken at will. That's not always true. Most such drugs contain antihistamines, which can aggravate glaucoma and cause urinary problems, especially in men. If you're using them regularly, check with your doctor whether it's safe for you to do so.

The most pressing question asked by insomniacs concerns sleeping pills. Most doctors, including myself, are opposed to the chronic use of hypnotics, sedatives and tranquilizers at bedtime. I have no objection to taking one now and then to help cope with an acute crisis—a bereavement, a major economic setback or some other disappointment. But routine reliance on these drugs is a crutch and is undesirable. Most of them are habit-forming and result in dependence—if not physical, then psychological. Once you are hooked, your chances of ever sleeping without them are remote. In chronic users, one pill rarely is enough. I have patients who have gone to the upper limit of safety for a given preparation, abandoned it, tried another and, still found themselves severely sleep handicapped, even after taking the most potent sleeping pills available. From time to time, such individuals graduate to narcotics, and then they're in real trouble.

There are other reasons why doctors discourage the use of sleeping pills. If you are an alcoholic or even a moderate social drinker, the interaction between alcohol and sedatives can produce very troublesome, indeed dangerous, side effects. If you're pregnant, these medications may have an adverse effect on the fetus. Remember thalidomide? Also, if you have a sick, elderly parent, friend, neighbor or a child who may need you during the night, or if you're on call for some sensitive or important job, taking a sleeping pill can impair your alertness in an emergency. Finally, there is the hangover that so many people have after they take sleeping pills, all the advertisements by the pharmaceutical industry notwithstanding. If you've been on such a product for more than a month, you will almost surely experience "rebound insomnia" when you stop.

So if you have trouble sleeping, try to determine the reasons. Are they psychological, physical, due to another illness or to some drug you're taking? In most cases the problem can be solved in consultation with your doctor. If it is not, then have him refer you to a sleep center, where more sophisticated analyses and forms of treatment are available.

How to Awaken the Dead

Can you name the one disorder in medicine that is characterized by the following? (1) The patient is totally unaware of the condition, denies that he has it and usually suffers no ill effects from it. (2) Those around him are perfectly miserable. (3) When convinced that he has a problem, the afflicted individual treats it as a joke, even though the impact on others may be devastating.

Those characteristics identify the snorer.

I'd never had any great personal or professional interest in the problem of snoring. As a child, I was always lucky enough to have my own bedroom. The first time I was ever exposed to the sleeping behavior of others on any significant or recurring basis was as a teen-ager, in an army barracks with fifty or sixty other men. Quite frankly, I was so exhausted at the end of each day, I couldn't have cared less about the decibel level around me. Later, I was fortunate enough to marry a woman who among all her other virtues does not snore. So —until a recent experience—I never gave much thought as to why some people snore, what can or should be done about it, and whether or not the "habit" has other than a social impact.

One day last winter I was called to see a patient who had rented a house in the Caribbean, and who had become sick there. I arrived at about 2 P.M., performed my examination, consulted with the local doctors and was through with the professional part of my visit by 4 P.M. So I went for a little swim, sipped a long rum drink and walked the pearly-white sandy beach. There were four of us at dinner that night, my patient, his wife, a houseguest who had arrived earlier that day and myself. After a delicious meal and a video-cassette movie, we all turned in.

Now, this house was situated atop a hill slightly inland. There was utter silence at night, except for the chirping of crickets and the sounds of other tropical insects.

The bottom half of my bedroom door was shuttered, permitting delightful cross ventilation. It had been a long day for me, although a very pleasant one, so I fell asleep the moment my head hit the pillow. Soon I had an unusual dream. I was on a jet runway beneath the engine of a departing Boeing 747. The roar was so loud it woke me up. I sat bolt upright, expecting silence with the end of my dream. The quiet lasted for only a moment, and then the noise recurred. Its vibration shook the walls of the room. Now wide-awake, I realized what was happening. This was not a jet, it was a snore—from the houseguest whose bedroom was next door to mine. I tossed and turned, but there was no way to escape the auditory assault. Apparently both our beds were similarly positioned with headboards against the dividing wall. Then a brilliant idea came to mind. I reversed position so that my feet steadied the wall. I hoped this would at least reduce the vibration. It didn't work.

What to do? I had no cotton with me, so I plugged my ears with tissue paper. Totally ineffective. Then I did something I personally reserve only for the gravest of emergencies—I took a sleeping pill. (Remember, I said earlier in this chapter it was all right to do so in an acute crisis. Boy, was this ever a crisis!) I waited for the merciful veil of sleep to descend, but every time it was about to do so, a staccato roar pierced it. Short of a general anesthetic, there was no way I could or would escape this noise. I then tried to make out some rhythm to the racket. I felt that if I timed it carefully, I might actually doze off between snorts. Of course, that expectation was ridiculous. It was as if he was playing cat and mouse with me. His noise pattern was totally unpredictable. Just as I began to float away during a ten-second period of silence, a machine-gun-like succession of six snorts erupted to jolt me back to wakefulness.

I now had only one alternative, my ace in the hole. I would move from that room. But where? The large villa was unfamiliar to me. It was dark and I wasn't sure who was sleeping where, except for that infernal noise generator next door. Then I remembered the living room, and its couch; that was obviously the place to go. I took my pillows, blanket, wrapper and slippers and wended my way through the darkened corridors.

The couch I was looking for was L-shaped. As I approached it, I was astonished to find it occupied. There, lying head to head on both limbs of the L, were my patient and his wife, sound asleep. They had also been driven from their own rooms.

I did accomplish one thing that unforgettable night. You know how some people count sheep when they go to bed? After returning resignedly to my room, I actually tallied the number of snorts in an eight-hour period. Would you believe 926? That's right. Over an interval of roughly 480 minutes, 926 snorts—in singlets, couplets and short bursts. That works out to approximately two bursts per minute.

In the morning, I never said a word about what had happened during the night. But when my patient invited me to stay the rest of the weekend, I suddenly remembered a very important appointment back home.

Snoring—The Road to Divorce

I have since thought many times about what it would be like to be married to or to live with someone who snored like that man behind my wall. Sharing a bedroom would naturally be impossible. Even separate rooms wouldn't work unless the house was big enough, or the walls adequately soundproofed. I then realized that a discussion of the prevention and/or management of snoring might be very much appreciated by millions of people who are exposed to the one in eight among us who are serious snorers.

In order to be able to do something about snoring, you must first understand the mechanism that produces it. Why, for example, don't we snore during waking hours? After all, snoring is part of the breathing process, and all of us breathe twenty-four hours a day.

Inspired air flows into the mouth and nose through the airways in the head and the pharynx on its way to the lungs. While we're awake, muscles in the area keep all these passages open, so the air rushes through them unimpeded. But when we sleep, those muscles relax, and the airway passages tend to collapse. Air now flowing through these constricted passages encounters resistance, requiring a greater inspiratory force. The resulting vibrations in the surrounding tissues constitute the snore. Its intensity, or loudness, depends on the degree of narrowing of the airways and on whether the tissues in the area are loose enough to "rattle in the breeze."

Snoring usually has no ill effects on the perpetrator. For example, my fellow guest in the Caribbean looked—maddeningly—great the following morning. Occasionally, however, respiratory pathways are so narrowed or constricted that the amount of air passing through them is very much reduced. This results in a condition called *obstructive sleep apnea*. An individual with this problem breathes in a characteristic cyclical fashion: first there is the familiar rhythmic snoring, followed abruptly by total cessation of breathing. The resistance in the airways is so great at this point that no air moves through them. The chest, however, continues to heave as if the person were still breathing, but he is not. The silence may last anywhere from a few seconds to as long as two minutes. During that time, since the lungs are not receiving air, the blood is deprived of oxygen, and so are the tissues throughout the body, including the heart and the brain. When the oxygen concentration in the blood drops below a certain level, sleep lightens and respiratory centers in the brain stimulate the breathing mechanisms vigorously, so that air once more moves through the constricted passages. The period of respiratory "arrest," or apnea, ends with a particularly loud snort, followed by a succession of other "bursts," after which the cycle repeats itself—snore, silence, snort, paroxysms of snorts, and silence. The recurring drop in oxygenation has health consequences that include hypertension, behavioral alterations the next day and even sudden death during the night. At the end of each cycle of apnea, the individual actually awakens, although he later has no recollection of having done so. Since this happens every few minutes throughout the night, the person with obstructive apnea is not only chronically oxygen-deprived, he also has a sleep deficit. He therefore tries to catch up during the daytime hours—sometimes involuntarily; literally falling alseep while conversing or even standing. This is called the Pickwickian syndrome, after the fat boy in Dickens' *Pickwick Papers,* where the description of this daytime somnolence was so classic!

Simple snoring and obstructive sleep apnea are really a spectrum, or continuum, in which men are afflicted twenty times more frequently than women. Such individuals tend to be stocky rather than tall and thin; they are likely to be overweight, to suffer from chronic lung disease, and, for some reason, complain of impotence. But perhaps the most important association is with high blood pressure. In a very recent study of some fifty men with hypertension, one-third were found to have sleep apnea—*of which they were unaware.* When the apnea was successfully treated (see below), blood pressure dropped in most cases. On the basis of this and other related research, which suggest a 30 percent coexistence of the two conditions, it seems reasonable to look for the presence of sleep-related breathing disorders in all middle-aged or older men with high blood pressure.

Anti-Snoring Remedies—"Stop Me Before I Snore More!"

Scores of household remedies have been suggested over the years to control snoring, none of which really work. I know patients who have tried all kinds of devices and contraptions varying from a neck collar to adhesive tape in order to keep their mouths closed. Since snoring is loudest when you are sleeping on your back, some desperate spouses have sewn little pockets on the back of their tormentor's pajamas in which they have inserted tennis balls or marbles to force them to sleep on their sides. There is no harm in trying these maneuvers; they may occasionally help.

Such simple measures as weight loss and regular exercise apparently do make a difference. You should avoid sleeping pills and/or alcohol at bedtime, since they increase the degree of muscular relaxation and so make the collapse of the airways more likely, thus increasing the obstruction to airflow.

An important caution: Most local surgical interventions used as a "cure" for snoring—for instance, correcting deviated septums, and removing tonsils and adenoids—don't really have much impact on the problem. So think twice before you subject a loved one (to the extent you can still love anyone who does this to you night after night) to an operation.

However, if none of the approaches I have mentioned above succeed, and if you are dealing with a true "mega-snorer," the level of intervention may have to be raised.

A relatively recent and effective technique for dealing with severe snoring and obstructive sleep apnea is referred to as CPAP—continuous positive airways pressure. This is a relatively simple and inexpensive treatment in which a small plastic mask is placed over the patient's nose. Room air, not oxygen, is delivered from a compressor at the bedside at a pressure slightly above normal (5 to 10 cms. of water). Synchronized with the patient's breathing, air flowing at such positive pressure keeps the airways from collapsing and hence stops snoring and sleep apnea. CPAP is the first route to follow. It often works.

If *all* else fails, and especially if the problem is one of sleep apnea, there is an operation that may help. This procedure, called UPP (which stands for uvulopalatopharyngoplasty), involves removing any excess tissue in the back of the throat that may contribute to the vibrations resulting from the construction of the air passages. The UPP operation is no more complicated than a tonsillectomy.

Finally, in some cases when the sleep apnea is life-threatening, a tracheostomy may have to be performed. An incision is made into the windpipe, and the patient breathes through a tube inserted into that opening, thus bypassing the constructed airways higher up. This is really an emergency procedure of last resort and is never used just for snoring, no matter how bad. The tracheostomy is left in place as long as the circumstances leading to the sleep apnea persist. Frankly, if I had to live the rest of my life as I spent that one night in the Caribbean, I would recommend surgery—any surgery—without hesitation, even for severe snoring without apnea. But don't you let yourself get talked into it.

CHAPTER 7

Cystitis—When the Honeymoon Is Over

Aside from the common cold, the most prevalent disease among females is cystitis—infection of the urinary bladder. Virtually every sexually active woman may be expected to develop cystitis at some time or other. I have patients who suffer recurrences every two to three months. This needn't be the case: cystitis *is* preventable or easily controlled.

The infection itself is usually caused by a bacterium called *Escherichia coli,* a normal inhabitant of the bowel. However, viruses and other infectious agents can also cause the trouble.

Cystitis is much more common in females than males because in women the rectum is only one to three inches away from the opening of the urethra. This makes it easy for the *E. coli* to travel from one to the other. Also, since the female urethra is only one-half inch to two inches long, after the bacteria gain access to it, they have only a short way to go to reach the bladder. Once there, unless eradicated, they establish a focus for chronic and recurring infection.

Cystitis is less frequent in men because the urethra in the penis is a long way from the rectum and not in physical continuity with it; and, unlike the short female urethra, that of the male extends about eight inches from the tip of the penis to the bladder. When cystitis does occur in men, it is usually after instrumentation or catheterization of the urethra, in association with prostatitis (infection of the prostate gland), or lesions in the urinary bladder.

Curiously, cystitis is not often accompanied by fever. Its chief symptoms are a painful, burning sensation on urination and a need to empty the bladder more frequently than usual. However, each time one does void, very little urine is actually passed, sometimes only a few drops. Although it may appear normal to the naked eye, when examined under the microscope, the urine is usually found to contain either blood or pus, or both. (I know that seasoned air travelers prefer an aisle seat, presumably so as not to disturb anyone should they wish to get up for any reason. Personally, I think a window seat makes much more sense. Imagine a long flight, especially during the night, sitting on the aisle beside a woman with cystitis—or a man with prostatitis.)

Since the urethra lies just above the vaginal canal, vigorous sexual intercourse commonly triggers cystitis, hence the term "honeymoon cystitis." The thrusting motion of the penis may irritate the urethra, causing it to swell, and also carrying bowel bacteria into it. Symptoms of cystitis usually follow anywhere from six to forty-eight hours.

Chlamydia, an organism that is responsible for a variety of infections ranging from blindness to genitourinary disorders, has recently been identified as one of the most common and important sexually transmitted diseases, and may also cause cystitis. Chlamydia used to be difficult to diagnose because of technical limitations, but it can now more easily be identified in a laboratory test that takes about an hour. A broad-spectrum antibiotic like tetracycline will usually eradicate the organism.

Some women, especially those with a "dropped bladder" are more prone to cystitis than others. Also in certain individuals, bacteria that would normally be washed away by urine or destroyed by the body's defense mechanisms hang on more tenaciously to the vaginal surfaces and resist being flushed out. Therapy of cystitis consists of an antibiotic to which the infecting organism is susceptible.

Every woman is vulnerable to cystitis and should follow these rules in order to prevent infection.

(1) Showering is more likely to wash bacteria away from the urethral opening than is bathing. Soap the vaginal and rectal areas thor-

oughly, then rinse them clean. When taking a bath, avoid bubble baths, vaginal sprays and bath oils. Their chemical ingredients may irritate the genital area and also alter the local acid-alkaline balance, permitting any bacteria in the vicinity to multiply and infect. Douching also helps keep the vagina clean.

(2) Bacteria thrive in a warm, moist environment. So wear cotton underpants rather than synthetic fabrics, since cotton absorbs moisture more effectively.

(3) Women with diabetes, whose urine contains sugar, are especially prone to recurrent cystitis because bacteria flourish in a sweet environment. Such individuals must pay particular attention to their personal hygiene, and make every effort to keep the blood (and therefore the urine) sugar levels within normal limits.

(4) Always empty your bladder before and after intercourse. This flushes out at least some bacteria, and makes it less likely that they will be forced into the urethra by the action of the penis. Those that do gain entry will be washed out afterwards, before they can cause infection. It's also a good idea to pour a stream of water over the vaginal area after intercourse to help remove the bacteria.

(5) Never ignore the signal to urinate. When the urinary bladder is full, its blood vessels are compressed. This reduces blood flow to the region and increases the risk of infection. Also, a stagnant pool of urine in the bladder is likely to favor the growth of bacteria that cause cystitis. So make it a habit to empty your bladder as frequently as is convenient. Voiding helps flush the bacteria out of the urethra.

(6) Don't wear tight pants, especially if you have a history of cystitis. They can irritate the vaginal area.

(7) Drink six to eight glasses of water every day.

(8) Some doctors recommend cranberry juice to make the urine more acid and therefore less hospitable to bacteria. I have found this to work in some women, but not in others. However, it's worth a try.

(9) A poorly fitting diaphragm can be irritating. If you have recurrent cystitis, make sure your diaphragm is inserted properly, or consider some other form of contraception.

(10) A dry vagina is vulnerable to infection and results in cystitis. This is most apt to occur in postmenopausal women, or those about to be, because of inadequate estrogen levels. If you fall into that category, you should know that estrogen therapy, by mouth or applied topically as a cream, is the most effective way to control the problem. Ask your physician about it. In any event, if your vagina is dry and irritated by intercourse, use a lubricant like K-Y

jelly. Avoid petroleum-based products. They irritate the vagina. If you're not trying to become pregnant, it's a good idea to apply a small amount of spermicidal gel around the urethral opening before intercourse. This creates an acid environment, which also kills bacteria.

(11) If you use sanitary napkins, change them frequently to reduce the opportunity for bacterial growth and spread from the rectal area.

(12) Women who practice anal intercourse are especially vulnerable to cystitis unless they make certain that vaginal penetration occurs first in the sequence of things.

If you follow all these simple precautions and still develop an attack of cystitis, here is what you should do while you are waiting to see your doctor. Make a solution of one glass of water and a teaspoonful of bicarbonate of soda and drink it immediately. (Take plain tap water if you have high blood pressure or heart problems.) This will help alleviate the burning sensation. Repeat the drink every hour for three hours. The idea is to urinate as often as possible to try to keep the infectious bacteria from reaching the bladder. Continue this regimen until you see your doctor, but if he is not available for several days, substitute plain water after your first three drinks with the soda bicarbonate. To help control pain, a simple analgesic like aspirin or acetaminophen (Tylenol, Datril) will offer some relief. After establishing the diagnosis, your doctor will prescribe the appropriate antibiotic.

For patients with recurrent cystitis, I often prescribe 50 mgs. of trimethoprim or 50 mgs. of macrodantin daily for several months in order to control attacks.

Cystitis is rarely serious, especially in women, but it can make life miserable. Common sense and the guidelines I have suggested above will help prevent this infection in most cases.

CHAPTER 8

Allergy in General, Asthma in Particular

Frankly, I wasn't sure whether to write this chapter at all. My concerns were these: Either you're allergic or you're not. If you are, you know it, and have by now learned the hard way how to cope with your environment. On the other hand, if you aren't allergic, you couldn't care less about the problem. But on further reflection, it occurred to me that allergic individuals might very well want to understand what makes them so and to know something about current research into the causes and prevention of allergy. Practical tips on life-style for the allergic person can be very useful. Also, several important new drugs have been developed that can prevent acute allergic attacks.

Nonallergic individuals, on the other hand, may not be aware that allergies can and do develop even late in life. They should know how this comes about and what to do about it. There is also the matter of the allergic child in whom proper health habits must be monitored and a reasonable life-style established. So I was finally convinced that the information in the following pages may be useful to enough of my readers to warrant its inclusion.

"Allergy," defined in practical terms, is "an immunological or defense reaction occurring in response to a normally harmless substance." Common offenders are airborne pollens, molds, house dust and animal dander; specific foods; insect venoms; and certain chemicals and drugs. The allergic response to any of these may be a stuffy nose, hives, itching of the skin, tearing of the eyes, temporary loss of hearing, wheezing and diarrhea. An allergic reaction can even be life-threatening when it induces anaphylactic shock, in which blood pressure drops and cardiac function is disturbed. Death may ensue unless treatment is promptly instituted. The nature of the symptoms any given person experiences depends on what provoked them, and the degree of that person's sensitivity, as well as how and when the offending agent entered the body—by inhalation, injection, skin contact or via the digestive tract.

The mechanism by which eating a delicious shrimp can threaten your life, or what makes you suddenly start sneezing uncontrollably while enjoying a golf game on the greens, is an interesting one. You can blame it all on the immune system. Normally, this collection of tissues and cells throughout the body protects us against countless life-threatening situations. But sometimes, and this is what happens in allergic persons, the immune system doesn't quite work as it should. It loses the ability to recognize right from wrong, to distinguish "friend" from "foe." As a result, it directs the natural defense mechanisms normally called into play to destroy an invading virus, bacterium or cancer cell against a perfectly innocent, harmless substance. The end result is the acute allergic attack.

The Care and Feeding of an Allergy

Although we understand how this happens, we don't know why it does. When an allergy-prone individual is *first* exposed to an "allergen" or "antigen" (the particular substance destined to make him or her sick), the immune system responds by producing a specific protein that functions as an antibody and is called immunoglobulin E (IgE). This event causes no symptoms, but has "primed" or "sensitized" the individual against the antigen. The newly formed IgE now waits for the next time this particular antigen is ingested, inhaled, injected or touched. When that happens, the immune system lowers the boom. The body releases a flood of chemicals called "mediators" to destroy the "invader." Unfortunately, these mediators also cause the symptoms of allergy.

The best-known mediator is histamine. Now you know why antihistamines are used in the treatment of allergic symptoms. They neutralize the mediator histamine. They don't always work because histamine isn't the only mediator around. There is a whole slew of them, which act in different ways and account for the many different kinds of allergic reactions. Some cause the bronchial passages to contract so that you wheeze; others make mucous glands secrete more heavily, thus aggravating an asthmatic attack; still others render small blood vessels (capillaries) more permeable so that fluid seeps out of them, causing the allergic area to become swollen. The exciting promise in allergy research is that new antimediators are now being made, to join the antihistamines in relieving or preventing allergic symptoms.

Why are 25 percent of Americans allergy-prone and the rest not? We now know that nonallergic persons have specific genes that block the manufacture of IgE antibodies. But even though the ability to do so is hereditary, all is not lost, because scientists are now working very hard to find ways to stop your body from making IgE—regardless of your genes.

Don't Pull the Allergy Trigger

If you are allergy-prone, you must follow certain basic rules in order to cope. For example, if you have hay fever, stay indoors as much as possible during the pollen season. Keep all windows and doors shut and equip your home with some filtering or precipitation device to trap the airborne pollens and mold particles.

Use blankets, pillows and rugs made of synthetic fibers. They are less allergenic than are natural fibers. Also, enclose the mattress and box spring of your bed in plastic.

Obviously, you should avoid those foods to which you are allergic. The most notorious allergens are eggs, shellfish, nuts, tomatoes and chocolate.

Molds are common allergens. They are found in spoiled bread and fruits, fermented alcohol beverages, cheese, mildewed clothing, and houseplants, as well as in such damp places as basements and laundry rooms. The growth of molds in such areas can be controlled by cleaning with products containing chlorine. There have also been reports of mold formation in air conditioners (at home, in the office and even in automobiles) and humidifiers. Spores from these molds are sent into the air when these units are turned on. If you're having acute allergic reactions for no apparent reason, have these air conditioners checked out.

Find another home for any pets to which you are allergic. But if you are too emotionally involved to give them away, then never allow them into your bedroom and keep them off your clothes.

If you are a new mother with a family history of allergy (and even if you are not), you can reduce the risk of the baby's become allergic by breast-feeding for as long as possible. Two years is not unreasonable. Don't give your infant cow's milk (and its products) for at least six months, and no eggs for the first two years. Also, delay the introduction of citrus juices and solid foods (particularly fish) into the diet for as long as possible. Don't smoke, during pregnancy *or* after. Infants of parents who are cigarette smokers develop all kinds of respiratory problems. Avoid wool fabrics and feathers. Finally, for the maximal protection of your child, eliminate molds and keep dust to a minimum in the home environment.

If you're allergic to the venom of insects, you can now be effectively desensitized by a series of shots. But don't rush to have this done just because you have some pain, redness or swelling when you're stung by a bee or a wasp. That's to be expected. The reaction of the truly allergic individual is overwhelming and can end in death. So if when you were previously stung you had difficulty breathing, your blood pressure dropped or you needed emergency treatment with Adrenalin, don't sit around waiting for the next bite. Get yourself desensitized. You can reduce the risk of being stung in the first place by wearing protective clothing and avoiding bright colors. Don't use enticing perfumes or after-shave lotions. These aromas attract biting insects, especially in late summer and early fall when for some reason bees and wasps especially become more aggressive.

Desensitization therapy is now successful not only against insect bites but even against hay fever. It will lessen the severity of symptoms in about 80 percent of cases, and afford permanent relief in 33 percent. Anyone whose life has been jeopardized by extremely severe reactions to certain stings and bites should arrange a course of desensitization, especially if he or she is continually exposed to the insect doing the biting. Also, if your hay fever is of such severity as to interfere with the quality of your life, you too should try being desensitized.

Asthma—The Classic Allergy—Treatable and Preventable

There are about thirty-five hundred deaths, most of which are preventable, from acute asthmatic attacks each year. Asthma, which affects ten million Americans, usually begins in childhood (symptoms appear before the age of five years in 65 percent of cases). About half of all chronic sickness in childhood is due to asthma, which accounts for more days lost from school than any other illness. One child in every forty has the disease, boys more often than girls. However, asthma can and often does have its onset in or persist into adult life. I have several patients who, without any previous history of lung problems, suddenly become asthmatic in their seventies.

At the outset, let me clarify a widely held misconception. Allergy in general, and asthma in particular, are not psychogenic in origin. While stress, anger, anxiety, fear and frustration can all worsen an asthmatic attack, or even trigger one, emotions are not the cause of the disease. However, once asthma becomes chronic, and interferes with one's life-style, it may then result in psychological stress and behavioral problems, especially in children. These youngsters are often rendered social and psychological cripples—a tragedy that is totally unnecessary these days.

In persons with chronic asthma, the major air passages into and through the lungs are somewhat narrowed most of the time, even in the absence of symptoms. This results from the fact that these airways tend to be inflamed, and their caliber reduced by swelling of the lining tissues. When an acute asthmatic attack occurs, these conduits become even more narrowed, thus interfering to a much greater extent with the movement of air in and out of the lungs. In addition, plugs of thick, sticky mucus further obstruct the airflow.

The IgE mechanism described earlier either causes or contributes to most cases of asthma. Asthma also tends to run in families. However, asthmatic attacks can be induced in certain persons without abnormal IgE by a variety of different stimuli—for example, vigorous exercise, cold air, aspirin, respiratory infections, other diseases, and toxic substances in the environment. Such individuals are vulnerable because of underlying inflammation of the mucous membranes lining their respiratory tree. This results in overreaction of the bronchi to what is for most people an innocuous agent. In these cases, avoidance is the best way to prevent the asthmatic attack.

Some asthmatics are so desperate, they try a change of climate. I know of several individuals who, plagued by severe, recurrent asthma due to pollens, actually moved, lock, stock, barrel, job and children, to start new lives far away. Six months later, many came back, not necessarily because they missed the old homestead, but because their IgE problem rendered them vulnerable to other asthma-provoking allergens in their new environment. So if you decide to move, don't burn your bridges. Try the new locale for a few months before making a final commitment.

In addition to attacks triggered by inhalants, asthmatic persons may get into trouble eating certain foods, notably shellfish. There you are, sitting in a seafood restaurant, enjoying a delicious shrimp remoulade, or a fresh Dungeness crab, or some succulent Maine lobster, and you suddenly break out in hives and start to wheeze. The next thing you know, you're acutely short of breath and are being whisked off to the nearest hospital emergency room. There you're given some Adrenalin, bronchodilators and perhaps steroids by injection, and you recover. But it's all quite frightening, and in the future, you vow you will shun shellfish like the plague. Unfortunately, even if you do, you may still develop an acute asthmatic attack while dining out on a "normal" meal. What will have done it this time? A sulfite or other additive. As many as 10 percent of asthmatics are sensitive to sulfites. Sulfites are preservatives and antioxidants commonly used in the preparation of a variety of foods and drinks to keep them edible and looking fresh longer, and even medications (ironically, some anti-asthma inhalants among them). Have you ever wondered why the salads left out in a restaurant always look crisp and green even into the next day, while the avocados and apples you serve at home turn brown so quickly? It's the sulfite the restaurateur has added to them. It takes anywhere from 25 to 200 mgs. to produce an adverse reaction in a vulnerable person.

The sulfite problem is so potentially serious that several communities have enacted local ordinances to forbid their addition in restaurants. After much debate, sulfites have been banned from many foods by the federal government. Where any remains—for example, in certain beers and wines—its amount must be listed on the label. So, even though you're now less likely to be exposed, still, if you're asthmatic and are eating out, ask about whether there is any sulfite in your food or drink—and how much. When shopping for groceries, look for the sulfite content on the labels of the foods you buy.

Sulfites are still sometimes added to asthma medications, as preservatives. The results can be disastrous. I recently read about a woman who was taken to the emergency room of a local hospital for treatment of an acute asthmatic attack. The aerosol therapy she was given was not only ineffective, it worsened her condition. In the end she died. It was later discovered that the anti-asthmatic inhalant she was given had sulfite in it. Don't be ashamed or too timid to ask the treating doctor whether the medication you're being given, especially in an asthmatic emergency, contains any of these sulfites.

There are children and adults, *with and without* IgE abnormalities, who develop asthma only after strenuous exercise. The attack is the result of cooling, evaporation and drying of the lining (mucosa) of the airways. Such exercise-induced asthma can be prevented by learning which physical activity and how much of it predictably provokes an attack in any given individual. Several of my patients, without any previous respiratory complaints, suddenly developed new-onset asthma. A careful history revealed that the attacks started after they'd begun to jog, run or perform some other strenuous exercise. So if you're asthmatic, limit your physical "rehabilitation" to those activities that are fun, are good for you and do not provoke wheezing. The sport most likely to fit that category is swimming. When you swim, your head, because it is in the water, is exposed to 100 percent humidity. So there is no drying, no evaporation, no cooling, and therefore no spasm of the airways. (However, the shock of diving into very cold water can also induce asthma, so it may be wiser to enter the pool toe by toe.) One of my sons is an IgE asthmatic. He was always athletically inclined and anxious to keep physically fit. Most sports provoked asthma, made him wheeze and left him short of breath. But he could swim virtually endlessly without any trouble whatsoever. So that's what he focused on, became a superb swimmer and ended up on his college swimming team.

If you do not have access to a pool, or don't happen to enjoy swimming, what are your alternatives? The sports most likely to give you trouble are those that involve sustained running, like football, soccer, tennis, handball or basketball. On the other hand, golf, weight lifting and bowling are almost always well tolerated. Whatever sport you choose, try to breathe through your nose, not your mouth. Doing so warms and moistens the air going to the lungs. But a great deal depends on how long you actually work out, under what circumstances, as well as the temperature and the humidity of the environment. It usually takes anywhere up to twelve minutes of continuous (as opposed to intermittent) exercise to precipitate asthma in a vulnerable person. The asthmatic attack itself begins a few minutes after the exertion ends, and may last for an hour or more.

If for some reason you must participate in physical activity that you know will give you asthma, certain medications taken beforehand may prevent it. The most effective is cromolyn (Intal) delivered from a nebulizer, combined with albuterol (marketed as Proventil and Ventolin).

Asthma frequently develops in some persons, regardless of their IgE status, as soon as they step into the cold. Such individuals should cover their mouth with a muffler in order to reduce the impact of the sudden cold shock.

Aspirin can also bring on an asthmatic attack in vulnerable individuals. In 1956, I reported in the *American Heart Journal* an account of two patients with chronic asthma who went into shock and came close to dying after taking two aspirin tablets each. I advise all patients with asthma to avoid aspirin and to use acetaminophen (Tylenol, Datril) instead. I also caution them about tartrazine, a commonly used additive for coloring food, which, like sulfites, can precipitate an acute attack.

Remember too if you are now or were at one time asthmatic, to avoid all beta-blocker drugs. The prototype of the group is Inderal. Others are marketed in the United States under the following names: Blocadren, Visken, Lopressor, Tenormin, Corgard and Sectral. These medications are very widely used in the treatment of several common conditions, including angina pectoris, irregularities of heart rhythm, high blood pressure, overactive thyroid, migraine, stage fright, hand tremors, and, more recently, in eye-drop form for glaucoma (Timoptic). If you require treatment of any of these disorders, especially high blood pressure or angina, ask your doctor whether you might take the calcium channel blockers instead (marketed in the United States as Procardia, Isoptin, Calan and Cardizem). Not only do they not cause asthma, they may actually protect against the exercise-induced form.

Rx: To Prevent (and Stop) the Wheezing

What are your medication options for the prevention of the asthmatic attack? Here is a list of the more commonly used agents. Their availability has changed the quality of life for many persons previously crippled by asthma.

There is a host of products in the United States related to aminophylline and marketed under a variety of trade names. Most are available only by prescription and include Unifil, Theo-Dur, Choledyl, Elixophyllin and Quibron. Be careful with any of them if you have liver trouble, heart disease or other chronic illnesses. The newer ones like Unifil seem to cause less gastric irritation and can be taken in once- or twice-a-day dosage. Be sure to follow the prescribing instructions very carefully, since adverse reactions can occur, especially among the elderly and when taken together with other medications. The best way to determine whether or not you are receiving an optimal dosage of these drugs and to avoid toxicity is for your doctor to obtain theophylline levels in your blood.

Another group of drugs used to prevent asthma belongs to the Adrenalin family. In addition to the time-honored ephedrine, their derivatives include Bronkosol, Bronkometer, Alupent, Metaprel, Brethine, Bricanyl, Proventil and Ventolin. They can be taken by pill, in liquid form or by inhalation. You may have to experiment to see which ones are most effective for you, and in what doses. But remember that all these agents can, to varying extents, cause an increased heart rate, elevated blood pressure, nervousness and muscle tremor. So be careful with them if you have hypertension, heart disease or thyroid trouble.

Although the main use of the steroid (cortisone) hormones lies in the treatment of chronic, severe and recurrent asthma, Vanceril (beclomethasone) is an effective preventive. It is delivered by aerosol, acts locally on the lining of the respiratory tree, and is rapidly inactivated by the body. In other words, it does not accumulate and cause the usual complications of oral steroids. Be careful, though, because chronic administration of this agent can leave you with a fungal infection in your throat.

The drugs listed above are not only useful to prevent an acute asthmatic attack; most constitute effective treatment as well. There is, however, another medication, called cromolyn (Intal), inhaled from a nebulizer, that is taken over the long term and is strictly for prevention. It is of no use whatsoever during an acute attack. It works best in children, and curiously enough, reports from England concerning its efficacy are much more glowing than they are in the United States. I recommend it highly—in either country.

Whether in prophylaxis or treatment, it's better to take two or more medications in combination, each in low dosage, than to depend on a big slug of any one, and thus risk unpleasant side effects or toxicity.

Very often, asthma follows on the heels of a respiratory infection, usually bronchitis—viral or bacterial. In these circumstances, lots of fluid together with vigorous and early antibiotic treatment will often prevent the asthmatic attack.

Asthma, whatever its underlying mechanism, is a chronic condition. Although it cannot be cured, the frequency and severity of attacks can be sharply reduced and in many instances prevented by a judicious combination of common sense, avoidance of known allergens and irritants, and the use of modern medications.

CHAPTER 9

Heart Valves That Leak and Flop— And Other Sites of Preventable Infection

Remember the woman with the infected heart valve whose case I described in Chapter 1—the one with a probable history of rheumatic fever as a child? She didn't think having her teeth cleaned was an especially noteworthy event (it isn't for most people), so she never mentioned to her dentist the fact that she'd had a heart murmur since her teens; and the dentist never asked. She was not given any prophylactic antibiotics, as she should have been, and ended up with a life-threatening infection (subacute bacterial endocarditis—SBE) of one of her heart valves. Had this occurred before the antibiotic era, she almost certainly would have died. (This disease is called "subacute" because it can smolder for some time, "bacterial" since the infecting agent is a bacterium, and "endocarditis" because the interior lining tissue of the heart, the endocardium, of which the valves are a part, is affected.)

What's the connection between undergoing dental work (or having a catheter inserted into your urinary bladder, or indeed any operation) and ending up with an infection in your heart? It happens this way. Whatever the provoking procedure, bacteria in the area enter the bloodstream. (Bleeding gums provide a good access route, since the mouth is teeming with organisms—ordinarily benign.) In healthy

90

persons, when these bacteria circulate in the blood, they are easily disposed of by the body's defense mechanisms. But heart valves previously inflamed and scarred by rheumatic fever have a reduced blood supply. (At this point, let me make it clear that a heart murmur does not always reflect an underlying cardiac abnormality requiring antibiotic prophylaxis. Many are "functional," or normal, and are due to the swirling of the blood within the heart chambers. Such innocent murmurs are especially common in early life. Characteristically, they come and go and frequently disappear as the child grows older. However, every murmur should be evaluated very carefully to make absolutely certain that it is, in fact "benign.") When the bacteria floating in the bloodstream come in contact with such devitalized tissue, they settle down quite comfortably on the free edges of the valve cusps, where the circulation is especially bad. Because of the poor blood supply to this tissue, the "bugs" cannot easily be reached by the body's antibacterial defenses. Once they've established a foothold, the bacterial colonies multiply, heaping up in little mounds. (These can often be "seen" by an echocardiogram, which may therefore be helpful in making the diagnosis of SBE.) As the organisms grow and spread on the valve, they chew it up, causing it to leak. The net result is a derangement of the usual way blood moves into, through and out of the various cardiac chambers. This abnormal flow pattern creates extra work for the heart, causing it first to enlarge and eventually to weaken and fail.

There are other ways these infected valves can hurt you. Little pieces (emboli) may break off from the bacterial vegetations, enter the bloodstream and travel to distant parts of the body, causing infection and malfunction of vital organs. If untreated, patients with such emboli will often die.

SBE can affect any portion of the heart's interior that has been devitalized, not only by previous infection such as rheumatic fever, but also by congenital malformations. Whatever the underlying condition, the end result is the same. Yet this disease can be easily prevented by taking an appropriate antibiotic *before* and after you undergo whatever treatment or test is planned. This knocks the bacteria out as soon as they enter the bloodstream and before they can settle down on the valve. Penicillin is the best antibiotic to use, if you are not allergic to it. Anywhere from thirty minutes to two hours before the procedure, for example, teeth cleaning or extraction, take four tablets together of penicillin V (the 500-mg. strength). When your dentist is through with you, take another tablet six hours later. That's all there is to it!

If there is any possibility that you might be allergic to penicillin, take erythromycin. Thirty minutes to two hours before the procedure swallow *two* 500-mg. tablets or capsules (not four, as with penicillin). Then six hours later take one more.

Patients who have had rheumatic fever should be on constant penicillin maintenance—usually into their forties—in order to prevent a recurrence. They take one or two tablets of penicillin daily, or receive an injection of the long-acting preparation once a month. In cases of penicillin sensitivity, a sulfa preparation may be used instead (providing, of course, you're not allergic to it too.) If such an individual is to undergo a dental procedure, or other manipulation (gastrointestinal, genitourinary), I then recommend a booster of the antibiotic given by injection into the muscle. (Some physicians, however, prefer merely to increase the dose of antibiotic via the oral route.)

If your diseased valve has been replaced by an artificial one, it's even more vulnerable to SBE. Here, antibiotic prophylaxis should preferably be administered by injection, not orally.

Bacterial Hide-and-Seek

If I had written this chapter a few years ago, I'd have stopped right here, because bacterial "seeding" was almost always thought to be limited to heart valves damaged by rheumatic fever or to congenitally abnormal cardiac structures. But in recent years, other sites have been found to harbor bacteria. Like "traditional" SBE, these infections can also be prevented. Here is an interesting example.

The call came from a doctor practicing in Bermuda. He and I had trained together, and he occasionally referred to me seriously ill patients who needed more sophisticated hospital facilities than are available in Bermuda. The problem this time was unexplained fever and weight loss, both of several weeks' duration, in a seventy-year-old man named Kevin James. His chest film, electrocardiogram, intestinal X rays, and scans of his liver, spleen and brain were all normal. There was some anemia and a modest increase in the white blood cell count, but these findings were "nonspecific," that is, they might reflect anything ranging from a trivial infection to cancer. I asked the referring doctor whether the patient had a heart murmur, because, as you now know, SBE can present that way. "Negative" was the reply.

Mr. James arrived the next day and was immediately hospitalized. Unlike the lady with SBE, this man looked and felt awful. He was weak, worried, wan and listless. His appetite was poor. He said he had no real pain anywhere, but felt "lousy" all over. We began the usual testing routine, repeating all the blood chemistries that had been done earlier. Like the Bermuda doctors, we too found nothing diagnostic. Then we drew blood for culture (a sample of blood is incubated at ideal temperatures to permit any circulating bacteria to stand up and be counted; in healthy persons, blood is sterile, that is, it contains no organisms). Five such cultures were obtained, the last three when the fever peaked to its highest values. The first two revealed "no growth." The third, fourth and fifth, however, all showed streptococcus viridans, the same bug that had infected our lady in Chapter 1! This puzzled me, for Mr. James had never had rheumatic fever. He had served in World War II as a combat officer, and a murmur had not been heard when he was inducted into the service. He had since been examined repeatedly for insurance policies, and in routine physicals over the years he was always found to be healthy. More to the point, on very carefully listening to his heart— with him sitting up, lying down, on his left side, on his right side, breathing in, breathing out, at rest and after some exercise—I could not hear any murmur. Just to check the accuracy of my findings, and in the event there was something blowing very softly in his heart that I did not hear, I ordered an echocardiogram, looking for vegetations on a valve. None were present. What on earth was going on? I asked Kevin whether he had undergone any dental work recently. Why, yes, as a matter of fact, he had, and rather extensive too, to repair an uncomfortable bridge. Had he been given antibiotics? No, why should he have? The dentist had asked him if he had a murmur and he denied it. "Do I have a murmur?" he wanted to know.

"No," I said wearily, "you don't." Of course, I wished he had. That would have made life much simpler. I was stumped.

At this point his wife walked into the room to visit and provided me with the diagnosis! "Good morning, darling, feeling any better today? And how's the hip?"

"The hip?" I asked. "What hip? What's this about a hip?"

"Oh, the hip he had replaced four years ago has been acting up recently. He now walks with a slight limp, which he never used to do. Didn't Kevin mention it to you?" He had not only forgotten to tell me, he never said a word about it to any of the other hospital staff who queried him—and we hadn't asked. After all, "Do you have an artificial hip?" is hardly a routine question.

Well, from then on it was easy. A prosthetic hip (indeed, any artificial organ or device) is no different from a scarred rheumatic valve as far as circulating bacteria are concerned. Originating in any site, including the mouth, they may settle down in and around the joint, infecting and loosening it. As happens in a damaged valve, too little blood reaches the prosthesis to eradicate the infection. So the bugs flourish there, seeding the rest of the body exactly as they do in SBE.

We treated this patient in much the same manner as we did the lady with SBE, but with one important difference. In order to eliminate the infection, the artificial hip had to be replaced. Whereas bacterial vegetations on a valve can usually be wiped out by massive doses of penicillin given intravenously, a prosthesis often needs to come out.

This story too has a happy ending. The new hip "took," the infection was cleared up, and our patient returned home without fever, and walking normally.

The point of describing this case is to emphasize the fact that whenever you undergo a procedure that may transiently release bacteria into your blood, be sure to inform the doctor or dentist not only of any murmur, but of any artificial joints, organs or valves you may have. The need to do so is not always appreciated by patients—and your doctor may not ask.

The next account dramatizes another preventable infection, much more common than that involving artificial joints, but one that is not yet fully appreciated by many patients or even all doctors.

Neurotic? Don't You Believe It!

A nineteen-year-old girl consulted her family doctor because, like the woman with SBE and the man with the infected hip prosthesis, she had fever, aches and pains, and some "weakness"—all of two months' duration, and for no apparent reason. She too had been to the dentist (a periodontist in this case)—twice, in fact, because her gums were sore and bled a little when she brushed her teeth. She had not received any antibiotics during either of these two visits, because when asked about rheumatic fever or a heart murmur, she denied both.

She was referred to me for clarification of the diagnosis. As in the other cases I've described, the blood culture was positive. On examination, I did hear a murmur, which she assured me most vehemently was "news" to her. An echocardiogram revealed vegetations on her mitral valve. But that's not all it showed. This young lady, in addition, had a prolapsed mitral valve, also known as a "floppy" mitral valve.

I want to tell you a little bit about this condition for several reasons. First, it's very common. According to some estimates, as many as 18 percent of otherwise healthy women have it. So do men, in whom, however, it seems to be less frequent. Second, it's a disease that has been recognized only fairly recently. Third, it is associated with a host of symptoms that previously were attributed to "neurosis" or "hysteria"—palpitations, chest pain, migraine headaches, fainting and weak spells, nervousness, feelings of panic and shortness of breath. Finally, and most importantly from this book's perspective of prevention, mitral valve prolapse leaves you vulnerable to SBE. Anyone who has a murmur due to mitral valve prolapse should therefore take prophylactic antibiotics as conscientiously as if he or she had had rheumatic fever.

What is a prolapsed mitral valve? In order to understand the answer, you have to know how heart valves work. There are four of them. Two (the mitral on the left and the tricuspid on the right) seal off the upper chambers (atria) from the lower chambers (ventricles). The other two valves (aortic on the left, pulmonic on the right) guard the exits from each of the ventricles. (Blood from the right ventricle goes into the lungs; blood from the left ventricle is squeezed out to the rest of the body via the largest artery, the aorta.) Each valve, when functioning normally, opens wide to let the blood out of the chamber, and then closes tight to prevent any from leaking back. When the mitral valve leaflets are prolapsed, they may fail to close properly, and billow out a bit when doing so. There are all gradations of this abnormality. At one end of the spectrum, the billowing results only in a clicking sound, which the doctor hears with his stethoscope, and there is no real derangement of blood flow in the heart. In other instances (the minority), however, the leak is important. If the leak is severe enough, the mitral valve may have to be replaced later in life. How or why this range of valvular malfunction causes all the other symptoms of mitral valve prolapse—the headaches, chest pain, palpitations, panic attacks and so on—is not clear. We assume that the valve disorder is probably only part of a complex disease involving several different organ systems.

How does one develop mitral valve prolapse? We don't know that either. It's not the result of an infection like rheumatic fever. It's usually not detectable at birth, but does appear to run in families.

Why was it only recently recognized? We've been hearing the clicks and seemingly innocuous murmurs of mitral valve prolapse for years. But since we had no way of knowing what they meant, we dismissed them as being of no significance. After all, persons in whom they were present were healthy, with normal electrocardiograms and X rays. So when someone with a click and a "harmless" murmur did end up with SBE, we merely concluded that they must have had childhood rheumatic fever without knowing it.

But then came echocardiography, a very important advance in cardiac diagnostic technology. Sound waves directed through the chest wall, sending echoes back which could be analyzed, opened up new vistas for the cardiologist and gave us a better understanding of the internal function of the beating heart. It showed us how the valves work, and indicated that in persons with the click and the murmur, there is prolapse or billowing of the mitral valve. And so a "new" disease was born. With it came the psychological emancipation of countless persons, mostly young women, who had gone through life labeled as hypochondriacs, because until now there was no physical explanation for their complaints—truly a classic case of "symptoms in search of a disease." Now that we've found the disease, the outstanding fact for you to remember is that if you are diagnosed with this condition, you should live a normal life but *take prophylactic antibiotics whenever you undergo any invasive procedure or dental surgery,* just as you would for a rheumatic valve. This is especially true for women having abortions and even normal deliveries. Some cardiologists, myself included, would prefer their female patients with any valve disorder that leaves them vulnerable to SBE not to use an IUD for contraception. Most of the symptoms resulting from the prolapse itself can usually be effectively controlled by various medications, and the great majority of patients with this condition live normally to a ripe old age.

CHAPTER **10**

From Seasickness to Jet Lag—
When Getting There *Isn't* Half the Fun

Travel ads tell us that "getting there is half the fun." Unfortunately, that's not always true. Ask anyone who has taken a cruise and become seasick, or developed a nasal hemorrhage after spending several hours in the cabin of a moisture-poor airplane. And once you've reached your destination, there is nothing funny about nausea, vomiting, fever and diarrhea, or trouble catching your breath at high altitudes, no matter how charming the locale.

This chapter tells you how to prevent these complications, what to do in the event you do develop them, and how, in fact, to have fun, not only getting there but also once you've arrived.

The Traveler's Traveling Kit

The kind of medical kit you should take on your trip depends on your state of health and where you are going. A healthy young man or woman of thirty-five visiting London for a week will not need nearly as many items as will someone of seventy with high blood pressure going on a month's tenting safari to Kenya.

But there are certain ground rules everyone should follow. If you're vacationing elsewhere than in the U.S. or Western Europe—

98

say, in Asia or Africa—check with your doctor about what shots are required by the specific countries you're planning to visit. He will also give you additional advice based on your particular health status. If you require a special diet, make sure it's available where you're going. If you are taking medication on a regular basis, or from time to time, take enough along with you to last the entire trip—and then some. You never know if your return will be delayed by a hijacking or some other unforeseen circumstance. And don't place all your medicine in one bag. If it's lost, you may be in trouble. I always put mine in my carry-on. Learn the generic (as opposed to the trademark) name of all your drugs: unless you do, you may find that no one in the country you're visiting knows what you're talking about. For example, nifedipine, a widely used cardiac medicine, is marketed as Procardia in the United States and Adalat in most of the rest of the world. If you ask for nifedipine, you'll get what you need, but the name Procardia may well be received with a shrug and "Sorry, we've never heard of it."

Aside from specific drugs for particular disorders, there are certain basic medicines you should always carry with you. These include pain-killers, sleeping pills, stomach sedatives, anti-nauseants, anti-diarrheal preparations, antihistamines (in the event of adverse allergic reactions), some basic antibiotics, mild laxatives (believe it or not, constipation occurs much more frequently on a vacation than does diarrhea), topical creams or ointments for the treatment of itches, bites or rashes, a cough medicine, and local antiseptics for cuts and bruises. Take along a few Band-Aids of different sizes, a roll of gauze bandage, some adhesive tape, a pair of scissors and a thermometer. Sexually active women should not forget their diaphragm, spermicidal jelly or pill. Premenopausal females should have extra sanitary napkins. Adventurous men with romantic ideas should take along a supply of condoms.

Now, to be a little more specific. With respect to medication for pain relief, aspirin and acetaminophen (Tylenol, Datril) are, of course, the old standbys. They're also effective in lowering fever. You can buy them over the counter. Bring something too that's a little stronger for pain not relieved by aspirin. I recommend ibuprofen (available as Advil or Nuprin), which can also be purchased without a prescription. Ask your doctor for some quarter- or half-grain tablets of codeine as well. These may be necessary if you experience more severe pain—a headache not responsive to aspirin, a sprained back or some other injury.

Although I normally advise against sleeping pills, they are occasionally useful on a trip. Something like Valium, 15 mgs. of Dalmane, 15 to 30 mgs. of phenobarbital or 0.25 mgs. of Halcion, a new short-acting sleeping agent, will help you doze off on a long plane flight while your biological time clock is in the process of adjusting.

For an upset stomach or abdominal cramping, for that queasy feeling that's not really nausea, Donnatal or Librax (for which prescriptions are required) are often useful, as are simple antacids like Gelusil, Mylanta, Rolaids or Maalox (available over the counter). If these don't work, a suppository of Tigan or Compazine may be necessary.

I like Imodium or Lomotil for the treatment of diarrhea (prescription required). These are small pills and don't take up much room in your kit. But have at least fifty or sixty per person, since as many as eight or more a day may be required for persistent diarrhea. If you still need them by the fourth or fifth day, you'd better see a local doctor.

There are many different antihistamines on the market to deal with minor allergic episodes. (Any attack that is severe or life-threatening requires drugs that should only be administered by a physician.) Most of these antihistamines result in drowsiness, which can be dangerous if you're driving or working around machinery. The very newest one, marketed as Seldane, causes little if any sleepiness. Take two a day. Patients of mine who've used it rave about its lack of side effects. However, it's much more expensive than the others.

Don't take along a dynamite laxative, one that's going to keep you close to the toilet for the better part of the day. Something mild and natural like Metamucil or Senokot (the latter, in capsule form, is somewhat more convenient) should be enough. Neither requires a prescription.

With regard to ointments or creams, I'd include one of the mild steroid preparations like Cortaid (available over the counter). They are useful for "nonspecific" itches, rashes and insect bites.

Some persons develop painful hemorrhoids while on vacation. If you are prone to this problem, take along a tube of Preparation H (over the counter) or a suppository containing a local anesthetic with some steroids, like Anusol-HC (prescription necessary).

A topical antibiotic (Neomycin, Bacitracin, Neosporin—now available without prescription) should also be included in your traveling medicine kit. In addition, take iodine or Betadine to cleanse breaks in the skin.

The antibiotics I recommend are tetracycline, cephalexin (Keflex), penicillin or erythromycin. But be careful with tetracycline if you are going to spend any time in the sun. It can cause a troublesome skin rash. These antibiotics cover most of the spectrum of common infectious organisms. (Make sure you're not allergic to penicillin before taking Keflex. These two antibiotics do have some cross-sensitivity.)

For cough medicines, I happen to prefer Actifed-C. It's effective and it doesn't taste too bad. But any over-the-counter preparation that contains dextromethorphan or codeine is acceptable. The former is just as effective as the latter, and much less constipating.

A word of warning: If there is some reason for you to have in your possession any narcotic medication, make sure you let the customs officers both here and abroad know about it. And it's a good idea to bring along a letter from your doctor justifying your need for this drug in the amounts you are carrying. One more reminder: Check the contents of your medicine kit with your own doctor to make sure you haven't left out anything important, and that what you have packed is safe for you.

The Anti-Jet-Lag Diet

One of the most common concerns of the traveler is how to avoid or at least minimize the effects of jet lag. Several complicated regimens have been proposed beginning days before you leave and continued after you've reached your destination. I will describe one of them later. However, here are some tips I have found useful for those of you who can't or won't follow such a protracted plan.

If you're going on a long flight to a different time zone, try to fly during the day. Sitting up in a plane all night adds weariness to the biological changes that take place in your body's time clock. While on board, eat lightly, avoid alcohol, drink lots of water and move about the cabin as often as you can.

I'm always amused at the advice about not resetting your watch and acting wherever you happen to be on the basis of whatever time it is at home. That's all right if you're the president of General Motors on a two-day business trip. You're the boss and your people had better meet you when and where *you* wish. But if you're not in charge or are simply on a vacation, you'll have a big problem asking room service to bring your breakfast at 2 P.M. and dinner at 2 A.M.

After you've arrived at your destination, don't worry about losing a day or two of your vacation to catch up on sleep. Get all the rest you can, keep your intake of food and alcohol to a minimum, and go easy while your body adjusts to the new time zone.

From a practical point of view, that's really all you can and should do about jet lag. Some of it is unavoidable—and the price you pay for going far from home.

If this simple advice does not seem to work for you, and you suffer from jet leg whenever you cross several time zones, you should try the recommendations of the scientists at the Argonne National Laboratory (one of the research centers in energy and basic sciences of the U.S. Department of Energy). According to them, jet lag is not only the result of lack of sleep. They attribute most of the trouble to the fact that your body continues to function as if it were daytime when it's actually night at your destination and vice versa. If you do nothing more than I suggested earlier, it takes about three or four days for your body to readjust, during which time you're not apt to feel your best. And you can look forward to more of the same after your return trip. These scientists say their plan resets the body's "clock," or biological rhythm, quickly. It's based on what you eat, how much and when. This is how they suggest it be done.

The program begins three days before your trip. On that day you "feast." (I'll describe what that consists of in a moment.) The next day you "fast." (I'll explain that too a little later.) The day before you leave, you feast again. Finally, on the day of your departure, you fast.

There are all kinds of scientific explanations why you should feast and fast on the days indicated and what each of these dietary regimens does to enzyme levels, sugar stored in the liver and so on. If you're interested in the biology of it, contact the Argonne National Laboratory. But if you merely want to arrive at your destination in good shape, read on.

On a feast day, breakfast and lunch should be protein rich. Eat meats, eggs, fish, high-protein cereals and green beans. Do not drink any coffee between 3 and 5 P.M. For dinner, have lots of carbohy-

drates, like pasta (but without the meatballs), potatoes, starchy vegetables and sweet desserts. They help you sleep. (This is not a diet
that should be followed by diabetics!)

The next day you fast. That doesn't mean you go without eating.
Just limit your calories. Eat small salads, have light soups, unbut-
tered toast, a little fruit and a glass of juice. Again, no coffee between
2 and 5 P.M.

On day three, you feast again.

Now, on the day of departure, you fast. If you are going west, for
example, from New York to Los Angeles, you need only do so for
half a day. Any coffee you drink should be taken before noon. If,
however, you are eastbound, for example, Chicago to London, you
must fast all day, and your coffee consumption should take place
between 6 and 11 P.M.

Once on the plane, get all the sleep you can. Take one of the short-
acting sleeping pills mentioned earlier. My preference is for Halcion,
whose half-life is only two hours. That reduces the likelihood of a
hangover continuing into the next day. *Do not drink any alcohol on
the plane*, even if it is free. The next step, on the day of arrival, is
very important. Make sure to wake up and have a high-protein breakfast when it's 7 A.M. at your destination. When you're finished, don't
go back to sleep. Read, or walk about the plane as much as you can.
Once you've arrived, follow the meal pattern in the city where you
will be spending the next little while. Go to bed early evening on the
day you arrive, not as soon as you get there if it happens to be
morning or afternoon.

One other piece of advice offered by the Argonne scientists is to
get a little extra sleep for a few days before starting your trip.

It all sounds complicated. Actually it's quite simple, and if you do
lots of flying, it might be worth a try.

Preventing Motion Sickness

Who hasn't dreamed, sometime or another, of a holiday cruise to
some faraway romantic island? But after boarding the boat, the fulfilled dream may become a nightmare—because of seasickness. The
wonderful sights, the great food, the sparkling entertainment, the
exciting gambling, even the shipboard romances, are nothing when
compared to the hours and days of nausea, retching, headache and

malaise. I know several people who planned and saved for years for such a cruise, and who left their "Love Boat" at the first port of call to fly back home, forfeiting the fare.

Let me tell you about my own seagoing experience, and how you can benefit from it. I love the sea, so a few years ago, my wife and I decided to get away from it all and take a ten-day cruise. She'd actually have preferred a view of the ocean from a white sandy beach on terra firma. The ship was a beautiful sleek ocean liner; the itinerary, several exotic Caribbean and Mexican ports. We were both looking forward to reading on deck, resting and having some fun in the sun—away from the cold, gray winter of New York.

We invited a few friends for a little farewell party in our cabin before sailing. While we were sipping champagne and nibbling on the hors d'oeuvres, the envy of our guests, my wife took me aside and asked if the sway bothered me. (Remember, the ship was still tied up in port, solid and secure.) I was incredulous. "Sway? How can twenty thousand tons sway anchored in New York Harbor? You'd better go easy on the champagne," I advised. After a couple of romantic blasts on the ship's horn advising all visitors to go ashore, we raised anchor and slowly pulled away from the wharf. By the time we reached the Statue of Liberty, a few minutes downstream, I realized we were in very big trouble. First, my wife did not seem to appreciate my keen sense of humor. Then, instead of remaining on deck to watch the magnificent New York skyline slip by, she told me she was going below to our cabin to lie down for a while. I couldn't believe it! Here we were, setting sail on a trip we'd been looking forward to for years; the band was playing, people were getting acquainted, everyone was in high spirits. Why on earth would she want to go to bed—at eleven o'clock in the morning?

But then I noticed how very pale she was; that she was perspiring, and yawning almost continuously—the classic signs of seasickness. Her wish (and need) to return to the cabin were obviously neither neurotic nor negotiable.

There's bound to be trouble when two people travel together and one becomes seasick while the other feels perfectly well. "It's in your head," I insisted. My "diagnosis" only added anger to her nausea. So I decided to be sympathetic. I also immediately instituted a standard anti-seasickness regimen, encouraging my "patient" to lie down, opening the porthole to improve the ventilation, making sure she couldn't see the moving horizon and securing her head firmly between two pillows. I then gave her some meclizine (Antivert), an antihistamine that is often effective against motion sickness, and waited, with fingers crossed. She soon became drowsy and fell asleep. Four hours later she awakened, feeling not great, but well enough to come on deck. During the next ten days her nausea came and went, but mostly came. I tried various other agents to help control her symptoms, including Marezine, Benadryl, Phenergan and even a little Valium. They all worked for a while, but none ever provided complete relief. Throughout the cruise, she always had a queasy feeling in the pit of her stomach. After ten grim days, we returned home.

My wife doesn't agree when I tell her so, but it could have been worse. She might have felt so miserable that we'd have had to leave the boat at our first port of call. In any event, not only did she never wish to discuss the possibility of our going on another cruise, she didn't even look at all the beautiful slides we (I) took on this one.

So for years we vacationed on shore—on beaches, in the mountains, in the desert, touring museums, visiting communes in China, shopping in Hong Kong for bargains that never fit after we brought them home—but we never, never went to sea. Then, one day, I read about a great new advance in the control of seasickness, Transderm-Scōp." "Scōp" stands for scopolamine.

A Patch in Time

Doctors have known for years that scopolamine is effective against seasickness. But its use had always been limited by troublesome side effects when taken orally, the only form in which it was available to the traveler—dry mouth, blurred vision, drowsiness and fatigue. Also, its duration of action was very short.

The new twist about scopolamine was its "transdermal" formulation—a small, flesh-colored adhesive patch the size of a dime, which one applied to an area of intact skin anywhere on the head. CIBA, the manufacturer, suggested it be put behind the ear. (However, if you wanted your friends to know that you were going on a cruise, you could, I suppose, wear it on your forehead.) Affixed a few hours before sailing, the patch would continuously release a measured amount of the medication. It was claimed to be effective in about 75 percent of persons, and more so than the antihistamines. Even our astronauts were wearing the patches in orbit.

As I read more and more about Transderm-Scōp, I could almost feel the salt spray on my face, hear the ship's horn and bells once more, taste the hot bouillon and see the momentary green flash of the setting Caribbean sun on the horizon. Here was my second chance!

I planned my campaign carefully, accumulating every written report I could find about Transderm-Scōp and its effect on seasickness. I even prescribed it for a few patients who happened to be going on sea voyages. They all returned with glowing reports about its effectiveness. None of them had experienced any nausea or vomiting. Then one day, when we were discussing a short vacation and my wife was in good spirits, I felt the time was ripe. I casually asked, "What about a cruise?"

Her facial expression underwent a series of transformations, from a smile, to puzzlement, to incredulity and finally to panic. "You're joking, aren't you?"

"No, I'm serious. There's this new medication that absolutely prevents seasickness," I said, extracting the Transderm-Scōp file from my briefcase, which I just happened to have with me. "Look at these reports. And everything they say here is apparently true. Patients of mine who've used it tell me it's terrific. Why, even the astronauts wear it in space. What do you think? Let's give it a shot—on a short trip. Please?"

Well, Mrs. Rosenfeld is a reasonable person, so she agreed, albeit reluctantly. Our first trip would be a short one, a trial run. Only seven days. Three weeks later, we were on board ship sailing to the Caribbean again after a six-year hiatus. No cocktail party this time: we were too nervous about what lay ahead. My wife had put the Transderm-Scōp behind her ear about two hours before leaving home. The ship set sail, swaying just a little as we left New York Harbor. Her reaction? Nothing. Three hours later, we sat down to our first meal. No problem. For seven glorious days (during which time she applied two patches), we ate, read, danced, and despite some rough seas, my wife, the sailor, the trouper, suffered no ill effects whatsoever.

We docked in New York Harbor tanned (lightly—see Chapter 18 on sun hazards), looking and feeling fit and healthy. We had done it! We'd not only survived but actually enjoyed an ocean cruise!

The next day, I returned to my office and my wife went back to her greenhouse and orchids. About four o'clock in the afternoon she rang me up. "I don't feel very well," she said.

"What's wrong? Do you miss the boat?"

"You won't believe this. It's almost as if I were seasick! I feel a little dizzy and I am nauseated. Can't stand the sight or even the thought of food. I just want to lie down with my eyes closed. Do you remember our first cruise? [Did I remember it? She must have been kidding!] Well, it's almost as if I had motion sickness ashore."

"Don't be ridiculous. No one gets motion sickness ashore," I responded. "It's probably the caviar they served us last night. Can't trust what the Ayatollah is sending from Iran these days. Take a ten-milligram Compazine. You'll feel better in a couple of hours." But she didn't. In fact, her symptoms persisted for almost four days. Frankly, I didn't know what to make of it, although the possibility of scopolamine withdrawal did occur to me.

In any case, after she felt better, we forgot about the entire incident. In the summer of 1984, we decided to take another cruise, this one a little longer, in the Mediterranean. Every three days on board ship my wife put on a fresh patch. Again, the Transderm-Scōp worked miracles. Even in the midst of an awesome *"meltemi,"* the evil Mediterranean wind that makes grown sailors cry, my wife felt no ill effect. As a matter of fact, *I* was minimally sick at one point, but not she.

We left the ship in Genoa and rented a car, to do some sight-seeing. Two days later, my wife once more became "seasick" on dry land. The pattern was now clear. She was, indeed, experiencing scopolamine withdrawal.

I was about to report this adverse reaction to the manufacturer of Transderm-Scōp, when there appeared a rash of articles and letters to the editor in the medical literature describing almost exactly what my wife had experienced.

Although this complication of "seasickness ashore" was not very common in the formal premarketing studies and testing of Transderm-Scōp, and none of my own patients has had any of these untoward sequelae, I suspect it occurs more frequently than we think. It's probably more apt to happen the longer the cruise and the more patches you apply. But there are ways to minimize these effects of withdrawal.

For those of you who want to try the patch, and I think that, in sum, it's well worth doing, here are some useful guidelines.

- Leave the patch on for two days instead of the recommended three. Since scopolamine is present in the urine for at least two days after a patch is removed, wait for a day or two before putting on a second fresh one. Also, you may actually need less scopolamine than the patch delivers. So instead of putting it behind the ear, apply it to some other part of the body where the skin is thicker and the medication less rapidly absorbed, such as the upper arm, the knee or the elbow. (This is recommended by Dr. G. Sienkiewicz, a dermatologist in Binghamton, New York, in correspondence published in the *New England Journal of Medicine*.)
- The scopolamine patch is for adults only. Its efficacy and safety have not been established for the young, so do not give it to children. Nor should you use it if you have glaucoma, an enlarged prostate, trouble with your urinary bladder or pyloric obstruction (a narrowing between the stomach and the small intestines that causes paroxysmal vomiting).
- Although there is no evidence in animal experiments to suggest that scopolamine reduces fertility or has an adverse effect on the fetus, I nevertheless advise against its use by pregnant women or nursing mothers.
- Side effects may occur not only after you remove the patch but while you're wearing it as well. The most frequent is dryness of the mouth. The package insert accompanying the drug states that it can also cause restlessness, giddiness, temporary confusion, drowsiness and blurred vision. Should you experience any of these symptoms, remove the patch immediately. An antidote is not ordinarily required, since these side effects wear off rather quickly. But in the event they do not, a drug called Urecholine will usually neutralize them. Check with your doctor about taking some with you if you're planning to use Transderm-Scōp.
- Remember to wash and dry your hands thoroughly before you apply the patch, and always clean the area of skin to which you will affix it. The last thing you want to do is to absorb any dirt or other impurities along with the drug. Then—happy sailing!

P.S. After I had finished writing this chapter, I read in a respectable medical journal that raw ginger is also effective in preventing seasickness. I've not yet had a chance personally to test this "breakthrough." If you try some, let me know if it works. But take some scopolamine along with you anyway, just in case.

How to Prevent Travelers' (and Some Other Kinds of) Diarrhea

The Word Association Test is a widely used technique in psychology. This is how it works. The examiner throws out a word that the patient is asked to match quickly and almost reflexly. For example, given "black" he might say "white"; "table" would be answered by "chair," "husband" by "wife"—and so on. I'll bet that if I gave such a test to any randomly selected group of adults and started with the word "Mexico," many of them would reply with "diarrhea."

Patients planning a vacation to Mexico or some other Third World country often ask me for prescriptions for the time-honored anti-diarrheals (Kaopectate, Lomotil, Imodium), anti-nauseants (Tigan, Compazine) and bowel sedatives (Donnatal, Librax, Bentyl) in case they develop "stomach upset." However, a new twist has been added in recent years. They now also want to take an antibiotic to *prevent* getting sick in the first place. Although some doctors comply with such requests, I usually discourage them.

The run-of-the-mill gastroenteritis, familiarly known as "turista," "Montezuma's revenge" or the "Aztec two-step," that tourists contract in developing countries is usually more of a nuisance than a serious threat. It is almost always due to *Escherichia coli,* a bacterium normally present in the gut. Strains of this organism vary from country to country. If you pick up a different form of *E. coli,* you may have some watery diarrhea and abdominal cramps (usually without fever) for a couple of days. (It's interesting that 7 percent of the visitors to the United States develop these symptoms when exposed to the good old American brand of *E. coli!*) If that happens, all you need do is drink some extra fluid. The symptoms will likely subside spontaneously. In my opinion, it's not worth loading yourself up with drugs to try to prevent them, except, of course, if you have a serious underlying disease that might be worsened by even mild diarrhea.

In addition, it is my impression that there is less turista around than there used to be. Hygiene is now much better in Mexico, especially in the larger cities and resorts. If, in addition, tourists follow commonsense measures, they are less apt to come down with diarrhea. So why swallow a batch of potent drugs, not without their own side effects, in anticipation of something that may not happen?

It is true that two tablets (100 mgs. each) of Vibramycin (doxycycline) taken the day before you reach your destination and once daily while you are there (but for no longer than three weeks) will probably prevent turista. Should you decide to follow this regimen, you must keep out of the sun, because doxycycline may cause a "photosensitivity" rash. Like all antibiotics, it can also result in a fungal overgrowth (whose symptoms are sore mouth, diarrhea and vaginal discharge), intestinal upset and nausea. So, if you take it and get sick, you may not know whether it was the *E. coli* or the antibiotic. If the latter was the culprit, symptoms may be more severe and persist longer than had they been due to simple travelers' diarrhea. Furthermore, an antibiotic designed to act on the bowel may kill virtually *any* organism it encounters. That includes the "normal flora" (the "good-guy" bacteria) that inhabit everybody's intestines and protect the intestinal environment against harmful invaders—bacteria, fungi, viruses and parasites. When you destroy these "guardian" bacteria with prophylactic antibiotics, you lose your first line of defense against serious bowel diseases, like dysentery and amebiasis. New "bugs" take over that are usually resistant to the "preventive" antibiotic you were receiving. Should they cause any problem later on, their treatment is more difficult.

Every so often patients tell me that they went on a tour somewhere and were the only ones in their group who did not get sick. They congratulate themselves on having taken antibiotics prophylactically —which their companions did not do. Of course, it's possible that the antibiotics did protect them, but their remaining symptom-free may in fact have been the result of more careful attention to what they ate and drank, or perhaps of natural immunity.

Now, if antibiotics and other agents are not recommended as prophylaxis, what should you do to prevent travelers' diarrhea? First of all, use common sense. Drink and brush your teeth only with bottled water. I've heard of empty bottles being refilled with local tap water (or worse), recapped and sold as "pure and safe." So carbonated water is the best bet. Dine only in restaurants recommended by your hotel. Avoid food from street vendors. All your dishes should be cooked, especially vegetables, and you should eat only those fruits you can peel. Shun creams and custards, especially in warm weather. Finally, take your cocktail without ice, since the ice is usually made from local tap water and the organisms it contains are not affected by the alcohol or the freezing. Don't ease up on any of these precautions, including the ice, on the homebound flight. The airlines usually stock up in the country you're leaving!

If and when diarrhea, cramps, nausea and a fever begin, then antibiotic treatment is appropriate. This is especially true if you are over sixty-five or have a chronic illness involving the heart, the lungs, the kidneys or your blood. I recommend you take Bactrim-DS or Septra-DS (prescription necessary)—identical products made by different companies. Two tablets a day for five days will usually clear things up. Do not take these drugs if you are sensitive to or allergic to sulfa, since this is one of their major ingredients. If there is no response after forty-eight hours, you'll have to try another antibiotic.

What anti-diarrheal preparations should be used and when? Bismuth subsalicylate (Pepto-Bismol) taken prophylactically is actually protective against diarrhea, even though it is not an antibiotic. However, in liquid form, the required dose is so large (four tablespoons four times a day) you'd almost need an extra suitcaseful if you were going away for any length of time. It's also available as a tablet, the recommended dosage being eight per day. Both the liquid and the tablets are likely to turn your stool grayish-black; the tablets are apt to do the same to your tongue, temporarily.

Tourists often begin taking Lomotil, Imodium or Kaopectate the moment they have a single extra bowel movement. I think that's a mistake. Certain symptoms, however unpleasant, are the body's way of dealing with trouble, and are in reality a defense mechanism. Fever is one such example. Elevated temperatures, which we rush to "normalize" with aspirin or acetaminophen (Tylenol, Datril), in fact make it more difficult for certain pathogens ("bad" bacteria) to survive. By the same token, diarrhea is also a protective response that rids the body of toxic or harmful substances. So in most cases, and certainly in the first few hours, it's probably not a good idea to try to stop the diarrhea. But if it persists, you should use Kaopectate, Lomotil or Imodium and drink lots of fluids as well (to replace what you've lost via the bowel). Imodium, in my experience, has fewest side effects of the three. You may take a dose with each abnormal bowel movement. If you notice any blood in your stool, call a doctor—wherever you are.

Nausea too may sometimes be beneficial, in that it deters you from eating—and so helps rest an embattled bowel. But if it continues for

more than twenty-four hours, try Tigan, either orally or in suppository form. If you're having diarrhea along with the nausea, you'd
better take the Tigan by mouth because the suppository won't remain
where it should be long enough to be effective. On the other hand, if
you can't keep anything down because you're vomiting, a suppository is the route of choice. Compazine is effective too, and also
comes both ways. However, it can give troublesome neurological
side effects, especially in older persons. I have several patients who
were thought to have Parkinson's disease because of tremor and
rigidity due to Compazine. These symptoms cleared when the drug
was stopped.

If your turista persists beyond four days, despite the measures
listed above, you have probably contracted something other than
travelers' diarrhea—possibly dysentery, or an amoeba or some other
parasite. You will then have to test your stool to see what the offending organism is and receive appropriate therapy.

In any event, have a wonderful trip!

Less Obvious Causes of Diarrhea

While on the subject of diarrhea, let me describe some other common
and preventable causes.

There are many different sugars in our diet—sucrose, fructose,
lactose, etc. Until fairly recently, very few people were aware of the
clinical disorder of *lactose intolerance*. It reflects an inability to digest the sugar "lactose," and is due to a congenital deficiency of
lactase, the enzyme necessary to break down lactose. This problem
occurs in about 5 to 6 percent of persons of European descent and
frequently among blacks and Asians as well. There are countless
thousands who suffer from lactose intolerance and who go through
life chronically complaining of gas, cramps and frequent diarrhea.
Because the diagnosis has not been made, they continue to eat the
wrong kind of food. Since repeated X rays, colonoscopies, sigmoid-
oscopies, proctoscopies and stool analyses are always normal in
such persons, they resign themselves to their symptoms and simply
assume that they were born with "nervous stomachs." They are so
labeled by their doctors, families and friends. These are the people
with whom you go out to dinner and who invariably have to leave

the table just after dessert to visit a rest room; they live on bowel sedatives and tranquilizers—none of which really help. Some days are worse than others—seemingly for no reason. Occasionally, however, an individual will come to realize that he or she is worse after drinking milk, or eating ice cream, or downing a dessert smothered in a delicious cream sauce. When they avoid such foods, they do feel better. And that's how the diagnosis is usually made.

If you suspect you have lactose intolerance, the most practical way to confirm your impression is to eschew lactose-containing foods—milk and all its products, including soft (but not hard) cheese—and see what happens. (Butter is okay, but not cream.) If this eliminates or reduces the severity of your symptoms, you've almost certainly got the disorder. However, if you want proof positive, you'll need a lactose tolerance test. A fasting blood is obtained and its lactose content determined. You then drink a measured quantity of lactose. Several additional blood samples are then drawn over a period of a few hours, and their lactose levels are obtained. In persons with lactase deficiency, the test dose of lactose is not absorbed, and so there is no rise in its concentration in the blood even after you've drunk a hefty amount of it.

Lactose intolerance is not easy to control because so many commercially prepared foods—breads, cakes, pastries, chocolate, and cream sauces—contain milk. This becomes a real problem for those who eat out most of the time: students at boarding school or college, soldiers, or people whose work involves much traveling or socializing.

There is good news for lactase-deficient persons. Several products are now available that contain this enzyme in liquid and tablet form, and they really work. Fifteen drops of the liquid marketed as LactAid (available in most pharmacies and health-food stores) are added to a quart of milk about twenty-four hours before drinking. The lactose in the milk is broken down during this interval, after which you may drink the milk directly or use it in cooking or baking without ill effect. Milk already pre-treated can also now be purchased. Or, you may take the tablet form before eating a "no-no" food and probably get away with it. Lactrase is another tablet form of lactase. If you swallow anywhere up to eight tablets before going on a lactose binge (the number will depend on the severity of your deficiency as well as the kind and amount of food you plan to eat), chances are you'll have little if any trouble. Unfortunately, neither the liquid nor the tablet comes cheap.

I was recently made aware that eating too much *sorbitol* may also cause chronic gas, bloating, cramps and diarrhea. Sorbitol is one of those ingredients (usually listed in fine print too small for the naked eye to see) found in many "sugar-free" products like chewing gum, candy, fruit juices, mints and canned fruits. You might call it a "non-sugar" sugar. (It's actually a polyalcohol sugar with the same caloric content as glucose, but only half as sweet.) Because it's less rapidly absorbed from the bowel than is glucose, it is more suitable than real sugar for diabetics. But in some people it has an osmotic effect on the bowel—in other words, it draws excessive water into the intestines. As a result, in doses of 10 to 20 grams a day, sorbitol may cause diarrhea. In order to see how much sorbitol one of the popular "sugar-free" mints contains, I examined the label on a well-known brand. I found that a single mint contains 2 grams. So anyone sucking five or more such mints per day (not an excessive number to keep the breath "fresh and clean" and curb the appetite somewhat) might develop diarrhea. I filed this information away for future reference. It wasn't long before I was very happy to have known about it.

A forty-seven-year-old woman consulted me for a general checkup. Her only complaint was a four-year history of chronic diarrhea and bloating, no matter what she ate. Two years earlier, amoebae were found in her stool, and were eradicated with the proper medications. Despite this her diarrhea persisted. Even though several barium-enema X rays, proctoscopies and stool cultures were all negative, it was assumed that some amoebae had been left behind. So she went through several more courses of an anti-amoeba regimen, enough to kill a horse, let alone a tiny amoeba. The diarrhea never did clear up. She was finally diagnosed as having an "irritable bowel," or "nervous stomach."

Now unless I had read that report on sorbitol, I would never have thought to ask this lady if she chewed gum or ate mints. Has your doctor ever fielded you such a question—what with all the really important ones there are to ask? Anyway, I did. Imagine my delight and surprise when she opened her purse and took out two packages of "sugar-free" mints. "You mean these? I suck them all day. I've been doing so for years.'' I had her stop them forthwith. A few days later her diarrhea cleared completely.

How High Is Safe?

Older persons, or those with heart or lung problems, often ask me if it's safe to vacation at high altitudes. I tell them that anyone who is fit enough to travel in the first place may usually have a mountain holiday. There are, however, a few simple rules to be followed if you're going to do so regardless of age or underlying health status. The following actually happened to me.

A few years ago my wife and I took a two-week vacation in Europe. After driving through the Italian countryside for several days, we decided to go to Switzerland. We left Milan in our Volkswagen early one morning feeling rested and relaxed, full of wonderful memories, pasta and Chianti wine. We enjoyed the breathtaking scenery as we drove higher and higher into and through the Swiss Alps. We arrived in St. Moritz about 6 P.M., a little tired but ready for a cocktail, a good dinner, some delicious local wine and a walk through the enchanting village. We checked into our hotel and rushed right out without even bothering to unpack. We walked briskly up a steep hill toward the quaint bistro recommended by our concierge. The mountain air was cool, crisp and clean, charming boutiques lined the streets, and the snowcapped peaks were silhouetted in the distance. It felt good to stretch my legs after having driven all day. In a few minutes, however, I began to develop a slight headache. It wasn't too bad at first, but the farther I went, the worse it became. Then I began to feel nauseated. Of course, I should have stopped then and there, or at least have slowed down, but how could I, what with my wife cheerily and effortlessly prancing up the steep incline. My complaining would only have emphasized the nine-year difference in our ages. As I continued with what was now an ordeal, I became a little short of breath. At this point, I just had to slow down. My wife, cheeks pink and the picture of health, happened to glance at me. ''What's the matter? You are absolutely gray!'' There is nothing worse, psychologically, than having someone confirm that you look as bad as you feel (except being told you look wonderful when you're feeling lousy). I now began to perspire—not the good clean sweat one gets during an invigorating workout, but a cold, clammy dampness. I rested on a stoop for a few minutes, until my shortness of breath eased a little, and then we walked very slowly back down the hill to our hotel.

Since my wife is the daughter of a cardiologist and also married to one, the first question she asked as I lay on the clean, crisp Swiss linen was whether I was experiencing any chest pain or pressure. I assured her that I wasn't—and hadn't (although I was expecting to any minute). I was still nauseated, somewhat short of breath, and had a sick headache. "Maybe you're just hungry," she said. "Of course, that's it! I'll bet some food is all you need. We haven't eaten all day." So down we went to the dining room where I had a light, simple veal paillard—grilled, without any sauce. I didn't feel any better. At this point, I couldn't resist some of the house white wine —dry and chilled. As I sat there sipping it, I broke out into a profuse cold sweat, became light-headed and dizzy, and then passed out! The hotel proprietor knew exactly what to do. He placed an oxygen mask (there were several tanks at hand) over my mouth and nose, and a few minutes later, after I had recovered somewhat, he helped me back to my room. Although I didn't sleep well that night, I did feel better the following morning. The innkeeper assured me that I would be all right, that it was not necessary for me to consult the local doctor, and that he saw this kind of thing all the time. He warned me against doing anything much that day or the next. (I suspect he probably had an aborted medical career somewhere in his distant past.) He was right on all counts. Within thirty-six hours, I was feeling perfectly well again.

I unburden myself to you about all of this because my symptoms were classic for mild altitude sickness—and they could easily have been prevented. I had done everything wrong, but have since learned my lesson well. Subsequent visits to St. Moritz (and Mexico City and the Rockies) have given me no trouble.

The symptoms I experienced occur in some 25 percent of people when they first arrive at high altitudes (usually above eight thousand feet) and are the result of a lack of oxygen. The body, and especially the brain, respond to decreased oxygen in much the same way as they do to too much alcohol—leaving you nauseated, with a headache and insomnia. Mountain sickness clears up spontaneously as one acclimatizes, very much as does a hangover. Shortness of breath (mainly on exertion but also to a lesser extent even when resting) is probably due to some excess fluid in the lungs, which is reabsorbed by the body in a day or two. This malaise, called *mountain sickness*, is usually mild and temporary, as it was in my case. How sick you become depends to some extent on how high you go, how fast you got there and what you do once you arrive, but no one can predict with certainty who will develop mountain sickness and who will not. And, as I have since told my wife repeatedly, the fact that she was fine while I fainted had nothing to do with the difference in our ages.

Occasionally, even in healthy persons, instead of the mild symptoms I experienced, the lungs fill up with water as they do during a severe heart attack. This is called *acute pulmonary edema of high altitude*. Unless oxygen and diuretics are administered immediately, death may occur within hours. Early return to a lower altitude is often necessary. There have been instances in which the shortness of breath, cyanosis (bluish discoloration of the lips, skin and fingernails), cough and confusion were mistaken for pneumonia, and instead of retreat to sea level, antibiotics were given—with disastrous results.

Another more serious but less common complication, usually at altitudes greater than ten thousand feet, is *cerebral edema*. Here the fluid accumulates not in the lungs but in the brain. Symptoms are what you might expect—severe headache, difficulty walking, confusion and behavioral changes. If untreated, these often progress to coma and death. In such cases, oxygen and diuretics are not enough. The individual must be returned to near sea level as quickly as possible.

All these problems, especially the milder ones, can be minimized or prevented by following a few simple guidelines.

(1) Wherever possible, mountain climbers should ascend to high altitude gradually.

(2) After arrival at your destination, avoid any vigorous activity for twenty-four to forty-eight hours. (I made the mistake of going for a brisk walk uphill as soon as I reached St. Moritz.)

(3) Carry with you some Diamox (acetazolamide) in the 250-mg. strength. Although Diamox is a diuretic widely used in the treatment of glaucoma, it also helps prevent or reduces the severity of symptoms at high altitude—probably because it stimulates deep breathing. Take three tablets the day before you arrive and two a

day for the next three days. You should have no problem tolerating this medication in such small doses, but be prepared to empty your bladder rather frequently. Some people have told me Diamox leaves them with a metallic taste in the mouth and a transient numbness and tingling of the fingertips. These side effects disappear once the drug is stopped.

(4) In addition to taking the Diamox, avoid all alcohol for the first two days, and drink lots of water instead.

(5) Eat lightly, mostly carbohydrates rather than fat and protein.

(6) Don't take sedatives and tranquilizers. Your brain, already working with less oxygen, doesn't do well with further depression of its functions.

(7) Since some people may develop clots in the veins of the legs (thrombophlebitis) at very high altitudes (fifteen thousand feet or more), women on the pill should stop taking it if they are planning to venture that high.

(8) If you tried Diamox on a previous trip, and still had trouble, discuss with your doctor whether or not to take small doses of steroids prophylactically.

Is there anyone who should *not* vacation at or visit locations above eight thousand feet? Yes. If you've done so before and barely escaped with your life because you developed high-altitude pulmonary edema or cerebral edema, look for your pleasures at the seashore. If you have coronary-artery disease with active angina, induced by emotion or slight exertion, or which awakens you at night, you are better off remaining near sea level. The same is true for anyone with severe lung disease requiring supplemental oxygen, for individuals with recurrent attacks of thrombophlebitis or those in congestive heart failure. Very fat people, who have trouble breathing deeply and cannot get enough oxygen into their lungs because of their obesity, had better reduce substantially before planning a vacation in the Alps or the Colorado Rockies. Finally, those black individuals with sickle-cell anemia should avoid high altitudes. Their red blood cells are genetically altered so that in the presence of decreased oxygen, they may develop severe vascular problems.

In reviewing the literature on this subject I came across a very amusing coincidence, one that is not uncommon in medicine. I know of an orthopedist named Dr. Bone, a surgeon named Dr. Slaughter, a gynecologist named Dr. Goldfinger and a distinguished neorologist named Professor Brain. And in the September 16, 1983, issue of the

Journal of the American Medical Association, there appeared an excellent paper entitled "Acute Mountain Sickness," authored by none other than Dr. Richard D. Mountain.

Noses Needn't Bleed

A "bloody nose" may be a traumatic event, such as occurs when you walk into a glass door you didn't know was there, or receive a well-placed punch. A "nosebleed," on the other hand, is spontaneous. There you are, just sitting, minding your own business, when suddenly blood begins to trickle, flow or spurt out of your nostrils and/or down the back of your throat. Almost everyone experiences a minor nosebleed now and then, usually from a little too much picking or other irritation. But some individuals, young and old alike, suffer recurrent nosebleeds for specific reasons—most of which are preventable, and some of which occur while traveling.

My own experience highlights one of the most frequent causes of nasal hemorrhage at any age.

A few years ago, I was a member of a United States delegation to the Soviet Union sent to discuss with their doctors the problems of sudden cardiac death. (Those were the days of détente, when the personal cordiality that has always existed among scientists of all countries was reinforced by a warmer political climate.) We flew first to London and, after a short layover, on to Moscow. It was late October, and very cold in Russia. If you think that American homes are overheated, try the Soviet Union. Our hotel room was stifling and oppressively dry, and my nose soon began to crust. After three days in Moscow, we flew to various areas in Soviet Asia. I spent day after day in the arid environment of either a jet aircraft or an overheated hotel room. On the ninth day of my trip, I was in Yalta, coming down in the hotel elevator, when what seemed like a torrent of blood suddenly gushed out of my nose. I immediately sat down in a chair, leaned forward, and pinched my nostrils between thumb and forefinger. Within five minutes, the bleeding stopped. The next day, the group continued its itinerary.

Four days later we left the Soviet Union for home, stopping over briefly in Paris. After a good night's sleep in that city, I was awakened early in the morning by another nosebleed, this one much more substantial than the first. It was Sunday, and there was no way I could find a doctor before my scheduled departure for the United States three hours later. So I went through the same maneuvers I had used in Yalta, and again was able to stop the bleeding. Although it was risky, I decided to take my chances on the transatlantic journey. My nose behaved during the next eight hours. And was I lucky, because the very first night at home, I had another nasal hemorrhage, this time a massive one. Blood poured out of both nostrils, down the back of my throat and even out of the corners of my eyes. There was no way I could stop it. I still shudder when I think what might have happened had that occurred aboard an aircraft on an eight-hour flight.

So with towels wrapped around my face to absorb the torrent of blood, I took a cab to the nearest hospital emergency room. The resident on call couldn't stop the bleeding by conventional methods. The unrelenting deluge precluded his finding the bleeding source, which was obviously an artery and not a vein. (You will read about the difference between them in a moment.) Finally, in order to control the hemorrhage, he tightly packed my entire nose—a very uncomfortable experience. After the hemorrhage had been arrested, he checked my hemoglobin level to see if I required a transfusion. Younger and/or healthy individuals can tolerate a substantial loss of blood, but someone with underlying coronary heart disease, other vascular disorders or chronic ailments may not. In my particular case, despite the fact that I appeared to be suffering massive blood loss, there was only a slight drop in the hemoglobin level—not enough to warrant a transfusion.

I remained in the hospital for twenty-four hours and was discharged with the nasal packing in place. After it was removed the next day, the surgeon examined my nasal passages and found them dry and severely crusted. Apparently, all that flying at low humidity, together with the overheated, arid hotel rooms, had left my nasal lining parched and cracked. One or more of the arteries in the back of my nose had then begun to hemorrhage.

There are two lessons to be learned from this experience. First, a great deal of flying in a short period of time, together with lack of humidity, can cause problems. Also, you should avoid all trips away from immediate medical care whenever you find yourself in a "bleeding cycle." For example, if you have had a cluster of two or three "minor" nosebleeds, such as I had in Yalta and Paris, do not plan a vacation until you have checked with your ear, nose and throat specialist.

In childhood, the most common cause of nosebleeds is the bad habit of picking. There are some children who always seem to have a finger in the very front of the nose, which contains a rich network of veins. When these are sufficiently irritated, they erode and bleed. A child is most apt to develop this habit when there are other problems in the nasal passages. For example, if the septum, or wall, of the nose (which divides it into right and left sides) is crooked or deviated, the free flow of air is interrupted. Any minor crust that happens to form at that site and that would otherwise be tolerated, reduces airflow through the nose and leads to the temptation to remove it with the finger. Also, allergic children whose nasal membranes are swollen and irritated often become "pickers" in order to increase the passage of air through the nose. In a dry environment, when the nasal membranes crust and interfere with ventilation, the child tries to solve the problem by picking rather than blowing into tissues. Finally, children —especially younger ones—like to stick foreign objects of all kinds up the nose, which is another common cause of bleeding.

In adult life, the preconditions for recurrent nosebleed also include excessive drying. But one should be on the alert for high blood pressure, tumors, medications, anticoagulants and abnormalities of blood clotting. Another factor to be considered these days in patients with recurrent spontaneous nasal bleeding is cocaine, whose chronic use eats away the septum of the nose.

Before discussing the prevention of nasal hemorrhage, a word about how one manages the garden-variety nosebleed. The commonest site of such bleeding is from the front portion of the nose, which has an abundance of small veins. But bleeding can also occur from an artery, as it did in my case. It is important to recognize the difference between a venous and arterial source since their management differs. Bleeding from a vein is generally not as violent or as profuse. Also, blood from an artery spurts, while a bleeding vein oozes or flows. When the source of bleeding is venous, most of the blood comes out the front of the nose and less goes down the back of the throat, especially if you tilt your head forward. Arterial bleeding, on the other hand, almost always presents both front and back, with equal force. When that happens get medical help immediately. There is no point calling your doctor and waiting for him to come to your home if you have easy access to a hospital emergency room. Before leaving and en route, do not take any medication. You run the risk, when you swallow a pill or capsule, of getting some of the blood into your lungs.

If the blood is simply trickling or flowing out the front of your nose and not coming out in spurts, chances are you can deal with the problem yourself. Sit upright in a chair and lean forward. (The natural tendency is to tilt your head back so that the blood will not pour out. But you are much better off having it come out in front than down your throat, whence you can possibly aspirate it into your lungs.) Then gently blow both sides of your nose to get rid of any retained clot that can continue to irritate the bleeding blood vessel. Now, put some cotton, or tissue paper soaked in cool water, about a half inch up both sides of your nose. Pinch the front of your nose tightly with your thumb and forefinger. That ought to do it in about five minutes unless you have some bleeding disorder, infection or arterial bleeding. But if, as you bend your head down, large amounts of blood continue to run down the back of your throat, then chances are the bleeding is arterial and originating in the posterior portion of your nose, as well as the front, and may require medical attention.

Some doctors advise the application of ice packs or very cold wet towels to the nose, face or back of the neck, presumably to facilitate clotting. As far as I'm concerned, all that does is increase the level of discomfort and anxiety.

After the bleeding has stopped, avoid unusual exertion or fatigue for at least forty-eight hours.

How can nosebleeds be prevented? First, neutralize the effects of a dry environment. When on a long flight, drink lots of water. Before boarding, put a tiny dab, no more than the size of a pea, of some bland lubricating jelly such as Vaseline on the tip of your little finger and introduce it just inside your nose on either side. Then massage it gently from the outside. This affords some lubrication to the area that is most apt to become dry and crusted and to bleed. If you have no ointment or cream on hand, wet some tissue paper and insert it into both sides of your nose for a few minutes every hour.

But dryness is not limited to airplanes or to the Soviet Union. Most of us overheat our homes in cold weather. Anyone with a history of nosebleeds should have a vaporizer, moisturizer or humidifier in those rooms where he or she spends most of the time. A less expensive alternative is simply to place a pan of water on a radiator, allowing the water to evaporate into the room. Also put a small amount of lubricating jelly into each nostril at night, especially if you've had chronic nosebleeds during the winter months.

If any of your younger children are "pickers" and cannot be taught to keep their fingers out of their noses, they may have to wear fingerless mittens at night, when the picking if often involuntary. This should never be presented as a punishment for the child.

Recurrent nosebleeds due to a deviated septum may require corrective surgery.

When nasal hemorrhage is the consequence of high blood pressure, those levels should be normalized by whatever means is necessary. Anyone who snorts cocaine should know that it eats away the lining of the nose and causes recurrent nosebleeds. In time, the cocaine erodes the wall that separates the right from the left side of the nose, leaving a gaping hole.

Anyone who suffers from repeated nosebleeds should be examined to rule out local causes, as, for example, a superficial blood vessel that needs to be cauterized, or even a tumor. But if there is no apparent source of the bleeding and it is recurrent, then a very careful general physical exam including an analysis of how your blood clots is necessary. I've seen several cases of leukemia and other serious hematological disorders present as "unexplained" nosebleeding.

So, whether you go by land, by sea or by air, the problems associated with every form of travel are usually preventable. Nor is there any need for you to become sick in your new environment—wherever it is. Commonsense rules of prevention will keep your brain, your bowel and your nose healthy.

CHAPTER 11

Diet, Hormones and Broken Bones— The Saga of Osteoporosis

When Columbus discovered America almost five-hundred years ago, most women did not live beyond age forty. For them, there was no such thing as the menopause; they continued to have their periods to the day they died. But a little girl born in the United States today may expect to live to age seventy-eight, and becomes menopausal somewhere near age fifty.

For the average modern woman who experiences the menopause, and goes on to leave it far behind, the result is a host of specific "new" medical problems. Among the most important of these is osteoporosis, an abnormal thinning of the bone due mostly to lack of calcium. It is now the second most common orthopedic problem (injury ranks first). Patients with osteoporosis suffer bone pain, spontaneous collapse of one or more vertebrae (occurring in a quarter of all women over sixty), and deformity of the spine. Each year, because of abnormal susceptibility to fracture, more than 200,000 older American females break their hips and other bones in some trivial injury. Though men are less vulnerable to osteoporosis, they are not immune to it. I have several with osteoporosis in my own practice. They're all in their sixties and seventies. Some have become osteoporotic because of excessive loss of calcium in their urine due to a kidney disorder; 10 to 15 percent are alcoholics. At particular risk are males who drink to excess and who use aluminum-containing antacids for ulcers or "hyperacidity." This combination of alcohol and these specific antacids causes severe calcium depletion of the bones. If you require antacids for whatever reason, and drink, I suggest taking antacids containing calcium carbonate and not aluminum. Their prototype is Tums.

Despite all the sophisticated newer techniques for welding broken bones in record time, a fractured hip in an elderly person is still a potential catastrophe—a landmark event that can transform a previously healthy, active individual into a helpless cripple. What's more, forty thousand women die each year from this particular injury and its complications. Yet osteoporosis can either be prevented or greatly reduced in severity by proper preventive measures—to which, unfortunately, too many doctors and patients remain indifferent.

The following account describes a typical case of osteoporosis from my own files.

Mrs. Martin was a seventy-four-year-old woman whose husband had died two years earlier. Since then she had fended for herself in a "nice" neighborhood of New York City. Her three children, all married, lived within a radius of one hundred miles, and they visited from time to time. She had many friends, went to the theater every few weeks, and was, to my mind, a model of what life in later years should be—fairly comfortable and completely independent.

She would come by my office once or twice a year, just for a checkup. Her past medical history was unremarkable and her health was good. At her last visit to me, she admitted that, although her appetite was "fine," her meals had been "less interesting" and somewhat haphazard since her husband's death. "It's not the same cooking just for myself. When Jack was alive, I prepared meals I thought he'd enjoy. We loved good food and it was fun dining together. Now that I am alone, I eat what's handy and don't fuss much in the kitchen anymore." There was one more dietary fact of note: she had avoided milk and milk products for many years because they gave her cramps and abdominal bloating. Her only "bad habit," she admitted, was smoking a pack of cigarettes a day. She had begun her menopause at age fifty-one, but had not experienced any mood changes, depression or hot flushes. She never took any female replacement hormones because she didn't think she needed them.

Mrs. Martin was in her usual state of health when, one evening, she went to the theater alone. She took the bus, which was quite convenient since it stopped only one block from her apartment. (Taxis had become too expensive for her now that she was on a fixed and limited income, and she avoided the subway because of the rampant crime.) She returned from the theater about eleven-fifteen, and began walking home from the bus stop. Soon she could see her doorman just a few yards away. What a wonderful sense of security that gave her. Suddenly, "out of the blue," a figure lunged at her from the shadows, grabbed her shoulder bag and, in so doing, threw her to the ground. She never did see her attacker, who disappeared as quickly as he came—with her handbag, its twelve dollars and an uncashed Social Security check. She lay there for a moment—stunned, weak, frightened—and then tried to get up. She couldn't. The pain in her left leg was unbearable. She said later that she had heard a snapping or cracking sound as she fell; she had fractured her hip.

The rest of the story is fairly straightforward. The doorman responded to her cries and called for an ambulance, and she was taken to a hospital. X rays revealed a nasty break in her left hipbone. The necessary surgery accounted for only the first two weeks of her stay. The heart attack that occurred five days after her operation and the subsequent complications kept her in the hospital for almost three months. When she was finally "ready" for discharge, this previously healthy, alert, vital woman was no longer able to look after herself alone in her apartment. She flatly refused to live with her children because she felt she'd be a burden to them and "they have their own problems." The hospital social-service worker finally found a nursing home that could take her. Her life's savings were assigned to pay for her new accommodation, since no one really expected she would ever go back home. They were right. She died a few months later. The cause of death was officially listed as "heart attack." As far as society was concerned, she was just another old lady who died "naturally" in her sleep. Only her children and I knew or cared about the truth.

This is the kind of heartrending scenario that occurs all too often these days. It reflects several problems facing so many of our senior citizens—problems that are only part medical, and which represent a great challenge to us all. I won't dwell on the obvious social aspects of this story, except to say that I ponder them as a citizen, a son and a human being. Mrs. Martin's experience was ultimately one of violence, loneliness, depression and malnutrition. In other elderly and infirm persons, there is also lack of family support and inadequate custodial care.

Mrs. Martin's *medical* problem was osteoporosis. All her bones were thin, brittle and calcium-deprived, making it virtually certain that she would break one of them in the event of a fall or other injury. A younger person would probably not have sustained a fracture in similar circumstances.

What were the clues to Mrs. Martin's special vulnerability? What could have been done to prevent or reduce the chances for her fracturing her hip? What should all the Mrs. Martins among us be doing to protect themselves from a similar fate?

This lady's case history provides several answers to these questions. She was a candidate for trouble for the following reasons.

(1) Her *age.* Although the various mechanisms that ultimately end in osteoporosis are not fully understood, it is rare among otherwise healthy young women before the menopause. Young persons do not develop it, unless there are some other underlying reasons for their bones to become calcium deficient. As we grow older, the ability of the intestines to absorb calcium is reduced. At what point and to what extent this occurs varies from person to person. But the older you become, the less calcium is available for your bones, which then become brittle, thin and fragile.

Other causes of calcium deficiency can occur at any age, and include parathyroid tumor (discussed in the chapter on preventing kidney stones), multiple myeloma (a malignancy that attacks bone and bone marrow), chronic use of large amounts of cortisone (as might be the case in someone with rheumatoid arthritis or severe asthma), untreated hyperthyroidism (overactive thyroid function), subtotal gastrectomy (in which ulcer disease or a gastric tumor has necessitated the removal of a large portion of stomach, thus reducing the area in which calcium can be absorbed) and inadequate secretion of male hormone (such as occurs in young men with a glandular disorder affecting the testes).

(2) *Lack of female hormone* plays an important role in the development of osteoporosis. Mrs. Martin was postmenopausal, and not taking estrogen supplements. I had never recommended them to

this seventy-four-year-old lady largely because she hadn't complained of hot flushes, painful intercourse (due to drying of the lining of the vagina), mood changes or bone pain. Certainly, if she had had an X ray in which I had seen evidence of osteoporosis, or if she was noted to be losing height in routine measurements due to "silent" collapse of her vertebrae, I would have done so without hesitation.

Some doctors now routinely advise their female patients to take estrogens just before or at menopause, regardless of symptoms, in order to prevent osteoporosis. (Unless, of course, there is a specific reason not to do so—previous history of uterine or breast cancer, vascular problems, or certain diseases of the liver or gallbladder.) That may be a good idea. I'm just not sure. I still worry that the possible risks may outweigh the benefits.

The current consensus, however, is that postmenopausal women *with osteoporosis* should be treated with estrogen, and the sooner the better. I usually prescribe it as Premarin in a dosage of 0.625 mgs, per day cyclically, that is, three weeks out of every four. Since estrogen increases the risk of cancer of the endometrium (lining of the uterus), any woman on this hormone who has not had a hysterectomy must have a Pap smear at least three or four times a year, and see her gynecologist whenever she has irregular bleeding. Avoid estrogens if you've had a tumor of the uterus or the breast, are troubled by clotting problems or have some form of liver disease. You might also double-check with your doctor about taking this hormone if you have gallbladder trouble. I also recommend adding 5 or 10 mgs. of progesterone during the last ten to fifteen days of the estrogen cycle in order to reduce the likelihood of uterine malignancy. However, the question of progesterone should be carefully weighed if you have any kind of cardiac or liver problem, on which it may have an adverse effect.

Tests are now available to determine who is at risk of developing osteoporosis *before* fractures occur. A technique called single-photon absorptiometry uses a low-energy photon beam (which exposes you to only very minimal radiation) to determine your bone density. The beam scans the bones of the forearm or wrist, and a radiation detector registers their mineral content. Once the base-line bone density is established, the test is performed annually, and the results are compared to the original readings to determine the need for hormonal or other therapy.

(3) Mrs. Martin was probably *malnourished*. Since her husband's death, she had not been eating a balanced diet. Remember too, she told me she had avoided milk and milk products, because they gave her gas and cramping. She probably had lactose intolerance. Although this condition may occur at any age and in both sexes (three of my four children are troubled with it), 65 percent of women with osteoporosis suffer from it to some extent. Lactose-intolerant individuals are deficient in an enzyme called lactase, which is necessary to digest the lactose in milk and its derivative foods. When such persons eat lactose in any form, they experience abdominal pain, gas and bloating because this sugar is not properly digested. And so they avoid eating what makes them sick, like milk and milk products. But these foods are rich in calcium, and so these individuals end up with too little of it, as did Mrs. Martin. Their bones then become osteoporotic and brittle. I had prescribed calcium supplements for this patient, but she never "bothered" to take them. (See pages 112–114 for a fuller account of lactose intolerance.)

(4) Mrs. Martin smoked *cigarettes*. We have come to realize that tobacco is an important contributory factor to osteoporosis. This bone disorder is more prevalent, at least statistically, among women who are heavy smokers. Tobacco exerts this adverse effect by virtue of its anti-estrogen properties. Women who smoke further decrease their estrogen level. Tobacco also constricts the arteries feeding the bone, thus cutting down the amount of calcium delivered to them. Finally, the nicotine and tobacco resins may in some way induce increased loss of calcium in the urine.

So, What's to Be Done?

If you are postmenopausal, how should you protect yourself against osteoporosis? Let's start with diet. Many persons follow a low-cholesterol diet these days in hopes of preventing arteriosclerosis (hardening of the arteries). The pros and cons of such a diet are discussed elsewhere in this book. But whatever its merits, a low-cholesterol diet is essentially one in which dairy products—milk, cheese and cream, among the richest sources of calcium—are avoided. Women who follow weight-reduction diets for long periods of time early in life also consume less calcium than they require, because calcium-rich foods are often high in calories. Since a low-calcium intake, both before and after menopause, promotes osteo-porosis, any adult, but especially any woman, over thirty-five who faithfully adheres to such a diet must have calcium supplements. If she doesn't, she's just begging for osteoporosis later on.

How much calcium you need depends on your age. Normal persons require at least 1,000 mgs. per day. I believe that the recommended daily allowance (RDA) of 800 mgs. is too low, even for elderly men. The average American female probably eats only 450 to 550 mgs. per day. And someone obsessively following a low-cholesterol diet ingests even less than that. Once she reaches the menopause, every woman should take no less than 1,500 mgs. of calcium a day. Anyone with obvious osteoporosis is well advised to consume two to three grams of calcium (2,000 to 3,000 mgs.) a day.

You can satisfy this requirement in a variety of ways. For example, drinking four glasses of milk daily will do it. (Use skim or low-fat milk to minimize the fat intake.) Five ounces of Cheddar cheese provide 1,000 mgs. of calcium. If you aren't taking enough calcium in your diet, either because you're on a low-cholesterol regimen or are lactose intolerant, then you'll have to get it in tablet or capsule form. The preparation I usually prescribe is a generic form of calcium carbonate in the 600-mg. strength. Check with your own doctor about his preferences. Make sure to look at the label on the bottle for the actual amount of *elemental* calcium delivered. For example, calcium-carbonate tablets are only 40 percent elemental calcium, while calcium lactate contains a mere 15 percent. You'd need four tablets of the former and twelve of the latter to end up with 1,000 mgs. of elemental calcium, even though each product is labeled as containing 600 mgs. of total calcium!

A word of caution: If you have severe osteoporosis and need 2,000 mgs. or more of calcium per day, have your blood and urine calcium levels checked from time to time to make sure you're not getting too much. There's no point in ending up with a kidney stone while trying to prevent osteoporosis.

Since the ability of the gut to accept calcium through its lining is reduced as we grow older, enough calcium may not actually be absorbed even though you are consuming as much as you need. So take some extra vitamin D, which promotes intestinal absorption of calcium. I usually prescribe no more than 400 units per day, an amount found in most "all-purpose" multivitamin supplements. More can be harmful. There is an unexpected spin-off from this calcium–vitamin D combination. A recent report from England suggests that women on an anti-osteoporosis regimen of calcium and vitamin D have less cancer of the lower bowel! And from the U.S. comes word that the same is true for men.

What else can you do to prevent osteoporosis? I've already mentioned that cigarettes seem to worsen it. So does too much alcohol, either because it results in bones losing their calcium, or by virtue of the malnutrition so common among heavy drinkers.

Here's some additional dietary advice. While it's important to eat enough protein and fiber, too much of either can result in depletion of body calcium. So can excessive salt, coffee, cola beverages, vitamin A and foods with phosphorous additives. That is not to say that these substances are to be avoided. Just don't go overboard on any one of them to the exclusion of other foods in your diet.

Physical inactivity promotes osteoporosis. The amount of bone mass a woman builds up by the time she is thirty-five years old will significantly determine her vulnerability to osteoporosis after the menopause. The greater that mass, the less likely she is to become osteoporotic. And the best way to augment it, in addition to diet, is by regular exercise. Stressing bones, like muscles, encourages the continuous absorption of old cells and their replacement by new ones. An individual confined to bed will lose as much as 4 percent of bone mass after a month. That's one of the main reasons we get our older patients up and about as soon as possible after an operation or a heart attack. But even if you're not old or bedridden, keeping physically fit helps your bones retain their calcium. The maxim "If you don't use it, you'll lose it" also applies to calcium and bone.

Do not go overboard about the kind and amount of exercise you try to do. Be practical. An elderly woman whose bones are already fragile is likely to break them if she does the wrong kind of exercise or "works out" too much. I have seen such women crack one or more ribs just coughing. So I recommend daily stretching to keep the muscles loose, and a two- or three-mile walk at a brisk pace to effect some weight-bearing.

Men with osteoporosis should follow the same dietary and exercise regimen as women. However, for them I additionally prescribe the male hormone, testosterone, because it reduces the amount of calcium excreted in the urine. But you must heed this warning. Any man taking supplemental testosterone over the long term for any reason, whether it's to treat osteoporosis or—as is more commonly the case —to increase libido and potency, should be checked at regular intervals by a urologist. A small, undiagnosed cancer buried deep inside the prostate gland, which might otherwise never cause any trouble, may be activated and spread by testosterone.

As of 1986, there is an ongoing evaluation in the United States of sodium fluoride for the treatment and prevention of osteoporosis. Although it is not approved by the FDA for this purpose, many doctors are now prescribing it. As a matter of fact, it's already in your toothpaste, drinking water and even some brands of chewing gum, and is credited with the drastic drop in the incidence of tooth decay in this country. It is possible that children who have been consuming this fluoride over the years may be protected against osteoporosis later in life.

When administered to patients with osteoporosis, the dosage of fluoride is 40 to 65 mgs. per day. I also recommend concurrently taking 1,000 mgs. of elemental calcium and 400 units of vitamin D per day, together with estrogens if there is no contraindication. Most patients tolerate fluoride without much problems, but some do complain of joint pain and vomiting, and become anemic. Although X rays of individuals following this regimen are quite impressive, some orthopedists are not convinced that all the new calcium they see actually adds to bone strength.

Another medication, calcitonin, is also available for the treatment of osteoporosis. Although derived from thyroid tissue, it is not thyroid hormone. Its major disadvantage is that it cannot be taken by mouth, and must be given by injection. It's probably only a matter of time before it will be available in other forms.

So bone thinning, or osteoporosis, is a common but not inevitable problem. But the time to begin preventing it is now, no matter what your age.

CHAPTER 12

Stones in the Kidney and Gallbladder— How to Avoid Them, and What to Do If You Don't

Solid particles can form in any body liquid. When these coalesce, and/or become visible to the naked eye, we call them "stones," or "calculi."

Stone formation commonly takes place in the gallbladder, where the body's bile is stored, or in the kidneys where urine is produced. It can also happen in the prostate gland (where the doctor can feel the stone during a rectal exam), in the parotid gland (which makes saliva) and in the urinary bladder itself. But gallstones and kidney stones are by far the most likely to cause attacks of pain.

As Painful as Childbirth

Once a stone develops in the kidney, it may just sit there indefinitely if it's very large, or, if it is small, it may travel down the ureter (the tube in which the urine flows from the kidney to the urinary bladder) on its way out of the body. The dimensions of a stone may vary from gravel or sediment to something the size of your thumb. Stones that remain within the kidney itself may damage it in the long run by obstructing the flow of urine out of that organ. But the smaller stones you pass are the ones that cause excruciating pain, and that are responsible for the term "an attack of kidney stones." Some women have told me that passing a renal (kidney) stone is as painful as childbirth. Men who have no such frame of reference have simply told me it's the worse experience they have ever had.

One of my patients was a forty-eight-year-old accountant, married and an athlete of sorts. At the time of his last routine visit to my office some months earlier, his medical history was most unremarkable. He had never been hospitalized, had had the usual diseases of childhood, considered himself quite healthy and always ate a "balanced diet." As a matter of fact, he'd recently passed a physical for a million-dollar insurance policy with "flying colors." His parents were in their seventies; three brothers and a sister had no medical problems as far as he knew.

In response to a standard question about any history of kidney trouble, he couldn't imagine what I meant! He emptied his bladder three or four times a day, no more and no less than other men his age. Once asleep, he never had to get up to void. Nor had he ever experienced any burning or pain when doing so. Blood in the urine? Heaven forbid! He couldn't stand the sight of blood—anywhere, least of all his own.

One day, subsequent to this last office visit, he played several sets of singles tennis. It was hot, and he had perspired profusely, but the workout left him feeling good. He came home that evening, had a good dinner, watched some television (an old Tarzan film) and went to bed at 11 P.M. He quickly fell fast asleep.

Some two hours later he started having a nightmare. He dreamed he had been captured by natives who were poking him with red-hot irons in the lower abdomen on his right side. ("This will teach me to watch Tarzan movies just before going to bed," he thought, even as he dreamed.) They would leave him alone for a couple of minutes, then start again. The pain became so unbearable it woke him. That ended his dream but not the agony, for every few minutes a knifelike pain would start in the small of his back on the right side and spread forward around to the front of his abdomen, reaching into his testicle. Each such spasm left him drenched in sweat. He had always thought himself a stoic, but he had never imagined such pain was possible. There was nothing he could do to ease the distress once the attack started—neither bending nor lying still nor breathing deeply made any difference. Nor could he prevent the onset of the next agonizing wave.

After thirty minutes of suffering, hoping each spasm would be the last, he awakened his wife, much as he hated to do so. But she had taken a Red Cross course in CPR and would surely know what the trouble was and how to treat it. She did. Having very confidently diagnosed acute appendicitis (because the pain was on the right side of his belly), she hustled him into a cab and to a nearby hospital emergency room. There the diagnosis of a kidney stone was made on the basis of his story, the clinical examination and the presence of blood in his urine (not apparent to the naked eye, but evident on chemical testing and microscopic exam). Mind you, his wife's suggestion of appendicitis was considered quite seriously by the emergency-room personnel. In fact, one of the interns raised the additional possibilities of an acute gallbladder attack or pancreatitis (inflammation of the pancreas occurring most frequently in alcoholics, diabetics or persons with gallbladder disease). However, the clinical diagnosis was confirmed when a small stone lodged in the ureter was seen on an X-ray film (intravenous pyelogram).

The patient was admitted from the emergency room to the urology ward. There were several reasons for keeping him in the hospital. The pain was so severe it required morphine injections. Also, although we expected the stone to pass spontaneously, it might possibly need to be removed surgically. Intravenous nourishment became necessary since the patient had begun to vomit and could not retain oral liquids.

At about eight o'clock that morning, about seven hours after its onset, the pain suddenly stopped. Two hours later, while emptying his bladder into a strainer, the patient saw a tiny stone. It was sent to the lab immediately, and the report contained no surprises. On the basis of statistics, we expected that it would be composed of calcium oxalate, and it was. Our friend went home that afternoon.

If you have a history of kidney stones, the following figures will be meaningful to you. Two to 3 percent of Americans have at some time or other passed a stone in their urine. I read one statistic that claimed such calculi develop in 12 percent of people in this country by the time they reach age seventy. This problem is responsible for one of every one hundred hospital admissions in the United States each year. Also, kidney stones are found in about 1 percent of all the autopsies performed in the United States, no matter what the cause of death. Most of these are "silent" during life, that is, they cause no symptoms and the individual is never aware of their presence.

Water, Water Everywhere . . .

Recurrent formation of kidney stones can be prevented in at least 50 percent of cases. Despite this, doctors and patients are generally apathetic about the measures necessary to do so. This is all the more surprising since almost seventy percent of patients who've had one attack will have another.

If you have ever had a renal stone in the past, in order to prevent a recurrence, you should know how and why they form. Normal urine contains a myriad of different substances—body wastes, chemicals and minerals. In the present of disease, additional, "abnormal" constituents are present. All urinary constituents usually remain "in solution." A kidney stone forms when one or more of these constituents that should have remained dissolved didn't do so.

There are basically two reasons why calcium or uric acid or oxalate or any of the other crystals normally present in the fluid phase in urine suddenly solidify. Either too much gets into the urine so that all of it can't remain dissolved, or some change takes place in the urinary environment that causes a *normal* concentration of the substance to crystallize out.

After your doctor has determined the composition of the stone, and which of these two mechanisms is operative in your case, and why, you can both begin to do something about it. For example, if stones have formed because your urine is either too acid or too alkaline, you can take something to correct the imbalance. If there is too much uric acid in your blood and urine (such as happens in gout), so that you repeatedly form uric acid stones, you may need to change your diet or take a specific medication.

If you're a stone former, regardless of the mechanism or the type of stone, the most important thing you can do to prevent a recurrence is to keep your urine in plentiful supply, flowing copiously, nicely dilute and pale. That means drinking lots and lots of fluids. It is more difficult for anything to solidify in very dilute urine. On the other hand, concentrated, or "strong," urine promotes stone formation, because it contains more solids relative to the amount of water in which they are dissolved. If you have a kidney stone problem, unless you have to get up at night to empty your bladder, you're not drinking enough water! The importance of water in the prevention of kidney stones has been documented many times. For example, soldiers on duty in a hot desert where water is sparse have a high incidence of kidney stones unless they "force fluids." Athletes and joggers who perspire profusely, especially in hot weather, are also vulnerable unless they replace the lost water. So are persons who become dehydrated from chronic diarrhea; tourists visiting tropical climates who avoid drinking enough fluid despite the heat because they're afraid of the local water supply; anyone, in other words, who loses excessive fluid and doesn't replace it.

Our patient played tennis, and perspired profusely. He was losing water not only through his skin but also in his breath as his respirations increased. Since he didn't drink enough water before, during and after tennis matches, he had less fluid for the formation of urine.

One of my urologist friends describes a good way to make sure your water intake is adequate if you're a stone former. Each morning put ten pennies in one of your pockets. Every time you drink a full eight-ounce glass of water take one penny and put it in another pocket. At the end of the day, all ten pennies should be in the second pocket (unless your fluid intake must be restricted for other reasons, as, for example, heart failure). It all seems so simple, yet it's not easy to get stone-forming patients to comply with such a drinking regimen. About 30 percent will take less than half of the two quarts prescribed.

And all water is not the same. If you happen to live in an area where the drinking water has a high mineral content, notably calcium, and you're a habitual stone former, you're better off drinking distilled water. The very popular mineral waters we consume may also enhance the development of stones because of their high calcium content. Some brands of artificially carbonated beverages—club soda and the like—may or may not have a high calcium content. Natural carbonated water invariably does—and should be avoided by anyone who has had a kidney stone. Its calcium source is the calcium carbonate in limestone. So if you're traveling to areas where you must drink bottled water, do not ask for the naturally carbonated variety.

Calcium is, in fact, a major concern for stone formers. Among American adults, 90 percent of stones are made up of calcium oxalate, 10 percent of uric acid, cystine, or struvite (magnesium, ammonium and phosphate). Although most stones contain more than one substance, calcium is found in more than 90 percent. So if for some reason the stone you passed was not identified, your best bet is to institute anti-calcium measures.

Blood and urine both normally contain some calcium. Why then, out of a clear blue sky, and after a lifetime of feeling fine, would you suddenly form a calcium stone? Occasionally, it's because the amount of calcium in the blood, and subsequently in the urine, has increased. These levels can be determined easily and inexpensively. A high blood reading may indicate the presence of a tumor of the parathyroid glands. The parathyroids are four pea-sized glands hidden adjacent to the thyroid in the neck. Too small to feel even when they are enlarged, they produce a hormone that regulates the calcium content of blood and bone by removing varying amounts of calcium from the bone. A parathyroid tumor produces too much hormone, which in turn sucks out excessive amounts of calcium from the bone. This ends up first in the blood and then in the urine, where it forms stones. When the tumor is surgically removed, calcium stone formation stops. About 5 to 7 percent of patients with calcium stones turn out to have such parathyroid tumors.

There are other circumstances in which the blood and urine come to contain too much calcium. A common example is when a cancer spreads to bone from anywhere in the body. A high blood calcium level may also be due to an overactive thyroid gland, to sarcoidosis (a disease of unknown origin that involves the bone, skin, eyes and lungs) or to too much vitamin D in your diet (something we are seeing more and more as megadoses of vitamins—usually self-prescribed—are consumed). If any of these conditions is responsible for your calcium stone, further stones can be prevented by treating the underlying cause—that is, correcting the hyperthyroidism, managing the sarcoidosis or cutting out the vitamin D supplements.

In most instances when there is too much calcium in the urine, the blood level is actually normal—a condition called idiopathic hypercalciuria. "Idiopathic" is a fancy word doctors use to say, "I don't know the cause"; "hyper" is "too much"; and "calciuria" means "calcium in the urine." So the most frequent cause of too much calcium in the urine is "I don't know why there is too much calcium in the urine"! In fact, many such cases are probably the result of renal hypercalciuria, in which the kidney extracts more calcium from the blood than it should. It ends up in the urine, and you end up with stones. In other cases, no matter how little calcium one eats, the intestines absorb too much of it, and so again it winds up in excessive amounts in the urine. If you fall into this latter category, ask your doctor about sodium cellulose phosphate (Calcibind). This is a non-absorbable resin, taken by mouth, which binds the calcium in your gut, and both are excreted in the stool. One of the possible complications of this otherwise useful drug is that it increases the amount of oxalate in the urine, making you vulnerable to the formation of that kind of stone—a real Catch-22! A newer preparation with the same mode of action but with supposedly fewer side effects is called Urocit-K.

Generally speaking, if you have too much calcium in your urine, due to whatever cause, you can reduce the likelihood of recurrent stone formation simply by drinking lots and lots of water—as much as two to three quarts every twenty-four hours, especially at night.

In addition to diluting the urine, you may also reduce your chances of recurrent stone formation by taking one of the thiazide drugs (a "water pill," or diuretic, commonly used for the treatment of hypertension and fluid retention). It acts by decreasing calcium extretion in the urine. One or two tablets per day of a preparation containing a combination of amiloride and hydrochlorothiazide (Moduretic) are probably more effective than the hydrochlorothiazide alone. More recently, potassium citrate has also been approved for this purpose.

Is there any special diet to prevent kidney stones? Given the excess of calcium either in the urine or the blood, why not simply reduce the amount of it you eat? This will work only if you are consuming too much calcium to begin with (large amounts of milk or milk products, or antacids that contain calcium carbonate, such as Tums). Otherwise, diet is not a key factor in calcium stone formation. So many patients go through life following a low-calcium diet unnecessarily.

Whatever you do, don't let your fear of forming kidney stones lead you to consume an inadequate amount of calcium. Deprivation of calcium has recently been shown to be a contributing factor in high blood pressure. More importantly, especially in women approaching or beyond the menopause, it may also facilitate osteoporosis—a thinning of the bones, which may then fracture easily (see Chapter 11).

Finally, it seems that the less calcium you eat, the more oxalate your intestines absorb, increasing the risk of oxalate stone formation.

What about some of the other kinds of kidney stones people form? You may have too much oxalate (a substance found mostly in tea) and so be especially vulnerable to making calcium-oxalate stones. This usually happens in persons who have a problem with fat absorption from the bowel. If that's the case, in addition to drinking plenty of water, avoid excessive oxalate in your diet by cutting down on chocolate and fruit juices, and especially tea.

If you have gout, with too much uric acid in your blood (and hence in the urine), recurrent stones are particularly likely—and especially easy to prevent. They can form only in urine that is highly acid. All you need really do is to take something to prevent such acidity, like sodium bicarbonate. (But make sure it is safe for you to take the sodium in this preparation. Patients with heart disease and hypertension should not. There is a better product called Polycitra. You can check on how effectively you are neutralizing your urinary acidity by dipping a specially coated test paper strip into your urine.

If you have gout, or continue to make stones even after you have rendered your urine alkaline, you will have to take allopurinol (marketed in the United States as Zyloprim) in a dosage of 200 to 400 mgs. a day. This drug, which is used in the prevention of gout, cuts down the manufacture of uric acid by the body, lowers its level in the urine and makes stone formation less likely. Allopurinol may not only help prevent a recurrence of uric-acid stones, but along with alkalinization it may also dissolve any that are present in the kidney. But remember, taking the allopurinol doesn't excuse you from drinking large quantities of water in order to keep the urine dilute. That's still a must.

In some patients who are prone to chronic urinary tract infections, the bacteria and other noxious elements in the urine predispose to stone formation. In such cases, the stone almost always consists of triple phosphates (struvite). The presence of such a stone makes the diagnosis of infection virtually certain. You must then take the appropriate antibiotic.

Cystine stones are an uncommon type, occurring in less than 2 percent of stone formers, usually between the ages of ten and thirty years. They develop as a result of a genetic abnormality in which the kidney allows large amounts of cystine to enter the urine. Treatment of this condition is difficult and complicated, and should be carried out under the supervision of a specialist.

Here's a practical tip that may make a difference to you. There are two widely prescribed diuretics in this country used in the treatment of hypertension and heart failure. Marketed as Dyazide and Maxzide, they consist of two different agents, hydrochlorothiazide and triamterene. Patients taking either of these products may form triamterene stones in the urine. So even though it doesn't happen very often, if you are a stone former—any kind of stone former—you're better off not taking a diuretic that contains triamterene.

Now, if you think you've grasped the big picture on kidney stones, let me say a word in defense of the doctor who tells you, "Yes, you've got stones all right, but I can't find the cause." Don't let that surprise you or diminish your confidence in him. Despite all I've said above, even after the most sophisticated work-up, we are unable to discover the underlying mechanism in about 20 percent of patients with kidney stones. There are probably some agents in the kidney or urine not as yet identified—some that prevent stone formation and some that promote it. You may have too much or too little of either. But for the vast majority of stone formers, the preventive measures described above are effective.

Gallstones—Treatable but Not Predictably Preventable

As you've seen above, even if you've never suffered from kidney stones, you can reduce the risk of developing them if you drink enough water, especially in warm weather. But there is nothing I can suggest that will predictably reduce your chances of forming gallstones. Here the goal is largely a matter of avoiding recurrent attacks once the stones have formed, to prevent them from irritating and infecting the gallbladder in which they sit, and to keep them from moving out into the duct that leads from the gallbladder to the intestines, for under those circumstances an attack of gallstone colic ensues, which can be very painful and is not without risk.

Gallstones are extremely common in this country, much more so than kidney stones. Some fifteen million women and five million men have them, and half don't even know it. One million new cases are discovered each year and 500,000 gallbladders are subsequently removed. Those most likely to have gallstones are American Indians, of whom seven out of ten suffer from this disorder. Patients with rheumatic mitral valve disease and women who take the pill are also especially prone. Individuals with high cholesterol, especially those who are taking Atromid-S (clofibrate) to normalize their blood lipids, have a higher incidence of gallstones, too. The rest of the population with gallstones consists mostly, but by no means exclusively, of those with the five F's—female, fertile, fortyish, fat and flatulent. In other words, the incidence is higher among women, especially those who have had children. It is a disease of adult life and its major symptom is gas—except when a small stone has moved out of the gallbladder and down its duct toward the intestines. Should that happen, you will experience severe colicky pain (the kind that comes and goes) in the right upper portion of your abdomen, radiating to the tip of your right shoulder or travelling around to the back. You may or may not have fever, and depending on the location of the stone in the duct, you may become jaundiced. In many cases, the stone continues its journey through the duct system and into the gut. Once it does so, and the duct is no longer obstructed by the stone, pain, jaundice and fever clear up. Unless it is very large, such a stone causes no problem once it has reached the intestine itself.

Just as kidney stones are the result of crystallization of some of the constituents of urine, gallstones are the result of a similar process taking place in the bile. So most gallstones, by far, are composed of bile's major constituent—cholesterol.

Bile, which is required to digest the fat in your diet, is made in the liver and is sent through the common duct to the intestines where it meets the fat you've eaten and helps emulsify it. The liver is constantly producing this bile, but you are not always eating fat. So to store the excess bile that is not needed at any particular time, there is a branch (cystic duct) of the main, or common, duct leading away from the liver to the sac we call the gallbladder. When bile comes down the common duct and there is no fat in the intestine, it backs up via the cystic duct into the gallbladder, where it is stored. When a fatty meal you have eaten reaches the small intestine, signals are sent to the gallbladder to send down some additional bile. The normal gallbladder then contracts and squirts out the amount necessary to digest the fat in the gut. If the gallbladder is loaded with small stones, one or more may slip out during such a contraction. That is why the key to preventing an attack of gallbladder colic is to keep fat out of the intestines, by avoiding fried or fatty foods.

It wasn't so long ago that anyone found to have gallstones either in the course of some unrelated X-ray examination of the abdomen or because he or she had suffered an attack of pain was advised to have the gallbladder removed. More recent experience, however, has shown that the great majority of such persons do not require surgery. However, if you continue to suffer repeated attacks of pain, fever and jaundice, then you have no alternative but to have your gallbladder taken out. Patients often ask me how they can live without this organ. Very easily—and comfortably. The body compensates by dilating the bile ducts, which assume the gallbladder's storage functions.

You may hear about—and consider—treatment for the *medical* dissolution of the stones. I suggest this only for people who are poor surgical risks, because despite the initial enthusiasm generated by the observation that certain chemicals (chenodeoxycholic and ursodeoxycholic acid) can melt away gallstones, subsequent experience has shown that this occurs in only a very small percentage of cases. Furthermore, with the drug now available in the United States, Chenex (chenodeoxycholic acid) side effects are beginning to appear that are quite troublesome. Also, in 50 percent of cases in which the stones have dissolved completely, there is recurrence within five years.

You may have wondered about the absence of any discussion on the influence of diet and gallstones. This was deliberate on my part, and not an oversight. Traditionally, all such patients have been given a low-fat diet. I still prescribe it in my own practice. The rationale for this advice is as follows: The presence of fat in the intestines stimulates the gallbladder to contract in order to provide the additional bile necessary for fat digestion. When the gallbladder squeezes out this extra bile, small stones within may gain entry into the bile ducts and obstruct them, causing pain and jaundice. Recent studies, however, purport to show that the passage of these stones into the ducts is a purely random matter, and occurs independently of what you eat. This is a revolutionary concept, and my advice to anyone with gallstones is to play it safe. Continue to avoid fat, and wait for confirmatory evidence for this new theory.

CHAPTER 13

AIDS—The Modern Plague

I am friendly with a general practitioner, an old-timer practicing in upper Manhattan. He is the prototype of a vanishing breed of doctor, dedicated, experienced and practical. He also knows when to ask for help, or as he puts it, "When I'm in over my head." Since he is not affiliated with any major teaching hospital, he sometimes calls me when confronted with a problem case that needs especially sophisticated testing and treatment.

One day, in early 1982, he telephoned because "I've got the damndest problem case of pneumonia I've ever seen. There's this thirty-year-old man, single, and working as a hairdresser. About two weeks ago, he asked for an appointment at my office 'as soon as possible.' He said that for the past two or three weeks he had been feeling poorly—a 'virus,' he thought. He was running a low-grade fever, was quite short of breath, had a persistent dry cough, had lost about eight or nine pounds without dieting, and he was so tired all the time he could barely finish a day's work.

"When I first examined him a few days ago, his temperature was one hundred and two degrees. I found some enlarged glands in both armpits and neck, and with my stethoscope I could hear abnormal moisture in the lungs. I diagnosed a respiratory virus of some kind. Routine laboratory tests in my office did not reveal any surprises. There was a slight anemia, which is what I would have expected in any chronic infection. But I was worried about the weight loss and the lung findings, so I took a chest X ray. It showed double pneumonia and looked viral. I tried to get him to cough up some sputum for me to send to the lab. I hated to prescribe antibiotics without knowing whether I was dealing with a virus or a bacterium.

"Well, after a couple of days, he called to say he'd been able to spit up a little something, which he'd kept in a jar for me. I prepared a smear in my own lab and looked at it under the microscope. There was something there all right, but I couldn't tell what it was. Strangest-looking organism I ever saw. So I ran it over to a bacteriology lab in the neighborhood. They called it *Pneumocystis carinii*. I don't think I've ever seen a case of pneumocystis pneumonia before, have you? I looked it up, and it says pneumocystis is neither a bacterium nor a virus, but a parasite. What's more, it's almost always seen in patients with some malignancy or whose immunity has been affected by lots of radiation or suppressive drugs. But this chap developed his pneumonia out of a clear blue sky! He's got no malignancy that I can find, is on no medication and has not been radiated. Anyway, since he was getting sicker and sicker, I tried some antibiotics. First I gave him erythromycin. That didn't work. Then I put him on tetracycline. That didn't touch his fever either. I tell you, there is something weird going on here and I don't understand it. I think he belongs in a hospital."

I agreed. In the hospital, further testing did not clarify the diagnosis. Repeat sputum analyses confirmed the presence of the *Pneumocystis carinii*. The patient's temperature reached 104°, his chest X ray worsened, and his respiration became labored. First he needed oxygen and then a ventilator to help him with his breathing. After ten of the most frustrating days I've ever known, during which time he was given every antibiotic we could think of, this previously healthy young man died—essentially undiagnosed.

One of my medical residents said he had recently read a report in the *New England Journal of Medicine* about a new disease called acquired immune deficiency syndrome (AIDS), and that this patient seemed to fit the bill. Our infectious-disease consultants agreed. Most of the doctors on the case thought that was too fancy a diagnosis, and that the patient had probably succumbed to some rare, lethal, unidentified virus. ("It must have been a virus" is a convenient wastebasket diagnosis for any unexplained illness with fever.)

In retrospect, of course, this case was typical of AIDS. It is interesting that in all the sixty pages of hospital records we accumulated on this particular patient, nowhere was there any reference to his sexual habits. Everyone involved in his care knew he was a homosexual, but so what? How could that explain his pneumonia? And our feeling was, why embarrass him with questions about promiscuity? He was feeling miserable enough without our harping on such sensitive and seemingly irrelevant data.

Now, by contrast, look at the details of this second case, three years later, when we are so AIDS-conscious.

The patient was an accountant in his late twenties. His illness was very much like the first man's—fever, dry cough, pneumonia, weight loss and enlarged lymph glands. There was, however, one important additional finding. He had several small, raised, reddish-purple plaques on his skin that were painless and did not itch. This time, before sending him to the hospital, I made the diagnosis of AIDS— without any fancy tests.

The history eventually obtained from this man was also much more relevant than was the first patient's. His hospital chart contained the following information, asked for by and freely given to the medical student, the intern, the junior resident and the senior resident who examined him. Yes, he was homosexual. Promiscuous? Absolutely. He had already had scores of lovers in his lifetime. He enjoyed anal intercourse, and was usually the "passive" partner. Two years ago, he had come down with a mild case of hepatitis B. Before that, when he felt well enough, he was a frequent blood donor, because he needed the extra cash.

The medical work-up revealed the presence of pneumonia, and the sputum again contained the *Pneumocystis carinii* organism. We now knew what that meant, and why this patient had it. (This parasite thrives when, for whatever reason, the immune system is not functioning properly.) A biopsy of the skin lesion confirmed the diagnosis of Kaposi's sarcoma, a form of cancer that involves not only the skin, but the lymph glands, and occasionally the abdominal organs as well. It is a slow-growing malignancy that may smolder for many years even in persons without AIDS.

Based on more recent experience with this disease, we administered Bactrim and then an antibiotic called Pentamidine. (The former is an antibiotic widely used in the management of urinary and upper respiratory infections, and, as you read elsewhere in this book, turista as well.) He began to respond to this therapy in about ten days, and a few weeks later the pneumonia cleared completely. He was discharged and arrangements were made for him to receive treatment for his Kaposi's tumor as an outpatient. His outlook? Statistically poor. Chances of survival beyond two years are very small—unless we come up with some effective therapy in the meantime. The pneumocystis pneumonia and the Kaposi's sarcoma are complications and not the causes of AIDS.

Homosexuals are at special risk for contracting several serious diseases, many of which are sexually transmitted. The most recent and deadliest infection they face is AIDS. Certain maladies—for example, Legionnaires' disease—have been around for years, but only recently identified and understood. By contrast, AIDS is really a new entity that appeared for the first time in the United States in 1981. Symptoms develop because of a specific defect in the patient's natural immunity. The presence of this abnormality can actually be detected in blood tests before any symptoms develop. As a result, we can often identify those at risk for clinical evidence of AIDS before they become sick. At the moment, there is not much we can do with this information, but given the momentum at which new knowledge is being obtained in this area, this ability to identify vulnerability will one day be very useful.

The immune disorder in AIDS primarily involves certain white blood cells called lymphocytes, which are important contributors to resistance. There are two kinds of these cells—"helper" T-cells and "suppressor" T-cells, and each plays its own role in the immune process. Patients with AIDS, or those vulnerable to it, have a deficiency in the number of helper T-cells. We think that the recently identified HTLV-III virus gets into the body of the AIDS patient and knocks out the helper T-cells. The affected individual then loses the ability to ward off certain specific infections and malignancies and succumbs to them. The "opportunistic" agents that cause these diseases include the *Pneumocystis carinii* (which results in pneumonia), certain fungi, various herpes and other related viruses. In addition, the malignancy called Kaposi's sarcoma also develops.

Analysis of the 14,000 individuals with AIDS thus far reported in the United States (and the number of new cases is more than doubling every year) indicates the following to be at "high risk"—homosexuals and bisexuals (who account for the great majority—71 percent), intravenous drug users (some 17 percent), children born of mothers who either have the disease or have been infected but are not yet symptomatic, hemophiliacs (1 percent), those with certain other blood disorders requiring frequent transfusions, and prostitutes. Haitian immigrants were formerly on this list, but were removed when their vulnerability was found to be due to their personal habits, not their national origin. What alarms researchers is the fact that at last count almost 6 percent of AIDS patients were heterosexuals with none of the other indications, individuals whom one would not expect to be at risk. Their number is also increasing.

Most scientists interested in the problem believe that the causative agent that wreaks all this havoc, that decimates the helper T-cells, is almost certainly the HTLV-III virus (called the LAV virus by French scientists who discovered it independently—and virtually simultaneously). Antibodies to this virus have been identified in patients with AIDS, in those at high risk and even in a few "normals."

How the AIDS virus is actually transmitted is still not clear. It has been found in virtually every body fluid—blood, saliva, semen, and even tears. Nevertheless, the current feeling is that somebody with AIDS probably cannot infect you by sneezing or coughing directly at you. Because of the presence of the virus in saliva, intimate kissing may constitute a route of infection but this has never been documented. The portal of entry of virus in semen may be the mouth, anus and probably the vagina as well. Ultimately, however, the AIDS virus reaches the bloodstream—as it now does mostly via transfusions, anal intercourse or infected needles.

Focus on Prevention

How can one avoid contracting AIDS? The most effective way is not to have intimate or sexual contact with any individual who has the disease or who is at high risk for developing it. That includes not only homosexuals but prostitutes and intravenous drug users as well. Homosexuals should abstain from anal intercourse "for the duration," that is, until there is effective treatment for AIDS or a vaccine to prevent it. Also, if you're on drugs, that's bad enough. Don't make matters worse by sharing your needles.

For physicians, nurses and other health-care personnel in contact with AIDS patients, how to avoid "catching" the disease is a very important problem. The number of cases is increasing dramatically, so that no matter what our specialty, many of us have already been called upon to help treat these patients, or soon will be. In the past year, four of my own cardiac patients have developed AIDS. These people need care, and someone has to deliver it. Fortunately, to date, there have been only scattered reports of the disease's being contracted by health providers. I do not believe that patients with AIDS need to be isolated. To protect myself, I always wear rubber gloves when in contact with any of their bodily secretions. I am extremely careful about how I handle needles used in their treatment. It goes without saying that I do not share their dishes or utensils. However, I do not wear a mask when examining them and I have no hesitation about doing so "bare-handed." I do not don a gown when entering their rooms, though some doctors do. Pregnant women should keep away from AIDS patients, because they may become infected by one of the "opportunistic" organisms that the AIDS victim harbors.

Until quite recently blood transfusions posed a real problem. We were worried about the consequences of administering blood to someone who had hemorrhaged during major surgery and needed replacement. There is no question that AIDS has been transmitted by blood from donors who have the disease or are carriers—infected persons who themselves have no symptoms. (Typhoid Mary was the most famous carrier in recent times. She was "healthy," but harbored typhoid organisms, and succeeded in transmitting them to countless persons with whom she came in contact.) In a major report from the Centers for Disease Control, which has been accumulating all the available information on this disease, 28 percent of all AIDS patients not otherwise at high risk had received blood during the previous five years. High-risk donors were identified in several of these cases. But we don't have nearly as much concern about blood transfusions anymore, because donor blood can now be screened for the presence of antibodies to the HTLV-III virus. In fact, it *must* be screened by law, and any positive specimens rejected. This should drastically reduce or eliminate the transmission of AIDS to patients receiving blood transfusions.

It all sounds so easy, but it isn't. This major advance has turned out to be a mixed blessing, because of the high incidence of "false-positive" responses in certain of the kits used to test for the antibodies. (A false-positive response is one in which a test erroneously comes back "abnormal.") Some people ostensibly in good health and without any evidence of AIDS are being notified after giving blood that they have antibodies to the virus!

The two most widely used tests for the detection of these antibodies are the ELISA (enzyme-linked immunosorbent assay) and the Western blot. The former is the less expensive, but some of its "positive" results are spurious. Most blood banks repeat a positive ELISA test at least once. If it comes back positive a second time, the Western-blot technique is employed. This particular kit costs about $100 per test, which is a prohibitive amount for a screening procedure. It is less sensitive but more specific in its results than the ELISA test. That means it picks up fewer positives, but when it does, you can depend on it. So any blood that is positive twice on the ELISA test and confirmed with a Western blot is assumed to contain the HTLV-III antibodies. Positive results are occasionally found in "normal" individuals, that is, not at high risk and without any symptoms or evidence of disease. But among high-risk persons still in apparent good health, the incidence of positive tests is substantial. For example, in some studies, up to 65 percent of "healthy" homosexual males, 87 percent of active intravenous drug abusers, 72 percent of patients with hemophilia A and 35 percent of women whose sexual partners had AIDS are found to have these antibodies.

What should such persons be told and how should they conduct themselves? In my opinion, despite all the potential sources of error in the test, any individual in whom antibodies are unquestionably present on repeated determinations must be considered a carrier or likely to develop the disease at a later date. The HTLV-III virus is a "retrovirus," which means it can hang around the body for years before causing full-blown symptoms. In various studies to date, as many as 19 percent of asymptomatic homosexuals with a positive test went on to manifest classical AIDS, while another 25 percent developed a milder form of the disease.

What to Do in the Meantime

So this is what I recommend to anyone who falls into that category. You must not only protect yourself; you should also think of others. Let your doctor and dentist know, so that you don't hurt them. Your doctor will also watch you more carefully for the earliest evidence of AIDS, which—when caught *very* early—may have a better chance of responding to treatment. You should look for the following warning signals: unexplained fever, diarrhea, headache, funny-looking rashes on the skin or in the mouth (especially those that are brown or purple), cough, shortness of breath, weight loss or swollen glands. Use condoms during any sexual contact you may have. Avoid intimate kissing and do not share needles, razors, toothbrushes or any item that may have blood on it. Hopefully, if you are indeed incubating AIDS, there will be a cure for it before it becomes apparent.

I believe a breakthrough is in the offing. But until a vaccine or cure is found, many of us will have to rethink our sexual practices, re-evaluate our personal habits and in the meantime keep our fingers crossed.

CHAPTER **14**

The Traveling Blood Clot—
When Rat Poison Can Save Your Life

I have bad news for you. There are thousands of people going about their business each day blissfully unaware that they are living under the sword of Damocles. For at any moment, they are vulnerable to sudden catastrophe in the form of a traveling blood clot, or embolism. An embolism may end up in the brain (causing a stroke), the lungs (severely damaging those organs), the kidneys, legs, spleen, eyes— indeed, in any part of the body supplied by blood vessels. Now here's the good news. You can, in large measure, be protected against such embolization, and that's what this chapter is about.

The following accounts will give you some indication of how problems can develop, and how they can be prevented.

Mary was thirty-seven years old, a career woman, the editor of a very prestigious fashion magazine. She was living quite happily with a successful lawyer. She used the contraceptive pill. Aside from some varicose veins, which she camouflaged rather well with the right color stockings and makeup, she was in good health. She used to visit my office once a year only because her employer insisted she do so. At each visit, I warned her to stop smoking cigarettes, which she refused to do. "Doctor, in my work, dealing with models, agents and the 'beauty' set, I can't afford to be fat. I had a devil of a time as a teen-ager. At college, I weighed almost a hundred and fifty pounds. That's when I started to smoke. The cigarettes helped control my appetite and I was able to drop to my present weight of a hundred twenty-four pounds. I am sorry, but what with all the two-martini lunches my job requires, I'd be as big as a house if I quit smoking.'' This was the gist of our conversation, year after year.

One morning, Mary called me, quite concerned. "Doctor, there is something very wrong. I think you should see me as soon as possible. Since breakfast, every time I take a deep breath I get a sudden sharp pain in the right side of my chest. I feel okay otherwise. I have no fever, and I don't have a cold, but I have noticed a little dry cough in the past few hours. What do you think it all means? Jim says it's probably a muscle spasm from the way I slept last night, or maybe a draft from the air conditioning.'' I had her come right over, because the association of sudden pain in the chest, made worse by taking a deep breath, and especially when accompanied by a new cough in someone with varicose veins, raised the possibility of a blood clot to a lung.

She had no fever, and she didn't look especially sick. When I examined her, I found her lungs were normal, even over the area where she had pain. Her breathing was somewhat shallow as she tried not to move her chest too much. Her right leg was fine. However, I found that a vein in her left leg was inflamed (phlebitis). There was a small area that was a little reddened, warm and tender to touch. A chest X ray and an electrocardiogram were both normal. Despite that, because the symptoms so strongly suggested a blood clot, I sent her for a radioactive lung scan. It revealed an embolism to the right lung, and so I had her admitted to the hospital. Fortunately, the clot was a small one, and she did well with bed rest and anticoagulants (blood thinners). After a few days, she was discharged and went back to work, still smoking, unfortunately, but with a spanking new diaphragm instead of her oral contraceptives.

The point of this story, as you may have guessed by now, is that the combination of ''the pill'' and cigarettes, especially in a woman in her mid to late thirties, is hazardous. Such women are vulnerable to disorders of blood clotting, which can result in a stroke or even a heart attack (when arteries are involved) or phlebitis (particularly in the presence of varicose veins). The latter is what happened in Mary's case.

Phlebitis is the inflammation of a vein, very commonly in the legs. It is usually accompanied by clot formation. If a piece of the clot breaks off, it may travel up the leg and through the system of veins in the abdomen into the heart and on to the lungs, where it finally lodges. If it ends in and blocks a large blood vessel within a lung, the amount of damage it causes to the pulmonary tissues can be life-threatening. Fortunately, in Mary's case, it wasn't.

The lesson? If you are thirty-five or older, it's better for you to use some form of contraception other than the pill—like the diaphragm we gave Mary when she left the hospital. If you insist on the pill, then you must stop smoking. You can't have it both ways if you hope to prevent blood clots, either in the arteries or in the veins.

This next case provides another good example of how a serious disorder to which many of us are vulnerable can be minimized or prevented.

Max was a fifty-four-year-old diamond broker. He was in good health except for his weight (he was 5 feet 7 inches and weighed 190 pounds—about thirty-five or forty pounds too much by my reckoning). He also had good-sized varicose veins, and about three years earlier had developed phlebitis in his left leg. Fortunately, it was not complicated by a blood clot to a lung.

This man's business took him to Europe quite often. Despite his wife's pleadings, and the fact that his expenses were tax deductible, he insisted on going Economy Class. There is no question that over the years the seats on planes have gotten narrower and narrower. Legroom is now virtually nonexistent. So Max had to sit with his knees almost up to his chest whenever the passenger directly ahead reclined the seat.

On one such seven-and-a-half- or eight-hour overnight trip to Germany, Max so dreaded the prolonged "torture," as he put it, that he took a sleeping pill as soon as he boarded the aircraft. The plane was full. He had the window seat. A portly lady sat beside him in the middle seat, and a Marine returning to duty after home leave was on the aisle. It was a real tight squeeze. Shortly after takeoff, Max asked the hostess not to disturb him for the movie or meal service, inserted earplugs and put on an eye mask. He was soon fast asleep. Four hours later, he was awakened by a full bladder, but didn't feel he should get up because the passengers beside him were now sleeping, and there was no way he could reach the aisle without awakening them. So he sat there for another hour or so, while his bladder signals became more and more insistent. The seating space was so tight he couldn't cross and uncross his legs, and so he remained virtually immobile. About forty-five minutes before landing, he was finally able to make his way to the toilet.

Two days later, while going about his business in Hamburg, Max experienced a sudden pain in his left chest, worsened by taking a deep breath. That same evening, he noted a low-grade fever. The long and short of it was that he had developed phlebitis in his right leg and suffered a blood clot to the left lung. He was admitted to a hospital, where a lung scan confirmed the diagnosis. Anticoagulant treatment was begun and continued for three months after his discharge. The phlebitis subsided and the lung clot dissolved.

Max's varicose veins had made him vulnerable to a pulmonary embolism. So had his overweight, and his prolonged immobility on that flight. The chances of his developing a blood clot could have been very much reduced or even prevented had he taken the appropriate measures.

Any situation in which blood flow is slowed favors clot formation. That's why such clots frequently occur in varicose veins. When legs with varicose veins are allowed to hang down for hours, as was the case in Max's long plane flight, gravity further promotes the likelihood of clot formation. Moving and walking about, so that the leg muscles can exert a milking action on the veins and assist the return of blood to the heart, helps prevent this from happening. So does wearing support hose or elastic stockings.

But Max did everything wrong. First, he should have flown Business Class, if only for the legroom. He should have asked for an aisle seat, as do most experienced travelers—so that he could at least straighten his legs from time to time. (What can you see out the window at thirty-five thousand feet during a night flight anyway?) He should not have taken a sleeping pill, but rather gotten up and walked about every forty-five minutes or so—to keep the blood moving through his varicose veins. Chances are that if he had done any or all of these things, he might have prevented the phlebitis and the resultant blood clot to his lung.

Straight from the Heart

Following is another common situation that I estimate leaves scores of thousands of persons vulnerable to emboli, not in the veins, as was the case with Mary and Max, but in the arteries. The consequences can be life-threatening. The condition to which I refer is an abnormality of heart rhythm called *atrial fibrillation,* a totally irregular heart action. Most normal persons experience an "extra beat" now and then. But in atrial fibrillation, it is as if every beat is "extra." There is no predictable pattern or rhythm of cardiac contraction. Actually, as long as we can keep the *rate* at which the heart beats within a reasonable range, say between sixty and ninety beats per minute (and we usually do so by prescribing a digitalis preparation), most people with atrial fibrillation can function quite normally despite the irregular cardiac rhythm.

Atrial fibrillation is a very common disorder not necessarily indicative of heart disease. I have several patients who are fibrillating all the time, yet who feel perfectly healthy. In fact, I understand that some years ago one of our astronauts, in superb physical condition, was found during a routine examination to have atrial fibrillation. In his case, it was intermittent. He was nevertheless permitted to go on one of the moon flights. I have also seen this rhythm disorder occur now and then, for periods ranging from minutes to days, in otherwise healthy individuals who drink too much coffee, smoke cigarettes, or are on excessive thyroid medication. However, atrial fibrillation is most frequently seen in older persons in whom it usually does reflect some underlying disorder, cardiac or noncardiac. For example, it may be due to an overactive thyroid gland, arteriosclerosis of the coronary arteries, or some abnormality within the heart, especially one involving the mitral valve.

Whatever the underlying cause, and despite the fact that the rhythm disorder may be well tolerated by the patient (a goodly number of these people aren't even aware they have it), we now know that anybody with chronic atrial fibrillation is at peril of throwing off a blood clot. Since most of these clots originate in the left side of the heart, which pumps blood to all parts of the body except the lungs (blood reaches the lungs from the right side of the heart), such a clot may end up in the brain and cause a stroke; in the arteries of the leg, cutting off the circulation there; to the kidneys, damaging those organs; and so on. Unless there is some reason why you shouldn't have your blood thinned (as for example, a bleeding ulcer, some underlying blood-clotting problem, liver disease or very high blood pressure), you should be anticoagulated indefinitely, or at least as long as you continue to fibrillate. The most widely used anticoagulant in this country is warfarin (Coumadin). When taking it, you must be certain to have your blood checked every three or four weeks to make sure you are not getting too much or too little of the drug. Interestingly, warfarin is used as a rat poison; it kills the rodent by causing it to hemorrhage.

In patients who need to be anticoagulated, but can't tolerate Coumadin for one of the reasons mentioned above, I prescribe agents that, though they are not, strictly speaking, anticoagulants, do reduce the clotting tendency in a different way. They interfere with platelet function. Platelets are microscopic particles in the blood whose job it is to facilitate blood clotting. Aspirin is one such drug; Persantine (dipyridamole) is another. I usually prescribe them together—Persantine in dosages of 50 to 100 mgs. three or four times a day, aspirin in the baby size, 80 mgs. once a day. In patients who *can* tolerate anticoagulants, combining Coumadin and Persantine is probably the most effective way of all to prevent embolism.

Persantine sometimes causes headache or gastrointestinal side effects. When that happens, an effective substitute is Anturane (sulfinpyrazone), administered in a dosage of 800 mgs. a day.

There are several other circumstances that may render you vulnerable to emboli, even when your heart rhythm is completely regular. Mitral stenosis is one such example. In this disorder, usually the result of rheumatic fever, the mitral valve in the heart doesn't open all the way. This interferes with the flow of blood out of the left atrium. As a result that chamber cannot expel all of its contents, and increases in size. Clots then form in this dilated chamber, break off and travel almost anywhere in the body. Therefore, some doctors anticoagulate patients with mitral stenosis whose left atrium is very big, even if their heart rhythm is regular.

Patients who have had one or more diseased heart valves replaced by a prosthetic one must also almost always receive anticoagulants for the rest of their lives. The reason was dramatically demonstrated in several of the artificial-heart recipients in this country. Little clots forming somewhere within the cardiac device broke off, traveled to the brain and resulted in a series of strokes. The same sequence of events can happen with a prosthetic valve. If, however, the artificial valve is a biological one—that is, made from tissue, as opposed to metal or plastic—anticoagulation may not be necessary. (The classic example of the biological valve is the very widely used pig valve.) Even in this circumstance, anticoagulants should be continued for a minimum of three months after its insertion.

When the Heart Is Weak

There are two other circumstances in which deadly blood clots can originate in the heart in the presence of a normal rhythm. The first is a condition called cardiomyopathy. ("Cardio" refers to the heart, "myo" to muscle, and "pathy" means "disease of" or "trouble with." So cardiomyopathy is a condition in which the heart muscle is not working properly—in short, a weak heart.) This can develop in several ways. The heart may have been "poisoned" by alcohol abuse (alcoholic cardiomyopathy); by a virus, which might have seemed innocent at the time (viral cardiomyopathy)—you might have thought you only had a bad cold, for instance—but which affected the cardiac muscle; by long-standing coronary-artery disease that deprived the heart muscle of nutrition (ischemic cardiomyopathy); by chronic infections; by high blood pressure that stressed the heart muscle over a period of years (hypertensive cardiomyopathy); or by the infiltration of certain body chemicals into the heart (amyloidosis). Whatever the cause, instead of contracting vigorously to expel the blood within its cavity, the heart muscle beats limply, like an old, stretched sac. Because the heart action is so weak, the blood within its cavities does not move briskly in and out, but swirls and eddies, permitting little clots to form. When one of these leaves the heart, there is no telling where it will end up. For that reason, I believe most patients with cardiomyopathy should be anticoagulated to reduce the likelihood of clot formation.

The treacherous thing about cardiomyopathy is that patients with this disorder are not always aware they have it. A fifty-eight-year-old man consulted me recently because of palpitations (an awareness of his heartbeat for which there was no apparent explanation). He was a schoolteacher, and not very athletic. His physical examination was unrevealing; blood pressure was normal; I heard no heart murmurs.

His electrocardiogram was all right. His chest X ray, however, revealed his heart to be considerably enlarged (which it almost always is in cardiomyopathy). But it was only on the echocardiogram that the diagnosis was made, by recognition of the flabby, poorly contracting muscle. This man had a serious problem, yet he had absolutely no indication aside from the palpitations that there was anything wrong with him.

Finally, there is another group of patients, those with a ventricular aneurysm, some of whom should also receive anticoagulants in order to prevent life-threatening emboli. The mechanism that makes them vulnerable is very similar to that of cardiomyopathy, but its origin differs. After a massive heart attack, especially one involving the front portion of the heart (anterior wall infarction), the injured wall balloons out with each cardiac contraction. Clots can form within this sac (aneurysm), much as they do in cardiomyopathy, and can actually be "seen" on an echocardiogram. Anticoagulants are protective in such patients.

If everyone vulnerable to emboli were anticoagulated, many thousands of deaths and much disability would be prevented.

CHAPTER **15**

Aging—You're Never Too Young to Stop Growing Old

Do you remember your reaction when you found the first single white hair on your head? And how the initial curiosity and amusement gave way to growing anxiety when more and more began to appear? Or your early attitudes toward cosmetic surgery? You understood completely why someone might want to correct a cleft palate, or a Cyrano de Bergerac nose, but to "go under the knife" simply to "look younger" was totally incomprehensible to you. Then one day you found yourself in front of the mirror straightening the creases in your forehead, the folds in your cheeks, the pouches under your eyes and the fat in both chins—just making believe. And you wondered . . . maybe, just maybe. Suddenly plastic surgery didn't seem so outlandish anymore. When did you first realize that you couldn't recall people's names so well anymore, or hear everything being said at the theater or at business meetings? And have you gotten over how you felt when your periods began to taper and finally stop, or when your golf game became more important to you than sex? These are but a few of the scenarios that made you—or will make you—aware that it's not only other people who grow old.

Individuals deal with aging in different ways. Some "adjust" to it. They plan for the "golden years," and accept their decreasing vitality as inevitable. Others deny. They try to alter their appearance with makeup, hair coloring or plastic surgery—face-lifts, buttock reduction or breast augmentation. There are those who develop the "seven-year itch" and then "scratch" for as many years as they can. The majority, however, simply continue looking for herbs, vitamins and magic potions to keep them young forever.

As far as the reality of aging is concerned, there is good news and bad news. First, the bad news: there is no way to stop the clock. We cannot now extend life beyond the maximum number of years for which our species has been genetically programmed. The good news, however, is that we have the potential to live longer than we now do, by as much as perhaps forty or fifty years. We fail to reach the 120 years that some scientists say are attainable because we're killed by accidents, cancer, hardening of the arteries, pneumonia and a host of other phenomena, none of which are either natural or the inevitable consequences of aging. Many of them can, in fact, be prevented or at least delayed.

Aging Is Not a Disease

When patients ask me how to cope with growing old, I advise them to follow the suggestions of the National Institute on Aging. They are not flashy or exciting, and they look so obvious. But believe me, they reflect where it's at today. Some of them will be explored in greater depth farther along in this chapter.

(1) *Don't smoke.* Cigarettes will shorten your life by causing heart disease, emphysema, cancer and virtually everything else under the sun.

(2) *Eat a balanced diet and maintain a desirable weight.* These are critically important goals, not only because they create a sense of well-being, but also because they influence what goes on in each cell of your body as you grow older, and help prevent a host of diseases.

(3) *Exercise regularly.* Fitness increases resistance to disease. Exercise is also the best tranquilizer there is.

(4) *Have regular checkups. See a doctor as soon as you've detected a problem and follow her advice, especially with regard to medication.* When you cannot prevent a disease, early intervention and cure are the next best things. Once a disease is diagnosed, its

outcome will depend largely on how well you comply with your doctor's orders.

(5) *Stay involved with family and friends and don't retire any sooner than you must.* Depression is a major curse of the elderly, and its main causes are loneliness and a loss of purpose in life. So many older persons look forward to retirement for years, and when they finally do retire, they're literally bored to death. Everyone must have something to wake up to and for in the morning. The excitement, the goals, the anticipation of each new day are what keep one feeling young. Without them, all you've got to look forward to is dying. So stay active, if not at work, then with hobbies, recreation or in community activities.

(6) *Make new friends of all ages.* Don't limit your social contacts to your own age group. The young can learn from the elderly. Older persons can continue to be stimulated by younger individuals. You will think better, eat better and feel better. Man is a gregarious animal, not meant to live alone. If your spouse has died and you feel lonely, remember if you're so motivated and have the opportunity, it's almost never too late to marry again. But in any event, make and retain close friendships.

(7) *Allow time for rest and relaxation* both before you retire as well as afterward.

(8) *Get enough sleep,* whether it's at night or a nap during the day.

(9) *Drink alcohol in moderation, if at all, and don't drive after drinking.* As we get older, we see less well and lose a little hearing. Our reflexes are not as quick either. The addition of alcohol, which interferes with coordination and attention at all ages, further compromises these faculties in older persons. It is just as important not to die in an accident as it is to avoid a fatal disease.

(10) *Use seat belts.* There is no use conquering cancer and heart disease if you're going to end up as a statistic on the road because you've gone through your windshield.

(11) *Avoid overexposure to sun and cold.* Older persons are more vulnerable to the excesses of heat and hypothermia because the aging body doesn't handle temperature variations as efficiently.

(12) *Practice good safety habits at home.* Falls and fires take the lives of many older people because their bones break more easily

or because they can't move quickly enough to escape a domestic catastrophe.

(13) *Plan ahead for your financial security.* Many disorders of aging are related to poor nutrition, and lack of money is often the culprit in these cases. Also, it's important to be able to afford the best care possible, and the most independence, in the event that you should become ill.

(14) *Maintain a positive outlook on life and expect to live a long time.* Your attitude in sickness and in health is extremely important in determining the quality and duration of life.

(15) *Finally, and perhaps most important, discover what makes you happy and do it.* Satisfaction and pleasure (including sex, which is too good to be left entirely to the young) contribute to good health and long life as much as does any pill or medication.

None of the above advice is often taken seriously. Instead, my patients want to know what I think about megadoses of vitamins, hormone supplements, lecithin, choline, zinc, copper, calcium, magnesium, kelp, alfalfa, dolomite, Dr. Aslan's procaine from Romania, scores of different herbal concoctions, and sometimes, believe it or not, even monkey-gland transplants. In my judgment, none of these can hold a candle to the rules laid out above.

Current Directions in Research to "Prevent" Aging

There *is* an ongoing, serious, worldwide scientific commitment to unlocking the door to immortality, to finding real answers and not Band-Aid solutions to the problems associated with aging. An interesting example of the kind of research being carried out involves the red blood cells, whose function it is to deliver oxygen to every organ and tissue in the body. These cells are formed in the bone marrow and live exactly 120 days, during which time they circulate into and through *every* nook and cranny of the body. Before its 120th day of life, the red blood cell passes through the spleen, as through other parts of the body, without any problem. However, on the 120th day of its life, as it courses through that organ, it is selectively filtered out and separated from the millions of other red cells with which it flows in the blood and is destroyed. That's why the spleen is referred to as the "graveyard of the red cell." The iron as well as other pigments and substances that the cell contains are recirculated and incorporated into new red cells, which are constantly being produced in the bone marrow. Scientists have been trying to fathom how the spleen knows to remove the red blood cell on its 120th day, and why it does so—or put another way, why the cell is "ready to die" at that particular time. If they do determine the cause, we may have a better understanding of aging and the limits of human life.

I could fill an entire book just summarizing the many ongoing scientific studies of aging and death. Although there are as yet no major breakthroughs, there are certain facts about growing old that have been well established. For example, we know that with time, all cells "wear out," and are not replaced. Older people generally become thinner and lose weight because of this gradual decrease in the body cell count. These same cells are not only reduced in number, they do not work as efficiently as when they were young. Stomach cells don't digest as well; lung cells don't extract oxygen the way they used to; and kidney cells lose some of their ability to make urine. The reason for this widespread reduction of function is probably a decrease in the enzyme activity within the cells. (Enzymes are proteins that speed up energy processes.)

Normal enzyme function depends on an adequate supply of vitamins and trace minerals in the diet. The elderly are apt to become deficient in some of these substances because of malnutrition, which can be due to any number of causes. They may not be able to afford a balanced diet; they may find it difficult to prepare adequate meals because they are infirm or don't see well, or have a tremor; they may have a dental problem that makes chewing difficult; they may be depressed; they may have a poor appetite because of some medication or illness. Whatever the reason, the fact is that a significant number of our senior citizens are malnourished, and this may have adverse effects on cells and tissues, accelerating symptoms of aging. Many of these are reversed when nutrition is improved. So supplementing the diet with the recommended daily requirement (RDR) of multivitamins and trace elements is very important to help prevent the consequences of aging in anyone at any age who may become deficient in these elements. But remember, supplementing does not mean megadosing. There is no evidence whatsoever that *excessive* amounts of any vitamins, minerals or other nutrients will improve health status or prolong life.

Radicals—Free and Dangerous

One popular theory of aging that has dietary implications relates to the "free radical"—a chemical by-product of cell metabolism. Free radicals are produced in energy processes that involve oxygen (not all do). Like some politicians, the body does not get along well with these free radicals. They're thought to speed up the aging process, and to play a role in the causation of cancer, hypertension, senile dementia and disorders of the immune system (impaired resistance). When we reduce the number of free radicals in small laboratory animals by manipulating their diet, three things happen. Their mean life-span is raised, overall resistance is enhanced, and certain cancers are inhibited. The diet that has these salutary effects contains only minimal amounts of polyunsaturated fats, and is sufficiently low in calories to reduce total body weight. (Remember when cardiologists were "pushing" polyunsaturates as a means of preventing coronary-artery disease? Only after several studies showed an increase in the incidence of cancer in persons taking large amounts of such fats was the advice withdrawn!) Selenium, a trace mineral that keeps cropping up in the anti-cancer literature, also appears to decrease the damage caused by free-radical reactions in these animal studies.

So it's possible that humans who follow a similar regimen, that is, consume a diet adequate in essential nutrients but low in calories and polyunsaturated fats and supplemented with perhaps 50 to 100 mcgs. of selenium a day, may live longer than they presently do.

Now a word about antioxidants, since they fit into the free-radical picture too. The best-known antioxidants, vitamins E and C, reduce the adverse effects of the free radicals in laboratory animals. Think of these two vitamins as free-radical "scavengers." They remove these undesirable by-products of metabolism from the body's environment. We know this is so because of the following evidence. We can produce cancer in laboratory animals by giving them certain chemicals. If, however, we first administer lots of vitamins E and C, we cannot induce the cancer. Also, the animals' mean life-span is increased.

What should you and I do with this information? Should we supplement our diet with extra doses of vitamins E and C, and if so, by how much? I have no scientific answers for you based on human experiments, but because of the available *suggestive* evidence, I prescribe 200 to 400 units of vitamin E and at least 500 mgs. of vitamin C per day for most of my patients, in addition to a daily multivitamin supplement. Such doses are not harmful, and may be protective in the long run.

Here's a theory proposed by other researchers. They refer to it as "undernutrition without malnutrition." In laboratory experiments, it has been observed that the life of test animals can be prolonged by keeping their weight down and reducing the total intake of protein. Apparently, the less protein there is for the cell to use, the smaller the chances of it becoming abnormal and transmitting adverse genetic information—or something to that effect. So it is suggested that all of us, no matter how old (it's apparently never too late to benefit from this diet), should cut our calories substantially but gradually over a five-year period to 60 percent of usual consumption. The diet must contain all the essential nutrients and amino acids. Enough protein should be consumed during childhood to permit normal growth, and in pregnancy to nourish the fetus. But beyond that, the amount should be progressively reduced. By the time we reach middle adult life, we should be eating mainly carbohydrates and very little protein and fat.

It's postulated that this low-calorie, high-carbohydrate, low-fat, low-protein diet is helpful mainly because it results in the generation of fewer "bad" free radicals.

Betrayed By Your Own Body—Deranged Immunity

In order to better understand the phenomenon of aging, you should also know something about how the immune system works. This is a complicated natural mechanism whose function it is to defend the body against hostile elements invading from the outside (bacteria, viruses, fungi, etc.) and from within (floating cancer cells that are not "permitted" to take root and multiply). As we grow older, the immune system gradually becomes less efficient. When that happens, it cannot always distinguish between the cells and proteins that are a normal part of the body ("self") and those that are foreign ("nonself"). It then manufactures antibodies that destroy the body's normal tissues. This process, called autoimmunity, is bad. (Immunity, on the other hand, which protects against harmful substances, is good.) So two things go wrong with the aging immune system. First, it doesn't combat invaders or handle toxic materials nearly as well as it did previously. At the same time, it embarks on its "anti-self," or "autodestruct," course. Scientists believe that dietary manipulation, especially protein restriction, as well as specific supplements of substances in which we are deficient, may counteract both these trends and protect us as we get older.

On the basis of the foregoing theories, it would seem reasonable for everyone to lose weight, to eat less fat and protein (that means reducing the amount of meat and fish), to concentrate on carbohydrates, and to add just enough vitamins and minerals to make sure we're not deficient.

My last word on diet and aging is a cautionary note about "herbal" concoctions that promise good health. While in most cases, they can't hurt you, I am wary of "herbal" products whose active ingredients are a mystery. For example, I know of one woman who was convinced that a certain herbal tea she bought at her health-food store was good for her. Drinking eight to ten cups a day helped curb her appetite. One day she noticed some vaginal bleeding between menstrual periods. She consulted her gynecologist, who couldn't find the cause. But when her blood was tested, it reacted as if she had been taking an anticoagulant. It was too "thin." The tea was analyzed, and found to contain warfarin, a potent blood thinner and a widely used anticoagulant (Coumadin). The woman stopped drinking the tea, and the bleeding cleared up. So be careful about any folk remedies whose ingredients are not listed on the package.

The Exercise Controversy

Is there anything other than diet that will forestall the consequences of aging? What about exercise and/or physical fitness? I'm always amused and surprised at the ongoing "controversy" about exercise. When the Harvard people or some other prestigious research group comes out with favorable statistics about exercise, we are all ready to jump on the bandwagon and conclude that it's good for us. But our enthusiasm is dampened when a Jim Fixx dies while running.

The fact is that none of these observations tells the whole story. Marathon running isn't exercise. In my opinion, it's madness, an obsession, an extreme. What I mean by exercise in these pages is maintaining a degree of physical fitness throughout life. I believe that that *does* improve the quality of life and does have a positive impact on the aging individual. There is no question that those of my patients who remain physically fit feel "younger" longer, look it—and act it.

Although the best time to start a fitness program is before your body functions begin to diminish (something that occurs in the early thirties), it's really never too late. I am convinced that a lifelong fitness plan that stresses bones so that they retain their calcium, and builds muscle strength to enhance endurance, coordination and flexibility, can slow many of the symptoms associated with aging. The breathing mechanism is a case in point. Physical fitness has a profound, measurable and positive effect on how well your lungs function. This is real, not theoretical. Starting at age thirty, the ability of the body to extract oxygen from the air we breathe begins to slow at a rate of about 1 percent per year. But a conditioned person at any age can extract the oxygen more efficiently than someone who is untrained. So in spite of the annual 1 percent decline, if you're seventy years old and fit, you may be able to pull oxygen into the lungs as well as an untrained individual of thirty.

Regular physical activity also improves the efficiency of the heart and helps prevent the formation of dangerous blood clots; it lowers cholesterol and raises the HDL levels; it has also been shown to decrease the level of stress hormones and to lower blood pressure. Stiffness of the joints, which increases with age, can also be counteracted with appropriate regular physical activity. Working out regularly has a positive effect on the nervous system as well. Physically active people are more likely to have quicker reflexes than do inactive individuals. The ability to respond promptly in a crisis can be lifesaving. There is no question that my older patients who are physically active have on the average a lower anxiety level, less depression, less nervousness, fewer sleeping problems, less fatigue, greater emotional stability and more self-assurance than those who are not. In short, they enjoy a better quality of life.

Then there is the protective effect of exercise on the pituitary and adrenal glands. These glands produce hormones that help us handle stress—both physical and emotional. If you're suddenly subjected to an unusual or unexpected challenge (a heart attack, major surgery, severe infection, profound emotional shock), you'll withstand it better if you're "in shape." But if your glandular, or endocrine, system has been dormant because you've always led a sedentary life, it may not be able to excrete enough hormone to withstand the challenge.

Furthermore, physical *inactivity* in itself causes several important symptoms. For example, older persons who have been sedentary for years and unfit are apt to drop their blood pressure and experience dizziness and blurred vision when they stand up suddenly—common complaints among the elderly. Nor is sugar as well handled in the physically untrained, who have a tendency to higher levels in the blood. They also excrete larger-than-normal amounts of calcium in their urine. Their muscles lose tone. All this contributes to many of the *symptoms* of aging.

So much for exercise of the body. What about the mind? The key is to develop those intellectual habits early in life that will keep you alert and psychologically alive as you grow older. For example, reading is important, not only because of the information it imparts, but because the more one's mental faculties are used, the stronger they become. It's a good idea continually to take courses in subjects that are intriguing, new and challenging as you get older. If you remain flexible and open to new experiences throughout life, you're apt to enjoy mental well-being when you grow older. Feeling that what happens to you is within your control and that you can do most things if you try are attitudes that will serve you well later in life. Low performance among the elderly is not a matter of the brain "wearing out" but rather lack of motivation. Old people stop caring. They just "don't give a damn" anymore. But the fact is, many faculties actually bloom in later years in healthy people. What you do with your mental machinery in early life can make all the difference as to how well it operates later on.

So with all the theories, the gimmicks, the fads and the folklore concerning aging, the *proved* ways to grow older better are a healthy frame of mind, doing what you enjoy, lots of friends, regular exercise, and a low-fat, low-protein diet complete with all the essential nutrients, vitamins and minerals—not in megadoses, but enough to satisfy the posted minimal daily requirements. You might as well add some vitamins E and C, maybe a little selenium, and calcium if you're an older woman. (See Chapter 11 on osteoporosis.) Above all *forget the calendar*. This should provide enough protection until the genetic engineers have us living to our full 120 years.

One of the most obvious manifestations of aging involves the skin.

Here is one area where common sense and certain guidelines can at least have us *looking* younger.

How to Keep Your Skin Alive

Your skin is more than just an inert wrapper that keeps everything inside the body from falling out. Stretching from head to toe, making its way in and out of every crevice and aperture, it is in fact the largest organ in the body—living, breathing, metabolically active tissue constantly undergoing repair and renewal. It helps regulate body temperature by dilating and constricting surface blood vessels and mediating perspiration; it determines body water content and mineral concentration; it reflects virtually every internal disease process. Look at the skin and you may find evidence of cancer or infection deep within the body, or of trouble with the lungs, kidneys or heart. But the skin is more than a mirror of what goes on internally. It is also vulnerable to insult and disease in its own right.

If I were limited to only two words on the subject of aging skin, I would sum it all up with "avoid sun." Excessive exposure to sun accelerates the aging process in the skin, especially in fair-skinned persons, or those with blond or red hair. If you have a darker complexion, you are less vulnerable to solar injury, because your skin cells contain more of a protective pigment called melanin, which guards against sun damage. However, with every passing decade, these pigment-containing cells decrease in number by about 10 percent. So as we get older, sitting in the sun is more harmful. Yet every winter, there is a mass migration to the South from cold-weather areas by millions of people, mostly the elderly. They not only seek the sun's warmth, but bake in its rays. On beaches, on golf courses and by swimming pools, as their exposed skin assumes the deceptive golden tan they mistake for "health," it loses its elasticity and tone. It is ultimately destined to become as wrinkled as a washboard—to say nothing of the hazards of malignancy. I am reminded of the story of one man who died while vacationing in Florida. His friends came to pay their respects to him at the mortuary. As he lay there, one lady looked admiringly at his tanned features, turned to her companion and said, "Now, that's what I call living!"

And among some who cannot afford to go south, or to stay there long enough to get a really deep, long-lasting sunburn, indoor tanning booths have become very popular. Remember, however, that such instant ersatz bronzing carries the same risk as does chronic overexposure to the sun.

Sometimes, when I remind a patient that a burned skin is an injured skin, she reassures me that she is using lots of moisturizing creams and other lubricants. With all due respect to the hundreds of millions of dollars spent on advertising by the cosmetics industry to convince you that its products make a difference, the fact is that while they may temporarily confer a softer feel to the skin, they in no way retard, prevent or even minimize solar damage.

To prevent premature aging of the skin, keep out of the hot sun. If for some reason or other you are not able to avoid the sun, then use a sunscreen. These ointments and creams block the sun's harmful ultraviolet light. The most widely used are those that contain para-aminobenzoic acid (PABA). Put some on about twenty to thirty minutes before exposure to the sun, and if you go swimming, reapply it frequently. Always check the label of the sunscreen you are using for the sun-protective factor number. Choose one with a value no less than 15.

Some persons are allergic to PABA and don't know it. So it's a good idea to apply a little of the sunscreen to a small area of the skin for a few days before leaving on your trip to the sun, just to make sure you can tolerate it. If you find you are sensitive, buy a product containing benzophenone, which is just as effective as PABA. Remember, using a sunscreen doesn't necessarily mean you will be coming home from that glorious Hawaiian or Caribbean vacation looking pale. Some sun does reach your skin, but not enough to harm you. Quite frankly, in addition to being a whole lot safer, I think a subtle tan looks more sophisticated than a deep one anyway.

I've found a great solution to the question of skin color. Years ago, I was chatting with that doyenne of beauty Estée Lauder. "You look so pale and tired," she said. (Pale, of course, because I was avoiding the sun whenever I could; tired—well, that's another story.) "Why don't you use some of my skin bronzer? It will make you look and feel so healthy." Well, I never much believed in cosmetics for men and was not impressed by her recommendation. But she remembered our conversation, and a few days later, there arrived a couple of tubes of one of her "male bronzers." I didn't think they belonged in my medicine chest, so I put them in my wife's cosmetic closet. The following week, one of my solicitous patients also expressed concern at my appearance. So, the next morning, when I was alone, I applied a little of Mrs. Lauder's bronzer to my face. I looked at myself in the mirror and I liked what I saw! I came down for breakfast, actually feeling younger. My usually observant wife was apparently unaware of the new me. "That's good," I thought. "It's nice and subtle." I went to the office, where to my surprise, patient after patient commented on "how well and rested" I looked. It was clear that no one suspected that my healthy color was of cosmetic origin. At dinner that evening, during a brief lull in the conversation, my wife looked up and said, "Well, did anyone notice?"

Frankly, I'm now hooked on male bronzers, even when I go down south. I try to avoid excessive exposure to the sun. If I can't, I wear a hat, I keep my skin covered, and I use a number 15 sunscreen. No more hour-after-hour broiling in the hot sun. Mind you, sitting in the shade, sipping a long, cool drink, reading, and never cursing the clouds anymore isn't all that bad.

CHAPTER **16**

Peptic Ulcers—More Than What You Eat

One of my friends invited me to a birthday dinner at his home a few weeks ago. His wife, who happens to be a gourmet cook, served a special meal to celebrate the event. As starters, there was Russian caviar with iced vodka, as well as crab fingers with cocktail sauce. The main course was a delicious veal Marsala accompanied by a perfect Caesar salad—anchovies and all. For dessert we had crepes Suzette soaked in Grand Marnier. The meal itself was accompanied by a vintage burgundy wine, Musigny (1971), and toasts were offered with Dom Pérignon champagne. The whole feast was spectacular, but I felt somewhat guilty and uncomfortable about it all because of another guest, a man in his middle forties sitting across the table from me. He passed up all the appetizers, and for his main course he alone was served a bland-looking custard dish. His dessert consisted of some plain yogurt. He drank none of the wine.

I wondered what his problem was. Perhaps he had an upset stomach from too much partying the night before. In any event, I thought it must be serious to make him turn down all those delicacies!

After dinner, while the rest of us were sitting around drinking our coffee, our "dieter" lit a cigarette. A few minutes later he sat down beside me and started another. Doctors are often buttonholed at social events by people with various medical problems, so I wasn't surprised when, after the usual preamble about how much he hated to bother me, this gentleman continued with "Did you notice what I ate tonight? Some life, huh? I'd have given anything for a little of that caviar, or the crepes. But I can't—not allowed."

"Why not?" I asked.

Half sighing, half inhaling, with the smoke pouring out of his nose and from deep within his lungs, he answered, "Stomach ulcers. I've had them for three years now. I used to be a great gourmet myself once. Now all I am permitted to eat is baby food. But even so, as good as I am about my diet and with all the pills I am taking, I still get ulcer attacks every spring or fall. I took Tagamet for three months. Great drug. I understand it's the biggest-selling medication in the United States. So I expected I'd never have any more stomach problems. Boy, was I wrong! Then my doctor prescribed this new drug, expensive as hell, but you only need two a day—I forget its name."

"Zantac," I volunteered. "It works very much like Tagamet, but it may have fewer side effects over the long term."

"Right, that's it, Zantac. Eighty bucks a bottle! Didn't stop the attacks either. Now I'm on something called Carafate. It's not absorbed by the body. Works topically, makes a beeline for the ulcer and covers it like a Band-Aid. A few hours later it peels off and is passed out of the gut. I take one every six hours. All these pills relieve the pain and shorten the attacks when I get them, but in my case, at least, they don't seem to prevent recurrences. Any ideas?" he asked, as he lit his third cigarette in an hour.

I am sure that some of you will identify with that unfortunate man, for there are thousands of persons in this country who suffer from recurrent peptic-ulcer disease. In many cases, despite faithful compliance with medication and diet, they continue to have repeat episodes. What can be done to prevent them, and why was our friend having such bad luck despite doing all he should?

How and Why Ulcers Form

To understand how to prevent ulcers, one must know what an ulcer is and why it develops. The basic problem is stomach acid; the TV commercials are correct on that account. All healthy persons have some stomach acid at all times; patients with gastric cancer, interestingly enough, do not; individuals with peptic ulcers may have normal acid content or too much. In someone with ulcers, whatever amount of acid is present has eaten away at the lining of the stomach or duodenum (the part of the small intestine that begins where the stomach ends), creating a hole, or ulcer. It is not clear why this happens. The answer may lie in the quality of the mucus that covers the stomach lining. It is the job of this mucus to resist the eroding action of acid. It does not do so as effectively as it should in someone with ulcers. The acid then penetrates the mucus and wears away the lining of the stomach beneath it. This occurs regardless of the amount of acid secreted. In other words, what causes ulcers is not the acid per se but some deficiency in the mucus.

The term "peptic" embraces both the stomach and the duodenum. Duodenal ulcers are never malignant, but may nevertheless cause serious complications. For example, they may hemorrhage; the hole may eat all the way through the intestinal wall, resulting in its rupture, especially in older persons; or the ulcer may penetrate the wall of the duodenum to involve the pancreas, which is situated directly behind it. Stomach "ulcers" don't "become" malignant either. What *looks* like an ulcer is frequently actually a cancer. If such a cancer is mistaken for an ulcer, precious time is lost trying to obtain relief of symptoms with anti-ulcer medications instead of undergoing the surgery necessary to cure the malignancy.

Age and sex patterns of ulcers are similar to those of heart disease. For example, premenopausal women do not get much arteriosclerosis—or ulcers. Men in their forties (and younger) may suffer from both. But after a woman's menopause, the incidence is the same in both sexes for both problems.

The classic symptom of ulcer disease is a gnawing hungerlike pain in the upper abdomen relieved by food or antacids. The pain of cancer of the stomach is usually aggravated, not improved, by food intake. But don't count on that observation to make the diagnosis yourself.

Ulcer symptoms may mimic those of other diseases, the most important of which is angina pectoris. So cardiac symptoms may be mistaken for evidence of ulcers and death following such an attack attributed to "indigestion." Although pain in the pit of the stomach may very well be due to ulcers, remember it may also reflect gallbladder trouble, hiatus hernia, a disc in your neck, or even heart disease. Therefore, it's important that the proper diagnosis be made early and appropriate treatment begun.

If you have an ulcer, it will hurt when your doctor presses on the upper belly. When the symptoms and findings are suggestive of an ulcer, I first order an X ray (upper-gastrointestinal series) in which the patient swallows barium. The barium outlines the ulcer on the film. If it is located in the duodenum, that's as far as I go diagnostically; I then begin treatment. However, if it is in the stomach, I arrange for an endoscopy—a procedure in which a thin tube, illuminated at its end, is swallowed. The "ulcer" is viewed directly and biopsied, just to make sure it isn't a malignancy.

Modern Treatment of Ulcers

If you're found to have an ulcer, and your doctor is "old-fashioned," he'll put you on a strict diet. And if you are a glutton for punishment, you'll suffer in silence. The fact is, what you ingest plays very little role, if any, in the treatment or prevention of most ulcers. There are four exceptions: (1) alcohol, (2) caffeine, (3) cigarettes and (4) aspirin and related drugs. All of these should be avoided completely during treatment of the acute phase and probably forever. Other than that, you may eat or drink whatever you want, including fruit juices, meat, even spices. Occasionally a patient will tell me that a particular food designated as permissible increases the pain. In that case, of course, it should be avoided.

In addition to a better understanding of the role of diet, we've made great advances in the past few years in the medical treatment of ulcer disease. The old standbys, of course, are still the antacids, of which there are many available. They work by neutralizing your stomach acid. Some contain a considerable amount of salt, so look for the contents on the label if you've got high blood pressure or heart trouble. Others may give you diarrhea, or constipation, and you may have to switch brands on those accounts. But in terms of efficacy, there is nothing really better than the antacids. Their problem is one of compliance. Most patients forget, or are too busy, to swallow a liquid antacid or chew one of the tablets every two hours—which is what you're going to have to do if you limit the treatment of your ulcer to antacids. So most doctors now prescribe a histamine II blocker, known as a "receptor antagonist"—Tagamet or Zantac—for people with ulcers. These agents prevent the stomach cells from making acid. There is also Carafate, the ulcer "Band-Aid." It's equally effective.

For some reason, the tricyclic antidepressants like Elavil and Sinequan are useful too, even in patients who are not apparently depressed. The mechanism of their anti-ulcer action is not clear.

Although ulcer patients traditionally drink milk for relief of pain, they are better off with an antacid. Too much milk will make you fat, and may raise your cholesterol. What's more important, the protein in the milk may stimulate the formation of even more acid, which means you will have more pain, not less. Avoid late-night snacks of any kind, because they too result in increased acid formation while you sleep. Keep away from specific gastric irritants like aspirin and all of the many nonsteroidal anti-inflammatory agents used in treatment of chronic pain. Best-known among these are Clinoril, Motrin, Nuprin, Advil, Dolobid, Indocin and so on. Instead, use acetaminophen (Tylenol, Datril) for any minor aches or pains.

Well then, suppose you've got upper abdominal pain, you see your doctor, you undergo the usual testing, and he makes the diagnosis of ulcer. He then prescribes one or more of the medications mentioned above. In a few days the pain clears up almost miraculously. You continue your Tagamet, or Zantac, or Carafate for a few months. Then, because we are not yet sure of the consequences of taking any of these histamine II blockers for prolonged periods of time (Carafate is not absorbed, so it's okay), you begin to reduce your dose. You are advised to stop the Zantac or Tagamet three to six months after your ulcer has healed. Were you to undergo a repeat upper-GI series (and there is no reason to do so if the ulcer was duodenal in location), it would probably be normal except for evidence of the ulcer scar. How can you prevent a recurrence?

Preventing a Recurrence

Many patients think that in order to avoid reactivation of their ulcer, they need only to follow a very strict diet and/or take medications indefinitely. Our friend at the party did not find such a regimen effective. Chances are that neither will you. What you eat has little bearing on the course of peptic-ulcer disease.

An important contributing factor to ulcer recurrence is cigarette smoking, because it results in increased acid production. Although we've long known that tobacco and ulcers go together, it wasn't until fairly recently that a *causal* relationship between the two was established. For example, there are three times as many smokers as non-smokers among ulcer patients. I have heard it said that cigarettes per se are not responsible for the ulcers. It's simply that the people who smoke them are more "nervous" to begin with. But a study in late 1984 clinched the cigarette-ulcer link, as far as I'm concerned. Some four hundred persons with chronic peptic ulcers were carefully studied for about a year. It was found that those who received Tagamet throughout the entire period were much less likely to have a recurrence than were patients who were taking no medicines. So Tagamet is protective. However, those who continued to smoke were three times as likely as nonsmokers to suffer reactivation of symptoms, even on the Tagamet. The investigators of this large, impressive study conclude that *the single most important thing you can do to avoid a recurrence of ulcer disease—more important than diet and medication—is to stop smoking.* Your best chance of staying ulcer-free is to eliminate tobacco, and also take the appropriate medications for whatever period of time your doctor prescribes.

Our friend who passed up the caviar, veal Marsala, Caesar salad, crepes Suzette and Grand Marnier need not have done so. He should have stopped smoking instead.

No one really knows why some people are ulcer-prone and others are not. We used to place a great deal of emphasis on personality types. I suppose one's emotional makeup does play some role, but it is certainly not the whole story. In fact, there is no one occupation that is associated with an especially high risk of the disease. But there does appear to be a familial predilection. If a close blood relative has ulcers, chances of your developing one are increased. Under those circumstances, avoidance of all tobacco is especially important.

CHAPTER **17**

Heart Disease—
Preventing Slow or Sudden Death

Cardiac disease is the number one killer in this and most other "developed" countries (with the notable exception of Japan, where stroke is the leading cause of death). About forty-three million Americans have some kind of trouble with their heart or arteries, trouble that will claim 550,000 lives this year. So when an ambulance tears down the street, siren wailing, on its way to a hospital emergency room, the statistical likelihood is that the patient in that ambulance is having a heart attack.

How any given individual approaches the management of this enormous problem depends on whether or not there is already any evidence of disease. Those with symptoms require medication—digitalis, beta blockers, diuretics, calcium channel blockers, nitroglycerin, just to name a few. Several hundred thousand people undergo bypass surgery each year. A handful receive heart transplants, artificial hearts, even the hearts of baboons.

Those who are still apparently free of heart disease and want to stay that way try to control the risk factors with which it is associated. In addition, they commit themselves to programs that they personally feel may be prophylactic, but concerning which there is no universal agreement. For example, if you should happen to be in any park or country lane in the United States—at the crack of dawn, during lunch hour, or when the sun's rays are receding—you will see men and women of all ages jogging or running. They're usually scantily clad and covered with perspiration, their faces contorted in agony. I remember too a visit to my local health-food store some months ago. There I saw an elderly couple who had just made a substantial purchase—lecithin, vitamin E, a high-potency multivitamin, and capsules of Norwegian salmon oil. The cash register rang up a whopping $126.45. I apologized for being nosy, but asked why they were buying these products, and who had advised them to do so. "The lecithin," they replied, "is for lowering cholesterol and to improve memory; vitamin E helps the circulation, and maybe even prevents cancer. We read somewhere that magnesium in this multivitamin lowers blood pressure and reduces the risk of heart disease. That's why people who live in areas where the water is 'hard' have fewer coronaries—because they get plenty of magnesium. The salmon oil is the latest breakthrough. That's what Eskimos eat, and they have hardly any heart trouble at all."

And here's a vignette that may be familiar to you. My wife and I were invited to a cookout last summer. Our host put a hunk of beef four inches thick on the charcoal broiler. He also cooked a number of pieces of pale, young, tender corn, fresh from the farmer's stall, in a pot of boiling water. The steak was served crisp on the outside, pink and cool on the inside; the corn was smothered with freshly melted butter. The saltshaker was optional, in deference to anyone there with high blood pressure. A man sitting beside me was clearly horrified by this lunch. "You're a cardiologist, aren't you? Why don't you tell Fred [our host] how dangerous it is to eat beef and butter, that they raise cholesterol and cause heart disease, and that charcoaling can give cancer of the stomach. He'd be insulted if I brought it up because I'm not a doctor, but he'd take it from you. I've been following a strict diet for several months now. I feel great, and I hate to ruin it all today. What do you think I ought to do?"

"Eat some to be polite," I suggested. "One meal isn't going to kill you. Trim any fat you can see from the meat, and next time invite him to *your* house." He picked his way through the steak, and found a piece of corn that had not yet been buttered. It goes without saying that he didn't touch the salt.

These are some of the ways people try to reduce the risk of developing premature heart disease—exercise, food supplements and diet. (The word "premature" is a joke. Do you know anyone at any age who has suffered a heart attack and who doesn't think it came too soon?) Which of these efforts are reasonable and proved, and which are not?

In order to answer that question, let's first clarify the term "heart disease." Exactly what is it we are all trying to prevent?

The Many Faces of Heart Disease

The heart can be injured in several different ways. Techniques of prevention that are effective against one cardiac disorder may have no impact on another. For example, retarding the development of arteriosclerosis, which progressively narrows the coronary arteries, requires intervention different from that which prevents infection of a heart valve.

The Kind You're Born With

In the spectrum of heart disease, the earliest form to appear is that with which you are born—like a hole in the heart, a defective valve, or some structure that's either missing or in the wrong place. Many of these "congenital" abnormalities can be prevented by the pregnant mother. I have discussed the appropriate measures in some detail in Chapter 24, dealing with birth defects. These measures include maternal vaccination (but almost never with a live organism), or avoidance of exposure to infections of all kinds—specifically German measles, toxoplasmosis (often transmitted by cats), syphilis, cytomegalus virus infection, herpes and, most recently, chlamydia.

But infectious organisms are not the only causes of congenital cardiac abnormalities. A variety of medications and other substances taken by the mother during pregnancy may also be responsible, such as Dilantin (for the treatment of epilepsy), certain antibiotics, alcohol, tobacco, "the pill," and even aspirin.

Some women who have not had any infections whatsoever during the entire pregnancy, and who have scrupulously avoided taking anything that might harm the unborn child, nevertheless give birth to babies with heart trouble. These tragedies sometimes run in families. I have one patient, for example, who was born with only two leaflets in his aortic valve instead of the usual three. (A "bicuspid" valve, as this anomaly is called, doesn't open or shut properly, and frequently requires replacement later in life. It is also vulnerable to infection, with serious consequences.) His two children were born with the same abnormality. A detailed history revealed that his paternal grandfather had died young of "some kind of heart trouble." It is extremely important to determine from the family tree the pattern of transmission on any congenital abnormality. This makes possible proper genetic counseling, so that you may be aware of the statistical chance of having an abnormal child. Given the odds, you can then decide whether or not you want to take the risk. There are more and more "defects," including a bicuspid aortic valve, that are now amenable to surgical correction, and thus in some cases becoming pregnant may be a worthwhile "gamble."

The Infected and Damaged Heart

If you're born with an intact heart, the next hurdle occurs during childhood and adolescence, when you become vulnerable to cardiac infections of various types. The most important and preventable one is acute rheumatic fever. The trouble starts with a "strep throat," one that's painful, looks beefy red and is covered with a white film. Since other organisms may cause the throat to look much the same way, we usually obtain a culture for positive identification. Penicillin promptly cures a strep throat.

And penicillin does more than relieve the immediate infection. It prevents its long-term consequences. For even though the strep germ *appears* to be limited to the throat, it may act on other parts of the body. For example, involvement of the joints, which is very common, causes acute arthritis; when the brain is affected, the patient has chorea (involuntary movements of the limbs, popularly known as "St. Vitus's dance"); when the kidneys are involved, they may, later in life, develop glomerulonephritis (which leads to high blood pressure and renal failure). And should the strep germ strike the heart, the result is rheumatic fever.

Strep throats are extremely common. Hundreds of thousands of youngsters and adults come down with them every year. The diagnosis is not always made, nor is penicillin always given as promptly as it should be. Despite that, rheumatic fever occurs in only

2 percent of the untreated "strep-throat" cases. Still, penicillin must be given to everyone with this infection, because we cannot, at this time, predict who those 2 percent will be. (A test to make that prediction has recently been developed, but is not yet available for clinical use.)

The Strep Throat and the Heart

Here is a scenario of how a strep throat may lead to rheumatic fever. The patient is usually between the ages of four and eighteen years. He or she suddenly develops pain on swallowing, the neck glands enlarge and become tender, and there is often some fever. (Before jumping to the "strep conclusion," however, be aware that infectious mononucleosis also causes a very painful throat and swollen glands —and in the same age group. If it is mistaken for strep or some other bacterial infection, and the patient takes an antibiotic called ampicillin, a widespread rash may appear.) If penicillin is not administered, a new heart murmur, soft, and sometimes difficult to hear, may develop within two weeks. Since the onset of the murmur is not usually accompanied by any symptoms, and may even have been missed unless the doctor listened very carefully, the heart involvement may not be appreciated at the time. The sore throat clears up, the patient feels better, and there is no apparent reason to see the doctor again. For many years there are no cardiac symptoms. Later, in the teens or as a young adult, the patient is surprised when told, during a routine physical exam, that he or she has an abnormal, or "organic," murmur. This murmur probably reflects the inflammation and scarring that follow the original infection. There may also be some ongoing sensitization of the cardiac tissues to constituents of the streptococcus. We're not really sure how it happens.

Why is valvular disease so important? Because the heart valves play a key role in the cardiac circulation. Their function is to channel the flow of blood from one chamber of the heart into another and/or into the circulation. When affected by rheumatic fever, the leaflets of these valves either stick together and lose their pliability, thus interfering with the free flow of blood across the valve, or they fail to close properly when they should. In the latter circumstance, there is leakage of blood across the "incompetent" valve back into the compartment of the heart from which the blood was ejected. In time, specific chambers of the rheumatic heart enlarge to accommodate the extra load of blood that has leaked back. Unless the valve is replaced, the heart becomes progressively bigger and at some point it "decompensates"—in plain English, it "fails." In addition, as the heart increases in size, the cardiac rhythm frequently becomes irregular, creating a potential for traveling blood clots, or emboli. (See Chapter 14.)

When symptoms of heart failure appear in a patient with rheumatic valvular disease (weakness, easy fatigue, shortness of breath—first on exertion and ultimately at rest—swollen legs, congestion of the lungs), medication is required. We prescribe digitalis and other drugs to deal with irregular rhythms, anticoagulants to prevent clots from forming in and leaving the dilated heart, and diuretics to get rid of the fluid retention that occurs in heart failure. But the major decision to be made is whether and when to replace the diseased valve(s). Operations to do so are now commonplace and if performed before it's too late are highly successful.

Although the incidence of acute rheumatic fever is declining, at least in our society, thanks to the widespread availability and use of penicillin, it is still an important disease. Among schoolchildren in the United States, 1 to 2 percent have heart murmurs due to rheumatic fever, and as recently as 1975, half of all the recruits rejected by the armed forces in this country for cardiovascular reasons had rheumatic heart disease. The key to its prevention lies in the administration of penicillin whenever streptococcal infection is suspected or proved in children with sore throats.

Arteriosclerosis—The Big Daddy of Heart Disease

But all those adult joggers and runners, dieters, vegetarians, vitamin poppers, weight watchers, smoke enders, nicotine-gum chewers and fitness enthusiasts are not concerned with rheumatic fever. Their preoccupation is with arteriosclerosis—the process that rusts, narrows and ultimately blocks arteries everywhere. This is the number one killer. It is what causes the almost 600,000 deaths from heart attacks (also known as "coronaries" or myocardial infarctions) every year in the United States.

Arterioslcerosis does not affect the heart muscle directly. It wreaks its havoc by blocking and narrowing the coronary arteries that nourish the heart and keep it pumping. As the amount of blood these arteries are able to deliver is progressively decreased, the heart muscle cries out for more oxygen. That cry is the pain we call angina pectoris. Angina first occurs on exertion, when the heart needs more blood (oxygen) and can't have it. As the blockage becomes more severe, the pain is felt even at rest. When the artery closes completely, so that a portion of the heart is receiving no blood supply at all, the usual result is a heart attack.

How can arteriosclerotic heart disease be prevented? The answer is complicated by the fact that its underlying causes remain unknown. Many theories have been offered to explain how and why the arteries become obstructed. The most popular one concerns cholesterol. However, while it is true that persons with high cholesterol levels are more likely to have arteriosclerosis than those with low readings, the latter develop the disease too—while many of the former do not. Another obvious culprit is smoking. But again, even though there is no question that cigarette smoking increases vulnerability to heart disease, and that quitting does reduce the risk, the fact is that many nonsmokers have arteriosclerosis, and large numbers of smokers do not. Hypertension accelerates the process of arteriosclerosis, and you are better off with a blood pressure that's normal, or even low, but many people, especially women, with long-standing hypertension do not suffer heart attacks. It's more fashionable to be thin (at least in our particular culture), and most doctors will exhort you to "watch your weight," but many fat people remain free of heart trouble well into old age. You can't choose your ancestors, and if several family members have had heart attacks before the age of sixty, you are at greater risk for having one too. On the other hand, many patients with coronaries in their forties and fifties have parents who are octogenarians. The streets are full of joggers and runners. Many of them live long lives, but so do the vast majority of sedentary individuals. And others, like Jim Fixx, drop dead in their tracks. Those with the so-called Type A personality, who are characteristically hard-driving, aggressive, hostile and time-conscious (the "time is money" crowd), appear to be at greater risk for developing heart disease, yet so many who fall into that category retire on large pensions from their senior executive jobs and attain ripe old age. By the same token, the placid, noncompetitive B types are certainly not immune to arteriosclerosis.

And so it goes for all the risk factors with which we are currently preoccupied. What does it all mean? Should you just resign yourself to the fact that you are going to "get yours" no matter what you do, live it up while you can and take your chances?

Of course not. The fact is that until we identify the specific agent or agents that really produce arteriosclerosis, our only options are to control the known risk factors as best we can. Even though they are probably not the basic mechanisms responsible for this disorder, they nevertheless play an important role in accelerating it. So as of today, prevention of arteriosclerosis means the successful reduction or elimination of these factors.

The Major Risk Factors

Let's start with *cholesterol,* a body fat with a very bad reputation. But did you know that it has many useful functions? For example, our sex hormones contain cholesterol, as does virtually every cell in our body. Despite our preoccupation with reducing the amount of cholesterol in our diet, most of it is actually made by the liver, so that it is entirely possible to have a persistently elevated cholesterol level even when you drastically cut down on how much of it you eat. For years a controversy has raged concerning who, if anyone, should limit his or her cholesterol intake. The "cholesterol is bad for you" activists advise we ingest as little of it as possible. Their reasons? (1) The plaques that obstruct the arteries contain mostly cholesterol (as well as some blood products and other substances, and (2) there is a higher incidence of coronary disease among populations with elevated cholesterol levels. If you have too much cholesterol, these activists say, it makes its way into the arterial walls and blocks the flow of blood within them. The counterargument runs that no one has *shown* that lowering cholesterol actually makes a difference. The late Nathan Pritikin, perhaps one of the earliest, most enthusiastic and most effective proponents of the "avoid cholesterol school," responded that those of his clients who adhered to the rigid low-cholesterol diet he devised not only dropped their cholesterol levels, but often lost their angina and even avoided or delayed the need for coronary bypass surgery. The puzzled health consumer has been buffeted and confused by these conflicting claims and counterclaims for a very long time.

Research reported between 1983 and 1985 appears to have lessened the controversy. There now seems to be credible evidence that lowering the cholesterol level *does* make a difference. For example, it has been shown that in patients whose femoral arteries (the large vessels going to the legs) are obstructed by arteriosclerotic plaques, as demonstrated and measured in an angiogram (arteriogram), reducing their cholesterol over a period of time either keeps the blockages from getting worse or, in a few cases, actually shrinks them. That's pretty impressive. Similar observations have been made on the coronary arteries.

Granted, then, that lowering the cholesterol in persons who already have vascular disease can make a difference, what about primary prevention—protecting those not yet stricken. More good news. In a five-year study conducted by the National Institutes of Health and concluded in 1984, several hundred men with elevated cholesterol levels, but no evidence of heart disease, were given a cholesterol-lowering drug. Results were compared with those in a similar group whose high cholesterol was left alone. The data were impressive. For every 1 percent drop in cholesterol, there was a 2 percent reduction of heart attacks. The drug used in this particular research was cholestyramine, marketed in the United States as Questran. It has been around for several years, and is considered to be nontoxic, that is, it apparently causes no serious or irreversible side effects. (There are those, however, who feel that the long-term use of this agent and certain other cholesterol-lowering drugs may increase vulnerability to cancer. The NIH vehemently denies this as far as cholestyramine is concerned.) Although scientists involved in the study were impressed, not only with cholestyramine's safety, but also by how well it was tolerated, many of my own patients complain of bloating, cramps, diarrhea or constipation and won't continue with it.

As a result of all the recent evidence that reduction of cholesterol does lower the risk of a heart attack, enthusiasm for such intervention has been greatly renewed. The questions now being asked are (a) at what level does it become important to intervene, (b) how long should one try diet alone, (c) if drugs are to be used, which are the safest and most effective, and (d) what cholesterol-level numbers should we aim for?

There is no unanimity concerning these four basic, practical questions. The suggestions that follow reflect my own opinion, experience and interpretation of the available literature.

How much cholesterol is too much? The "normal" range is still reported by many laboratories to be between 180 and 300 mgs. per-cent. They consider these values "normal" because the thousands of people from whom they were obtained were assumed to be "healthy." We now know, however, that even though someone may *appear* to be "healthy" with 300 mgs. of cholesterol circulating through their arteries, the chances of remaining so five, ten or fifteen years later are statistically not as good as when the cholesterol read-ing is 200 mgs. or less.

Most doctors now aim to have their patients maintain cholesterol values under 200 mgs. percent. My own target is 180 mgs. percent below age thirty and no higher than 200 mgs. percent above age thirty. Some physicians believe that the less cholesterol you have, the better off you are, and they encourage their patients to achieve the very lowest possible readings. I'm not sure that's reasonable. Extremely low values of cholesterol usually require a dedication to a dietary regimen and/or medication that, over the long term, is im-practical or unpleasant for most people. So they pack the whole project in in disgust and frustration. There is also the lingering suspi-cion that when the cholesterol level drops too much, the risk of cancer of the bowel is increased. The evidence for this association is by no means documented. Furthermore, a recent report suggests that the low cholesterol levels found in some patients with bowel cancer are evidence of that cancer and not its cause. Still, why tempt fate? If you can get your cholesterol between 180 and 200, count your blessings and don't push your luck!

Recently, there has been a lot of talk about other blood abnormal-ities in addition to cholesterol which are said to be markers for vul-nerability to arteriosclerosis. The best-known of these are HDL, LDL and the apolipoproteins. What's it all about?

HDL (high-density lipoprotein) and LDL (low-density lipoprotein) are proteins to which cholesterol is attached in the bloodstream. Their job is to transport the cholesterol molecule in the circulation. Think of them as the canoes in which the cholesterol "passenger" sits. Your cholesterol reading includes the amount bound to both HDL and LDL. Now, HDL is good for you. The more you have, the better off you are. The reverse is true for LDL. The HDL canoe, when it approaches the wall of an artery with its cholesterol "passenger," is refused "landing rights." The "passenger" does not get out of the canoe. In other words, the cholesterol stays in solution within the bloodstream. As long as it does not enter the vessel wall to form plaques, it won't do you any harm. HDL not only hangs on to its cholesterol, it may actually suck out some that's already in the wall and thus, at least theoretically, reduce the size of the plaque. So you may not have any problem even if your total serum cholesterol is higher than we would like to see it, as long as the HDL is also elevated. The important number to look for is the cholesterol/HDL ratio, which should be no higher than 5 to 1. The lower the ratio the better we like it. For example, someone with a cholesterol of 270 mgs. percent (that's high) but with an HDL of 90 has a ratio of 270/90, or a value of 3. On the other hand, a cholesterol of 220 with an HDL of 22 will give you a ratio of 10, which is much too high. In this instance, you're better off, at least theoretically, with a 270 cholesterol than with one of 220. Reasoning from an ideal cholesterol "ceiling" of 200 mgs., HDL values should be higher than 40.

By contrast to HDL, the LDL "canoe" promptly discharges its cholesterol "passenger" into the arterial wall, where it contributes to plaque formation and narrowing of the vessel. So the more LDL you have, the worse off you are.

Now, let me tell you something about apolipoprotein B (apo B), which may be the most important new "marker" for spotting vulnerability to coronary heart disease—more sensitive than the amount of cholesterol in the blood and perhaps of greater prognostic value even than the HDL level. Apo B is a protein found in the shell of the "bad guy," LDL. It is not identified by current techniques that measure HDL, LDL and cholesterol. The apo B phenomenon may at long last explain why so many persons with normal or even low cholesterol levels have arteriosclerotic heart disease, and those with high levels do not. We may have been looking at the wrong indicator all these years! Recent studies have shown that individuals with high apo B are at predictable risk for heart attacks, regardless of their other lipid parameters, including cholesterol. In an interesting study of children in families with a high incidence of premature heart disease, those with increased amounts of apo B, regardless of their cholesterol readings, went on to develop premature arteriosclerosis, while those whose values were normal or low did not. When an inexpensive and accurate method is devised to measure apo B, it may become the screening test you'll be getting instead of cholesterol and all others.

Eating Your Way to a Lower Cholesterol

Suppose, then, that your cholesterol is 270 and your HDL is 45, so that the ratio is 6. That's too high. You also happen to have a lipid scientist friend who arranges to test your apo B, and he tells you it too is elevated. You're at risk. What should you do?

Let's start with your diet. In order to make any impact on your cholesterol level, you'll have to be faithful and persistent in your efforts to lower it. Cholesterol is found mainly in food of animal origin, particularly eggs, red meat, fat, and organs like liver, kidney or brain. So the less beef, lamb, ham or pork you eat, the better. Avoid eggs. Drink skim milk. Eat cheese and ice cream made only from skim milk or tofu. When baking cake or bread, discard the yolk and use only the egg white. (Commercially baked products are almost always made with cream and the whole egg, unless otherwise specified.)

Saturated fats are loaded with cholesterol. These are usually of animal origin, for example, butter, cream, whole milk and its derivative cheese. Such "bad" fats are also present in nonanimal sources like coconut oil and palm oil (the stuff they put in nondairy "cream substitutes" and some frozen desserts) as well as in the cocoa butter in chocolate. Margarine made from unsaturated vegetable oils (corn or safflower) is a popular substitute for butter among low-cholesterol enthusiasts. But remember, the fat in margarine may also be saturated, if it is "hardened" for marketing convenience. So eat only that margarine which is "soft," or the "tub" variety.

A word of caution. Not so long ago, doctors were advising their patients not only to avoid saturated fats, but to go out of their way to eat *extra* amounts of polyunsaturated fats of plant origin, because these substances were thought to be protective against arteriosclerosis. Don't do it. There is evidence that *excess fats of any kind probably increase the risk of cancer.*

What can you substitute for all the high-cholesterol no-no's? Foods of plant origin, like beans, vegetables and fruits. Replace beef, lamb, ham and pork with fish, poultry and veal. Lobster is okay. So are scallops, clams, crabs and oysters (all forbidden in the older low-cholesterol diets), but limit their intake to 9 ounces a day. Avoid shrimp and caviar too, even if you can afford them. Whatever meat or poultry you do eat should be (and look) lean—all muscle, without visible fat. Marbling, in which the fat is evenly distributed throughout the meat and which makes steak taste juicy and tender, is especially bad. Since most "prime" cuts are marbled, you will be buying less expensive meat. Chicken should be eaten without the skin. If you are a hamburger lover, keep away from regular ground. It's rich in fat. Use only the lean cuts, like lean round.

In preparing meat, fish or poultry dishes, you may barbecue, pan-broil and oven broil them. (But just to make life a little more complicated, the cancer experts tell us that smoked and charcoal-broiled foods eaten to excess may predispose to malignancy of the intestinal tract.) When roasting or baking meat, use a rack so that the fat can drain off. To provide the fat-free meats with some moisture, you'll want to add some gravy. There is no point using gravy made from the fat that dripped from the meat in the first place. The way to avoid that is to refrigerate the drippings. This hardens the fat, and separates it from the rest of the juice. Remove the fat and use what's left for the gravy. If that doesn't leave you enough juice, you may add up to 1 ounce of vegetable oil for every 3 ounces of meat.

In the real world of low-cholesterol diets, what else should you avoid, and what may you eat? Flavored crackers like potato chips, corn chips, and cheese crackers are verboten. You'll have to nibble on something else while watching TV. Any biscuits you haven't made yourself, sweet rolls, pancakes, waffles and French toast must also become fond memories. But graham crackers and breads like whole wheat, pumpernickel, rye, Italian, oatmeal or raisin, as well as English muffins, are permissible. Drink anything you'd like except whole milk, malteds and milk shakes. Cereals are great, but egg noodles are not. Eat all the fruit your heart desires (no pun intended). Vegetables are good too, but they should not be creamed, buttered or fried (farewell to fried zucchini). Most nuts are permitted except cashews and macadamias, and none should be covered with chocolate. If weight is not a problem, you may eat mints, any pure sugar candy, jam, jelly, honey, gumdrops and marshmallows—but nothing made with chocolate or fat.

If you love soup, make sure it's fat-free. Stay with bouillon, clear broths, dehydrated package soups—or soups you make yourself.

In my experience, most motivated individuals can live with and on this kind of diet, and many Americans do. How rigorously you do so will depend on how abnormal your blood fats happen to be. Strict adherence can drop your cholesterol by as much as 30 percent. As you will see later in this chapter, the most recent recommendations of the American Heart Association will help you decide just how dedicated to be about what you eat.

Many doctors also measure *triglyceride* levels. Triglycerides are the "neutral" fats circulating in the blood. The normal upper limit is about 150 mgs., but test results must be interpreted carefully. Unless your blood is drawn after you have been fasting for at least fourteen hours (except for water, black unsweetened coffee or tea), a high reading may not be significant. The same is not true for the cholesterol test, in which blood may be obtained at any time, regardless of what you ate and when.

Now, if your triglycerides *and* cholesterol are both high, then there are more restrictions. You'll have to cut down on carbohydrates, that is, sugars and starch. Goodbye to all those desserts and sweets, and no more than 1 ounce of hard liquor, 2½ ounces of dry table wine or 5 ounces of beer per day. (You are better off without any alcohol at all if your triglycerides are really up, like 400 mgs. percent or more.) You may have virtually all the vegetables you'd like, but fruit is limited to one serving of ½ cup of any fresh unsweetened variety. What does that leave for dessert? In addition to the unsweetened fruit, gelatin, angel food cake or sugar-free fruit ice.

With the growing evidence that dietary cholesterol should be effectively reduced, the American Heart Association has taken another look at its old, fairly permissive "prudent diet." It has announced a new set of recommendations with which it hopes Americans will seriously comply. This most recent advice consists of a three-phased dietary plan, depending on your blood-test findings.

Phase 1, the most liberal of the three, is meant for anyone over the age of two years whose cholesterol level is less than 220 mgs. percent and whose family history is not bad for heart disease. The goal of this diet is to lower fat intake by 20 percent, and reduce the amount of cholesterol consumed to two-thirds the present level. The average American eats anywhere from 500 to 750 mgs. of cholesterol per day. Adhering to these latest guidelines would cut that down to about 300 mgs. per day. Only 30 percent of total calories should come from fat, equally divided among saturated, polyunsaturated and mono-unsaturated. (Olive oil is a mono-unsaturated fat; peanut and corn oils are typical polyunsaturated fats; any animal fat is saturated. Forty to 45 percent of the calories in the typical American diet are now derived from fat, most of it saturated.) Increase the intake of carbohydrates from the present 40 to 45 percent of total calories to 55 percent. This should come mostly from complex carbohydrates—namely, vegetables, fruits, dried peas and beans, and whole grains. Fifteen percent of your caloric intake should be of protein origin, much as it is now.

The *Phase II diet* was designed for those individuals whose cholesterol level ranges between 220 and 275 mgs. percent and/or whose families are riddled with coronary-artery disease. If you fall into this category, you should reduce your fat intake to 25 percent of total calories, again, equally divided among the three different types. Even more of your calories, 60 percent, should be derived from carbohydrates. Maintain your protein intake at 15 percent. In practical terms, this means no egg yolk—ever. And at least three days a week, instead of red meat, eat "heart-healthy foods"—fish, skinned chicken, fresh fruits and vegetables. Phase II, if carefully followed, will give you a total cholesterol intake of between 200 and 250 mgs. per day, as compared to 300 mgs. in the Phase I diet and the 500 to 750 mgs. per day now consumed nationally.

Phase III is where they really lower the boom. It's for anyone whose family history of premature coronary disease is very bad, whose cholesterol level is higher than 275 mgs. percent, or whose LDL is greater than 170 mgs. As you look wistfully back to the earlier recommendations in Phase I and Phase II, which you may have thought were stringent, consider this latest diet. Here, the total intake of fat may not exceed 20 percent of total calories; cholesterol is restricted to 100 mgs. per day. That means only 3 ounces of meat, fish or poultry each day, no red meat whatsoever, plenty of dried beans, peas, lentils, egg substitutes, peanut butter and tofu (soybean curd). The latter is available in a tasty product with ice-cream-like consistency that comes in several different flavors and lots of calories.

Drugs to Lower Cholesterol

If you can't or won't adhere to whichever diet is appropriate for you, but want to lower your cholesterol level, then you'll need medication. There are several different agents on the market and more are on the way. I've already mentioned cholestyramine (Questran), which was used in the recent NIH-sponsored cholesterol–heart-disease study. Others available at this time, each with its own mechanism and side effects, include gemfibrozil, colestipol, probucol, nicotinic acid, clofibrate (Atromid-S) and Neomycin (still listed as experimental for this purpose). Some doctors also prescribe L-thyroxine, a form of thyroid hormone. I don't advise it. Large-scale studies have found its use to be associated with higher cardiac death rates. The most effective and safest combination in my experience is cholestyramine or colestipol and nicotinic acid.

The Pritikin Approach

Nathan Pritikin was a nutritionist, not a physician. In 1958, he was diagnosed as having a malignant lymphoma (cancer of the lymphgland system). In addition, a routine electrocardiographic stress test is said to have been distinctly abnormal. His cardiovascular evaluation was otherwise unremarkable except for a cholesterol level of 280 mgs. percent. In the ensuing years until his death in 1985, Mr. Pritikin received treatment for his lymphoma. He is best remembered for the dietary and exercise program he formulated, which continues to influence the life-style of thousands of Americans.

If you prefer to go the Pritikin route, instead of following the American Heart Association diet, there are two ways you can do so. (But remember that the Pritikin people think Phase III doesn't go far enough!) First, you can live at home and read up on their diet described in any one of the books written by Nathan Pritikin. Several of my patients have done it this way and found it satisfactory. They formulate their own walking programs, which, incidentally, are an integral part of the Pritikin regimen. However, if you need more discipline, motivation and monitoring, you can go to a Pritikin live-in center where you remain for up to three weeks as part of a captive population, so to speak.

If you plan to do so, you must first arrange for your own doctor to send along a summary of his findings and recommendations. When you arrive, you will be examined, with emphasis on the cardiovascular system.

A very important aspect of the live-in center is motivation. Session after session is held in which the importance of the cholesterol theory and exercise are stressed. You will learn how Mr. Pritikin's concepts and experience evolved.

The Pritikin diet is not impossible. It's just tough. It approximates Phase III of the American Heart Association program, with the following similarities and differences. The total fat intake is 10 percent (rather than 20 percent), total cholesterol consumption is less than 100 mgs. per day, protein is kept under the 15 percent recommended by the American Heart Association, and the carbohydrate content is over 75 percent. What's more, Pritikin reduces salt to under 3 grams. (The typical American diet is often in excess of 10 grams. The American Heart regimen does not require sodium restriction.)

There are two dietary levels at a Pritikin center. You start with the more stringent "regression" diet and, after certain biochemical, blood pressure, blood sugar and weight objectives have been attained, graduate to the somewhat more permissive "maintenance" diet. You will be served eight low-calorie meals a day, consisting mainly of cereal, fruits, salad, potatoes, soup, wild grains, dried beans, an entrée and dessert. There's not an egg yolk in sight; only the whites are used. No organ meats are ever served, and the consumption of other meats and fish is drastically reduced. The only sugar you'll eat is that present in fresh fruits, vegetables and grain. No fatty sauces are added to any of the dishes, and foods are never fried. To add to the taste of the dishes, you'll be offered a selection of herbs, spices, garlic, onions and lemon juice. One glass of wine per day is permitted, if you must. Smoking is absolutely out of the question. Mr. Pritikin decided that you get enough natural vitamins in this diet so that you need not, and indeed should not, take any supplements.

This diet, if you stick with it, will surely lower your cholesterol, blood sugar, weight and blood pressure—and perhaps your joie de vivre. Is it safe? I have heard some concern expressed that the severe fat restriction may result in a deficiency of the fat-soluble vitamins, especially A and D. Also, since much of our dietary zinc is in shellfish and poultry, too little of that mineral may be available. I don't think anyone can predict the effects of adhering to the Pritikin diet over the years, with respect to diseases other than those that affect the heart.

There is one thing of which you will have an abundance if you are a Pritikin follower, and that's gas. Because of all the fiber in the high-complex-carbohydrate diet, you will feel bloated for many weeks. Ultimately, however, you, as well as those around you, will learn to adjust.

Among the forty-five or so of my patients who have gone to Pritikin centers, only a handful have been able to follow the regression diet for more than a few weeks or months after getting home. But most do adhere to the basic recommendations. They eat less beef; they cut down their chicken and fish intake and are basically vegetarians. Most do feel better. Blood pressures are generally lower, especially among those who have lost weight and kept it off. Diabetic control is also improved, because of the decreased weight (especially in noninsulin diabetics), the reduced sugar intake and the greater consumption of fiber. Patients with leg pain on walking are able to go farther, though I have not been able to document objective measurements of increased blood flow to the lower extremities. Those with angina pectoris have fewer symptoms—mostly, I think again, because of weight loss.

Nathan Pritikin himself rigorously practiced what he preached. His last recorded cholesterol level, taken three months before he died, was 94 mgs. percent. The postmortem examination of his heart revealed his coronary arteries to be remarkably free of arteriosclerosis.

When Should Dieting Begin?

Let me anticipate your next question. If cholesterol in fact contributes to arteriosclerosis, and if lowering its levels is important, when should we start being careful about what we eat? In early adult life or in childhood? If the latter, at what age? Should we focus on diet alone or give our children cholesterol-lowering agents as well?

The American Heart Association advises that we begin to teach "healthy eating habits" to "healthy" children when they are as young as two years of age. This recommendation seems reasonable in view of the fact that when our soldiers killed in World War II, Korea and Vietnam were examined postmortem, early stages of arteriosclerosis were already present in their coronary arteries in anywhere from 45 to 77 percent of cases.

As in the adult diet, it is suggested that children eat lots of fresh fruits and vegetables, complex carbohydrates, and lean cuts of meat, fish and chicken. Thirty percent of caloric intake should be derived from fat, equally distributed among mono-, poly- and unsaturated fats, 55 percent from complex carbohydrates and 15 percent from protein. As in healthy adults with "normal" cholesterol levels, the total intake of cholesterol should not exceed 300 mgs. In actual fact, at age ten, "average" American boys eat 391 mgs. of cholesterol per day, and by nineteen that figure rises to 505. Interestingly, cholesterol intake is not as high in girls. By age nineteen, they consume only 280 mgs. percent per day.

Some pediatricians are worried about the long-term impact on growth if early on our children start drinking only skim or low-fat milk, eat only the whites of eggs and avoid the yolk with its concentrated cholesterol. (The American Heart Association recommends no more than three eggs per week.) In fact, the American Academy of Pediatrics has refused to endorse the Heart Association's dietary advice for children. Its members are concerned with the diet's effect not only on growth but also on brain development. They point out that our kids have never been healthier, at least during childhood, even though when they reach adult life they are vulnerable to coronary-artery disease. Resistance to disease among the young is good, growth is at its highest level, and our lengthening life-span is due largely to better health statistics early in life. They remind us of the studies over the years suggesting a relationship between very low serum cholesterol levels and cancer. The cardiologists concede that men with low cholesterols who are also underweight appear, at least statistically, to be at high risk for malignancy, but add that the ringer in the equation is heavy cigarette smoking, without which the association does not appear to be true. It has also been suggested that the low cholesterol level is a marker for cancer, and not its cause.

Given all the pros and cons, my own opinion is that the American Heart Association diet makes sense, both for adults and children, and I recommend it to my patients and their families. However, I think age ten or twelve is time enough to start adhering to it.

An Interesting New Cholesterol Theory

Very often in my practice I find that there are patients who, no matter how closely they follow the dietary instructions for lowering cholesterol, continue to have high levels. Others, who eat whatever they like without any restraints, enjoy a persistently normal or even low cholesterol. Researchers at The Rockefeller University in New York City have come up with an explanation for this phenomenon. They suggest that there are several different ways in which the cholesterol we eat is handled. As I understand it, in some individuals, it goes from the stomach directly to the liver, which then excretes it via the bile into the intestines and out of the body. So no matter how much cholesterol such persons consume, they retain very little, there is virtually no impact on the blood level, and none of it gets into the walls of the arteries. If you are lucky enough to fall into that category, you've got it made. There is no need for you to bother with any diet. Another way the liver, which produces its own cholesterol, can respond to the cholesterol you eat is to reduce the amount *it* makes, thus compensating for any excess of butter, cheese and fat meat consumed. So again, there is no net increase in the amount of cholesterol entering the bloodstream. Again, if that's how your body responds, you too can eat pretty much anything you want. But then, alas, there is a third category, those persons who do get into dietary trouble. For instead of excreting cholesterol into the bile, or compensating by synthesizing less of its own, the liver delivers the ingested cholesterol directly into the bloodstream, whence it can accumulate in the walls of the arteries to form the plaques that ultimately cause heart attacks. Finally, in some persons, the liver continues to make large amounts of cholesterol no matter what you eat, so that here, too, dieting is of no avail.

Now, if each of us could predict into which of the above categories we fall, we would know whether or not we need to follow a diet. Unfortunately, this cannot yet be done on any large scale. So for the moment, it's safest for everyone to be pessimistic, to assume that their dietary cholesterol is heading straight for their arteries—and to eat as little of it as possible. That will protect those who are vulnerable, though unfortunately at the expense of those who really are not.

An alternative clinical approach has been proposed based on this theory. Instead of assuming you are at risk, stop whatever diet you're now following. Eat what you wish for a few weeks. Then have your cholesterol level measured. If it is normal or low, there is no need to follow any restrictive diet. You would merely be subjecting yourself to an unnecessary diminution of gustatory pleasure. But if the numbers are high, carefully follow a low-cholesterol diet for the next six weeks and then recheck your level. If it has dropped significantly at the end of that time, let's say by at least 10 percent, then dieting *does* make a difference. However, if there has been no change, your liver is making more cholesterol when you eat less, so there's no point punishing yourself.

So much for diet. What other preventable factors can increase your risk for heart disease?

The Evils of Tobacco

In a word, *smoking cigarettes* is probably the best way to give yourself a heart attack, or, for that matter, to accelerate the arteriosclerosis process anywhere in your body. I don't think there is anyone anywhere who can read or hear who is not aware of the hazards of smoking. But such are the vagaries of politics and the power of the vote that an American President (Carter) whose own Secretary of Health (Califano) launched a national anti-smoking campaign, himself assured tobacco farmers that he had no intention of supporting legislation which would interfere with their livelihood. We put warnings on the package that cigarettes can virtually kill you, and, at the same time, subsidize the tobacco industry with taxpayers' dollars!

You know that if you want to hear something badly enough, you can always find someone who will tell it to you. So there are even a few physicians who insist that "the whole story" has not yet been told about cigarettes, heart attacks and cancer. In my opinion, and that of the overwhelming number of doctors everywhere, there is more than enough evidence to justify never starting the habit in the first place, and giving it up if you have. Yet so many Americans continue to smoke. What's even worse, thousands of youngsters, especially girls, are still starting the habit because they think it's chic and sexy!

No one knows what it is in the weed that does you in—the heat of the smoke, the products of combustion in the paper, tar, resins, carbon monoxide, nicotine, radioactive particles or any of the hundred other ingredients in tobacco smoke. But whatever it is can cause a heart attack, even in someone without any other risk factors. Just the other day, one of my patients, a forty-eight-year-old man, was admitted to our hospital with an acute coronary. He had "never been sick a day" in his life. Both parents had died in their late eighties. His cholesterol level was usually about 220 mgs.—certainly not bad. He was an ardent fitness fan, but a reasonable one. His blood pressure was normal and his weight was average for his age. He had everything going for him—except that he was a three-pack-a-day smoker.

Some people do get away with it, but smoking is a crapshoot with the dice heavily loaded against you, especially if you harbor other risk factors like hypertension, high cholesterol, abnormal blood fats, overweight, diabetes, a totally sedentary existence or a Type A personality. Don't kid yourself about "safer" cigarettes either. If you're addicted to nicotine, your body needs—and you crave—a certain amount of it each day. The less nicotine any of the so-called "safer" brands contain, the more frequently you'll puff, the more deeply you'll inhale and the more cigarettes you'll smoke in order to satisfy your nicotine quota. In the end, you're not really getting any less nicotine with the "safer" cigarettes, and since you're smoking more of them, you're inhaling more tar, resins and carbon monoxide. (Some scientists think it's the carbon monoxide, not the nicotine, that's the real toxin in cigarettes anyway.)

If you're a smoker, and want to stop, don't do it in fits and starts. Go "cold turkey." If you smoke only casually, you should have no real problem quitting abruptly. Even if you are seriously addicted, withdrawal symptoms will last for a few days, but then you're done with it. The alternative, tapering or "cutting down" gradually, simply keeps you in a chronic state of withdrawal from which you never recover.

For those who have tried time and again and can't quit, but who are truly motivated, there are several aids—hypnosis, psychotherapy and behavior-modification techniques. Even acupuncture may work.

A few of my patients have used nicotine gum, available by prescription, with mixed results. Clonidine, a drug for the treatment of high blood pressure, also helps reduce the craving for narcotics, alcohol —and cigarettes. Ask your doctor about it.

Hypertension—The Silent Killer

High blood pressure promotes arteriosclerosis, particularly in the arteries supplying the brain, the eyes, the kidneys, the legs and probably the heart as well. Most doctors agree it's important to normalize elevated pressure, but how high is high? And what's the best way to lower it? Diet, weight loss, exercise, drugs—or all four?

Blood-pressure readings are reported in two numbers, a higher one (called the systolic) and a lower figure (the diastolic). The systolic is the pressure at which the blood flows through the arteries after the heart thrusts it out with each beat, or contraction. The arterial pressure, between beats, when the heart relaxes, is the diastolic reading.

The significance of the numbers depends on your age. A reading of 160/90 in a "healthy" man or woman of sixty years may not require intervention. In a thirty-year-old, however, it almost certainly does. The "upper-limit" figures around which one works are 140/90, but again, these must be interpreted on an individual basis.

If your doctor tells you your readings are too high, make sure it's not the result of "the white-coat syndrome." I know several patients whose pressure is a perfect 130/85 when their spouse or a friend measures it, but which rises to an abnormal 160/95 when I do. If your blood pressure is high only when recorded by your physician, or when you're being examined for an important insurance policy, or in other stressful situations, but is normal the rest of the time, you probably don't need any drug treatment.

If, however, your blood pressure is truly and persistently elevated, the first cardinal rule to follow is not to rush to medication, unless, of course, it is dangerously high—above 200 systolic and 110 diastolic. In that event, you don't have the luxury of time. But if you do, then first lose weight by calorie restriction and exercise.

Salt and Hypertension

Most Americans consume ten to twenty times more *salt* than they actually need. For years this was thought to be a major cause of hypertension. We now know that "normal" people may eat as much salt as they like without it affecting their blood pressure, and excessive salt probably doesn't play much of a role even in some patients with hypertension. But it does in others. Despite this individual variability in response to sodium, most doctors still routinely recommend that *every* hypertensive cut down salt intake. In so doing, they unnecessarily restrict those in whom it is safe. In my own practice I initially restrict the salt when blood pressure is high. If, after a few weeks, I find that the low-salt regimen has not made a significant impact on the elevated levels, I permit the use of as much salt as is necessary to make the food palatable. (The only exception is in patients with heart failure or fluid retention.)

Your pressure may be high because your *calcium* intake is low. Ironically, this is especially likely if you're following a low-cholesterol diet, which is virtually free of dairy products rich in calcium. Persons who avoid milk and its products, because they are lactose intolerant, may end up calcium-deficient and hypertensive. This association with high blood pressure is not sufficiently appreciated.

There is also a relationship between *potassium* and *magnesium* deficiencies and hypertension. These two substances are lost in the urine when you take diuretics, or have chronic diarrhea, so be sure to replace them in adequate amounts.

Chronic *tension* and anxiety may contribute to hypertension. Before embarking on medications to lower your pressure, try relaxation techniques or a biofeedback program, especially if you think you're not handling your stress well.

Exercise will make you feel better, but I do not believe it is an important method of lowering blood pressure.

If nondrug intervention isn't effective, I prescribe medication. I start with the mildest agents in their lowest doses, increasing them as necessary and adding other medications until the target reading has been reached. In their zeal to get the right numbers too fast, some doctors hit patients too hard with excessive therapy. This may reduce the blood pressure too abruptly, and at the same time induce a host of side effects ranging from dizziness and weakness to impotence. If you develop these, or *any* symptoms, after being given a new medication, don't suffer in silence. Let your doctor know.

Heart Attacks and the Kind of Person You Are

I have noticed over the years that after a woman has had a heart attack, and comes to see me with her husband in tow, we discuss her medication, her physical activity, her diet—but rarely her behavior and "outlook" on life. But when it's the husband who's had the coronary, the main reason wives come along is to impress upon me how "you must change him."

In the usual scenario, my secretary hands me a confidential message from Mrs. Smith, who would like to speak with me privately before I examine Mr. Smith. At this surreptitious meeting, she unburdens herself. "Doctor, Jim must have a death wish. You probably didn't know that while he was still in the coronary-care unit, he was calling the office! And that his secretary was there taking memos three days after his attack. You told him not to go back to work for a month, right? That's a joke. He might as well be at the office with all he's doing at home. Ten days after leaving the hospital, he was already rushing through meals to get to his business mail. He's fifty-eight years old, and still thinks he's going to conquer the world. You've got to straighten him out, doctor! But please don't tell him I said anything."

All this raises an interesting question. Should Mrs. Smith really be worrying about her husband's behavior? Isn't he sufficiently protected if he continues to abstain from cigarettes, watches his weight, does what is necessary to control an elevated blood pressure, reduces his cholesterol intake, and takes all the medications prescribed? Is it really important, as his wife thinks, that he stop being "crazy"?

I must confess that all these years I've gone along with the wives who complained to me. As per their instructions, I have sternly admonished their husbands to slacken their pace. Subconsciously, I was probably doing this more to keep the wives happy, and to maintain a good relationship with them, than for their husband's benefit. But recent developments lead me to believe that these concerned women may have been right after all.

Back in the 1960s, two doctors in San Francisco, Meyer Friedman and Ray Rosenman, described the "coronary-prone" personality, and labeled it "Type A." Such individuals are characteristically aggressive, ambitious, time conscious, angry and hostile. They tend to have a higher blood pressure than the norm. Their major goal in life is success rather than contentment. Of course, there is a spectrum of such behavior. But the full-blown Type A's rarely carry on a two-way conversation. They talk to, not with you. They don't really listen to what anyone else has to say. If you've got the floor at a meeting, they can't wait for you to sit down so they can take over. They speak rapidly and are likely to finish your sentences for you because they're in such a hurry. They're never without a watch, are always on time and are very annoyed if you're late. They find it hard to delegate authority because they're convinced no one can do the job quite as well as they. They literally can't sit still; they are always drumming their fingers on the tabletop or moving their knees or swinging their legs. When they do take time out to play, they must win, even when the opponent is a child. It doesn't take much to make them fly off the handle. They lean on the horn in traffic if the car ahead of them delays but for a moment after the light has turned green. They cannot bear to follow in a traffic pattern, they simply must pass any car in sight. Every other driver is "a damn fool who shouldn't have a license because he's stupid." Vacations? Only when absolutely necessary, and even then, they usually take some work along or "combine business with pleasure." I could go on and on, but looking over my shoulder, my wife thinks I'm writing my autobiography.

Persons who are easygoing, less competitive, less pressured, more philosophical, less aggressive, more contented and, believe it or not, no less successful than Type A's are called Type B.

Rosenman and Friedman, in their psychological testing of hundreds of men who had suffered heart attacks, found that the majority were Type A's. They satisfied many if not all of the key behavioral criteria. These investigators are convinced that the Type A personality is an independent risk factor for coronary disease, and an important one to identify before and after a heart attack. Before, so that behavioral modifications can be instituted to prevent it, after, in order to avoid a recurrence.

Quite frankly, cardiologists who agree in principle with this theory, including me, have, for the most part, paid no more than lip service to it over the years. We have our hands full just trying to get our patients to comply with more easily definable goals than changing their personality. It's hard enough to get them to stop smoking, take antihypertensive or other medication, lose weight, or follow an appropriate diet. Nor does everyone agree with Rosenman and Friedman. Other investigators have not confirmed their theory. Indeed, they claim to have disproved it.

But, like Pauling and Vitamin C, Friedman is not to be deterred. In mid-1984, he reported additional findings that strengthened his case considerably. Supported by a grant from the National Heart, Lung and Blood Institute, he and his associates monitored the clinical course of some nine hundred Type A men who had sustained heart attacks. They separated them into two groups. The first received the usual care. Their doctors examined them regularly and advised them about controlling the conventional risk factors. However, the second group, in addition, received psychological counseling. When both categories were re-evaluated after three years, there were some statistically impressive results. In those Type A men whose behavior patterns could be modified (and this was possible in 75 percent of the cases), the heart-attack rate was reduced by 50 percent. That's actually better than what was effected in the cholesterol-lowering study! So Friedman reaffirms that attitudes and behavior *can* be altered, and that when they are, all other things being equal, the risk of a second heart attack is substantially decreased.

Some investigators claim the Type A personality can be modified more quickly and effectively by administering a beta-blocker drug than by protracted psychological counseling. (Beta blockers, the prototype of which is Inderal, lower blood pressure and slow heart rate.) I've been unable to document this in my own practice. Some of my Type A patients who take beta blockers for other reasons (angina, disturbances of cardiac rhythm, increased blood pressure) often complain of feeling like "zombies." They are slowed down, frequently have bad dreams, cold hands and feet, and are impotent, but they are rarely contented or less aggressive.

Do Friedman's specific behavior patterns apply to women too? Probably, but again, there is no unanimity. In one study, however, Type A women did have a higher incidence of stroke than did their Type B counterparts.

By what mechanism(s) might Type A behavior end up giving you a heart attack? One theory holds that it is associated with chronic stress, that such individuals are constantly keyed up and act as if life were one long emergency. In the course of evolution, animals, and indeed primitive man, often found themselves in emergency *physical* situations—for example, when threatened by some predator animal or other enemy. When that happened, it was a matter of life and death. The available alternatives were fight or flight, and both required extra adrenaline. If the decision was to run, the adrenaline provided the instant energy and strength to do so quickly. If, instead, there was to be a fight, the greatest risk was bleeding to death from a wound inflicted by the enemy. Now think for a moment about the last time you had a tooth pulled. What did the dentist inject into your gums to reduce the bleeding? Adrenaline, because it constricts the blood vessels. This increased secretion of adrenaline in an emergency situation is nature's way of protecting the endangered animal against fatal hemorrhage. In the jungle, crises were generally of short duration. Primitive man either evaded his enemy by flight or he won the fight for survival. In either event, he went into "neutral," as far as his adrenaline secretion was concerned, until the next crisis.

By contrast, threats facing modern man, be they real or imagined, are mostly emotional or psychological. They are neither as obvious nor as short-lived as the physical encounters of his predecessors. The body, however, cannot make the distinction. It responds as if this perpetual crisis in which the Type A individual lives was really life-threatening. Several complicated hormonal reactions are called into play—including an increased secretion of adrenaline—and they never really stop. The net effect of the chronic oversupply of adrenaline is constriction of blood vessels and increased "clottability" of the blood. That's great in the jungle, but not in America, where it sets you up for a heart attack.

Since all the attention given behavioral modification, many of my patients have asked me whether "changing" is worth the trouble. "After all, doctor, who wants to be a Type B anyway? There is no fun going through life like a vegetable. I'm the chief executive officer of a Fortune 500 company. I didn't get there by being complacent, easygoing and late for appointments. And you can be sure I'm not going to stay there very long if I go fishing whenever there's a crisis." Well, that's a misconception. Those who have been able to make a "value transition" or reappraise their priorities after their heart attack, who have been able to put first things first, have found that anger, hostility and a constant sense of pressure—the key ingredients of Type A—are not what makes for success. These "new" Type B's, who have psychologically bowed out of the rat race, are no less "successful" than they were before—but much happier.

So here's the bottom line. Whatever you do that's good for you *after* you've had a heart attack is doubly valuable *before* you've gotten sick. If you're still well, why not prevent trouble now? Take a hard look at how you're living your life. If you need help doing that, inquire of your doctor or your local heart association about a Type A counseling service in your own community. I recommend it.

The Exercise Controversy

For the last several years this nation has been consumed by a passionate debate about *exercise*. Should we or shouldn't we? Doctors, scientists and laymen have taken strong positions on both sides of the issue. Exercise enthusiasts point to the countless books, magazine articles, and studies documenting its benefits. On the other hand, proponents of the sedentary life, ranging from those who actually loathe anything physical to those who are simply bored by it, refer to many equally convincing conclusions that exercise will not help you live any longer, and that too much can kill you.

Jim Fixx was America's running guru. His sudden death while running brought the issue to a head in 1984. Doctors were flooded with calls from their patients asking what to do. Those who wanted permission to continue running or jogging concluded from the facts that "his father died at age forty-three. Jim lived to age fifty-two, so running prolonged his life by nine years." But the antijoggers and antirunners didn't see it that way. "We were right all along. Running killed this poor man prematurely at fifty-two. If he hadn't continued his lunacy, he'd still be alive today." The fact is the case of Jim Fixx does not support either point of view. As I understand it, he had coronary disease with lots of warning symptoms, yet he never consulted his physician about it, and he continued to run.

Even as I sit looking out my window, I can see an endless procession of runners and joggers. So all the debate has changed nothing. Runners will continue doing their thing; the rest of us will go for an occasional walk when we feel like it.

So who's right? Should we be exercising regularly? And if so, how much and what kind? Will exercise actually prevent heart attacks and/or prolong life?

If you were to list and evaluate all the pros and cons, you'd find that the great preponderance of evidence favors exercise. The body of negative opinion on the matter, though not to be dismissed, nevertheless represents a minority viewpoint at the present time.

Even among the proponents of exercise, however, few claim that it will prevent heart attacks or even delay death. They simply love to exercise. They feel great doing it. For them, it's the best tranquilizer there is. They find that their workouts increase physical tolerance. Whether or not they suffer from angina, have had a heart attack, or are still healthy, they can do more before becoming short of breath.

Regular exercise raises the HDL level (the "good" cholesterol fraction thought to protect against heart disease). Individuals who keep fit are apt to be health conscious, so their weight is usually closer to the ideal than it is among the sedentary. They are also less likely to smoke. Exercise helps prevent osteoporosis. If you're in "condition," your chances of surviving a heart attack when you do get one are somewhat better than if you are flabby and overweight. And if you have had a heart attack, and were encouraged to get out there and be "physical," chances are that your mental state and self-image are more positive than if you simply sat home waiting for the next chest pain or spasm. Such a psychological boost is in itself important to the quality of life. If you regularly take time out to exercise and enjoy what you're doing, you're also beginning to modify your Type A personality. The determination to do something for your well-being, unrelated to work, ambition or the daily grind, is a big plus in itself.

Despite all of the above, I cannot tell you for sure that your exercise program is going to shrink, dissolve or prevent progression of any plaques in your arteries, or help you develop the kind of collateral circulation necessary to prolong life. The truth is that at the present time we simply don't know these to be facts. It's entirely possible that exercise may have these effects—and why not think so as you're exercising? But don't do it for these reasons alone.

Can exercise hurt you? Of course it can, if you do more than you should, and especially if you already have a heart problem. For those over sixty-five years of age, or anyone with a chronic disease—cardiac, kidney, liver, whatever—exercise should be prescribed and "taken" as carefully as any potent medication. Your doctor, alone or in conjunction with an exercise physiologist, can determine the amount and kind of exercise most appropriate and safe for you. He will base these recommendations on a careful history, thorough physical examination focused on the heart and circulation, and an electrocardiogram at rest and one taken after physical stress. In some cases, a twenty-four-hour Holter monitor, in which an electrocardiographic tracing is continuously recorded throughout a range of daily activities, may be useful too. In my opinion, anyone older than forty-five, even in good health, should undergo such an evaluation before embarking on a rigorous exercise regimen.

If despite the foregoing discussion you're still not sure about exercising, make the analogy with sex. Most people do both for enjoyment, not to prolong life. Sex and exercise make you feel better; they improve the quality of life. You shouldn't do either unless you feel like it. Exercise and sex performed under duress are not very satisfying. The kind of exercise you choose, like sex, is a matter of personal preference. There are those who like it alone; others prefer company. Is either activity dangerous? People die exercising, as well as during sexual activity. But such occurrences, though dramatic, are almost always a matter of chance—coincidence. Fear of death during sex or exercise is not a valid reason for abstaining from either. But there are times and circumstances when both must be temporarily modified or held in abeyance. When to restart, with what frequency and intensity, and in what manner are matters that you and your doctor, and, in the case of sex, your partner, must decide together.

Is Fat Unhealthy?

In America, thin is beautiful. Fat is viewed as either ugly, unhealthy or both. But in other cultures, the more portly the male, the higher his social status; the plump female is more desirable, sexy and attractive (the Yiddish word "zaftig" sums it up). Esthetic preferences aside, is being fat bad for your heart?

Officially, overweight used to be designated a "minor" risk factor, that is, not as statistically risky as the major risk factors like cigarette smoking, elevated blood pressure and high cholesterol. But in 1985, a federal study panel in the United States found that persons weigh-

ing 20 percent or more above "desirable" levels were prone to premature death and such serious illnesses as adult onset diabetes, heart
disease, arthritis, respiratory problems, gallbladder disease, menstrual abnormalities and high blood pressure. They also have elevated cholesterol levels. Even as little as five to ten pounds of
overweight was an increased risk to health. Similar data have been
reported from Framingham, a community of several thousand in
Massachusetts. In the 1960s, this town was selected as a "laboratory" to evaluate the impact of various factors on health and longevity. Virtually everybody living there has over years been repeatedly
questioned, measured and examined. Their blood has been analyzed
by every conceivable test, and their living habits carefully studied.
During this ongoing twenty-six-year project, it was found that adults
who were only 10 percent overweight suffered from a higher incidence of coronary disease and death from all causes—independent
of any other risk factors.

How would you know whether your weight is optimal or ideal?
From the cosmetic viewpoint, that's purely subjective. But the best
objective guide is the table put out by the Metropolitan Life Insurance Company derived from ongoing actuarial data that are periodi-
cally revised. The most recent one, published in 1983, is considered
by some to be too "permissive" in its definition of ideal weight. I
nevertheless find it very useful in helping my own patients attain their
weight objectives. According to this table, an adult woman who is 5
feet 4 inches tall and weighs 160 pounds is 20 percent overweight; a
man 5 feet 10 inches weighing 192 would also be 20 percent overweight.

———— 1983 METROPOLITAN ————
HEIGHT AND WEIGHT TABLES

To Make an Approximation of Your Frame Size . . .

Extend your arm and bend the forearm upward at a 90 degree
angle. Keep fingers straight and turn the inside of your wrist toward
your body. If you have a caliper, use it to measure the space
between the two prominent bones on *either side* of your elbow.
Without a caliper, place thumb and index finger of your other
hand on these two bones. Measure the space between your fingers against a ruler or tape measure. Compare it with these tables
that list elbow measurements for *medium-framed* men and

women. Measurements lower than those listed indicate you have a small frame. Higher measurements indicate a large frame.

Height in 1" heels Men	Elbow Breadth	Height in 1" heels Women	Elbow Breadth
5'2"–5'3"	2½"–2⅞"	4'10"–4'11"	2¼"–2½"
5'4"–5'7"	2⅝"–2⅞"	5'0"–5'3"	2¼"–2½"
5'8"–5'11"	2¾"–3"	5'4"–5'7"	2⅜"–2⅝"
6'0"–6'3"	2¾"–3⅛"	5'8"–5'–11"	2⅜"–2⅝"
6'4"	2⅞"–3¼"	6'0"	2½"–2¾"

Weights at ages 25–59 based on lowest mortality. Weight in pounds according to frame (in indoor clothing weighing 5 lbs. for men and 3 lbs. for women; shoes with 1" heels).

Men					Women			
Height Feet Inches	Small Frame	Medium Frame	Large Frame		Height Feet Inches	Small Frame	Medium Frame	Large Frame
5 2	128-134	131-141	138-150		4 10	102-111	109-121	118-131
5 3	130-136	133-143	140-153		4 11	103-113	111-123	120-134
5 4	132-138	135-145	142-156		5 0	104-115	113-126	122-137
5 5	134-140	137-148	144-160		5 1	106-118	115-129	125-140
5 6	136-142	139-151	146-164		5 2	108-121	118-132	128-143
5 7	138-145	142-154	149-168		5 3	111-124	121-135	131-147
5 8	140-148	145-157	152-172		5 4	114-127	124-138	134-151
5 9	142-151	148-160	155-176		5 5	117-130	127-141	137-155
5 10	144-154	151-163	158-180		5 6	120-133	130-144	140-159
5 11	146-157	154-166	161-184		5 7	123-136	133-147	143-163
6 0	149-160	157-170	164-188		5 8	126-139	136-150	146-167
6 1	152-164	160-174	168-192		5 9	129-142	139-153	149-170
6 2	155-168	164-178	172-197		5 10	132-145	142-156	152-173
6 3	158-172	167-182	176-202		5 11	135-148	145-159	155-176
6 4	162-176	171-187	181-207		6 0	138-151	148-162	158-179

Source of basic data: 1979 Build Study, Society of Actuaries and Association of Life Insurance Medical Directors of America, 1980.

Once a desirable weight is defined, how to achieve and maintain it is often a continuing problem. For the eleven million Americans who are severely obese, it may, in fact, not even be possible. Such massive overweight—defined as 250 pounds and above—is not simply a matter of chronic overeating. It's a disease—one we neither really understand nor are able to treat successfully in most cases: not by diet, pills or exercise. The less such an individual eats, or the more calories he or she expends, the fewer calories the body burns. In other words, as one diets, the body lowers its energy requirements and output almost as if it were doing its darndest to maintain the excessive weight. What's more, when such patients are carefully studied in a hospital, most of their conventional tests are "normal."

The only time I've seen very fat people lose weight and keep it off is after an operative shunting or stapling procedure. The most successful one involves tacking down the end of the stomach to the beginning of the large intestine. This bypasses the small intestine, where much of what we eat is absorbed. As a result, the caloric intake is markedly reduced. It's a dramatic treatment for a serious disease. Unfortunately, the operative consequences are tolerable in only 50 percent of cases. Among the remainder, the surgical complications are crippling and occasionally life-threatening.

So if you suffer from such massive obesity, and usually weigh in excess of 250 pounds, don't waste your time, hope and money on fad diets, cytotoxic testing, fancy fat farms or expensive "weight" doctors. Try to do what you can on your own. For example, eliminate any other risk factors from which you may suffer, like hypertension, cigarette smoking and high cholesterol levels. And remain optimistic, because there is a great deal of active research now going on at specialized centers throughout the country. Scientists are searching for as yet unidentified substances in the bloodstream or intestinal tract that may be responsible for your problem and that may one day be neutralized.

Most people who want to lose weight aren't terribly fat. Everyone has a basic body weight, below or above which we do not fluctuate more than fifteen or even twenty pounds. The desire to lose weight in such cases is more often for cosmetic than medical reasons, although it may be for both.

Unlike the morbidly obese, the run-of-the-mill "heavy" individuals *can* usually achieve and maintain close to optimal weight, although a certain amount of fluctuation is almost inevitable. But that involves a lifelong commitment to watching what you eat, being conscious of every dessert you're offered, limiting alcohol intake, knowing the caloric content of all foods, avoiding binges, and weighing yourself daily so that you can compensate after you've indulged too much. Exercise is important because it helps burn off excess calories. This amounts to "behavioral modification," which I believe most people can do for themselves. Once you've learned what to eat and to eat less of it, and follow such a regimen for the *rest of your life,* you'll remain thin. If you can't, look for the necessary help from legitimate sources, such as behavioral-modification clinics or practitioners. Ask your own doctor to refer you to one.

Diet Pills? Safe? Effective?

Physicians used to prescribe "diet pills" much more often than they now do. When the most effective of them (at least over the short term), the amphetamines, were found to be both habituating and, in some circumstances, dangerous, their use for this purpose was prohibited by law. They have been replaced by a profusion of over-the-counter drugs available to anyone in any amount, advertised as effective appetite killers. They fall into three groups. The largest-selling are those that contain phenylpropanolamine (PPA). Chemically related to the amphetamines, PPA is the ingredient in many cold remedies and decongestants. When first used for treating stuffy and/or running noses, these preparations were serendipitously noted to suppress the appetite somewhat. To fill the vacuum created by the withdrawal of the amphetamines, PPA was introduced for weight control. The FDA has verified the claims made by its manufacturers, and decided that PPA is both safe and effective when taken as recommended. However, the package insert warns against its use by persons with hypertension, coronary-artery disease, diabetes, cardiac arrhythmias and thyroid disease.

There are consumer activists and physicians, including myself, who would like to see PPA withdrawn from the market. While I believe that it probably is minimally effective over the short term— that is, four to six weeks—taking it for weight reduction is like trying to close a large surgical incision with a Band-Aid. It solves nothing, and distracts from the real problem. But what's more important, millions of people who should not be taking this drug, because they have one or more of the contraindications mentioned above, are not aware of their underlying disease. When they take PPA, especially in excessive doses, they may have problems. The medical literature is sprinkled with accounts of persons who sustained brain hemorrhages and other serious complications from such overdosage.

Results of most of the evaluations of PPA for weight reduction are not really impressive, at least as far as I am concerned. The majority of persons lose only half a pound per week more than those who take placebos. In fact, in one study, the individual who lost the most weight of all was actually taking a blank pill, not the PPA! For all these reasons, I advise my patients not to use this substance.

Another "appetite suppressant" that is popular, despite its unfortunate trade name "Ayds," is a tasty candy containing a mild local anesthetic, benzocaine. Each cube has 25 calories. The manufacturer recommends you take two before eating. That's supposed to numb your mouth and tongue, decreasing your desire for food. Out of curiosity, I tried them myself. I was not able to detect any of the alleged "numbing" properties. In my opinion, they can do you no harm, but I have not found them effective either.

The most recent addition among the appetite-suppressant agents is a food, not a drug. It is actually a fiber derived from the konja root grown in Japan. Two capsules taken when you are hungry dissolve in the stomach, where they absorb water and form a pastelike substance. The resulting distension "fools" your body so that it thinks you've eaten. Hunger signals are then muted. Frankly, I don't know how effective this preparation is. Not surprisingly, the makers are very enthusiastic about it, but I have not seen scientific, impartial validation of their claims. Although there would appear to be no danger in taking it, I suspect that as the fiber moves along the gut on its way out of the body, the fermenting action of the intestinal bacteria may cause distension, gas and perhaps cramping, Also, taken on a regular basis, to the exclusion of a normal, balanced diet, this fiber may lead to a deficiency of zinc, iron and other trace metals.

Is there any special diet you can follow that will make it easier to lose weight and keep it off? Hundreds of thousands of Americans are convinced that the low-calorie balanced diets prescribed by most doctors are of no use. What's more, they are skeptical of how much doctors really know about diet, vitamins and nutrition. On the other hand, they are quite prepared to follow the advice of countless "authorities" who write diet books by the score. Depending on how far back you go, you've probably heard about or perhaps even tried the

Drinking Man's Diet, the water diet, the Mayo diet, the Atkins diet, the Scarsdale diet, the "I Love New York" diet, the Beverly Hills diet, the Royal Canadian Air Force diet or any combination of these. You may even have survived the liquid protein diet—many did not. In each case you likely lost some weight for a few days or weeks, then bounced right back.

Several of my patients have gone to various "fat farms." They found some better than others, and were able to lose anywhere from ten to fifteen pounds (depending on how long they could afford to stay) by a combination of exercise and starvation. But unless they underwent behavioral modification, every single one of them gained it all back within three months.

What about seeing a doctor who specializes in weight reduction— a bariatrician? Some of them can help, especially if they educate you, motivate you and teach you good nutrition. Unfortunately, many of these doctors run "mills," not clinics. Some of them employ questionable or fraudulent techniques. A patient recounted to me an experience she had with one such "specialist." When she called for an appointment, before she could say "Jack Robinson" or even identify herself, she was told exactly what it was going to cost her, and "by the way, it's payable in advance. Bring the money with you." The figure quoted seemed excessive to her. When she dared ask "How come?" she was told it was because of all the analyses she would need that had never been done before—hair, nails, other body secretions, hormones, cytotoxic testing and so on. She decided to go ahead with it. At her first visit, as promised, her hair and blood were analyzed. A few days later she was sent a very scientific-looking print-out indicating everything she was "missing" or to which she was "allergic." The bottom line, after two or three sessions, was (a) she had been eating "all wrong" her entire life, (b) she was "allergic" to virtually everything, and (c) her body needed supplements and "purification." She was given a special diet. More important, she was told she required medications that she could only buy right there, and not at any drugstore. They were not sold anywhere else because they were this doctor's own formula, which only his patients were privileged to have. They were expensive, because they contained so many costly ingredients, and, of course, their price was not included in the original fee quoted.

"What's in these pills, just for the record?" she asked.

"Never mind, but in case anyone should ask you, there is no thyroid or 'speed' in them."

She followed the diet, took the pills and did lose six to eight pounds in the first month. But she had to discontinue both because she became terribly nervous, experienced palpitations, and her hair began to fall out. So, if you decide to go to a bariatrician, check him or her out with your own doctor or with the local medical society. I am sorry to say there are a lot of phoneys out there, immune to the arm of the law.

According to some researchers in the field of bariatrics, one's predisposition to obesity and the ease or difficulty with which extra pounds are shed or gained are determined by the number of fat cells in the body. Anyone who has too many will have a hard time losing weight. And when they do, however briefly, it's tough to keep it off because these cells constitute an avid reservoir for the reaccumulation of fat. Once you've got these fat cells you're stuck with them. But they are the result of overeating. Vulnerability starts in childhood and continues into adult life. So we may be able to prevent obesity later in life by keeping our children thinner than we do. The more we stuff them, the greater the number of fat cells they will develop and the more difficult it will be for them to lose weight in the years to come. Parents should know that a fat baby is not necessarily a healthy baby, but rather a candidate for being a fat adult.

But the number of fat cells is not determined solely in infancy and childhood. It's apparently an ongoing process, one that continues to reflect your diet into adult life. If you've been careless about your caloric intake, and have gained weight, you can at least prevent the problem from getting any worse by changing your eating habits now so as not to accumulate even more fat cells than you already have.

Exciting Fishy News

Attention was first drawn to the possible beneficial effects of oily saltwater fish (salmon, sardines, haddock and mackerel) when certain populations whose diets were rich in these foods were noted to be remarkably free of coronary-artery disease. For example, the coronary death rate among Greenland Eskimos is only 3.5 percent, as compared to 50 percent among neighboring Danes. Analysis of the diets of these two populations reveals that while Eskimos consume anywhere between 5 and 8 grams per day of the polyunsaturated fats found in oily saltwater fish, the Danes (and we) eat less than 1 gram per day. The total lipid profile of Eskimo blood is also much more desirable: their cholesterol and triglyceride levels are lower and their HDL is higher; their blood clots less easily and even their blood pressure is somewhat lower. All this is attributed to the polyunsaturated fats that the Eskimos eat—and we don't.

Polyunsaturated fats are of various types, depending on their molecular structure. Most of those in our diet are of the Omega-6 group, derived mainly from vegetable oils. By contrast, the polyunsaturated fatty acids from fish are of the Omega-3 variety, and are structurally and biochemically different. There are two kinds—EPA (eicosapentaenoic acid) and to a lesser extent DHA (docosahexaenoic acid).

Given these observations, scientists then wondered what effect a diet rich in Omega-3 fatty acids would have on Westerners. They found that volunteers given supplemental EPA and DHA ended up with lower cholesterol and triglyceride levels and higher HDLs. And that's not all. As was true among the Eskimos, the Omega-3 fats rendered the blood of the Western subjects tested less "sticky," by acting on their platelets. Some scientists consider this "anti-platelet effect" the most important action of the Omega-3 fatty acids. Normal blood clotting is a very important mechanism to prevent bleeding to death after an injury. But such enhanced coagulability is not good when your arteries are clogged. EPA and DHA have much the same effect on platelets as does aspirin. They retard clot formation, thus helping prevent heart attacks and strokes in susceptible persons. Another desirable consequence of the Omega-3 fatty acids is a reduction of blood pressure.

What a package of benefits from simple fish oils—improved cholesterol, triglyceride and HDL levels, reduced tendency to blood clotting, and lowered blood pressure! Patients with angina pectoris, given EPA and DHA, not only manifested these positive chemical changes, they also reported less chest pain and the need for fewer nitroglycerin tablets.

The most recent data concerning fish in the diet were published in mid-1985. A twenty-year study begun in 1960 involving some 850 middle-aged men living in the Netherlands revealed that death from heart disease was more than 50 percent lower among those who ate at least 30 grams of fish a day (that is about half a pound per week) than among those who did not.

So should you or shouldn't you add these Omega-3 fatty acids to your diet? I leave it up to those of my patients who are in good health, with cholesterol levels under 200, HDLs 50 or higher and who have no blood pressure problem. But I recommend them for anyone who has already had a cardiac event, be it angina or a heart attack, or whose risk factors are bad.

The best way to obtain EPA and DHA is to eat fish. But you can also buy capsules containing these oils in most health-food stores. They are marketed under various trade names. Look for a brand that has mostly EPA, and some DHA, and in which each capsule contains 1 gram of fat. Because so many of the data obtained thus far are experimental, there is no "recommended" dose on the labels. Most say "One or more capsules a day." I recommend two or three capsules daily. Why not take more? Largely because the safety of *any* fat in large quantities is in question. There is the lingering suspicion that too much—be it mono-unsaturated, polyunsaturated, fully saturated, Omega-3 or Omega-6, of animal, fish or vegetable origin—if taken long enough may increase the risk of malignancy, especially of the breast and the bowel. Also, despite their decreased rate of coronary disease, Eskimos and Japanese (who also eat lots of fish and who have similar favorable statistics for heart trouble) both have a very high incidence of vascular disease of the brain. The incidence of strokes due to hemorrhage in both groups is higher than it is in this part of the world. Do not take these supplemental capsules if you have any bleeding problem.

There are several other supplements and minerals alleged to be of value in the prevention of heart disease.

For example, the trace element *magnesium* has been under considerable scrutiny in recent years. Its deficiency has been proposed as contributing to the development of coronary-artery disease. It has long been known that persons living in "hard-water" areas have less coronary disease than do those where the water is "soft." This may be due to the larger amounts of magnesium in hard water. Magnesium plays an important role in as many as three hundred human enzyme processes. Low levels may contribute to high blood pressure, and adding some to the diets of hypertensives has been shown to be therapeutic. Animals deprived of magnesium develop abnormal blood fats, which promote arteriosclerosis. When magnesium is with-held from a rat's diet, its heart develops a life-threatening arrhythmia. But to what extent these animal observations apply to humans is not clear.

How should you act on this information? If you think you have low magnesium (because the water you drink is "soft," or if you're on diuretics and losing magnesium in your urine, or are taking an anti-biotic in the aminoglycoside family), have your blood level checked. If it is low, supplement your diet with magnesium, available in tablet form. Remember too that certain foods, for example, fat, sugar, so-dium, phosphates and vitamin D, increase your magnesium needs. If you drink alcohol regularly and to excess, you may be losing magne-sium in your urine. If you fall into any of these categories, supple-mentary doses of magnesium are a good idea.

I remember my mother telling me when I was very young how healthy it was to eat lots of *garlic* and *onion*. These two vegetables are synonymous with good health and long life in the folklore of many different cultures. Over the years, there was never any scientific documentation to support these assumptions. Recently, however, it has been found that onions contain ingredients that lower blood pres-sure and decrease the tendency of the blood to clot within the arte-ries. Garlic also apparently reduces blood coagulability by acting on platelets. What's more, eating it will raise your HDL, and you don't have to become a social pariah either: you can buy garlic tablets, which have no impact on your breath or on your immediate environ-ment.

It was observed some years ago that teetotalers have a higher incidence of coronary-artery disease than those who drink in moder-ation. Most doctors now recommend that unless you're an alcoholic, two ounces of hard liquor a day (and that does not mean four, six or eight), or two glasses of wine, will probably raise your HDL. How-ever, if your triglycerides are very high (regardless of the cholesterol level), you should forgo any alcohol, because it further raises the triglycerides. I have mixed feelings about recommending alcohol as cardiac therapy. For many people, even small amounts depress heart function and increase blood pressure. In others, liquor induces rhythm disturbances. And in some, it may knock them off the wagon.

If you're a woman who is no longer menstruating, you may be confused as to whether estrogens protect you against heart disease or render you more vulnerable to it. According to one recent report, women who had been taking estrogens after the menopause had less heart disease than those who didn't, especially if they'd previously had their ovaries removed. A more recent study, however, revealed a 50 percent increase in vascular disease in a similar group of women. How can these disparate findings be reconciled? If we look at the data very carefully, we see that in the women who were protected by estrogen therapy, it was started by age forty. In the group in whom the cardiac risk was increased, the hormone was not begun until after fifty. It would therefore seem that young women who have become menopausal after surgical removal of their ovaries benefit from estrogen supplements, but that those in whom the menopause is a "natural" one may not.

Preventing the Second Heart Attack

Let's now consider "secondary prevention" of heart disease. Suppose you're an established cardiac, that is, you've either got angina pectoris or have had a heart attack. Is it too late to do anything worthwhile, and should you just enjoy what life you have left?

The truth is that prevention is now more important than ever. That means establishing proper priorities in life and controlling all the risk factors we've discussed throughout this chapter—cigarette smoking, high blood pressure, cholesterol and overweight.

But is there, in addition, anything specific you can do or any drug you can take that will help improve your chances of reaching old age comfortably? Most definitely. Any medication that makes your blood clot less easily by reducing the stickiness of your platelets will probably help prevent recurrence of heart attacks. Such anti-platelet agents include (1) aspirin, (2) dipyridamole (Persantine), (3) Anturane, and to a lesser extent, (4) beta blockers (Inderal and related drugs), (5) calcium channel blockers (diltiazem, nifedipine and verapamil), (6) vitamin B-6 (but not in megadoses), (7) onions, (8) garlic and (9) the Omega-3 polyunsaturated fish oils.

Make sure that it's safe for you to take aspirin before committing yourself to long-term therapy. For example, avoid it if you have bronchial asthma, a history of bleeding ulcers or are pregnant. And even if you've gotten the okay from your doctor, don't take too much. The smaller the dose, the better the results as far as your vascular status is concerned. In early studies of the effectiveness of aspirin in the prevention of heart disease, which showed it to be useless, we were using too great a dose. You see, aspirin has two opposite actions with respect to the coagulability of blood: one prevents clotting, the other promotes it. The more aspirin you take, the greater the adverse effect. I recommend the "baby" aspirin (80 mgs.) strength once a day or even every second day. This dose has been shown to result in a 51 percent reduction in the incidence of acute heart attacks in patients with severe unstable angina—the kind that usually progresses to a heart attack.

Persantine (dipyridamole) also interferes with the ability of platelets to clump together in the blood, but in a different way. It's very well tolerated, and although some doctors believe aspirin alone is all you need, most prescribe them together.

Anturane, used in the prevention of gout, has also been found to reduce the death rate of patients who continue to take it after they've had a heart attack. Its mode of action is not clear, but probably involves an anti-platelet effect. The FDA has not, however, approved its use as a preventive. Despite this, many doctors do prescribe it for that purpose.

Everyone agrees on the value of beta blockers *after* a heart attack. There are several kinds available, each with its own special characteristics. However, they have certain major properties in common. For example, they all improve angina pectoris, reduce high blood pressure, slow heart rate, prevent migraine headaches, suppress "extra" heartbeats, minimize symptoms of overactive thyroid and decrease eye pressure in glaucoma. There is also evidence that if you start taking one of these beta blockers within three weeks after a heart attack, your risk of dying during the next two years is virtually halved. Whether or not you should continue this therapy for longer than two years depends on your symptoms. If you still have angina, high blood pressure or some disturbance of heart rhythm, there is no reason to stop taking them. If you're completely without symptoms, most doctors feel you've gotten all the protection possible in those first two years and may safely discontinue them after that time. But beta blockers do have their problems. They're excellent as long as the heart muscle is strong. But when cardiac weakness or heart failure sets in, they can worsen it. They can also produce or aggravate bronchial asthma, obscure the evidence of an insulin reaction in diabetics, slow the heart rate excessively, and cause impotence, fatigue and cold extremities. But these side effects are overshadowed by the usefulness of the beta blockers in the treatment of angina pectoris, hypertension and certain cardiac rhythm disturbances when the chips are down and you need them.

The *coronary bypass operation* is now one of the most frequently performed surgical procedures in the United States. It is generally undertaken for the relief of angina pectoris. The obstructed portion of one or more coronary arteries is bypassed by inserting part of a leg vein (or an artery removed from within the chest wall—the internal mammary) at a point above and below the occlusion. Is this operation prophylactic, that is, will it prevent a heart attack or decrease your chances of dying? It will, but only under certain circumstances. In order to understand what these are, you need to know something about the coronary circulation. The heart is supplied by three arteries. One of them, the right, is a single vessel. The other two (the left anterior descending and the circumflex) originate in a common trunk called the left main stem. Significant obstruction of that artery, regardless of the severity of the accompanying symptoms, is life-threatening, and a bypass operation may be lifesaving. Diagnosis of blockage of the left main coronary can be made with certainty only by a coronary angiogram (in which dye is injected into the cardiac circulation and the arteries visualized).

There are many possible combinations of coronary-artery disease. One, two or three vessels may be obstructed. The narrowing may be located proximally, that is, high up in the artery in which event most of the vessel and all the cardiac muscle it supplies are deprived of blood; or it may be situated lower down (distal disease) or in a twig of one of the branches. As a rule, the larger the artery involved, the more proximal (or closer to its origin) the disease, the greater the significance and more severe the symptoms.

Our attitudes toward bypass surgery, its value and when to have it have been changing over the years. Soon after the procedure came into use, cardiologists were very conservative in their recommendations. Only those patients whose chest pain could not be controlled with anti-anginal medication were selected. But with increasing surgical skill and experience, the pendulum began to swing the other way. More and more patients whose arteriograms revealed obstructions in two or three coronary arteries were referred for bypass, regardless of symptoms. Currently, we have once more modified our stance, so that most cardiologists now recommend operation only to those patients who have left-main-stem blockage or who have documented evidence of obstruction in two or more arteries *and whose symptoms persist despite optimal medical management.*

There have been several studies over the last fifteen years dealing with the efficacy of bypass surgery. The results have been conflicting. In my own practice, I recommend bypass surgery not to improve survival (except in the case of left main stem obstruction), but to control symptoms and to enhance the quality of life.

It is often difficult to assess the impact of an operation like the bypass in a condition whose course is as unpredictable as that of coronary-artery disease. For example, I remember one of my patients who consulted me back in 1970. He was then fifty years old; he had already had two heart attacks. He had just returned from a very famous heart center where he had undergone coronary angiography (a relatively new procedure at the time). It revealed severe disease of all three of his coronary arteries. A ventricular aneurysm was also detected. That meant that a portion of his heart muscle was dead and ballooning out ineffectually every time the uninvolved part of his heart contracted. He was scheduled for bypass surgery, which had to be postponed when the nurses at the hospital went on strike. Unwilling to wait away from home for the resolution of the labor dispute, he returned to New York. While he was cooling his heels, so to speak, he consulted me for a second opinion. Remember that in 1970 there were very little data about the long-term impact of coronary-artery bypass surgery. In those days, too, the risk of the operation was substantially higher than it is today. For these reasons, and because he was totally without symptoms, I suggested that he delay surgery for the time being, and that we evaluate his progress at regular intervals. In these ensuing sixteen years, this man has not experienced a single attack of angina, has had no cardiac-rhythm problems and has not suffered another heart attack. He works hard, travels extensively and even plays doubles tennis. Had he undergone and survived the bypass operation in 1970, we would now be congratulating ourselves about our wisdom in sending him for surgery at that time. So one must be very careful about drawing conclusions concerning the effectiveness of any intervention on the basis of an individual example or even a small number of cases. The fact is that the majority of persons with mild-to-moderate angina pectoris do well regardless of the route they follow—medical or surgical.

Even when the arteriogram looks horrendous, with seemingly severe obstructions all over the place, patients often live for many years with only minimal symptoms. This is probably due to collateral circulation, a network of tiny vessels that develops and helps take over from the larger diseased vessels.

I believe that in the next few years the coronary bypass procedure will be increasingly supplanted by more sophisticated, less traumatic techniques. For example, we are rapidly becoming more expert with the use of the balloon catheter, with which we are now able to enter the coronary arteries and compress the obstructing plaques; laser techniques to disintegrate these plaques are presently being developed; we can now synthesize substances to dissolve the fresh clots that cause the acute heart attack. As this progress continues, it is inevitable that fewer bypass procedures will be done. At the moment, however, this operation is the best there is for most patients with obstructive coronary disease not responsive to medical management.

Sudden Cardiac Death—A Great Way to Die?

Sudden cardiac death is the most serious public-health problem in the Western world. Every year in the United States alone, at least 350,000 people die suddenly, or without much warning. They are, literally, alive one moment and dead the next (or, at most, within one hour). What happens in the first few minutes after the onset of symptoms or the occurrence of death is critical. If you make it to a hospital because of appropriate treatment at the scene, chances are ten to one that you will survive.

On December 5, 1963, at 7:30 A.M., eighty-five-year-old Herbert H. Lehman, four-time governor of New York, former Director General of UNRRA, and most recently United States senator, stood in front of his bathroom mirror, a rich foam lather on his face. Downstairs, his car was waiting to take him to Washington, where President Lyndon Johnson was to bestow upon him America's highest civilian award, the Medal of Freedom. Mrs. Lehman was already at the breakfast table. "Herb, don't be long. There'll be lots of traffic this time of day, and we don't want to be late." His "Down in a minute" was followed almost immediately by a dull thud. "Herb, what was that?'' No answer. "Herb, are you all right?'' Again, no reply. Dreading the worst, Mrs. Lehman ran quickly up the stairs. There, motionless on the floor, without pulse or any other evidence of life, was her husband. Whatever efforts Mrs. Lehman made to "revive" him were futile. The first doctor on the scene, who arrived some fifteen minutes later (something of a record in New York), was no more successful. The governor, without any previous history of significant heart disease, had died literally within an instant of speaking to his wife.

Lawrence S. was a forty-eight-year-old attorney. At forty-one, he'd had a minor heart attack from which he recovered completely. In the ensuing year, he had changed his life-style dramatically. He gave up that portion of his practice that involved pleading in court— the stress was simply too much for him. He also stopped smoking, lost weight, exercised regularly, and was very careful about what he ate, and how much. In short, he tried to do everything right. He was symptom-free over the years and neither required nor took any heart medications.

One day in May, Lawrence's daughter presented him with his first grandchild. This gave him enormous pleasure. On a beautiful Saturday afternoon, he bought some flowers and walked to the hospital to visit mother and child. As he entered the lobby, he suddenly collapsed without any warning in full view of the receptionist, the telephone operator, scores of visitors milling about and two cardiology residents who happened to be going by. For all intents and purposes, Lawrence was dead. There was no pulse; there were no respirations. The telephone operator summoned the "arrest team" while the two young doctors on the scene began CPR (cardiopulmonary resuscitation). As one rhythmically depressed the breastbone, the other delivered mouth-to-mouth breathing to the hapless new grandparent. Moments later, the rest of the team arrived. An airway was inserted through the patient's mouth into the pharynx, and respiration was continued by machine. The electrocardiogram showed "ventricular fibrillation"—a condition in which, instead of contracting normally, the heart just wriggles like a bag of worms. It is unable to pump any significant amount of blood, and the net result is tantamount to its simply stopping. ("Cardiac arrest" is the term applied to any condition in which blood does not leave the heart. Ventricular fibrillation is one such circumstance; cardiac standstill is another.) Electrodes were applied to Lawrence's chest. A shock was delivered to the agonized heart from the portable defibrillator. No response. Then another jolt was applied. Seconds later, normal cardiac rhythm was restored, blood pressure was soon measurable, and Lawrence "awakened"—literally from the dead. It was subsequently determined that his cardiac arrest was due to an acute heart attack. He recovered uneventfully and left the hospital three weeks later. That was twenty years ago. He is now sixty-eight years old, has not had any subsequent cardiac problem, and the grandchild he went to visit that day is a premed student.

Andy was eighteen years old—a high-school senior who was built like a bull. He loved football and was considered the strong man on the team. That was fortunate, because he would need an athletic scholarship in order to be able to go to college. Andy had never been sick, rarely needed a doctor, and had limitless energy. When he was examined pro forma by the school physician in order to qualify for the football team, he was asked whether he had ever had rheumatic fever, growing pains or any serious childhood diseases. He hadn't. Had any other doctor told him or his mother anything about hearing a heart murmur? No, why would they? Andy wondered why all these questions were being asked. The doctor explained that Andy had a "functional" murmur. He went on to tell him that heart murmurs are either "functional" or "organic." The functional kind is harmless, and not the result of disease. It reflects blood swirling around in the heart or across a particular valve. It is often heard in children, and they usually "grow out" of it. An organic murmur, on the other hand, indicates a problem within the heart—a valve that isn't working normally, or in kids, some abnormality with which they were born, like a hole in the heart. "So, if I have this functional murmur, can I be on the team?" asked Andy, who had no interest in medicine but a passionate desire to play football.

"Of course. I just thought I'd mention the murmur to you in case some other doctor tells you about it in the future, and worries you unnecessarily."

That evening at dinner, Andy told his parents and his younger brother about his functional murmur. "You know," said his mother, "now that I think about it, I seem to remember your pediatrician saying something about a murmur when you were born. He said there was no cause for concern but to have it checked from time to time."

"Well, I'm glad this is nothing new, and that I can still play football."

Just before graduation, in the last game of the season, whose outcome was nip and tuck, Andy intercepted a pass on his own thirty-yard line and ran for all his worth for what would have been an incredible touchdown. At the other team's twenty-yard line, he was free and clear. The fans were standing, cheering, hysterical, "Go, Andy, go!" At fifteen yards he stumbled, and at ten yards he fell to the ground. He was dead.

One day in 1961, a twenty-eight-year-old woman was referred to me because of troublesome palpitations. They would come on at any time, and even awaken her at night for no apparent reason. She described these "attacks" as a sensation of rapid, forceful thumping in her chest. She couldn't think of anything that brought them on. They would last for anywhere up to an hour or two and then stop as suddenly as they had started. Once they got going these palpitations seemed to run their course regardless of any measures with which she tried to stop them. In response to my questions, this patient told me she'd never lost consciousness, did not experience what she would call "pain" in her chest during an episode of the rapid beating (although from time to time they did make her somewhat short of breath), and was not aware of any family history of premature coronary heart disease.

When her symptoms had begun—some two years earlier—she had given up all caffeine and tobacco. Although alcohol did not seem to make things worse, she took no more than an occasional drink. These life-style changes had no impact whatsoever on the frequency of the attacks. Other doctors whom she had consulted could find no significant abnormalities, and so they told her to ignore her symptoms and lead a "normal" life. Despite this reassurance, she was worried, and so she stopped playing tennis and badminton. She also confided to her husband that she would rather not have a baby until the cause of her palpitations was diagnosed. He then requested that her doctor arrange yet another opinion, and that's when I saw her.

Well, like the four or five other cardiologists who had already examined this lady, I could find nothing wrong. There were no heart murmurs. Her blood pressure was normal. During the entire physical examination in my office, her heart rate was never more than eighty per minute, and the rhythm remained completely regular at all times.

I was unable to detect even a single extra beat! Her electrocardiogram was normal. Her chest X ray revealed her heart to be neither enlarged nor misshapen. I evaluated her with other blood tests—cholesterol, thyroid function (an overactive thyroid gland can frequently cause palpitations), kidney status and liver function. They were all normal. I had her walk up and down the Master Two-step, which was then the standard exercise test. (Today, most doctors use the more rigorous treadmill.) That was entirely normal, too.

I reviewed her many previous electrocardiographic tracings and other reports, which had been accumulated over the years. I could find no clues to help make a diagnosis.

When a patient, particularly a young woman, presents with elusive symptoms that defy explanation, and all the tests are "normal," doctors unfortunately are likely to conclude that the problem is of emotional origin. And in this particular instance, several cardiology consultants actually did suggest that she see a psychiatrist. They almost had her convinced.

"Well, what do you think?" asked Dr. C., who called me to discuss his referral.

"Sorry, I can't help you. I don't know what she's got, but my gut feeling tells me that whatever it is, it's real."

"That's all very well, but what do we tell her?"

"Just that. Don't add insult to injury by suggesting that it's all in her head. Keep an eye on her. I'll bet something will show up one day. And don't push her too hard about leading a normal life either. Let her set her own pace."

Some six years later, Dr. C. called to tell me that his patient had died suddenly while walking outdoors. No diagnosis had ever been made during her life.

The four cases I have described—the old governor without any previous cardiac history; Lawrence, who'd had a heart attack years before; Andy, the young athlete with an unexplained heart murmur; and the young, otherwise "healthy" woman who had bizarre heart symptoms—are all representative of the kinds of people who die suddenly. As you can see, there but for the grace of God goes any one of us.

Governor Lehman's only risk factor of which I was aware was his age. It's very difficult to anticipate and prevent sudden cardiac death among such elderly "normals." After all, one has got to die sometime of something, and who could have improved on the way Lehman did it? He was eighty-five years old, and on his way to receive a presidential citation. His was a sudden end to a life of satisfaction. By dying in his own home, he was spared the ambulances, operations, medications and inevitable indignities of hospitalization. Would (and should) I have attempted to resuscitate him had I been on the scene? I would, because life, even at eighty-five, is precious. And if someone who has always been healthy dies suddenly, an attempt should be made to prolong that life if possible. But his death was not a tragedy except to those who knew and loved him.

Sudden cardiac death in an eighty-five-year-old man is not a problem. What concerns us here is its premature occurrence in apparently healthy persons in their teens, twenties, or even fifties and sixties. Why do such individuals die suddenly? Usually, but not always, from a heart attack. Sometimes, however, a heart suddenly "goes crazy" —beating so fast and irregularly in the lethal rhythm called ventricular fibrillation that it cannot effectively pump blood to the rest of the body.

Lawrence, the man who suffered a cardiac arrest and had had a coronary many years earlier, was already vulnerable. Anyone who has had a heart attack in the past, or currently has angina pectoris, or suffers from a cardiac rhythm disturbance that may lead to lethal ventricular fibrillation, or has moderate-to-severe high blood pressure, falls into a high-risk group. Attempts at prevention here are *secondary* rather than primary. Although one should still try to control risk factors associated with heart disease, especially elevated pressure, cigarette smoking and cholesterol levels, that's not nearly as critical as identifying specific cardiac abnormalities that may predispose such persons to sudden cardiac death.

Years ago, we were unable to identify these characteristics with the same precision as we can today nor could we do anything about them once they had been discovered. Fortunately, this is an area in which some progress has been made.

Who Will Die Suddenly?

This is how we now determine who is a candidate for sudden cardiac death:

(1) A careful history should be taken at frequent intervals, and

patients should be educated to report the onset of any symptoms indicating "instability" of the cardiac circulation. For example, an increase in the amount of angina or troublesome palpitations, the onset of dizziness or light-headedness, or an actual fainting spell may all reflect changes in heart rhythm that are possible forerunners of sudden death.

(2) We have such individuals perform a treadmill or other monitored stress test in order to see whether the work load imposed on the heart produces any evidence, however brief, of a rhythm disorder suggesting susceptibility to ventricular fibrillation.

(3) We obtain a Holter monitor. The patient carries a small combined ECG machine–tape recorder, usually on his or her belt, connected to electrodes placed on the chest. This unit records a continuous electrocardiogram for twenty-four hours during a broad range of activities—work, play, eating, sex, sports, sleep, etc. Again, we look for evidence of cardiac irritability of which the patient may be unaware and which may lead to the kind of rhythm disturbance that can cause death.

These two techniques should be performed routinely at least once a year in anyone with established heart disease, regardless of the presence or absence of symptoms. Those who have recently had a myocardial infarction should be so tested before leaving the hospital. If the results are positive, preventive measures described below should be instituted prior to discharge.

Once vulnerability has been determined, patients should be told to avoid stimulants like caffeine, alcohol, compounds containing epinephrine derivatives (often found in cough mixtures and nasal decongestants), and, of course, tobacco.

There are also specific drugs that may reduce the life-threatening irritability of the cardiac muscle. Unfortunately, many of those currently available have potentially serious side effects themselves; they require careful supervision by a physician who is expert in their use. Although the number of these agents approved for prescription in the United States is limited, there are others that are promising, but still experimental.

The anti-arrhythmic agents approved in the United States at this time are the various forms of digitalis, quinidine, procainamide (marketed as Pronestyl, Procan); several beta blockers (Inderal is the prototype); disopyramide (Norpace); calcium channel blockers—nifedipine, verapamil, diltiazem; Dilantin, tocainide and flecainide. The experimental list includes Aprindine, Mexiletene, amiodarone, encainide and others.

Can anything be done to reduce the chances of dying suddenly after recovery from a heart attack, even if none of these special tests indicates particular vulnerability? Bearing that goal in mind, I prescribe the following regimen for all my patients who have suffered heart attacks.

(1) A beta blocker (Blocadren, Inderal, Tenormin, Lopressor, Corgard). There is evidence that such medication after a heart attack reduces the chances of a second heart event and death by almost 50 percent. I advise the beta blocker be continued for at least three years, assuming, of course, there is no other reason not to take it (asthma, heart failure, very slow heart rate, cold extremities, impotence, fatigue and unstable diabetes requiring insulin).

(2) Aspirin. If you've had a heart attack, take 80 mgs. every day (the dosage in one baby aspirin), unless there is some reason for you not to do so. For example, you might be allergic to aspirin, especially if you're asthmatic; you may have a bleeding problem or stomach ulcers, or you might be taking some other anticoagulant. Many doctors administer aspirin in conjunction with dipyridamole (Persantine), but there is no conclusive evidence that the two together are any more effective than the aspirin alone.

(3) Recent studies have indicated that a drug used in the prevention of gout, sulfinpyrazone (Anturane), when given after certain kinds of heart attacks, especially those involving the undersurface of the heart, reduces the incidence of sudden cardiac death. This agent affects the platelets, as does aspirin, making the blood less sticky. It also appears to render the heart less irritable.

The third case I described, the healthy boy who died suddenly during a football game, represents a relatively small but important group—usually athletes, apparently in top form, in the first, second or third decade of life without any previous cardiac history or symptoms—who die during a vigorous athletic event. What kills them? As a rule, it's not hardening of the arteries, which is rare at that age. These boys and girls usually die because of congenital cardiac disease, which was never diagnosed, but which could have been in 90 percent of the cases. Andy was found, at autopsy, to have thickening of the muscle fibers in the septum of the heart, the wall that divides the left side from the right side. This condition, called asymmetric septal hypertrophy, may be associated with lethal disturbances of heart rhythm. One tip-off to its presence is a murmur present from birth. This diagnosis, if suspected, is easy to confirm with an echo-cardiogram—nonpainful, noninvasive and without risk.

Any suspicious murmur should be thoroughly investigated before permission is granted to engage in strenuous competitive athletics. If there is a finding of which the physician, especially if he's not a cardiologist, is not absolutely certain, the patient should not engage in vigorous sports until the diagnosis has been clarified.

The last tragic case, the young woman with palpitations who died suddenly, still undiagnosed, years later, was medically fascinating. She was a medical examiner's case because she died on the street. An autopsy revealed that she had only two instead of the three coronary arteries normally present. Her right coronary artery was congenitally absent. As a result, her heart was not receiving enough blood. This may have left it "irritable" and vulnerable to a life-threatening arrhythmia. There was no way that diagnosis could have been made back in the early 1960s. It can only be established by a coronary angiogram, a procedure that was then not routinely available. Subjecting a woman in her twenties, whose only complaint was palpitations, to a coronary angiogram, then (and even now, for that matter), would not have been justified. And, even if we had established the diagnosis, there's nothing we could have done about it. However, we would at least have had an explanation for her symptoms—small comfort to the patient. What can be done for a missing coronary artery today? Attempts have been made to refashion the coronary circulation, but the chances of success are marginal.

Some years ago, in Seattle, a voluntary program to teach cardiopulmonary resuscitation (CPR) was launched for the benefit of the general public. At one point, one person out of every seven living in that city was able to perform CPR, and the sudden cardiac death rate did, in fact, drop. So a community educational effort, together with risk-factor control, is the most effective way at the present time of reducing or preventing premature sudden cardiac death in the population at large. The advice I give to families in which there is someone at high risk for sudden death is to have one or more members learn how to perform resuscitation. You never know when you're going to need it. Ask your own doctor or your local heart association where you can be taught how to do it.

I recently read some very impressive statistics about out-of-hospital resuscitation. At least 60 percent of those "revived" on the street or in a public place are alive for periods as long as 105 months after the "fatal" event. Several of my own patients, including Lawrence S., are among them.

What's new or on the horizon for preventing sudden cardiac death? In addition to a variety of anti-arrhythmic drugs to suppress the irritable foci in the heart which trigger the deadly rhythm, there are also electronic devices that can terminate ventricular fibrillation. These are implanted within the chest very much like an ordinary cardiac pacemaker. The conventional pacemaker is inserted to prevent the heart from actually stopping, a condition called heart block (which, incidentally, can also cause sudden cardiac death). When the heart fails to beat under those circumstances, the pacemaker sends a charge into the cardiac muscle stimulating it to contract. Similarly, in the implanted defibrillator, there is a sensing electrode that detects and signals the presence of the lethal ventricular fibrillation as soon as it starts. Shocking electrodes within the heart jolt the cardiac muscle into a regular rhythm, very much like the external "paddles" on the machines that you may have seen in the coronary care unit of a hospital. This implanted ventricular pacemaker is already available and in use. It is lifesaving for those persons who, even without suffering a heart attack, are for some reason prone to go into ventricular fibrillation. Such individuals live under the sword of Damocles. So if you or anyone in your family has this problem (primary ventricular fibrillation), inquire about the implantable defibrillator.

CHAPTER 18

When It's Blowing Hot and Cold—
Frostbite and Heatstroke

When the Temperature Drops

Mention frostbite and most people conjure up images of stranded mountain climbers, injured skiers, or survivors of a plane crash lying in deep snow in the bitter cold in some remote mountain area. In the media version, the first rescuer on the scene is apt to be a friendly St. Bernard dog with a brandy flask hanging from its neck. But in the real world of frostbite and hypothermia—life-threatening exposure to cold—people freeze in circumstances not nearly so exotic or romantic. And when this occurs, it may either involve some exposed part of the body, like the nose, feet or hands, or result in a drop in body temperature affecting overall function.

Years ago, when I was doing my hospital training, first-year interns fresh out of medical school were assigned to emergency ambulance duty. Today, that job is performed by specially trained paramedics. Whenever I went out on an emergency call, I was accompanied by an elderly gentleman who had but two responsibilities—to drive the ambulance and to help me lift the stretcher. He knew nothing about medicine or first aid. In those days, we carried no resuscitation equipment or miracle drugs—only some oxygen tanks, pain medication and a few splints. Whenever I sat in the ambulance racing toward my destination, I worried, with good reason, about my ability to handle whatever problem might be waiting for me there. If somebody was hemorrhaging, would I be able to stop it? Could I deliver a baby coming down as a breech, buttocks first? Would I splint a fractured limb properly, so as to keep the patient comfortable en route?

My internship was served in Montreal, built around a mountain whose gentle slopes attract many skiers on weekends. On weekdays, however, the runs are virtually deserted, so that anyone who is injured may well lie around for a long time before being found. In the wintertime, Montreal can be as cold as Alaska. I recall temperatures of −30° F., with lots of snow.

One such winter weekday, when a strong north wind made the cold almost intolerable, I received an emergency call to pick up an "injured" skier on Mount Royal. No other details were provided. Since my hospital was situated on the mountainside very near the ski slopes, it took us less than five minutes to reach the scene. On the way, I prepared various splints, expecting to treat a broken leg or arm. When we arrived, I found the patient lying on the ground, covered by the police rescue blanket. The left leg was askew and obviously broken. But the situation was much more serious than that. The body, that of a man in his late fifties, was rigid and cold; the lips were blue. I could not feel a pulse, and he was not breathing. When I lifted the blanket to listen to his heart, I was puzzled by the fact that the ski jacket was open and the shirt beneath it unbuttoned, as if the patient had felt too warm in this subzero weather. I went through a few routine maneuvers looking for signs of life, and found none. I was about to declare the victim dead to the waiting police when suddenly I heard a gasp. Fifteen seconds later, there was another. I felt for the pulse once more and now counted thirty very faint beats per minute (the normal range is anywhere from sixty to ninety per minute). I had almost declared a living, albeit very frozen, man dead! At this point, I wasted no time. I immediately covered the patient with more blankets, quickly lifted him into the warm ambulance and we sped to the hospital—siren wailing, lights flashing—desperate to get there in time to save his life. As soon as we arrived, the patient was given the standard rapid rewarming therapy and other emergency procedures for resuscitating victims of hypothermia.

The story has a happy ending because the patient survived, but I have never forgotten that experience. Ever since, on other ambulance calls, as a resident in hospital emergency rooms, or as a practicing doctor, I've always made sure to think of hypothermia whenever I encountered an elderly person "dead" in an unheated apartment, or a skier lying immobile in a snowbank, or someone "dead drunk" on the street in cold weather.

A more subtle example of cold exposure was Max, a seventy-five-year-old retired printer with a "heart condition." He lived alone in a three-flight walk-up. His one-bedroom flat was "heated," technically speaking, and rent-controlled. The landlord had several times tried to persuade Max to move out, telling him the stairs were "no good for a man of your age, and anyway, the neighborhood is changing." The real reason, of course, was that if Max left, the next tenant could legally be charged a higher rent. But Max didn't move. He couldn't afford to. In any event, whether it was deliberate or (as alleged by the landlord) a "breakdown in the outmoded heating system, which I can't afford to fix because the tenants don't pay me enough rent," there were several cold days when the apartment received no heat.

On one especially frigid winter morning, Max was brought to the emergency room of our hospital by his son, who thought his father had had a stroke. He wasn't rigid and unresponsive, as was the man on the ski slopes, but he was shivering and confused. He didn't recognize his son and was "talking gibberish." Nor was this the first time Max's son had noticed such behavior. On several other occasions that month, he had found his father acting strangely. When he told their family doctor about it, a tranquilizer was prescribed over the phone to "settle Max down, because older people can become agitated." Both Max's son and his doctor assumed that this was the beginning of senility, or Alzheimer's disease. But this particular morning, the symptoms were so bad his son was sure Max was having a stroke.

Actually, it turned out to be nothing of the kind. Max was suffering from the cold. Some older people react after a few hours of exposure to low temperatures by shivering and altered behavior, especially if their nutrition is poor and their circulation not so good. In any event, we warmed Max up, and he recovered after a couple of days. His "Alzheimer's disease" and "stroke" both disappeared. But he might well have died, had he been left in that unheated flat.

Max, with the help of his son, could have prevented the dangers of cold exposure by (1) making sure the apartment was adequately heated, or moving temporarily to a lodging that was; (2) wearing proper clothing when the apartment was cold; (3) drinking warm fluids at frequent intervals; and (4) at the first sign of change in his father's behavior, his son should have *taken* him to the doctor instead of relying on a telephone impression. The correct diagnosis of cold exposure would then have been made. Tranquilizers prescribed over the phone further depressed Max's already compromised cerebral functions.

The next case reflects yet another variation in the hypothermia theme, with equally important lessons to be learned.

Jack was a traveling salesman in the Northeast. He covered his territory of several hundred square miles by car. One cold winter day, during a heavy snowstorm, he decided he needed extra traction. So he pulled over, took the tire chains out of the trunk, and got down on his knees to put them on. He was wearing a business suit, and his knees got cold and wet. But he wasn't concerned about that because he knew he'd soon be in his warm car. He also had to remove his gloves in order to put the chains on. It took him longer than he had expected, and when he got into his car, it wouldn't start. So there he was, in 0° F. temperature, with cold, damp knees, wet trousers, very cold hands—and no heat. He stood out in the biting wind, trying to flag down a passing car. There were very few vehicles on the road, and none stopped for him.

As he stood out there in the storm, Jack didn't know what to do. He had no extra clothing in the car. At first, his knees and hands ached and burned, but soon the pain disappeared. His limbs became hard, white, cold and numb. Then he remembered some advice he'd heard years ago about rubbing the frozen areas with snow. That only made matters worse. Finally, about an hour later, a cruising highway patrol car came by and took Jack to the nearest hospital. On the way, he asked the cop for a drink. To his delight, he was given some brandy. Imagine, boozing in a patrol car! The friendly policeman also offered him a cigarette, but he couldn't hold one in his frozen fingers.

As he sat there in the cruiser with the heater on, Jack's numb hands and knees began first to tingle, then to burn and finally to throb. He was thawing out! When he got to the hospital emergency room, the staff immersed his knees and hands in warm water (about body temperature, i.e., 98° F.). He was observed for a few hours and then discharged home. Like Max, in the previous account, he was lucky to have been helped in time. A little longer out in the cold and he might have ended up losing his hands and possibly his legs. Even so, it wouldn't surprise me to learn that years later Jack had developed arthritis. People whose joints have been severely frostbitten sometimes do.

I could tell you other stories of frozen persons—not only the sick, the elderly and the injured, but also athletes collapsing during excessively cold weather. Most of the medical problems induced by cold can be prevented. Here are some useful pointers for you to remember.

In addition to a drop in temperature, wind velocity and dampness also increase the danger of freezing. The "wind-chill factor" we hear about on radio and TV weather broadcasts is a very real thing. In fact, it is much more important than the actual thermometer reading itself. When the meteorologist says, "It's 20° F. above zero and the wind velocity is twenty miles per hour," he is telling you that as far as your body is concerned it is − 10° F.! The higher the wind speed (up to forty miles an hour—beyond that it makes no further difference), the greater the impact on "coldness." For example, when it's a balmy 50° F. and the wind is blowing at thirty-five miles per hour, it feels like a nippy 28° F. (4° below freezing). A cold 40° F. in the presence of a forty-mile-per-hour wind will feel like a frigid 10° F. So don't be lulled into a false sense of security in terms of how you dress for what you plan to do just because the thermometer reading is not too low.

And all wind-chill readings assume you are dry. If any substantial portion of your clothing or body becomes damp (from perspiration, such as occurs in a long race, or from water, snow or ice), the danger of either frostbite or hypothermia increases dramatically.

Other factors that increase vulnerability to cold include fatigue, hunger, malnutrition, dehydration (all of which interfere with your body's temperature-regulating mechanisms), tobacco and alcohol. Once he was rescued, Jack should not have asked for alcohol, and the cop should have known better than to give him any. A warm, nonalcoholic beverage would have been permissible, but alcohol dilates skin vessels, thus shunting blood away from critical interior areas of the body, which need it to sustain life. Jack was also lucky that he was unable to hold a cigarette. Tobacco constricts blood vessels so that the already frozen limb is further deprived of potential warmth. Narcotics of any kind should not be administered, since the brain of the frozen victim doesn't always function as well as it should, and narcotics further impair judgment and the ability to do the right thing for yourself. Certain medications lower body temperature, and so can worsen matters. The most commonly used are Valium, Librium, barbiturates, and tranquilizers in the phenothiazine group, the prototype of which is Thorazine. Several diseases may leave you more sensitive to cold, for example, low thyroid function, insulin-dependent diabetes, kidney trouble and certain glandular abnormalities.

Suppose you expect to be in the cold for one reason or another; here are some additional tips on how to prevent cold injury.

Dress warmly and appropriately. There are several cardinal rules for proper attire in cold weather. Do not rely on bulky, tight outerwear. Your clothes should provide adequate insulation to keep you warm, yet permit the evaporation of perspiration (remember that dampness from any source is to be avoided). Wearing several layers of loose, lightweight clothing permits both insulation and evaporation. Air is trapped between the layers, helping retain body heat and allowing ventilation. From a practical viewpoint, this is how you do it. (1) Underwear should be woolen or made of synthetic propylene (rather than cotton). (2) Wear a second layer of wool or propylene between under and outer garments. (3) Avoid waterproof outer jackets or coats. They prevent evaporation of any dampness generated by your body. Instead, use water-*repellent* and windproof material. (4) If you like down, use the synthetic material rather than the natural goose or duck down. The latter trap the moisture when you or they become wet. (5) Cover your head (especially if you are bald), face and other exposed parts of your body so as not to lose heat through those channels. (6) Wear mittens, not gloves. This allows the fingers to keep each other warm. If you expect to use your hands for fine movements, as Jack did when he put on the tire chains, wear lightweight cotton gloves under the mittens. (7) If you are apt to be walking in snow, avoid low shoes. Wear boots—the higher the better, and never below the ankle. (8) Socks should be woolen, not cotton—and wear two pairs if it is going to be really cold. (9) If you are stranded in a snowstorm, stay in your car, especially if you are elderly. Keep the heater on, the motor idling and the windows slightly open. (10) If you do much driving in rural areas, install a CB in your car so that you can summon help from the police or a passing motorist without being exposed to the wind. (11) Don't touch cold metal with your bare hands. That increases heat loss. Also avoid getting gasoline on your skin (it takes on the temperature of its environment).

With the onset of frostbite, the affected areas (tip of the nose, cheeks, hands, feet, ears) will first be a healthy pink, as blood rushes to them in your body's attempt to keep them warm—and they will hurt. With continued exposure, however, the skin will turn white and the pain will begin to lessen as the frozen part becomes numb. This numbness results from the fact that the blood vessels to the skin go into spasm, and, also, cold is a good anesthetic. Sometimes the frozen part will also swell or blister. When that happens, get out of the cold as quickly as you can. Delay may result in serious and irreversible damage to the exposed area. As you warm up, and thawing sets in, the numbness will be replaced by a burning, throbbing pain.

Other important don'ts include:

- Don't rub the affected area with snow or anything else in order to "warm it up." That's what we were told to do when I was a boy. Whoever started that rumor was wrong. If the nose or ears or fingers are frozen, rubbing them with snow is a good way to damage them permanently.
- Don't, for goodness sake, put the frozen part in an oven. You think I am joking? If you work long enough in the emergency room of a Montreal hospital as I did, you will see all kinds of bizarre approaches to frostbite—and that's one of them.
- If blisters do develop on the exposed portion of your body, don't try to break them or bandage them. Just cover them lightly to protect them from the cold. As soon as possible, immerse the affected limb in warm water, with a temperature somewhere between 90° and 100° F., but no hotter than an unaffected part of your body can tolerate comfortably. However, and this is very important, if there is any chance of refreezing, it's better to delay the thawing process, since the moisture released by rewarming causes increased damage when refrozen.

Frostbite is a serious matter. I have seen patients hospitalized for weeks and months because of it. Some have lost portions of their limbs as a result. Those who don't may end up with arthritis or Raynaud's syndrome (a condition in which the arteries become sensitized to cold, so that even in only slightly cool temperatures, they constrict and cause pain in the fingers and toes). In children whose leg joints are affected, growth may be stunted.

The kind of generalized hypothermia I described in my ambulance experience is life-threatening—and requires expert, meticulous, sophisticated care in the hospital. Most deaths in such patients are due to cardiac arrest of one kind or another. If you come across someone so affected, remember that (1) he or she is not necessarily dead, even if they look it. (2) Warm him or her up as fast as you can. If you do not have additional blankets, use your own body. (3) Getting to a hospital is the number one priority. (4) If the patient is breathing at all, no matter how slowly, do not perform CPR, even if you can't feel a pulse. The heart is already beating as fast as the low temperature permits. A well-meaning attack on the chest isn't going to help matters and may only result in some broken ribs and further cardiac damage.

Everything you've read above really pertains to persons exposed to excessive cold in rather classic and fairly common ways. But there are other situations that can result in cold injury—immersion in cold water for a long time is one, as when a boat capsizes or sinks. Another, especially these days, is long-distance running, which may cause important heat loss through prolonged, excessive perspiration. The net result, even when the outdoor temperature is as high as 45° or 50° F., may be enough cooling to cause hypothermia, or even loss of consciousness.

You may be wondering why the skier on Mount Royal tried to get his clothes off even as he was freezing to death. When the body is exposed to cold for any length of time, the smaller blood vessels supplying the skin constrict. They do so in order to shunt blood away from the cold surface of the body, sending it to the interior, where it can nourish and keep warm those organs critical for survival—the heart, kidneys, liver and intestines. This redirection of blood from the body's exterior is what accounts for the cold, white, hard skin in the areas of frostbite. But this surge of blood to the body's core may result in a signal to the brain telling it not to worry—that it is not really so cold after all. And so the patient may actually "feel" too warm, despite the fact that his extremities and the rest of his body are frozen. This false sensation of heat may result in "paradoxic undressing" (which is what that man on the mountain did before he lapsed into coma).

In the Good Old Summertime—The Risk of Heatstroke

All this talk about freezing to death is enough to make anyone shiver. For a change of pace, let's go to the other end of the spectrum and consider how to prevent the consequences of too much heat (hyperthermia). As with cold injury, those most vulnerable are the elderly, the sick, the very young and athletes. Problems are most apt to occur in the setting of intense physical exercise, since 75 percent of all the energy we produce during physical effort is converted to heat. That heat is normally dissipated in several ways. First, blood vessels in the skin dilate, bringing the warm blood to the surface, where some of the heat is lost by *radiation*. On windy days, *convection*—in which the wind blows the heat away—is responsible for additional cooling. When the temperature is pleasantly warm or cool, these two mechanisms, radiation and convection, are the most important ways the body deals with excess heat production during exercise. But as it gets hotter and hotter, and the outside temperature approaches or exceeds that of the body, *sweating* becomes the most important way we cool off.

Normally, the body is pretty good at regulating its temperature. But the complicated mechanisms responsible for maintaining the steady 98.6° F., come hell or high water, can break down in the following circumstances: (1) When the temperature outside the body is greater than that of the blood being carried to the skin surface. Since heat is no longer lost by radiation in these conditions, one of the three cooling mechanisms is lost. If, in addition, the sun is shining, the body *absorbs* heat instead of losing it. (2) When the humidity is also increased, the ability to sweat is impaired. If in this setting, you don't drink enough fluids, you're in real trouble. The body now doesn't have the wherewithal to sweat, and so the amount of heat it can lose via the skin is drastically reduced. *Avoiding dehydration is key to the prevention of heat injury.* (3) If you're overdressed, of course, the heat will get you more quickly. (4) In some older individuals, the temperature-regulating mechanism in the brain, like other bodily functions, is less efficient. Challenged by excessive heat, the signals necessary to initiate the sweating, the blood shunting and the fluid shifting are delayed or inadequate. That's why older people must be very careful on very hot days. The newborn and the very young are also vulnerable to prolonged, excessive heat because their body surface area is much higher relative to their weight, and so they absorb more heat than does the adult. (5) Just as there are medications that lower body temperature and present a danger when you are exposed to excessive cold, so are there drugs that increase your susceptibility to unusual heat. These include (a) agents that interfere with the brain's ability to regulate body heat (the phenothiazines, like Thorazine or Compazine, which some psychiatric patients take fairly regularly); (b) drugs that reduce your ability to sweat (here the list is long and includes antihistamines, certain medications used in the treatment of Parkinson's disease, a whole variety of antispasmodics taken for intestinal irritability, e.g., belladonna, and a long list of substances used in psychiatry); (c) medications that actually increase heat production, like amphetamines ("speed") and cocaine; and finally, (d) diuretics, which remove body water—during a heat wave, that is precisely what you don't want to happen. Alcohol increases the body's heat production and so should also be avoided in hot weather. Certain diseases like diabetes and heart trouble interfere with the body's ability to lose heat. Finally, when the heart is weak and can't pump the blood adequately, less of it gets to the skin, where heat is dissipated.

Now that you know how and why problems can arise from excessive heat, let's look at what can happen in such situations and consider how to prevent it.

Just as the consequences of freezing may range from frostbite of a finger or a toe to overall hypothermia, so the severity of hyperthermia may vary from simple heat cramps to fainting to heat exhaustion to heatstroke.

Heat cramps are painful spasms that athletes experience in the muscles they use most. For example, runners get such cramps in the legs; a weight lifter will feel them in his arms. Usually all one needs do about it is rest, apply ice packs and gently stretch the affected muscle. But how can these cramps be prevented? The key is drinking enough fluid before, during and after the exercise. Many of my patients think heat cramps are due to salt deficiency, so they take extra salt in the form of tablets before a heavy workout. That's not necessary if you have been eating normal amounts of salt with your meals right along.

Once the hot weather sets in, every athlete should gradually work back up to peak capacity over a few days, because that gives the body a chance to get its heat-regulating mechanisms acclimatized. Also, it's best to engage in sports early in the morning and late in the afternoon or early evening, before it gets too hot or after the sun has gone down.

A more severe consequence of excessive exposure to heat than muscle cramps is *heat exhaustion*. This occurs not only in athletes generating too much heat during intense exercise, but to anyone—the elderly without access to air conditioning, infants and small children (a child left in a car on a very hot day with the windows closed while the parents are shopping is an excellent candidate for heat exhaustion). The symptoms of heat exhaustion are nausea and vomiting, muscle cramps, fainting and a rapid, weak pulse. Prevention here involves keeping cool (the elderly poor should spend as much time as possible in cooled areas like shopping malls if they don't have air conditioning at home), applying cold compresses and drinking plenty of fluids. Extra salt is not usually necessary and should be avoided by cardiac patients and those with high blood pressure.

The most serious form of heat injury is *heatstroke*. This usually occurs in the setting of very high outdoor temperatures (usually greater than 95° F.) and high humidity, especially in bright sun. The stroke itself is often sudden, and results from the total breakdown of the body's heat-regulating mechanisms. At first, the individual stops sweating, then confusion sets in, followed by coma and seizures. Body temperature, which remains near normal in heat exhaustion, shoots up above 106° F. in heatstroke. This condition is a prime medical emergency, and unless treatment is started early, the victim will die. That treatment consists of anything that will cool the patient. After arrival at a hospital, he or she will be given the appropriate intravenous fluids, may be immersed in a bath filled with ice cubes, will have cool compresses applied or be subjected to a warm-water mist with a fan blowing air over the body.

In summary, how can one cope on a very hot day and prevent all the complications of excessive heat? If you are an athlete, (1) get into condition gradually over a period of days before striving for peak performance; (2) try to engage in sports in the early morning or late afternoon; (3) avoid running when the wet-bulb-globe temperature is greater than 83° F. (the wet-bulb-globe temperature is analogous to the wind-chill factor in cold weather; it is calculated on the basis of the outdoor temperature, humidity, and radiant heat from the sun);

(4) drink 6 to 8 ounces of fluid before competition and again at frequent intervals during it; (5) douse yourself with water frequently; (6) wear light-colored, loose-fitting short clothes; (7) best of all, postpone your game or workout in very hot weather.

CHAPTER **19**

Sight and Sound—
Preserving Two Great Gifts

Preventing Blindness—Never Look at an Eclipse

Despite thirty million office visits every year to eye specialists in this country, someone becomes blind every eleven minutes. Five hundred thousand Americans are legally blind, 3.5 million persons cannot see out of one eye, and twelve million are "visually impaired," among whom are 1.5 million who are not able to read a newspaper even with the strongest available glasses. One of every five blind individuals in this country was born that way because of hereditary or congenital causes.

The solution to this enormous problem ideally lies in prevention. Mind you, if we were able to select our parents, we'd be well on our way, for who will develop what kind of eye trouble—and when—is largely genetically determined. But until such time as we are able to manipulate genetic material, we have no choice but to focus on a more practical approach. Fortunately, timely treatment of many eye disorders will prevent blindness.

Glaucoma—The Road to Blindness

The leading cause of blindness among adults in the United States is *glaucoma*. Although this disorder itself is not preventable, when early treatment is instituted, blindness does not occur. So in effect, one out of every seven cases of blindness in this country can be prevented by proper diagnosis of this disease in time.

Glaucoma exists when the pressure of the liquid in the eyeball is increased. This compresses the retina, whose function is to transmit to the brain the light rays entering the eye. As the pressure within the eye rises, the retinal nerve cells and fibers become progressively more compromised, and vision begins to deteriorate. This can happen acutely, with sudden pain in the eyes and clouding of vision, or, more commonly, very gradually. The chronic course is often so insidious in its progression that it has been referred to as the "thief in the night."

As glaucoma continues untreated, eyesight is progressively impaired. Typically, such individuals have difficulty adjusting their vision in dark rooms, as when entering a movie theater from a sunlit street. They may see rainbow rings around bright lights, and images become blurred or foggy. The next stage is the loss of side vision, so that one is able to see only what is directly in front. (Side vision goes first because the increased fluid pressure within the eyeball initially affects the retinal nerve cells and fibers involved with peripheral sight.) Later, complete blindness sets in when central vision is affected.

Another form of glaucoma is "iatrogenic," or doctor-induced, and occurs in 10 to 30 percent of patients ("steroid responders") receiving steroid therapy for serious ocular inflammation or acute allergic reactions. This problem is less apt to occur when the steroids are taken orally, not topically. But in any event, if you are on long-term steroid therapy for whatever reason and via whatever route, you must have the pressure within your eyes monitored frequently and carefully.

You can avoid being among the six thousand adults who go blind every year as a result of glaucoma if you maintain a high degree of suspicion for this disorder. This alone will lead to early diagnosis and prompt treatment. Glaucoma rarely strikes before the age of thirty-five, and is most prevalent in the forties to the sixties. Anyone with a family history of the disease is more vulnerable to it (glaucoma has a strong genetic predisposition), and it is often associated with diabetes and myopia (shortsightedness). Remember that blindness cannot be reversed. So if you're over thirty-five, are myopic, diabetic and/or have a family history of glaucoma, have your eyes checked *every two years*. Although some internists can and do measure eyeball pressure (which, incidentally, has nothing to do with blood pressure), you're probably better off going directly to an eye doctor.

If the intraocular pressure is found to be high, chances are you'll first be treated with eyedrops. If that doesn't work, surgery may be necessary.

Here are some other important tips for anyone with glaucoma. You should know that the latest medication for its treatment is a beta blocker called timolol, marketed as Timoptic. Like all beta blockers, Timoptic can decrease heart rate and lower blood pressure. It may worsen heart failure and precipitate asthma in vulnerable individuals. Several deaths among asthmatics taking Timoptic have already been reported. So, if your eye doctor prescribes it for your glaucoma, be sure to tell him if you have asthma or a cardiac condition.

There are several commonly used medications that can increase the pressure within the eyeball in patients who already have glaucoma. In other words, they don't cause it, as do steroids, but they make it worse. Such agents include antihistamines, nitrates (used in the treatment of angina), and antispasmodics (for an irritable bladder or intestinal tract). If you have glaucoma, make sure to keep the lines of communication open among you, your ophthalmologist and any doctor treating you for some other ailment.

Senile Macular Degeneration

The second major cause of blindness (one of every nine cases) is senile macular degeneration (SMD), responsible for three thousand new cases in this country each year. This is essentially a disease of aging, but although most patients are over sixty-five, there is a hereditary form sometimes present in young people.

Blindness due to SMD results from damage to the macula, that area of the retina responsible for sharp, central vision. But here the cause is vascular, and has nothing to do with eyeball pressure. The small blood vessels that nourish the retina become diseased, burst or leak fluid. As a result the macula is blood- and oxygen-deprived. The typical scenario goes something like this: A man or woman, almost always over sixty-five years of age and more likely seventy-five or older, notices that the center of his or her visual field is obscured by a dark spot. Because the macula is smaller in size than the head of a thumbtack, the remainder of the retina is not involved early on. So these individuals can pretty much see everything except what's straight ahead. Side vision remains unaffected until much later (in contrast to glaucoma, where peripheral vision is lost first). Patients with SMD prefer to have you beside them rather than directly in front. Also, when watching TV, such individuals prefer to sit almost at right angles to the set rather than facing it.

Aside from their visual problems, patients with SMD may enjoy good health. In other words, the disability is not part of some general disorder. Occasionally, there is a history of eye injury or of excessive exposure to very bright light—but usually not.

Unfortunately SMD is neither preventable nor, in most cases, really treatable. However, the loss of vision usually progresses very slowly. Most patients continue to see well enough to get along for many years after the onset of symptoms. They can be helped by a variety of "low vision aids" which include magnifying lenses, some of which are illuminated with high-intensity lamps, and even telescopic lenses. Your ophthalmologist can decide which will benefit you most in any particular stage of the disease.

I have recently referred several of my patients with SMD for krypton laser treatment. A pinpoint of light directed at the diseased blood vessels can stop bleeding. When done early enough in suitable subjects, such laser therapy can sometimes prevent or at least delay total blindness.

Cataracts—The Timing Is Up to You

The third major avoidable cause of blindness in this country is cataract formation. Timing (by you) and skill (of your doctor) are of the essence in the management of this disorder. Forty-one million persons among us over the age of forty have already begun to develop cataracts. But in only 5 percent of cases will surgery be required. Among the 600,000 operations performed each year for cataracts, 97 percent are successful.

The image you see is focused by the lens, "passed on" to the retina and then to the brain. When the lens behind the pupil becomes cloudy, very much as egg white does after boiling, you have a cataract. Since cataract formation interferes with the transmission of the light rays through the lens, it impairs vision. Objects are blurred, new glasses don't help much, there never seems to be enough light by which to read, and rubbing the eyes does not remove the "film" or "veil" before them.

We do not know precisely what chemical changes cause the lens to become opaque. Although diabetics are more prone to cataract formation than those with normal sugar metabolism, most individuals with the disorder are apparently healthy. Like senile macular degeneration, cataracts are usually associated with aging. However, certain hereditary conditions, maternal infection with German measles, or herpes during pregnancy can result in cataracts early in life.

In contrast with glaucoma, where early diagnosis and immediate treatment are necessary to prevent blindness, it is *usually the patient who decides if and when a cataract is to be removed.* And when it is, vision is restored. I am so often told, "My eye doctor wants me to have my cataract surgery as soon as possible. I don't know whether I should or not." Anyone in that kind of quandary probably doesn't need surgery. A "ripe" cataract means it is *ready* to be removed, not that it *needs* to be. If your vision is adequate *as far as you're concerned,* waiting won't usually do you any harm. Of course, if you're an airline pilot and want to continue flying, that's a different story.

Cataract surgery involves removing and replacing the diseased lens. The kind of substitute you get is very important. Remember the days when so many of the elderly among us stumbled around looking like owls after cataract surgery? In place of the diseased lens that had been removed, they wore thick eyeglasses, which caused a great deal of distortion. One rarely sees such glasses anymore, because of several newer options. There are contact lenses that fit directly on the eye. The newest ones are gas-permeable and permit oxygen to pass through them to the cornea, allowing the eye to "breathe." However, some older persons may find it difficult to take the lens out and replace it every day or two. For them there are *extended-wear* gas-permeable lenses, which can be left in place for as long as three months, and then changed by either the patient or the doctor.

The most revolutionary advance in lens technology is the lens the

Giant Cell Arteritis

Among the elderly, giant cell arteritis is another important cause of blindness. I've seen enough of it in my own practice to justify telling you about it. This is how my last patient with this problem presented. She was sixty-seven years old and had been quite well all her life. About two weeks earlier, she had developed a low-grade fever accompanied by aches and pains throughout her body. She was sure it was just the flu. She began to have a headache, her muscles started to hurt and then her left temple area suddenly became sensitive to touch.

When I examined her, the only significant physical finding was diffuse muscular soreness. Blood tests, however, revealed evidence of anemia, not uncommon in ladies this age, and an unusually high sedimentation rate. (The sedimentation rate is a "nonspecific" test. Its elevation is an indication that something is wrong, but the test doesn't tell us what it is. It might be anything from a cold to cancer.) In any event, my diagnosis in this case was giant cell arteritis, an inflammation of the large arteries in the area of the temples. A biopsy is almost always necessary to confirm this diagnosis. Giant cell arteritis is a potentially serious disease, which if not treated correctly and quickly can lead to blindness. Therapy consists of high doses of steroids as soon as the diagnosis is made. Sometimes medication must be continued in maintenance doses for one or two years.

Other Eye Hazards

When we add up all the cases of blindness, only half are due to disease. The rest result from some accident at play, school, home or work. Nine times out of ten, the injury could have been prevented had appropriate safety practices been observed and protective eyewear used. There are 160,000 eye injuries each year in children between the ages of five and seventeen, two-thirds of which happen during unsupervised play. It's most likely to occur in a baseball game, as well as in football, basketball, or one of the racket sports like tennis, badminton or squash. Wearing protective eyewear or a helmet in any of these sports means you're smart, not a sissy.

Every Fourth of July, about 1,200 kids are brought to local emergency rooms because a firecracker exploded in or near an eye. Many of these children end up blind in that eye. Ophthalmologists in our emergency rooms remove BB shots from the eyes of more than six hundred children each year, and arrows, darts and slingshot pellets from yet another six hundred. These are the kinds of injuries that can and should be prevented by caring and careful teachers and parents. You're not being good to your children by giving them toys they're too young to handle. Warn them of the dangers of throwing a pencil or scissors or a paper clip at someone across the room.

Are you safer at home than you are at work or at play? Apparently not. Almost half the eye injuries in the United States happen right in your own bailiwick. Here's how: Suppose you're cleaning your oven, polishing some furniture, unclogging your drain or doing the laundry. If the chemical you're using gets into your eyes, it may injure them. Be particularly careful when the cleansing agent is in a pressurized can. Always look for the hole in the nozzle. Should you get a faceful of this stuff after pointing the can in the wrong direction, you not only have the contents themselves to worry about but also the force with which the substance hits your eye.

One of my patients enjoyed making furniture in a workshop in his basement. One day, he rubbed some glue on his finger into his eye. He very nearly lost it—the eye, that is, not the finger. Other patients have suffered eye injuries from flying sparks during welding, from splashed molten metal, solder, acids, splinters, metallic fragments, broken tools, flying nails and screws. So wear goggles whenever you're in your workshop. I'm a fuss-duddy, am I? Tell that to the thirty-five thousand people whose eyes are injured every year in their home workshops.

Is working in your garden safer than the workshop? Not much. Chips of wood from an ax or a chain saw, flying clippings from pruning a bush, a pebble flung into your eye by a lawn mower, can all injure your eyes, while toxic chemicals, pesticides, fertilizers or herbicides can burn them. I advise my patients always to wear goggles when gardening.

Industrial eye accidents are, of course, almost always preventable. All the available preventive measures are too numerous and varied for me to cover in this chapter. Suffice it to say that were the laws that already exist always observed, 90 percent of the industrial mishaps that cause blindness would never happen.

One of my patients visited me the other day in the dead of winter sporting a beautiful tan. "Been to Florida?" I asked.

"Are you kidding? With what my boss pays me?"

"How'd you get your tan?"

"Sunlamp, how else?"

"Wear goggles?"

"Naw, they leave me looking funny with a white rim under the eyes. That makes the whole tan look phony. No, I just shut my eyes."

That patient is a prime candidate for impaired vision. Sunlamps are not only poison for the skin, but anathema to the eyes.

Persons who wear contact lenses can damage their eyes too, if they're not adept at putting in the lenses. This is especially true in the elderly, whose coordination may be impaired. If you're not absolutely comfortable doing it yourself, either use regular glasses or ask your eye doctor for the newer gas-permeable extended-wear lenses, and have *him* remove and clean them for you every few weeks or months.

Incidentally, if some harmful substance (anything is harmful until proved otherwise) does get into your eyes, act immediately. *Do not rub your eyes.* Flush the affected eye continuously for fifteen minutes with water from a clean container. Then go to the nearest emergency room or to your own doctor's office, if he's in. Don't add insult to injury by using any "neutralizing" chemicals.

If a solid particle gets into your eye, lift the upper lid outward and bring it down over the lower lid, letting the tears wash the speck out. If that doesn't work, don't rub the eye. Keep it closed, put a light bandage over it and get to the nearest eye doctor or emergency room as quickly as you can.

Now that I've got you thinking, maybe a little worried and hopefully more careful about your precious vision, let's test your knowledge about some commonly given eye advice. Are the following statements true or false? You can find the answers after the last statement.

1. It's okay to look directly at the sun provided you wear dark sunglasses.
2. A cataract is a film over the eye, and the film can be peeled off with surgery.

3. The eyes should be cleaned regularly with eyewash.
4. Watching a bright television picture in a dimly lit room for long periods of time will harm your eyes.
5. People who wear glasses should be checked every year to see if they need new ones.
6. Cataracts can sometimes grow back after surgery.
7. Crossed eyes will likely correct themselves as the child grows older.
8. If your eyes are weak, you should rest them for long periods of time in order to strengthen them.
9. Older persons with poor vision should not use their eyes too much because that wears them out sooner.
10. Children who sit too close to the television set or hold their books too close when reading can harm their eyes.

The answer to every single one of these ten statements is false. Following is some elaboration on those answers.

1. It is dangerous to look directly at the sun, and dark glasses, though they may help with the glare, offer very little protection against the harmful ultraviolet rays that damage the retina and may ultimately blind you.
2. A cataract is not a growth or a film that can be peeled off. It's a clouding of the lens, which must be entirely removed and replaced with special glasses, contact lenses or an implanted lens.
3. Don't waste your money on eyewashes. Nature has provided us with enough fluid to keep our eyes as moist as necessary. (There are some diseases, however, associated with a marked decrease in tear formation. Such patients require special treatment, not eyewashes.)
4. The eye is never harmed by the way the light enters it. Although you may not be comfortable watching TV with such contrast, it does you no harm to do so. But suit yourself.
5. This one may surprise you. I've said earlier that everyone over thirty-five years of age should have his or her eyes checked at least every two years to detect glaucoma. But if you're comfortable with your glasses, there's no need to be examined for new ones. Unlike shoes, glasses don't wear out. If your refraction has changed, you'll know it soon enough. That's the time to see your ophthalmologist.
6. A lens, like an appendix, uterus or gallbladder, once removed, never grows back.

7. This is an important question—one you should know the answer to if you're the parent of a "cross-eyed" child, or one with "lazy" eyes. If truly crossed and left unattended, one eye will become blind. The images from two normally positioned eyes merge and fuse in the brain to give you one stereoscopic picture. When the brain is presented with images falling in different fields, the result is double vision, and one of the two images is suppressed. Unless the condition is corrected by special exercises or surgery, that portion of the brain that constantly suppresses an image will in time never be able to represent one properly.

8. You probably need glasses, not rest.

9. There is no truth to this old myth. Most organs of the body, including your eyes, are strengthened, not weakened, by use. Imagine the consequences of sitting around always resting your muscles, your heart or, for that matter, your brain. The eyes are no different.

10. You and your children should hold your reading material or choose a seat in relation to a movie or television screen at whatever distance is most comfortable for you. As long as you do that, you will not harm your eyes.

Preventing Deafness—Diet, Drugs, Decibels and Other Hazards

Helen Keller, who was herself both blind and deaf, once compared these two disabilities in the following way: "Blindness," she said, "separates man from things, but deafness separates man from man." There are about thirty-two million people with impaired hearing in this country, making this our most prevalent health disorder. Many individuals are either not aware of their hearing loss or won't admit it. A child who doesn't hear normally may mistakenly be labeled as having a "learning disability" or a "behavioral problem." Among the elderly, deafness can result in suspicion, paranoia, depression and withdrawal, simulating senility.

The ability to hear is the result of several complicated mechanisms that are set in motion by sound. The structures involved include the ear canal, which carries the noise to the eardrum. This vibrates in response, making three little bones behind the drum wiggle and oscillate. This movement stimulates the hair receptors in the inner ear, which then convey the impulse to special auditory nerves. These in turn relay it to specific areas of the brain, where it is finally interpreted as a meaningful message.

Deafness may be caused by trouble anywhere along the way. For example, your hearing may be affected if your ear canals are plugged with wax. Because chewing slows the formation and accumulation of ear wax, older persons with poor teeth who eat mainly soft or mushy food are especially likely to accumulate wax in their external canals. Deafness may result when the eardrum loses some of its ability to vibrate because of previous infection, when ear ossicles (bones) fuse so that they can no longer move in response to such vibration, when nerves that convey the sound to the brain are damaged, or when the brain itself has been injured.

Loss of hearing may be temporary (for instance, from blowing your nose too vigorously when you have a cold) or permanent (as when nerves going from the ear to the brain are affected by some toxic agent like the antibiotic streptomycin). It may be sudden (someone discharging a pistol near your ear) or gradual (because you love to go shooting and fire your shotgun too close to your ear too often), congenital (because your mother developed German measles when she was pregnant) or acquired (from the noise in your job as a riveter).

One of the most common, important and *preventable* forms of hearing loss is *nerve deafness,* or presbycusis. By age fifty-five, one person in four no longer hears normally. The high-pitched tones go first, followed by a loss in low-frequency perception. There is difficulty hearing women's voices, the sounds of music are less rich and full, one cannot discriminate among high-frequency consonants like *s, f, ch, th, sh,* especially when they're followed by high-frequency vowels like *ee.*

You can often identify this problem in others, although you won't always admit it in your own case. Where others are concerned, their speech is apt to be indistinct or unnecessarily loud; they always turn up the volume to hear the TV, car radio, or hi-fi; they frequently don't get the point of a joke that breaks up everyone else; they ask "What?" much too often; they smile inappropriately during a conversation, especially at noisy cocktail parties; and they seem to watch your lips unusually intently as you speak with them.

Unlike other causes of deafness in which surgery is often curative, there is, presently, no really effective treatment for nerve deafness.

Hearing aids help a little, but are often more trouble than they're worth. They are, however, becoming smaller and less obvious. (Some now fit snugly in the ear canal and are barely visible, so that only your hairdresser knows for sure.) And what with President Reagan's disclosure that he wears one, they have won increasing public acceptance. I can't resist telling you the story of one man who was telling a friend how well his hearing device worked. "I'm sorry I was so vain so long," he said. "I should have worn one of these years ago, even when they were obvious. I mean, so what? Who cares? It's fantastic what I can hear now. To think what I've missed all these years. Look how small this hearing aid is. You can't really see it, can you?"

"No," said his friend, "not really. What kind is it?"

"Sixty-thirty," he replied, looking at his watch.

The answer to nerve deafness lies in prevention. We used to think that decreased auditory acuity was an inevitable consequence of aging. It is to some extent, but it can be minimized and delayed. The key to doing that lies in the three D's—diet, drugs and decibels.

Diet: The Mabaans, a primitive tribe only recently "discovered" in southeast Sudan, retain normal hearing well into old age, and for several reasons. They live in a quiet environment, certainly by our standards; their blood pressure is lower; and their diet, unlike ours, contains very little saturated fat.

We tend to think of saturated fats, found in marbled steaks, butter, egg yolks, dairy products and certain shellfish, as conducive to arteriosclerosis and, more recently, to certain forms of cancer. But researchers in the field of hearing are now convinced that a high-fat diet also accelerates the development of nerve deafness. Dr. Samuel Rosen, an old friend who died recently, was one of America's most distinguished authorities on diseases of the ear. He evaluated the possible impact of environmental factors on hearing in many different countries and cultures. In one study conducted in Finland (where the diet is very rich in saturated fats), he was able to correlate hearing acuity with blood fat levels. The more fat there was in the blood, the less good the hearing. He also demonstrated that when the intake of saturated fat was reduced, there was a measurable improvement in hearing. Similar reversibility has been shown in other studies in this country. Given the now apparent cardiac benefits of lowering fat, it seems reasonable to recommend the same diet to reduce the risk of deafness as well.

Drugs That Can Make You Deaf: A wide variety of drugs, including some very commonly used ones, are potentially "ototoxic." (Three of every thousand hospitalized patients suffer some temporary hearing loss because of a drug they've been given. Years ago, one of my hospital patients was a teen-age girl with cardiac problems. We were giving her several medications to strengthen her heart and keep it beating regularly. One morning, on rounds, I asked her how she was feeling. She looked uncertain. "What? I can't hear you with all this construction going on outside. It really shouldn't be allowed during the night near a hospital. I haven't slept a wink." I agreed with her in principle, except I couldn't hear any of the hammering or pounding of which she complained. Just to be sure I looked out the window: the courtyard was empty. The noise this girl heard, as well as her deafness, were quite literally all in her head—from the quinidine she was taking for her heart. When we stopped the drug, her symptoms cleared up. She happened to be lucky, because her problem was reversible, and she drew immediate attention to it. But in other circumstances, drug-induced deafness is insidious, progressive, often unrecognized and occasionally permanent.

I have known patients who lost their hearing, usually temporarily, but sometimes permanently, after taking aspirin. That happens in eleven cases per thousand. Several different antibiotics may induce hearing loss, the most important of which are streptomycin (six per thousand), neomycin (widely used to reduce elevated cholesterol levels—twelve per thousand), kanamycin (sixteen per thousand) and gentamicin (twelve per thousand). In rare cases, ampicillin, chloramphenicol, polymyxin-E, vancomycin and viomycin will also do it. Ototoxicity may be induced too by diuretics like ethacrynic acid (twelve per thousand) and occasionally the very widely used furosemide (Lasix). The quinine you take at night for your leg cramps or in your tonic water with your gin, and the quinidine I gave the young lady for her heart may also be responsible (three per thousand). Finally, some of the newer nonsteroidal anti-inflammatory drugs prescribed in the treatment of arthritis, drugs such as indomethacin (Indocin) and Nalfon, can result in hearing loss too.

So if you're taking any medicine for whatever reason, and you've noticed a change in your hearing, or if you've become aware of a buzzing, ringing, pounding, whistling or roaring noise in your head, ask your doctor about the possible ototoxicity of any of the medication he has prescribed for you, particularly if you're over sixty years of age and/or have some kidney problem. And don't forget to check out whatever over-the-counter drugs you happen to be taking as well.

Decibels: With all due respect to diet and drugs, the most important cause of nerve deafness in our society is noise. Each and every one of us is exposed almost every day, for varying periods of time, to noise levels hazardous to our health. While the hearing apparatus bears the brunt of the punishment, noise pollution affects the body generally.

We are conditioned to respond defensively to certain stimuli. When a loud, unexpected noise results in fright, certain natural defense mechanisms, involving hormonal and chemical responses, are called into play. When the threat is over, the physiological responses end too, and the "startled" feeling disappears. But if the threat (or noise) becomes chronic, so do these responses. The consequences of a persistent or frequently recurring alarm mechanism such as loud noise are elevated blood pressure, an increased heart rate, muscle spasm and vulnerability to certain diseases, including deafness. Whether these consequences are mild or severe, transient or permanent, depends on the intensity of the sound, as well as how long and how often you are exposed to it. The Environmental Protection Agency (EPA) estimates that about half of us are subjected to a level of noise that has untoward effects. Nor do you need a decibel meter to know when that's happening. If you must raise your voice to be heard above the background noise, that's *too* loud.

I avoid the New York subway system whenever possible—not only because of the crime, filth, derailments and breakdowns of the equipment, but because while standing on the platform I become dizzy at the sound of an approaching train, especially when it's coming around a curve. (Trains in the underground transit systems in London, Paris, Montreal and Moscow are fitted with rubber wheels in order to eliminate that loud screech.) There are countless other sources of harmful "deafening" noise in our environment—airplanes (persons over seventy-five living within two miles of the Los Angeles airport were found to have higher blood pressure and more incidence of stroke than age-matched controls whose homes were situated farther away from the airport); jackhammers; and occupational noises.

Among those at risk are riveters, rock musicians, punch-press operators, traffic policemen, soldiers—especially those in the artillery—airport employees, particularly those working on the tarmac, and many, many more. Unless they wear ear coverings to protect themselves, these individuals are likely to become deaf. The human hearing apparatus was simply not designed to withstand the noises of "civilization."

So what is safe? The Occupational Safety and Health Administration (OSHA) says exposure to 85 to 90 decibels (dB) for eight hours per day is not harmful; 115 dB are safe for only fifteen minutes. All of us can probably tolerate constant exposure to about 80 dB, the threshold of hearing being zero. Here is the number of decibels generated by some everyday phenomena:

A quiet whisper	25 dB
Driving in an open convertible on a highway	95 dB
Conversational speech	60 dB
Roar of a motorcycle	90–100 dB
Power mower	106 dB
Disco	100–140 dB
Jet engine overhead at 100 feet	140 dB
Food blender	93 dB
Live rock concert	90–130 dB
New York subway train rounding a curve (the noise that makes me dizzy)	104 dB

If you cannot avoid these noises because they're part of your job, earplugs or earmuffs will reduce their intensity by 25 dB and bring most of them into the safe range (less than 90 dB).

But we are gluttons for noise punishment. We deliberately subject ourselves to what *is* avoidable. How many people, young and old, spend hour after hour listening to portable radios or tape recorders, often through earphones, to noise as loud as 130 dB? I can't remember going to a large public dinner or wedding party without being exposed to an almost painful din from amplified music, either live or canned. Our kids with their cap pistols, firecrackers, stereo sets and passion for discos are insuring the onset of nerve deafness much earlier in life than did preceding generations. A campaign to educate the public about the dangers of noise, its avoidance and the proper measures to reduce its intensity is the most important action we can take to prevent or delay deafness—and probably strokes and heart attacks as well.

One recent gadget, the cordless telephone, poses potential hearing problems too. The ring of a normal phone stops when you take the receiver off the hook. But a cordless phone continues to ring or chortle when you raise it to your ear unless you first flip a switch. Since the bell is situated in the earpiece, deafness is being reported, especially in children, who put the ringing phone close to their ears. The problem is of such magnitude that the U.S. Consumer Product Safety Division has issued an alert on portable phones. Keep them out of the hands of children and learn how to use them yourself.

Tobacco: It's interesting that the major risk factors for heart disease (increased blood pressure, abnormal blood fats, and cigarettes) have all been implicated, in one way or another, with hearing loss. In one study comparing auditory acuity among 150 smokers and 150 nonsmokers, 83 percent of the latter had normal hearing as compared to only 30 percent of smokers. So I give the same advice to the hard of hearing as I do to my patients with heart disease, stroke or blocked arteries in the legs: Don't start smoking in the first place. And if you have started, it's never too late to stop.

Flying: Changes in atmospheric pressure in airplanes can impair your hearing, especially if you fly when you have a cold. The problem is usually mild and temporary, but can occasionally be severe and permanent. In order to prevent this complication: (1) don't fly when you have an upper-respiratory infection or when your nose is running or stopped up; (2) if you must fly under these circumstances, take a nasal decongestant, preferably in the form of nose drops, a half hour before taking off and a half hour before landing; (3) swallowing, or chewing gum, can minimize the adverse effects of the changing pressure on your ears as the plane loses altitude. So don't sleep when the plane is in descent—this is especially important for infants.

Deafness is the end result of a wide variety of causative agents, operative from fetal life through senescence. Contaminants in our environment—what we eat, the pills we take, the kind of work we do, the type of recreation we prefer, the sounds we seek out for our pleasure or to which we are exposed at work—all have an impact on the fragile hearing mechanism. Identifying those that are preventable

—the atherogenic diet, specific medications, and a host of noise pollutants whose impact can be modified by either avoidance or the wearing of protective ear coverings—can effectively reduce the growing incidence of deafness.

CHAPTER **20**

Preventing Stroke—We Must Be Doing Something Right

A stroke is not a heart attack, as some people think. The term refers to damage to a part of the brain. Any process that interferes with or cuts off the blood supply to the brain can result in a stroke. Nervous tissue is very sensitive and requires constant nourishment, which is provided by a network of arteries that course over the surface of the brain and penetrate deep into its interior. All kinds of things can go wrong with this vascular network. How a stroke manifests itself— whether in paralysis, loss of speech, blindness, coma or even death —depends on what caused the attack in the first place, the particular area of the brain involved and how much tissue was injured.

Clot Formation in the Arteries of the Brain

Thrombosis, or the clotting of an artery due to arteriosclerosis, is popularly referred to as "rusting of the (vascular) pipes." When this process takes place in the heart, it causes a "coronary" (heart attack). In the legs, it gives pain from walking. When it strikes the eyes, blindness may result; in the kidneys, there is retention of the body's waste products—and so on through every organ and tissue. In the brain, thrombosis causes stroke.

In most cases of stroke you usually don't know what hit you. Warning signs occur in less than a quarter of the cases, and are called "transient ischemic attacks" (TIAs). They are characterized by short-lived numbness of a limb, weakness, slurring of speech, or double vision. Usually, however, a patient will say, "There I was watching TV"—(or talking to my wife or husband or having dinner) —"when I suddenly developed a headache. It lasted for an hour or two, and then I couldn't move my right arm"—(or my left leg, or talk, or hold my fork)—"I was perfectly healthy until that very moment." Of course, such individuals weren't really "perfectly healthy"—they only thought they were. If for some reason we had done any of the tests available to evaluate the cerebral circulation, we would have found evidence of vessel narrowing somewhere in the arterial circulation of the brain.

If the artery involved by the thrombosis is small, or is only a twig of a larger vessel, the area of brain damaged is also small. In these circumstances, recovery is likely to be early and complete. But the larger the artery, the more serious the symptoms and the greater the risk of permanent disability or death.

When Brain Arteries Burst

A stroke may also occur when one of the arteries in the brain suddenly bursts (instead of closing up gradually or "thrombosing"). Such rupture usually takes place after years of untreated hypertension. The constant, unremitting pounding of the blood under increased pressure against the walls of arteries everywhere in the body, including the brain, gradually weakens them. At some point, one of these vessels may suddenly burst. When this happens in the brain, the symptoms are instantaneous, as blood pours into the surrounding tissue from the torn vessel (unlike the warning headache that precedes the "thrombosis" stroke by several hours). Whether the patient lives or dies, and the quality of life if he or she survives, will depend on the size and location of the vessel that ruptured.

Brain arteries can burst even in persons with normal blood pressure but who were born with a congenital weakness of the wall of an artery. The rupture is associated with the sudden onset of a terrible headache, paralysis and often death. Occasionally, however, premonitory symptoms permit the diagnosis to be made before the blow-out occurs. In such cases, emergency surgery may be life-saving—as happened in the following case.

A married woman in her early thirties was referred to me for evaluation of a heart murmur that had been detected by her family doctor. The findings in my exam and in the corroborating echocardiogram indicated the presence of a mitral valve prolapse. This is a malfunction of the leaflets of the mitral valve in the left side of the heart (as discussed in Chapter 9). In a great majority of cases, it does not in any way limit or interfere with one's life-style.

Some months later, her doctor called to tell me that she had developed a severe headache in the preceding two weeks. He thought it was probably a migraine (frequently associated with mitral valve prolapse) but asked if I would see her. When I did, what she described was in no way suggestive of migraine headache. There was no "aura," or constellation of symptoms that usually precedes a migraine. The headache was not one-sided as it normally is in migraine; there were none of the accompanying visual disturbances, and there was no nausea or vomiting. Also, migraine associated with mitral valve prolapse normally starts much earlier in life, in the teens. This patient's headache was blinding, involving her entire head, and though it had waxed and waned somewhat over the previous two weeks, it had never really abated.

When I examined her, she impressed me as looking a lot sicker than someone with migraine. When I asked her to put her chin to her chest while lying on her back, she was unable to do so because of the pain it caused. This evidence of meningeal irritation (the meninges are the thin covering of the brain) is due either to infection or hemorrhage within the brain.

I rushed the patient to a hospital, where she was immediately examined by a neurologist. The appropriate tests indicated that she was bleeding into her brain tissue. Fortunately, it was not a massive hemorrhage, but rather an oozing leak from a cerebral blood vessel. Left unattended, she probably would have died. But we were fortunate in that there was still time to operate and repair the congenital aneurysm, or weakening of the wall of one of her brain arteries—and her life was saved. (The mitral valve prolapse was a red herring.)

Clots on the Move

There are still other causes of stroke. A cerebral artery may become obstructed by a blood clot originating elsewhere in the circulation. Here too, the outlook depends on the size of the artery in which the clot (embolism) lodges. A large clot in a major vessel spells disaster. But when the fragment is tiny, and the brain vessel in which it ends up is small, the neurological symptoms produced are minimal and clear up after a few days. However, this event serves as a warning that more clots may be on the way. Incidentally, such emboli always travel within arteries. You need never worry about getting a brain embolism from a clot in the varicose veins of your leg. These go to your lungs, not your brain.

Emboli to the brain can originate in several different locations as a result of a variety of conditions. For example, a heart previously damaged by rheumatic fever may develop a chronic irregularity of rhythm called atrial fibrillation. When this happens, clots may form within the enlarged left atrium. (That's the small chamber sitting atop the left ventricle, the main pump of the heart.) When a piece of this clot makes its way into the left ventricle and out into the circulation, it can lodge virtually anywhere in the body—in the eye, causing blindness; in the spleen, giving pain; in the kidneys, damaging that organ; or in the brain, producing a stroke. As you will see below, such embolization can often be prevented by the long-term administration of anticoagulants.

These days, surgeons have become expert at replacing congenitally deformed heart valves or those damaged by rheumatic fever. The sick valve, one that either doesn't open all the way or that leaks after it's supposed to have closed tight, is cut away, and a substitute "prosthetic" valve is inserted. Most such artificial valves are made of metal or plastic. Some, however, consist of tissue obtained from other species, the best example of which is the porcine valve. The former are called heterograft valves; the latter, homografts. These valves function well, and are lifesaving—opening and closing as they're supposed to. But bits and pieces of the solid constituents of the blood can attach themselves to various portions of the artificial valves, especially the heterografts, and later break off, lodging in the brain and causing a stroke. Again, proper anticoagulation is highly (though not completely) effective.

Embolism to the brain can occur under other circumstances, also preventable, as this next case illustrates.

Martin F. was a seventy-year-old man who loved to tell anyone who would listen that he played hard, worked hard and loved good food. "I've never been sick a day in my life" was his favorite expression. The only time he visited me was to get some shots before his yearly trip abroad or to be examined for a life insurance policy. This particular June he and his young second wife were leaving for Europe. They made no bones about it—they planned to eat their way through France.

So off they went on Air France—"where I can begin to get into my French mood"—expecting nothing worse from this entire trip than a few additional pounds. I'll get right to the point of this story. Six days after nonstop eating and drinking, Martin had a heart attack.

He spent two weeks in a hospital in Nice, and a few days later flew home.

Shortly after he arrived back in the United States, he called my office for an appointment and brought with him all the electrocardiograms and lab data obtained in France. He told me he'd had recurrent chest pains and pressure for several days before consulting a doctor. Although he had survived, I found that the damage to his heart was considerable. (As soon as the diagnosis of a heart attack is made, everything is done to limit the amount of cardiac muscle destroyed. That includes reducing the demands on the heart by restricting physical activity, giving supplemental oxygen and appropriate drugs, none of which Martin had received at the time he needed them most. He had made it through his heart attack all right, but the portion of heart muscle that was damaged was now very thin, and ballooned out every time his heart contracted.)

I didn't see Martin again for four months. He kept canceling his appointments. "I'm fine. The attack was a fluke. I must be very strong to have survived it without treatment."

At six o'clock one morning, I received a hysterical call from Martin's wife. "Doctor, I can't wake him. I think he's dead." Sadly, she was right. I wondered about the cause of death: Could it have been a sudden disturbance of heart rhythm, which sometimes occurs weeks and months after a substantial heart attack? Had the cardiac aneurysm that he had developed burst, causing instantaneous death? Or had Martin simply had another heart attack, this one massive and instantly fatal? It was none of these. The medical examiner requested a postmortem examination, and the cause of death turned out to be a massive stroke. A blood clot had formed within the damaged sac, or aneurysm, that had resulted from the heart attack. Because that portion of cardiac muscle doesn't contract normally, blood swirls around within it and doesn't get squeezed out as it should, permitting clot formation in this chamber. This clot is friable, and in Martin's case, a small piece of it broke off, was pumped out of the heart, made its way into the carotid artery on the left and lodged there, cutting off the blood supply to the brain. The result? A massive, sudden stroke and death. You'll see in a moment how that could have been prevented.

So emboli, or traveling clots, which can cause a stroke, may originate within the heart in certain patients who have had a previous coronary. Actually it's not even necessary for an aneurysm to have formed, although it's more likely to happen when it does. Even in an uncomplicated myocardial infarction, clots can form within the heart cavity, break off and lodge in the brain.

Another subtle, treacherous, often unrecognized condition can also result in a stroke. This is how it happened in one of my patients. He was a sixty-four-year-old man who had had mild high blood pressure for years, but who had it under very good control. He suddenly went blind in one eye. By suddenly, I mean, there he was, reading a newspaper one moment, and the very next, the top half of his visual field was completely obliterated. He had occluded a blood vessel behind one eye. The last time he had been examined was about two years earlier, when I had found nothing to indicate that he was a candidate for that kind of trouble. But now, when I listened to his neck with my stethoscope, I could hear what we call a "bruit," the French word for "noise," over the large carotid arteries coursing up each side of his neck. Also, when I felt for the pulse in these same carotids, it was somewhat reduced in volume. What to do about such a finding in someone who has no symptoms has always been a source of disagreement among doctors. Over the years, they have been split down the middle in terms of whether or not to intervene surgically. Most neurologists have generally taken the position that as long as the patient feels well and has no neurological symptoms, the best course of action is medication, not surgery. By contrast, neurosurgeons and vascular surgeons usually recommend reaming out the affected artery, since the noise one hears over it is due to blood flowing across a narrowed portion of the vessel. They contend that the plaque that reduces the flow can fragment, sending little pieces upstream to various parts of the brain, and thus cause a stroke. They believe that if the patient can tolerate an operation, he should have one. These days, you see, we don't have to guess about the plaque, where it is situated, or how big it is. Using techniques that are simple, safe and painless, we can obtain this information with great precision. These procedures include a CT scan or a Doppler device that records the velocity of flow across a vessel. The latter enables us to calculate the caliber of the artery at any given location. The location and magnitude of the blockage in the artery can further be established by injecting a dye, not into the arteries of the neck, as we used to do some years ago, but into a vein (a procedure called digital intravenous angiography, or DIVA). This dye ends up in the involved arteries, permitting them to be visualized. Had my patient come to see me in the past two years, and had I heard this bruit, I would have worked him up to see whether he needed this operation, or whether anticoagulants might have sufficed. In either event, we may well have reduced the risk of the stroke.

I decided to see even at this late date whether there was anything we still could do surgically to prevent another embolism elsewhere in his brain. While we were arranging for the various tests, I prescribed daily aspirin. We then did the Doppler and DIVA studies, which showed major narrowing of both carotid arteries at points the surgeon could easily reach. It was clear, both from the location and size of these plaques, that this man was at great risk for a sudden, massive stroke. He underwent surgery without complications and remains well, except for the partial blindness in his left eye.

This experience highlights the fact that important vascular disease can be present in the blood supply to the brain and that the disaster of a stroke can be prevented by routine examination, early diagnosis and effective intervention, medical or surgical.

How the Heart Can Affect the Brain

Finally, stroke can occur in the elderly in another set of circumstances without clots, without hemorrhage and without an embolus. Remember that the brain needs a constant supply of blood to carry on its sensitive functions. That supply can be reduced below a critical level if the heart fails, even briefly, to pump enough blood. That is most apt to happen in an older individual who experiences a sudden disturbance of cardiac rhythm, that is, the heart beats either very quickly or much too slowly. In either event, the amount of blood it ejects during that time is drastically reduced, causing a transient "mini" (or not so mini) stroke. That's why when a patient comes in with a recent "strokelet," TIA (transient ischemic attack) or any temporary neurological event, we always (1) do a complete neurological exam, (2) listen to the neck arteries for bruits, (3) get a CT scan of the brain to see if any and/or how much tissue has been damaged, (4) record an echocardiogram, looking for any "vegetations" that might have broken off a heart valve and traveled to the brain, and (5) record an electrocardiogram for evidence of a recent heart attack or rhythm disturbance. If the latter is normal, we (6) usually get a twenty-four–hour Holter, or ambulatory, tracing, looking for bursts of irregular heart action that may have been responsible for the symptoms. When such an arrhythmia is found, there are medications with which to prevent its recurrence.

How to Prevent Strokes

Now that you know the bad news, that is, how strokes can happen, here's the good news—how to prevent them. You will have noticed that the subtitle of this chapter is "We Must Be Doing Something Right." I added that because the incidence of stroke has been decreasing dramatically here and in many other countries for the past thirty-five years (except in Japan, where it is the number-one cause of death, presumably because of the high salt content of the diet). And the downward trend continues.

There are several explanations for this good news. Most doctors think it's the result of looking for, finding and treating high blood pressure. Another theory holds that it is due to the decreased salt intake resulting from the more widespread use of refrigerators, salt no longer being used so frequently as a preservative. It has even been suggested that the drop in stroke deaths stems from the increased consumption of vitamin C and riboflavin found in the fruits and vegetables we are eating in greater amounts.

Despite the decline, however, 400,000 strokes still take place every year in this country, and 200,000 of them are fatal. Two million Americans have survived strokes, some of them not very happily.

Preventing Strokes Due to Thrombosis

How to prevent thrombosis is discussed more fully in the section on heart attacks. The most important intervention, in my opinion, is cessation of cigarette smoking. If you are particularly worried about stroke because so many of your blood relatives have had one, then the best thing you can do to protect yourself is to stop smoking. On April 12, 1960, I learned a lesson that caused me immediately to get rid of my cigarettes, and never to resume smoking. My wife and I were demonstrating a radiotelemetered electrocardiogram, which, in those days, was quite new. The prototype we used was one that had been developed by NASA and affixed to monkeys going into orbit. This device made possible the transmission of the electrocardiogram from outer space to radio receivers in Houston. I was particularly interested in radiotelemetry to monitor patients who had had heart attacks, and also to permit us to perform an electrocardiographic stress test with the patient unattached to an ECG machine. So there we were in a large auditorium. My wife was at the receiver while I walked around several hundred feet away wearing my ECG radio transmitter—and smoking a cigarette. At one point, some of the doctors attending the meeting stopped by the oscilloscope screen and drew my wife's attention to the fact that there, clearly visible, were a large number of "extra beats."

"Who's your subject?" they asked her.

"My husband," she said.

"Really? Is he sick?"

"No, he isn't." She found me and brought me back to the base station to look at the premature contractions in my tracing. They occurred every time I inhaled my cigarette.

At the booth next to ours was another doctor who was interested in evaluating circulation in the extremities. He had developed a small cuff that fit over a finger and that was able to estimate the amount of blood flowing within the tiny vessels supplying the fingertips. He suggested that we determine the impact of the tobacco on the digital blood flow. So he applied his little cuff around my index finger, obtained a base-line measurement and then had me inhale deeply. When

I did, the volume of blood in my finger dropped dramatically. "That decrease of blood in your fingers," my colleague told me, "is happening in your heart, in your brain, and everywhere blood flows in your body." That was enough for me. The extra beats, together with the evidence of decreased circulation every time I took a puff, convinced me to remove the fresh pack of cigarettes from my shirt pocket and throw it into the wastebasket. I have not smoked a cigarette since.

A word about diet, discussed in greater detail in Chapter 17. I have long advised my patients, especially those with high cholesterol levels, to reduce their intake of cholesterol and total fat. Recent data strongly suggest that whether or not you already have evidence of arteriosclerosis (a heart attack, stroke, etc.), effective lowering of cholesterol by diet and/or medication does reduce the chances of your suffering some kind of vascular event—including a cerebral thrombosis.

I advocate "ideal weight" and "plenty of exercise" because they make you look better and feel better. I suspect that they really do retard the process of arteriosclerosis, although there are no hard data to prove it.

If your blood pressure is high, it must be lowered—by diet (decreased salt, increased calcium, increased potassium) and decreased weight; other nonpharmacological techniques (relaxation and meditation, biofeedback); and if all else fails, drugs.

Supposing, then, that you've lived the good life with respect to preventing thrombosis, and it hasn't worked. One day, for no apparent reason, you find your speech garbled. As you look at yourself in the mirror, your mouth is drooping to one side, and when you stick your tongue out, it too falls over. You consult your doctor, who confirms the diagnosis of stroke. Your symptoms last three or four days, then more or less clear up. I say "more or less" because, even though you can move your hands and feet normally and no stranger would know anything had happened to you, your handwriting remains a bit shaky, and you don't quite look or feel yourself. But you're grateful that what we call the "residua" of your stroke are minimal. Your main concern now is to prevent a recurrence. What are you going to do? Well, first, you'll redouble your commitment to controlling your risk factors. If you had previously compromised by merely cutting down on your cigarettes or switching to a pipe or cigars, you'll eschew tobacco in all amounts and forms.

What about anticoagulants? Will thinning your blood *after* a stroke help prevent another one? Most neurologists do not think so. Once a particular blood vessel has closed, that's that. The symptoms have run their course, and although it may take months before you will know the extent of your impairment, if any, the stroke itself is over, finished, done with.

In contrast, the TIA, or transient ischemic attack, in which symptoms last for only moments or hours, and then clear completely, is a warning that the worst is yet to come. The blood vessel is only partially closed. Most doctors feel that under these circumstances some kind of anticoagulation is justified.

But anticoagulants are themselves not without hazard. The biggest threat they pose is internal hemorrhage, especially if they've been taken in concert with other drugs that potentiate their blood-thinning action, or if you have a history of easy bleeding anywhere, or an ulcer, or have high blood pressure.

So what I advise my own patients who have had a TIA is to take the anticoagulant warfarin for three or four months, then switch to aspirin in small doses, an 80-mg. tablet (baby aspirin) every day. (See Chapter 14 for more on the effects of warfarin and aspirin.) I have them continue the aspirin indefinitely. One word of caution, however. Anyone with a TIA must also be evaluated for the possibility that surgically correctable plaques in a carotid artery are throwing off emboli.

Even if the stroke was a completed one, rather than a TIA, I still prescribe an aspirin a day in the event that one or more other arteries are diseased and may give trouble in the future.

You may also have heard of the use of dipyridamole, more popularly known as Persantine, its commercial name. "Aspirin and Persantine" are terms used together almost as frequently as "Mutt and Jeff" or "bread and butter." Both affect the "stickiness" of the blood by interfering with the function of platelets. Platelets are tiny elements in the blood responsible for one of several mechanisms of normal coagulation or clotting. Aspirin and dipyridamole interfere with this function, but in different ways. Most doctors continue to prescribe them together, even though there is no proof that adding the dipyridamole to the aspirin makes any difference. But the dipyridamole is particularly useful when a patient cannot tolerate aspirin for some reason (history of a bleeding ulcer, asthmatic attacks due to aspirin sensitivity) and needs anti-platelet therapy.

Treating High Blood Pressure to Prevent Brain Hemorrhage

Preventing stroke due to a cerebral hemorrhage is a matter of controlling high blood pressure. One reads from time to time in lay articles, and even in medical journals, that some elevation of pressure is "permissible" or "not dangerous"—that it may be left alone. In my own practice, I have seen too many patients with modest elevation like 170/95 who subsequently developed massive strokes due to brain hemorrhage after refusing to continue treatment because of side effects from the drugs used. While it's true that the higher the pressure, the greater is the risk, *mild to moderate elevation is not safe and should not be left untreated*. In my opinion, even borderline readings should almost always be normalized. In doing so, however, one should not start off with the most potent drugs in high dosage. Instead, this is what I recommend. First, make sure the hypertension is real, and that we're not dealing with "the white-coat syndrome." That's the phenomenon in which the pressure is elevated only in the doctor's office, but is perfectly normal the rest of the time. If you're told your pressure is high, have several readings done in different places at varying times of the day. There are now reliable automatic blood-pressure recording devices available that not only measure the blood pressure but print out the reading as well. Try one of these yourself, but make sure to check its accuracy against other models, including the one in your doctor's office.

If your pressure is indeed elevated in several readings, then it's time to act. Unless the readings are dangerously high, like greater than 200/110, hold off on the drugs for a while. If you are overweight, *cut down on your calories* (and alcohol) and *exercise* more. *Decrease your salt intake*. Make sure your *calcium consumption* is adequate. There is an inverse relationship between calcium and blood pressure. In other words, the lower the calcium, the higher the pressure. Dairy products rich in cholesterol and saturated fats are also full of calcium. So if you're trying to *lower your cholesterol level* by cutting down on your consumption of dairy products, you can supplement your calcium intake with tablets. *Potassium deficiency* has also been implicated in elevated blood pressure, so add some extra apricots, prunes, bananas and orange juice to your diet, especially if you are also taking water pills on a regular basis.

Stop smoking. In combination with increased blood pressure and raised cholesterol, tobacco is lethal to the vascular tree.

Try *biofeedback* and other *relaxation techniques*. They sometimes help.

Give yourself five or six weeks. If your pressure has not come down, it's time for medication. But don't start with the heavy artillery. I usually prescribe low doses of the mildest medications first. If there is no response, I then start a second, third or sometimes even a fourth drug—all in low doses. The stories you hear about the side effects of medication used in the control of high blood pressure, though probably exaggerated somewhat, are basically true. These agents can cause everything from dry mouth to utter fatigue, from bad dreams to reverse ejaculation (where the seminal fluid during orgasm goes back into the urinary bladder instead of out the penis), from intolerable frequency of urination to loss of sex drive and erectile capability. But most of these symptoms can be prevented by choosing the right drug for a particular patient and administering it in the lowest dosage necessary. It sometimes takes sophisticated testing and patience, but I know of not a single man or woman whose elevated pressure could not be effectively and tolerably controlled. It's important, however, that you not approach the treatment of your hypertension with fear and prejudice about drugs. A good deal of the side-effect phenomenon can be psychological. You'll be starting with two strikes against you and will strike out, particularly in the sex department, with the very first pill if you anticipate the worst.

Every doctor manages hypertension differently. I usually start either with captopril, a substance that neutralizes renin, responsible for many cases of high blood pressure, or a beta blocker (Lopressor, Tenormin, Inderal). Then, if necessary, I add Apresoline or a diuretic. Incidentally, of all the medications used in the treatment of hypertension, the ones I find least likely to cause potency problems in men and decrease of the sex drive in women are Apresoline (hydralazine), Minipress (prazosin) and Capoten (captopril). In my experience, agents like Aldomet and Aldactone are particularly bad in those respects.

Let's look at some of the other preventable causes of stroke described earlier. Remember Martin? After his unrecognized coronary, as a result of which he kept on going instead of receiving treatment, he developed a ventricular aneurysm. However, because of his built-in denial mechanisms, he broke his office appointments with me. Had he in fact kept them, I might well have detected that aneurysm, which is often not formed until several weeks after the heart attack. The diagnosis can be made on the clinical exam, it may be apparent in the electrocardiogram, the aneurysm is often visible on the chest X ray, and its presence can almost always be confirmed in the echocardiogram. We check all these parameters in patients who have had a heart attack. If the echocardiogram had indicated clot formation within the aneurysm, I would have prescribed anticoagulants to prevent the sudden fatal stroke Martin suffered.

The other causes of stroke, atrial fibrillation with or without valve disease, or clots or fragments breaking off a prosthetic valve, require long-term anticoagulation. With respect to atrial fibrillation, all the available data indicate that persons with this rhythm disorder should be anticoagulated regardless of its cause. We used to think that embolic strokes occurred only in those cases of atrial fibrillation associated with valve disease. That's not so. I now anticoagulate almost every one of my patients with chronic atrial fibrillation—everyone, that is, who will accept it. Unfortunately, some won't.

Most heterograft prosthetic heart valves using animal tissue do not require anticoagulants. I administer these agents for the first three months after surgery, then discontinue them. But to be doubly sure, I recommend aspirin over the long term.

In those patients whose strokes or TIAs are due to prolonged bursts of very rapid heart rates (including, but not necessarily limited to, atrial fibrillation) or periods of "heart block" (during which time the heart rate is so slow as to be inadequate to supply the brain), drugs are available for the first type, and a cardiac pacemaker is useful for the second.

This seems like a good place to end this chapter on prevention of stroke. But for those who have had one, and survived with residual paralysis, it is the beginning of a new kind of life. With the proper outlook and rehabilitation, many such patients can be *prevented* from ending their years as vegetables. I have so often seen return of virtually normal function despite problems with movement, coordination or speech. I have learned, in caring for and observing these individuals, that one can never predict the degree of recovery after a stroke. It depends very much upon the patient's will to live and determination to fight on. These are neither platitudes nor empty words. Ask anyone you know who's had a stroke, or for that matter, any doctor who has treated one. There are two keys to the successful return to living by the stroke victim, regardless of his or her disability. The first is a vigorous, optimistic and ongoing physical rehabilitation program supervised and/or prescribed by experts. The second and equally important aspect of treatment is antidepressant therapy. Practically every stroke patient has been psychologically devastated and depressed, and for good reason. Such depression is most acute in the first three or four months after the event. In my experience, positive psychological support, together with the liberal use of antidepressant drugs for as long as is necessary, can prevent the worst outcome of all—a living death for the unfortunate victim.

CHAPTER **21**

Herpes and Shingles—
Viral Birds of a Feather

One of my patients, a forty-year-old stockbroker, married, usually in good health, burst excitedly into my waiting room one day some months ago. "I must see the doctor right away!" he insisted. He had not phoned for an appointment ahead of time, the usual procedure in my practice except in an emergency. My receptionist knew him to be a staid, quiet, rather conservative type who kept his emotions to himself. This public agitation was very much out of character for him.

"The doctor is with a patient at the moment. He'll be another few minutes, but if you are in pain, or are short of breath, I'll call him right out."

"No," he said. "It's nothing like that—but it's still an emergency. Can you squeeze me in before he starts examining the next patient?"

A few minutes later, this very worried man was ushered into my office. He dispensed with the usual formalities. "Doc, I am in terrible, terrible trouble. I went to Boston a couple of weeks ago to attend an investment seminar. Blanche wouldn't come along. Too short a trip for her, and she doesn't like Boston anway. Look, I am not going to beat around the bush. There I was, alone in the hotel. The meetings had ended. I was at the bar relaxing with a drink when this nice-looking gal sat down next to me, and we got to talking. She was well dressed, really classy. It turns out that she was in town for only a couple of days. She said she was a buyer for a department store or something like that.

"I was such a damn fool. I knew nothing about her, and had no business even talking to her. Believe me, doc, I don't usually pick up strange women. I guess I had too much to drink. Anyway, she really seemed to like me. It was kind of exciting, you know, after all these years of married life. Not that I'm complaining about Blanche, or anything like that. Anyway, I fell for it hook, line and sinker. One thing led to another and—look, doc, I've got this wet little sore on my privates. I am sure it's herpes. It will never go away. They say 'herpes is forever.' My god, how will I explain it to Blanche? There goes my marriage. Doc, help me. Tell her I got it on a toilet seat, or from a towel in my hotel room. Tell her you see patients all the time who catch herpes from nonsexual contact. Doc, tell her anything, but please help me."

I could well appreciate his panic and anxiety, and I tried to calm him down. I assured him that there are many sexually transmitted diseases, as well as other causes of "cold sores," that have nothing to do with herpes.

In examining the "cold sore" on his penis, I noted that it was painless. That's unusual for herpes. Actually, it looked more like syphilis to me, but I couldn't be sure. I hadn't seen a case of primary syphilis for some time in my own practice. So I sent him right over to an infectious-disease specialist. I asked for a confirming dark-field illumination test, in which the spirochete, the organism that causes syphilis, can be looked for directly under a microscope. (The blood test for syphilis, the VDRL, might not be positive so early in the disease.) My colleague called back in a few minutes. Sure enough, this man had syphilis.

Now it was not so long ago that telling a patient that he or she had syphilis left them feeling guilty, ashamed and worried. All that has changed, what with herpes (and now AIDS) on the scene.

I gave my patient the news, fully prepared to support him emotionally. But it wasn't at all necessary. "Thank goodness," he said, "that it's only syphilis." And with a smile, his old self-confidence restored, he bent over to receive the first of his intramuscular penicillin shots.

"Some 'buyer' she was, eh, doc? Should have introduced herself as a seller, not a buyer!"

Why was my patient so relieved to find he had syphilis and not herpes? Because syphilis is treatable and curable, provided the correct diagnosis is made early enough and penicillin is given in appropriate dosage. Syphilis, untreated, remains potentially fatal. It can affect almost any organ in the body, but if it strikes the brain, it may cause insanity years later.

Our stockbroker friend was right: as of today, herpes *is* forever. Once you've been infected, you never know when the next attack will recur. And it has nothing to do with re-exposure. Even if you forswear sex for the rest of your life, and take ice-cold showers instead, you are still going to have recurrent herpes infections. That's because once the herpes virus gets into your body in the initial infection, it never leaves.

The usual clinical course goes something like this. First, you have sexual contact with someone who is infected. (Forget about toilet seats and all that nonsense. You can use those ploys in a desperate marital confrontation, but don't for a moment believe them yourself.) Several days later, you find a painful sore (or sores) where the virus entered your body—usually the genitals or rectum, depending on your particular sexual preferences. After ten to fourteen days of local discomfort, the skin lesions clear. But that's not the end of it. The virus that caused the infection now takes up residence elsewhere in your body. It makes its way from the skin up along a nerve fiber and travels to the nerve ganglion or cell body near the spinal cord where the fiber originates. There it remains for an unpredictable period of time—three weeks, four months, six months—there's no telling how long. Then, whenever the spirit moves it, or when you are under some kind of stress, become pregnant or have an infection somewhere, the virus retraces its steps along the nerve fiber, reappearing at the site where it entered in the first place. When it does so, the sores reappear. And so the virus goes, up and down, up and down—indefinitely.

In most cases, herpes is just a nuisance, a stigma and a social embarrassment. However, there are some exceptions. For example, it may cause meningitis, which can be life-threatening. In women, it may predispose to cancer of the cervix. That's why any female with herpes should have a Pap test at least once a year. And there is an almost 50 percent chance that giving birth while she has a vaginal herpes eruption in full bloom will infect her baby, for whom it can create a host of problems, ranging from blindness to death. As a matter of fact, even if the eruption is not obvious, but the mother is known to have been infected with herpes at some time in the past, the infant is still vulnerable to trouble. So if you become pregnant, and have herpes, either active or in remission, let your gynecologist know. He may advise a Cesarean section. If you're not sure whether that "cold sore" you had in the vaginal area some months ago was herpes, and have become pregnant in the meantime, there is a new test to diagnose this infection. It is accurate, and the results are available in only two days.

In persons whose resistance generally is poor—as for example, those with organ transplants receiving immune suppressants to prevent rejection, cancer patients on chemotherapy or homosexuals with Kaposi's sarcoma (the illness that often accompanies AIDS)—a herpes infection, instead of presenting as sores at the site of contact, can be disseminated throughout the body, with life-threatening consequences.

The herpes infection to which I have been referring is caused by the herpes simplex virus, of which there are two types, 1 and 2. Type 1, which is for the most part acquired "innocently," involves the mouth, eyes, lips and skin above the waist. Type 2 is the genital form. It strikes below the navel. But with so much variation in sexual activity these days, we are finding more 1's where 2's should be and vice versa. There is some evidence, for whatever small comfort it may provide, that when a type 1 infection hits below the belly button, it is not likely to be as severe as is a type 2. The recurrence rate for the type 1 is also much less than that for type 2.

There must be at least fifteen million people in the United States with genital herpes. There were 30,000 visits to doctors' offices for this disease in 1966, 260,000 in 1979, and these days 500,000 new cases are documented every year. So herpes *is* a real and increasing problem, not merely a matter of media hysteria.

Can it be prevented? What can be done to reduce the frequency of the recurrences and their severity? Also, are there any "measures" we are currently taking that represent a waste of time and money?

When Prevention Is Boring

If you want absolute prevention of herpes, a guarantee that you won't get it no matter what, there is only one course to follow—abstinence from sex. However, unlike absence, abstinence does not make the heart grow fonder, and it's neither widely acceptable nor realistic.

After abstinence, prudence is the best way to reduce your chances of getting herpes. Fear and temperance are companions. The current panic over herpes and AIDS has resulted in fewer cases of syphilis, gonorrhea and other sexually transmitted diseases, because "consenting adults" are now more discriminating in their choice of partners. But remember, you can't tell just by looking at someone whether he or she is infected, and few lovers are qualified or motivated, in the passion of a sexual embrace, to perform the appropriate physical exam. The disease can be transmitted even when lesions are not apparent. Also, if you have herpes, you are not necessarily safe from additional infection, as the following account dramatizes.

One of my patients, a forty-four-year-old man, had recently been divorced. His wife, for whom he still carried a torch, had left him for another man. In the midst of great emotional turmoil, he suddenly developed severe pressure behind his breastbone, began sweating profusely, and felt weak and nauseated. It was a heart attack. He was hospitalized, and recovered well physically, but was very depressed. When it was time to go home, he expressed considerable anxiety to me about his future. "I am a bachelor again now and I don't want to be alone forever. Do you think I'll ever be able to date, to lead a normal sex life and get married again?" His heart attack had actually been a minor one. I reassured him all would be well. Now where does herpes enter into all of this? It seems that he and his former wife both had the disease. So long as they lived together, there was no problem. But he was now worried that his "affliction," as he called it, would interfere with any relationship he might develop in the future. Being a decent sort, he had no wish to infect some unsuspecting young woman.

A few months after his heart attack (he had already returned to work and was feeling fine), he happened to be thumbing through a popular magazine when he came across a notice that in effect said, "Good-looking woman of 30, intelligent, etc., etc., *with herpes* seeks company of exciting but lonely man, etc., etc."—the message being "Why don't we two herpetics get together?" Since his infection had been preying on his mind, this ad interested him. He contacted the young woman who had advertised and they hit it off, at least to the extent that they were soon in bed together. Two weeks later, he developed an attack of herpes that was unusually severe for him. He was puzzled. Wasn't it okay for two people with herpes to have sex? Weren't you supposed to be immune to reinfection once you got the virus? The answer, I told him, is yes and no. Types 1 and 2 are actually different strains of the herpes simplex virus that can be distinguished one from the other only by sophisticated lab testing. Infection with one does not render you immune to the other. Furthermore, with all the sexual gymnastics these days, one never knows for sure whether genital herpes is the type 2 that belongs down there or a type 1 that has gone astray. Now, if you have type 1 herpes, and join a herpes club, then make contact with a type 2, you are in for a double whammy. That's probably what happened to our friend. Supposing he now has both types 1 and 2 under his belt, is he really as free as a bird and may he safely deal with anyone? Surprisingly, the answer is still no, because within each major type, 1 or 2, there are enough variations to make exposure to another person with herpes risky. So much, at least in my opinion, for the herpes clubs and dating services.

After abstinence and prudence, there is the condom. Among all the contraceptive devices and techniques available, a sheath, although it is far from foolproof, provides the greatest protection against genital infection. (However, it is not as effective against herpes as it is against gonorrhea.) If there is any question at all, especially during a casual encounter such as our friend in Boston enjoyed, a condom should always be used by the male and demanded by his female partner. Any woman who has had a herpes infection, and who cares about her mate, should use a contraceptive foam or a diaphragm with jelly when having sexual intercourse, even in the absence of herpetic sores. As mentioned earlier, a substantial number of women without obvious lesions do continue to shed the virus. Under these circumstances, the diaphragm with jelly and the contraceptive foam offer some protection to the male partner since they may kill the herpes virus.

There is a great deal of scientific activity directed at developing a vaccine that will protect against herpes, so that exposure will not lead to infection. At the time of writing, at least two such anti-herpes vaccines are in research.

Let's move along in our consideration of the natural history of the disease. Supposing you've gone and caught it! It's now too late for prevention. Our next objectives are to (1) try to minimize the severity of the infection; (2) shorten the period of viral shedding (that is, the duration of the sore); and (3) prevent or delay the otherwise inevitable recurrences. Your options are now greater than they were just a short time ago.

The most recent breakthrough in treatment, and to some extent prevention, is the availability of oral acyclovir. This drug, marketed as Zovirax in the United States, was initially introduced in intravenous form for use in severe, generalized infections. It was followed by the topical preparation and now can be taken by mouth. It's the best medication yet for herpes, and this is what it does.

In first infections, oral acyclovir will reduce the time the virus is actually present in the sores from nine days to two; the lesions will heal in twelve days rather than the average sixteen; you will experience discomfort for five days instead of the usual seven; after forty-eight hours your chances of developing new sores will decrease from 62 percent to 18 percent.

If you're an old-timer as far as your herpes is concerned, and have been suffering from recurrences, oral acyclovir can drop the likelihood of your having an attack within four months of your last one from 94 percent to 29 percent. What's more, any flare-up will be of shorter duration. But you've got to continue taking the drug. Once you stop, you're back to square one. Because this is a new medication, you'd better not continue it for more than six months until more data are available regarding its long-term safety. Also, if you're pregnant or nursing, do not take acyclovir.

If you decide to limit the use of acyclovir to the treatment of actual recurrences, take it at the very onset of symptoms. It will substantially cut the duration of viral shedding and the time it takes lesions to heal, and will reduce the tendency to form new sores. Always have some acyclovir on hand so that you can start it immediately. If you wait until you contact your doctor, especially on a weekend, and then have to go out to buy the drug, you will have lost forty-eight hours and the effect will not be nearly as great.

Acyclovir comes in 200-mg. capsules. The usual dosage is about five capsules per day. If you're taking it for an initial attack, you should continue it for ten days. That will cost you $30 or more, depending on your druggist's markup (he pays about $26). For treatment of recurrent attacks, you need the acyclovir for only five days. To prevent recurrences you will require anywhere from two to five capsules a day (most patients respond well to three). But remember, limit therapy to six months. I wouldn't embark on a prophylactic regimen unless your repeat attacks are really severe.

The drug itself is fairly well tolerated, although some patients do complain of headache, intestinal upset, dizziness and joint pains, all of which disappear when treatment is stopped.

Interferon is also being tested against herpes. Early reports suggest that it is useful for both the treatment and prevention of recurrences.

Because herpes is a chronic problem for which—until recently—there was no effective treatment, millions of sufferers the world over have been wasting effort, time and money on ineffective therapy. Here are some of the interventions that I suspect are useless: various vaccines—smallpox, BCG, polio and influenza, topically applied ether (which can be toxic), and chloroform. L-lysine, an amino acid taken orally, is very popular with some herpes patients, who have told me they "feel better" taking it and deny any side effects. However, I know of no scientifically documented benefit from this agent.

By the way, you might be interested in a follow-up on my stockbroker patient with syphilis. We cured him. Also his wife. It seems he didn't notice the wet little sore soon enough!

Shingles: Another Herpes Virus—Worlds Apart

For most people, the term "shingles" brings to mind a mild disease of the middle-aged or elderly, consisting of a rash and some fever, both of which clear up in a few days. And very often that's all there is to it. But in a substantial number of cases, shingles is a deadly, debilitating infection that can cause grief, chronic severe pain, blindness, deafness and even suicide.

I will never forget John R. He was a seventy-year-old stockbroker who had enjoyed good health all his life. He was active and productive in his work, and hadn't missed a day at the office in years. On one of his routine annual visits to me, I noticed the presence of a tremor, mostly in his right hand. The shaking was apparent when he just sat there. But when he began to use his hand—for example, to pick up a pencil—it almost disappeared. In short, this was a "resting tremor" (as opposed to an "intention tremor," one that occurs with purposeful movements). John's appearance also seemed to have changed since his checkup a year earlier. His usually crinkly, mobile face was now almost expressionless. These two findings—tremor and a masklike appearance—usually add up to Parkinson's disease.

John asked what the tremor meant and what we could do about it. I reassured him that it probably reflected a mild and not necessarily progressive form of Parkinson's disease. This all happened years ago, before the availability of L-dopa and its derivatives, and I prescribed what was available at the time. John and I could do nothing more than hope for the best, but the best didn't turn out to be so good. Not only did the tremor become worse, but his limbs became progressively more rigid, and he began to find walking difficult. The medication I had prescribed made his mouth dry and blurred his vision. But John was a remarkable man. He was determined to "overcome." He signed up for physiotherapy to help his spasm and bore the world no grudge because of his affliction. He was grateful that his mind was intact, and that he could continue to work at his job.

About two years later, John's son called at midnight to tell me that his father was experiencing severe chest pressure, was sweating profusely, felt very weak and looked ashen. My tentative diagnosis of an acute heart attack was confirmed thirty minutes later in the emergency room. The patient was admitted to the hospital, where, after treatment, his cardiac status improved within the hour. A few days later, his electrocardiogram stabilized and John was on his way to recovery. This second illness did not faze him either. He was confident he would recover and return to work, as had several of his partners who'd also had heart attacks. They seemed all right. Why shouldn't he be?

On the fifth hospital day, however, John developed a new symptom —one that had nothing to do with his heart attack. He complained of a burning sensation on the left side of his forehead and in his left eye. I examined him very carefully, and also arranged for an eye specialist to see him in consultation. Neither of us could determine the cause of his symptoms. The next day, the burning sensation was replaced by sharp, severe, shooting pains every few minutes, as if someone "was jabbing my face and eye with a hot poker." Again, there was nothing to see, either in his eye or on the skin of his forehead above it. But now, his temperature was slightly elevated, to 100°, and although (and because) there were no objective findings, we suspected John was developing shingles. We treated him with everything we thought might help—anesthetic eyedrops, large doses of B-12 by injection, various lotions with calamine and phenol, ice compresses —but nothing seemed to do much good. After five or six days of gradually increasing pain, the characteristic red pimply rash of shingles appeared on his forehead, and small ulcerations formed on the cornea of his eye.

John was now in agony most of the time and required narcotics for relief. I hated to introduce these addicting substances for a disorder that might become chronic, but I had no choice. His heart would not long withstand such severe suffering. Again, I reassured him that in most cases of shingles the pain lasts only a couple of weeks, although I forewarned him that his eye might be permanently scarred and his vision reduced. He was grateful for this favorable prognosis. He would carry on again, he said, so long as he could expect the pain to end at some point. Well, my predictions were only half right. He did become blind in that eye, but the sharp, shooting, agonizing spasms did not abate.

He left the hospital after two weeks, a physical and emotional shadow of his former self—not because of the Parkinson's disease or the heart attack, but from the unrelenting pain of his shingles. His suffering persisted even after the rash had completely disappeared as he continued to be racked by the lancinating shocks, virtually without respite. He called every day begging for relief. All I could do was give him more narcotics.

Two months later, John R. died by his own hand. His life was no longer bearable.

Most cases of shingles, of course, are not that severe. But the disorder should never be taken lightly. Even though its course is often unpredictable, and its treatment for the most part unsatisfactory, there are some things we can do to reduce the likelihood of its becoming chronic and crippling, as it did in John's case.

The formal name for shingles is herpes varicella-zoster. It is caused by a virus related to, and which acts very much like, the herpes simplex virus. It strikes the vulnerable young, but more importantly, the frail aged. Its cause is an old childhood acquaintance, the chicken-pox virus, returned to plague us in our senescence.

Some 90 percent of Americans have at one time or another had chicken pox, usually during childhood. This is a mild infection with a diffuse rash that blisters, crusts and disappears after a few days. In most children, that's the end of it. In some, however, this usually benign form can become virulent and spread to the lungs or the brain and result in death. This is most likely to occur when the immune mechanisms are impaired by some malignancy or blood disorder like leukemia, lymphoma or Hodgkin's disease, or when the individual is receiving chemotherapy or agents to suppress rejection of transplanted organs. In fact, 7 percent of children with leukemia who are under treatment and otherwise responding die after contracting chicken pox. But the norm for chicken pox is the uncomplicated case.

After the rash clears, the virus does not just disappear into thin air. As in other forms of herpes, it enters nerve fibers in the skin and moves along them to their origin, ending up in cells near the spinal cord. And there it sits. In normal healthy children and young adults, an intact immune system keeps the virus in this dormant state, and you'd never even know it was there. But as we get older, and our resistance begins to diminish, the virus may become re-activated, and retrace its path along the affected nerve, emerging once more onto the skin. The nerve is irritated by this viral migration, causing pain, itching and a burning sensation in the skin the first few days prior to the appearance of the rash. These symptoms may be perplexing to patient and doctor alike, since initially there are no other clues to the diagnosis. If the painful area involves the back of the chest, it may be mistaken for pleurisy; if it's in the front of the chest, pericarditis (inflammation of the lining of the heart) may be considered, or even a heart attack. But the truth becomes apparent four or five days later when the characteristic rash appears exactly where the pain was felt. The little red, raised pimples follow the distribution of the nerve fibers. Since nerves do not cross the midline of the body (one set emerges from each side of the spinal cord), the rash of shingles stops abruptly at the midline. It is almost never present on both sides of the body.

No one knows what specific factors activate the dormant virus. As I mentioned earlier, shingles develops mostly among the elderly because of their decreased immunological capability. But sometimes, as was the case with John R., some distinct stress or trauma will do it—an operation, emotional crisis, acute gout, a heart attack, radiation or chemotherapy.

The shingles rash usually lasts for about a week. Pain is apt to be more severe at the onset, and begins to diminish as the rash crusts. That's often the end of it. But various different complications can occur. For example, in someone with low resistance, the virus, instead of being limited to the skin, may spread throughout the body and cause death. Or it may involve the nervous system, resulting in encephalitis (inflammation of the brain). Again, when the nerves that supply the eye are affected, there may be exquisite pain, scarring of the cornea and blindness. Ear involvement may end in deafness.

But the most common complication, one we can sometimes prevent, is called postherpetic neuralgia. In such cases, the pain persists even after the rash clears, and may continue for several months or even indefinitely. About half the patients over sixty years of age develop such postherpetic neuralgia. (Shingles is uncommon below forty years, begins to increase at age fifty and is most common in those over sixty.)

Preventing the Painful Aftermath

The key to preventing postherpetic neuralgia is early diagnosis. The sooner you and your doctor determine that you're coming down with shingles, and the earlier the intervention, the less is the likelihood of prolonged pain. Such intervention with interferon (in the first four or five days) has been shown, at least in immunocompromised children, to reduce the chances of a long and painful aftermath. Interferon is no longer costly or difficult to obtain. Originally, when it was derived solely from animal sources, literally gallons of blood were needed to produce tiny amounts. But now, with recombinant DNA techniques, it is being turned out in large quantities at reasonable cost. Most doctors have access to it, even though it is still listed as an experimental drug.

Another preventive step, this one available to every doctor without legal restriction, is large doses of steroid hormones (corticosteroids), given as early as possible after the onset of symptoms. Mind you, not everyone can tolerate or safely take such steroids, but if you can (and that is something your doctor will have to decide), treatment for several days may reduce the chances of your being plagued with pain for a prolonged period of time.

An antiviral product called vidarabine (marketed as Vira-A) has also been shown by some researchers to soften the impact of herpes zoster. Ask your doctor about it, too.

Treatment of shingles is not very satisfactory. Fortunately, pain usually ends spontaneously, despite what we do, not because of it. Some patients have told me that injections of B-12 have made them feel better; others say it has no effect. Cold compresses may afford temporary relief, as do various pain-killers. Wherever possible, avoid narcotics, because they are habit-forming or addicting when taken for any length of time. Various lotions help the rash, but are of little use once the skin is clear and postherpetic neuralgia has set in.

I have found one simple technique useful in pain control—transcutaneous nerve stimulation. Electrodes are placed on the painful area, and electrical stimulation is applied from a portable battery. The relatively benign impulse competes with pain sensation in the affected nerves, affording some relief. The patient carries the small battery wherever convenient, during the day, for example, on a belt, and places it on a bedside table at night, activating it at will whenever necessary.

As a last resort, it is sometimes necessary to cut the pain nerves to the affected area.

Oral and intravenous acyclovir are now being used in acute shingles and are very effective, but doses higher than those being given for herpes seem to be required. Also, although the acute phase is modified by acyclovir, this drug does not appear to have an effect on postherpetic neuralgia.

For most individuals, shingles is just an annoyance. But its course is unpredictable, both in terms of whom it strikes and with what severity. If you are above fifty years of age and have developed herpes zoster, it behooves you to discuss with your doctor, as quickly as possible, how to reduce the likelihood of falling victim to its worst consequences.

I am sometimes asked by patients with shingles whether they're apt to have another attack, or if the first one confers immunity. In most viral infections, a single exposure does confer lifelong protection. But in shingles (and in herpes), recurrences of symptoms are not due to reinfection but to reactivation of a virus that is already present in the body. So repeated "episodes" of shingles can and do occur, although not nearly as frequently as in herpes simplex.

This chapter describes two common and debilitating viruses. Herpes and shingles are related, but they are very different in how they are transmitted, treated and the nature of the symptoms they produce. Their prevention awaits the development of vaccines—and these are very much in the offing.

CHAPTER **22**

Constipation—Keep Moving

Regular bowel movements are a very important cultural preoccupation in this country. Most of us expect to be "blessed" with at least one good evacuation a day. I have heard them described as "beautiful," "fantastic" and "wonderful." And if it doesn't happen when expected, it may become the source of great anxiety.

Late one evening a few weeks ago, I went to the coronary care unit in our hospital to visit one of my patients who had been admitted earlier that day with a heart attack. She was a seventy-two-year old woman whom I had known for years. From a technical point of view, coronary care units are wonderful. They provide immediate nursing and medical attention for any crisis that may occur in the course of a myocardial infarction. There is no question that they have been responsible for reducing the in-hospital death rate from acute coronary events. But they are also frightening places, what with all the technology enveloping the patient—intravenous infusions, invasive catheters and wires, and bedside monitors with flashing lights that frequently sound alarms for no apparent reason. I thought I would stop by at about ten o'clock to see how things were going and to reassure my patient. Before entering the unit, I looked into the waiting room just outside. Sure enough, there were her husband, two children and four grandchildren, sitting quietly in what they feared might be a death vigil.

When I entered the patient's room, she was dozing lightly. I chose not to wake her, and evaluated the various parameters being monitored—heart rhythm, blood pressure and electrocardiogram. Everything was going well. Just as I was about to leave, she stirred, opened her eyes, looked at me, smiled and said, "I'm so glad to see you. I was hoping you'd come. I'm in trouble, you know."

"No, you're not," I replied. "You're going to be just fine. Don't worry about all these wires. They're routine. Everybody gets them."

"Oh, I don't mind them. I don't expect any trouble from my heart. What's worrying me is the fact that I haven't had a bowel movement for almost two and a half days!"

I'm not sure how we came to focus on regular, daily evacuations to the extent we do. It may have started with the myth of "intestinal autotoxicity." I remember my mother telling me that unless I took the time to have a movement every day, I would somehow be poisoned by the retained wastes. I suspect most people believe that to be true. It isn't. In fact, bowel rhythm varies widely from person to person. Some normally have as many as three movements a day; others enjoy three a week. How frequently you "go," with what volume and with what regularity, depends on a host of different factors—your age (things slow down a bit as one gets older); your commitment (if you ignore early signals because you're too busy doing something else, you may have missed your chance and won't be due again for several hours or until the next day); how much water or other fluids you drink (those persons who tend to avoid water like the plague are likely to have more problems with constipation); the nature of your diet (natural fiber in plentiful amounts will almost surely result in a soft, bulky stool at least once a day); the level of your physical activity (a previously active individual who is suddenly confined to bed will have fewer bowel movements). Certain medications, discussed below, will also cause intermittent or chronic constipation; the presence of other diseases not associated with the bowel (for example, low thyroid function) may result in chronic constipation; a stroke may also slow intestinal motility.

In this particular discussion of constipation, I refer to those bowel irregularities that occur from time to time for no apparent reason, and/or which may lead to chronic constipation. An abrupt change in bowel habits is a different matter. It is ominous when someone who has always been regular suddenly becomes constipated, and/or in addition experiences alternating diarrhea; has narrowing in the caliber of his or her stools, so that they become ribbonlike; passes blood (old and black or fresh and red); has difficulty evacuating the stool despite a strong urge to do so; or, when all's said and done, experiences a feeling of incomplete emptying. These symptoms and findings raise the possibility of a growth somewhere in the bowel and should be investigated immediately, even if they do clear up temporarily.

Don't worry about occasional constipation. But if it becomes chronic, the consequences can be serious. These may include impaired function of the nerves and muscles responsible for control and continence, especially in the elderly, as reflected in the following anecdote. Two elderly gentlemen who were waiting in a doctor's anteroom, struck up a conversation.

"What's your trouble? I mean, why are you here to see the doctor?"

"Oh, I'm terribly constipated. Sometimes I don't move my bowels for a week or more."

"You know, I used to have that problem, but thank goodness, I don't have it anymore. I now go regularly every morning at seven o'clock."

"Well, then, why are you here?"

"Because I don't wake up until eight."

Long-standing constipation may also result in impaction, so that the stool literally has to be dug out, a painful and unpleasant business. It may even play a role in the development of cancer of the lower bowel.

You can, by modifying your life-style and personal habits, prevent constipation and avoid the symptoms that sometimes accompany it —the loaded feeling, dull headache, furry tongue, bad breath, lack of appetite and abdominal distension.

The best way to insure bowel regularity is to heed the "call to action." Many bodily functions are cyclical and almost automatic. They should not be thwarted. For example, we normally get hungry at a set interval after our last meal, give or take a few minutes; women's periods generally come in fixed cycles of exactly twenty-seven, twenty-eight or twenty-nine days; if you were to measure your body temperature every hour, you would find variations within one or two degrees occurring at almost exactly the same time every day. Most of us have built-in internal "alarm clocks," which wake us up at almost precisely the same time every morning. All the complex internal mechanisms that make us tick are quite orderly, and the signal to empty your bowel is one of them. You may be forgiven for ignoring it occasionally, but if you make a habit of it, you're destined ultimately to become chronically constipated. That often happens in the Type A personality, the high-powered, driven individual who has more important things to do than move his or her bowels. But we also see it among hospital patients, the elderly in nursing homes, and even youngsters in school, all of whom deliberately delay going to the bathroom because of the desire for privacy, the lack of cleanliness in the facility they must use, shyness or whatever. And so many of us are in such a hurry in the morning. We rush through breakfast so as not to miss the school bus or the next train. There never seems to be enough time to cultivate healthy bowel habits. Having ignored the early signal at home after breakfast, a youngster will go off to school, where circumstances are usually not conducive to a leisurely evacuation—he's embarrassed to ask the teacher for permission to leave the room, or is worried about taking too long or suffering the gibes of classmates, or the toilets are either dangerous or dirty. And so the student contains himself or herself until arriving home later in the day. The longer and more frequently you ignore the feeling of "being ready," the more your lower bowel stretches to accommodate the retained feces. A distended bowel wall ultimately begins to signal to you less frequently, that is, at longer intervals, storing the waste products for longer periods of time. This leaves the stool harder and more painful to pass when you finally decide to do so.

Sometimes there are physical reasons for ignoring the message to empty one's bowel. A painful rectal or anal condition, like hemorrhoids or a fissure, may make movements so uncomfortable that they are deliberately delayed. It is important to correct these problems as soon as they develop and not allow them to fester and result in chronic constipation. The other reason to do so is that the disorder itself can become worse if left unattended. For example, fissures may become deeper, longer and infected, while hemorrhoids can bleed subtly and chronically, causing serious anemia, especially in the elderly or chronically ill.

In terms of your life-style, you should also develop the habit of drinking plenty of water each day, at least eight full glasses (but check with your doctor before doing so if you suffer from a heart or kidney disorder). One patient of mine, a man of seventy-six, informed me not long ago that he had recently become constipated. His movements, which he had heretofore enjoyed every morning "like clockwork," now occurred at three or four-day intervals. They were hard and painful but not reduced in caliber, and there was no evidence of bleeding. There was nothing in his history to suggest a serious problem, but we "worked him up" anyway to rule out the possibility of a hidden bowel tumor. None of our studies revealed any abnormality. It finally turned out that this man was troubled by frequent urination due to an enlarged prostate. Because he had to get up three or four times a night to empty his bladder, he thought that reducing the amount of water he drank might help. It was shortly thereafter that his constipation began. He underwent prostate surgery from which he made a good recovery. His urinary frequency no longer troubled him, and when he resumed drinking his usual amount of water, his constipation cleared up promptly.

Exercise stimulates the bowel to contract and move out the feces. You must remain physically active to avoid becoming constipated. This is especially true among older persons. Those in their sixties have the same number of bowel movements as do younger individuals—if they remain active. One of the complications of confining a patient to bed for whatever reason—a heart attack, operation, infection, injury—is the development of constipation.

Diet has a great deal to do with how regularly your bowels move. Enough roughage and a high-fiber diet are necessary to prevent constipation. Grains are the richest sources of fiber, followed by fruit and vegetables. I advise any patient who complains of constipation to start with one teaspoon of unprocessed miller's bran every day, and to increase that amount gradually until he or she can tolerate about one-half cup a day. That's usually enough to insure normal bowel function. But remember, these foods are most effective when you drink plenty of water too.

Avoid taking laxatives on any regular basis. They perpetuate, never solve, the problem. I see so many laxative "junkies" who need to have their bowels whipped into action daily by ever-increasing doses of laxatives. If you feel you must have something because of temporary bowel malfunction, start with the bulk-forming agents like bran or methyl cellulose, psyllium or polycarbophyl. They're very much like dietary fiber in that they combine with water in the intestine to form a gel or emollient that is easily passed.

It is not a good idea to use mineral oil. It's an irritant, and if some accidently goes down "the wrong way" into your windpipe, you may develop a serious pneumonia. The body has trouble dealing with oily substances. What's more, when taken with meals, mineral oil reduces the absorption of the fat-soluble vitamins A, D and E.

Lactulose, a widely used synthetic sugar, is one of the better laxatives. It works by sucking water into the bowel and making the stool softer and bulkier.

If you suddenly become constipated, make sure it's not from some medication you're taking. One of the best ways to prevent constipation is to avoid repeated use of the following:

(1) *Any preparation containing codeine,* such as is found in various cough mixtures, narcotics and analgesics.

(2) *Antacids containing aluminum.* Many persons chew antacid tablets every few hours to relieve "acid indigestion." Those preparations containing magnesium or calcium carbonate will not cause constipation, but any that contain aluminum may.

(3) *Cholestyramine* (Questran). In 1984, a government report indicated that lowering cholesterol levels with cholestyramine prevented or delayed the onset of coronary-artery disease. Since then, I have prescribed this drug to many of my patients with high cholesterol. Many of them have become chronically constipated as a result. This can be avoided by adding lots of fiber to the diet.

(4) A wide variety of *tranquilizers and other psychotropic agents,* including the phenothiazines (Compazine, Thorazine); tricyclic antidepressants, such as Elavil; anticholinergics, like atropine and Donnatal; and antihistamines, used for allergies.

(5) *Iron preparations,* widely prescribed to correct anemia ("tired blood"), will not only make your stool look as if you've been bleeding high up in the gastrointestinal tract by turning it black, they are also likely to give you constipation. Most people in good health can obtain enough iron in their diet without resorting to supplements, although women with heavy menstrual flow may require them.

(6) *Diuretics,* by removing water from the body, which is what they are supposed to do, also leave your bowel "high and dry."

So if you become constipated, look carefully into your life-style and reflect on some of your personal habits—what you've been eating and drinking, and the medications you've been taking. It's always a good idea to check with your doctor if you suddenly become constipated. It's his job to make certain there is no significant disease in the bowel itself.

CHAPTER 23

Cancer—When It Can Be Prevented

Although there has been some progress with respect to earlier detection, treatment and cure of cancer, its prevention is still your best bet. The sad truth is that the overall survival rate for most cancers has not changed much. Your chances of being alive five years after the initial diagnosis of lung cancer has increased by only 1 percent since 1976—from 12 to 13 percent. Survival rates for colon cancer during that time have risen from 49 to 52 percent, and in prostate cancer, from 64 to 70 percent. Among those unlucky enough to have cancer of the pancreas, a mere 2 percent will live another five years. Ninety-five percent of patients with cancer of the esophagus will be dead five years after the diagnosis is made.

All these statistics add up to the fact that cancer is the second leading cause of death in this country. But this need not be so, for many malignancies are either caused or provoked by factors in our environment which we can control. So while the scientists continue their search for a cancer cure, each and every one of us should be practicing prevention.

At least thirty-five percent of malignancies are diet-related. In fact, Burkitt, the man who educated us about the benefits of the high-fiber diet, believes that the number of cancers could be cut by two-thirds by dietary manipulation alone—reducing the amount of fat we eat by one-third, sugar by one-half, doubling our intake of starch and eating

40 grams of fiber every day. Thirty percent of cancers are due to tobacco use, 4 percent are related to occupational factors, 3 percent result from excessive intake of alcohol and 2 percent are the consequence of air pollution. The remaining preventable causes include some of the medications we consume (estrogens, immunosuppressants) and the X rays to which we are exposed.

In preparing this chapter, I came across a myriad of fascinating observations. The more I surveyed the massive data before me, the more insurmountable the task of organizing it appeared. It began to look as if virtually everything we eat, drink, breathe, wear and do can cause cancer—if not in humans, then certainly in other forms of life, including rats, guinea pigs, dogs, monkeys and cows, to name but a few. Also an overwhelming number of facts about cancer apparently bear no relation to one another. For example, people who smoke cigarettes and drink too much alcohol are prone to develop cancer of the mouth. That seems straightforward enough, until we're told that women who neither drink nor smoke but who use mouthwash regularly also develop oral cancer. Are you dusting your baby's "privates" with talcum powder? That's okay for little boys, but female infants so groomed may develop cancer of an ovary later in life due to the irritant effect of the talcum particles. Cabbage, it is said, protects you against certain forms of malignancy, but beets, on the other hand, may increase the risk. Just as we had begun to believe that large amounts of fiber protect against cancer of the bowel (you can even read that statement on some of the cereal boxes on your breakfast table), the prestigious National Academy of Sciences, after reviewing all the data on cancers and nutrition, concluded that the cancer–fiber link has not, in fact, been established. One researcher even implicates fiber in the *causation* of cancer! Worried about the pill? It apparently will protect you against cancer of the ovary and the endometrium (the lining of the uterus)—but not of the breast. In fact, there are still some diehards who believe that despite all the negative studies so far, estrogens probably do increase the risk of breast cancer. And so it goes, fact after apparently unrelated fact, to the extent that I initially decided that the only way to present the available information was simply to list the most reasonable, credible observations and theories, and to leave their interpretation up to you.

But that didn't seem quite fair. So I decided on what I hope you will find is a better way. I have reviewed and digested all the important information on which I could lay my hands concerning the most common malignancies in the United States. I then organized this chapter by specific cancer, in descending order of frequency, emphasizing how best you may be able to prevent each one.

Nonmelanoma Skin Cancers—Preventable and Treatable

From a practical point of view, we can divide skin cancers into two main types: the melanomas, which are lethal unless detected and removed very early (20 percent of all melanoma patients are dead within five years); and the rest, the nonmelanoma skin cancers, with an estimated 400,000 to 500,000 new cases every year—the most common cancers among whites in this country. (Incidentally, the latter are not included in the American Cancer Society's ranking of tumor incidence.) They consist mostly of basal-cell or squamous-cell cancers and are highly curable—more than 90 percent of the time. That's an important fact to know. I remember one patient who consulted a dermatologist because of a suspicious-looking pigmented pimple on his skin. The lesion was biopsied and the report came back "basal-cell carcinoma." It sounds ominous, but all one really has to do is to have it removed and that's almost always the end of the problem. Unfortunately, the dermatologist never told that to the patient. His final comments to him were "The pathology report reveals skin cancer, but we've got it all and you should be all right."

The patient didn't believe him. "Cancer is cancer," he thought. "What a terrible way to die." So he settled his affairs, began reading about all those brave people who, given the diagnosis of cancer, took their own lives before the real suffering set in, and went into a deep depression. For a time, he considered suicide. Of course, it was ridiculous in his case, as it is in virtually every instance of nonmelanoma skin cancer. (For a discussion of melanoma skin cancer, which is much less common but much more deadly, turn to page 335.)

The Sunny Road to Cancer: The single most important and preventable cause of all skin cancer is prolonged exposure to sunlight, and to a lesser degree to ultraviolet rays and other forms of radiation. As you might expect, 90 percent of skin cancers occur on areas of the body that are usually left uncovered—the face, ears, neck, backs of the hands and so on. As a result, people who work outdoors—

fishermen, farmers, ranchers, sailors, construction workers and athletes are most vulnerable. In the United States, where drivers sit on the left-hand side of the car with the sun beating down on the left side of the body, more skin cancers occur on the left; in England and Australia, with the right-wheel drive, right-sided skin cancers predominate. You should be especially careful of the sun if you are a redhead, fair-skinned and fair-haired, light-eyed, freckled and of Celtic descent, and also if you blister easily when trying to get a tan or have some disease that has left you intolerant of sunlight. (There are genetic disorders that do so—for example, xeroderma pigmentosum.)

The latitude and altitude at which you live are also important determinants of vulnerability to skin cancer. The amount of ultraviolet light is greatest near the Equator, where the sun is directly overhead more hours of the day and more days of the year than elsewhere. So the incidence of skin cancer increases the closer one is to the Equator. As you might expect, it is more prevalent in tropical and subtropical regions than in, say, Alaska, or even New York. There is twice as much skin cancer in Australia and Arizona than in northern regions. Altitude is important, because the higher you go, the less radiation the atmosphere absorbs, leaving more of it to play havoc with your skin. We are protected to some extent from the dangerous rays of the sun by ozone, a form of oxygen that begins to appear in significant amounts at about thirty-five thousand or forty thousand feet, where jet aircraft fly, and increases as one goes farther out into space. Unfortunately, this protective layer is being depleted by industrial components, like fluorocarbons, which used to be found in spray cans before they were banned for that purpose. Smog, which is harmful for other reasons, is actually protective against the sun's rays. Remember, those rays are most intense in the northern hemisphere during the summer between 10 A.M. and 3 P.M.

If you must spend time in the sun, make sure to cover exposed portions of your body with a strong sunscreen, one that contains PABA (para-aminobenzoic acid) and has a solar protection factor of at least 15. Apply it one hour before being out in the sun; reapply after swimming or if you perspire a great deal. (Please also read the portion of Chapter 18 dealing with the aging skin.)

But It's Not Sun Alone: Keeping out of the sun is the first step in preventing skin cancer. But you can do more. Avoid all contact with specific carcinogenic substances, as for example, coal-tar derivatives in petrochemicals used in roofing or construction. Arsenic can also cause skin cancer. It was formerly found in certain "tonics." Although you are no longer apt to buy it to pep you up, you may still be exposed to arsenic in certain pesticides and fungicides. Always determine the ingredients of any products with which you come in contact frequently, for whatever purpose.

If you have scars from burns, cuts or even surgery, remember that they are prime sites for the subsequent appearance of skin cancer. So examine all scars very carefully and at frequent intervals to make sure they are not discolored. I saw a patient recently who developed a skin malignancy in an appendectomy scar that had been there for twenty years.

Early detection of nonmelanoma skin cancer is virtually synonymous with prevention. That means *you* and your doctor should examine your skin frequently. You can learn to recognize a basal-cell cancer by its appearance. It is usually a small, shiny, flesh-colored nodule, crisscrossed with tiny blood vessels and surrounded by pearly borders. It may crust, ulcerate, bleed and resemble eczema or even psoriasis. Squamous-cell cancers have a different appearance. They are also nodules, but are scaly, platelike, with sharply outlined red patches. Regardless of what the "sore" or "rash" looks like, if it doesn't heal, or if you have any doubts about it, see a dermatologist without delay.

Cancer of the Lung—Legacy of the Cigarette

In 1984, colorectal cancer yielded its place as the most common nonskin malignancy. Cancer of the lung is now the number one cancer in the land. It owes its ever-increasing frequency to one major factor—the cigarette. This malignancy, which used to be uncommon in women, now kills more of them than any other cancer—all because of female involvement with the weed. At a time when virtually every other sector and age group in American society is "kicking the habit," teen-age girls are taking it up in unprecedented numbers. One-third of all male cancer deaths are due to cancer of the lung. If everyone were to stop smoking right now, the number of new lung cancer cases each year would drop by 75 percent, from 140,000 per year to 35,000—perhaps even less.

Cigarette smokers are at ten times the risk of developing lung cancer than are nonsmokers. The death rate among those who consume
two or more packs a day is fifteen to twenty-five times greater than
in nonsmokers (the risk increases with the length of time you've been
doing it, how deeply you inhale, and how much tar and nicotine your
favorite brand contains). There is said to be some "benefit" from
using filtered, low-tar cigarettes, but the incidence of lung cancer
among those who use these brands is still many times that of the
nonsmokers. Nicotine is addicting. The less your cigarette contains,
the more deeply you'll inhale, and the more you'll smoke to satisfy
your daily need. So in the long run, the filters and other gimmicks
probably end up giving you the same amount of nicotine but you'll
be absorbing more of the other cancer-causing substances found in
smoke.

A word about clove cigarettes, which have become increasingly
popular among teen-agers as the herbal alternative to tobacco. Don't
you believe it. The two brands sold in this country, imported from
Indonesia, contain 60 percent tobacco and twice as much tar and
nicotine as the average cigarette. Their other ingredients include
cocoa, caramel, licorice and eugenol, all of which are perfectly safe
when eaten. (Eugenol is what your dentist applies to an aching tooth.)
But no one knows what effect they may have when burned and inhaled. A few deaths have already been reported from their use. So if
you plan to switch from tobacco to clove cigarettes, don't.

It is not easy to stop smoking once you're hooked, so, given these
awful statistics, why start the habit in the first place? When I tell it
like it is to some of my patients who have been smoking for years,
they reply with "It's too late to quit now, after all this time." They're
wrong. It's never really too late, either from a cancer or a cardiac
point of view. Within ten years of stopping, a previously heavy
smoker has the same overall risk as a lifelong abstainer.

We used to think that whether or not a given individual chose to
smoke was very much a personal decision, that it was one's right to
do so. Given all the facts, if you were prepared to shorten your life,
well, that was entirely up to you and no business of society's. In my
opinion, this attitude is not justified. Several recent studies have
shown that nonsmoking wives of heavy smokers are at greater risk
for developing lung cancer than are wives of nonsmokers. The nicotine present in their urine is evidence that when their husbands

smoke, they do too, passively. In fact, if you live in the same house as a two-pack-per-day smoker, you inhale the equivalent of up to ten cigarettes a day!

Not long ago, one of my patients, a forty-six-year-old woman, came to see me complaining of a chronic, dry cough and weight loss of three months' duration. She had delayed her visit because she wasn't really worried about cancer since she was a nonsmoker. So we were both surprised when her chest X ray revealed a "shadow" that looked very much like, and in fact turned out to be, cancer of the lung! The only risk factor I could find in this lady was her husband's three-pack-a-day habit—and they had been married for more than twenty years.

Not only do cigarettes render you vulnerable to cancer of the lung, they also increase the danger from other occupational carcinogens like asbestos and radon. For example, we have seen that cigarette smoking alone can increase the risk of lung cancer by ten times. Persons exposed to asbestos have a five times greater chance of developing this malignancy. But when cigarette smokers are also exposed to asbestos, their cancer risk is fifty times that of non-smokers.

In my opinion, and that of virtually every other doctor and oncologist I know or whose work I have read, the cigarette–lung-cancer link is a documented fact—cut and dried. There are nevertheless some puzzling statistics for whose explanation an interesting theory has been offered. Lung-cancer deaths have increased by some 75 percent between 1960 and 1980 despite the fact that during that interval the consumption of cigarettes actually dropped by 15 percent, and 90 percent of those smoked were filtered. What's more, the amount of two important carcinogens in cigarettes, benzopyrene and nitrosamine, has also been cut in half. So why the increased lung cancer? One explanation is that most deaths among cigarette smokers occur in the sixty-five and older group, who are set in their ways, who would "rather fight than switch," and so they stay with their high-tar, high-nicotine weed. Another theory I came across is very thought-provoking. Tobacco crops are treated with fertilizer rich in phosphates that are derived from radioactive apatite rock. This high-phosphate fertilizer contains a substantial amount of radioactive polonium, which adheres to the tobacco leaf throughout the entire manufacturing process, and ends up in your cigarette. When you inhale the smoke, the radioactive polonium particles pass directly into your lungs, where they remain for about six months. Their concentration in the lungs of smokers is four times greater than in nonsmokers. Nor are passive smokers free of these particles, which hang in the air for some time after being blown out of the smokers' lungs. The alpha radiation emitted by polonium, which is more carcinogenic than are gamma and beta radiation, penetrates the cells of the lungs, where it disrupts the DNA in the cell nuclei and ends up causing cancer. Translated into practical terms, this theory holds that a thirty-ciga-rette-per-day smoker is exposed to the same amount of radiation in two years of smoking as if he or she had had three hundred chest X rays per year.

Well, it's an interesting theory, whether or not you believe it. But it does offer yet another fascinating explanation of how cigarettes may cause lung cancer, and why the most effective prevention against this terrible disease is abstinence from tobacco. Remember, smoking two packs per day will decrease your life-span by some eight years.

If You Can't Stop Smoking: My patients know how strongly I feel about cigarette smoking. No one leaves my office without hearing (but not always listening to) an impassioned dissertation on the subject. Some who can't or won't quit never come back to see me because they're too embarrassed or "afraid." The fact is, although I never give up in my attempts to get everyone to stop, I have made peace with the hard-core smokers who don't. They are a fact of life. I have heard other doctors say that they will not treat anyone who continues to smoke. That, in my judgment, is not only wrong, it's unforgivable. First of all, the threat of discharging these patients doesn't mean much, because there are enough doctors who do (and should) continue to take care of them. After all, smokers are not criminals. What's more, the risk of smoking is so great that these individuals need more, not less, medical care. Sending them packing will not prolong their lives. For example, smokers who already have heart or other vascular diseases are at special risk if, in addition, their blood pressure is high, their cholesterol level is elevated and they are obese. Keeping these other parameters within normal limits does reduce the dangers of tobacco somewhat. Smokers should also be constantly reminded of lung cancer's earliest symptoms. Typically, the victim has had a "chronic" morning cough for years that has recently become more troublesome. Spitting blood and weight loss are advanced signs of lung cancer, so too is the appearance of a "shadow" in a chest X ray.

I believe that cigarette smokers should take *beta-carotene* supplements. Although the evidence is not yet conclusive, there are strong indications that they, as well as persons whose diets are low in vitamin A are at increased risk for lung cancer. Foods rich in vitamin A and its chemical cousin, beta-carotene, are thought to reduce the chances of lung tumors' starting in the first place, and also to slow their growth once they occur (not only in the lungs, but in the oral cavity and larynx as well). This is probably the result of the fact that vitamin A and its derivatives enhance DNA repair within the cells.

Normal tissue consists of differentiated cells. Cancer cells, on the other hand, are undifferentiated, that is, they grow wildly in every which way. Beta-carotene exerts what you might call a "disciplinary effect" on the lining of the respiratory tree, where many of these cancers start, by keeping the cells there growing in an orderly way, that is, differentiated. So the smoker's diet should contain lots of carotene, found in dark-green and deep-yellow vegetables, like spinach and carrots, all plants that contain chlorophyll, and the cruciferous vegetables (cabbage, broccoli, cauliflower and Brussels sprouts). It's probably also a good idea for everyone, but especially smokers, to take small daily supplements of beta-carotene in capsule form—not extra vitamin A capsules. The concentrated therapeutic forms of the latter can in high dosage cause serious toxicity.

There is so much evidence to suggest that beta-carotenes are protective against lung cancer that Harvard researchers have been funded by the National Institutes of Health to conduct a long-term study to test the validity of the theory. Some twenty-five thousand doctors across the United States (myself included) have volunteered to participate in a double-blind ten-year study. That means I don't know whether the red capsule I take every other day is beta-carotene or a placebo. After ten years, the code will be broken, and we will see whether there are fewer cases of lung cancer among those of us who took the beta-carotene.

Other Risk Factors for Lung Cancer: Although tobacco is far and away the leading cause of lung cancer, other agents, mostly occupational, are also responsible for this malignancy. You can avoid them if you know what they are. The greatest risk in this category is airborne asbestos. Those most vulnerable to its hazards are workers in contact with it in such industries as milling, mining, textiles, insulation and the manufacture of cement. Anyone currently so employed knows the risks and what precautions to take. But forty-five years ago, the dangers of asbestos were not generally appreciated by Rosie the Riveter—and her friends. So new cases of lung cancer are now cropping up in men and women who worked in this country's shipyards fireproofing vessels with asbestos during World War II. Unfortunately, there is no longer any possibility of prevention for these individuals. For them, the die is cast. But any facility—schools, public places and even homes—in which asbestos is known to have been used as insulation when it was built may cause lung cancer among those who live or work in it. This asbestos continues to be shed into the environment and inhaled by schoolchildren, housewives and office workers. Every one of these structures should be stripped and the asbestos it contains removed.

Radiation is another important environmental carcinogen. Whether you're a survivor of Hiroshima and Nagasaki, a uranium miner inhaling radon particles, or a patient receiving too many X rays from your doctor or dentist, you're at risk for cancer of the lung. Unfortunately, there is nothing an atomic-bomb victim can do about it after this late date, but the rest of us can. For example, if you are offered a diagnostic X ray, always make sure it's for good reason. Too many X rays are done too often for routine purposes and without sufficient clinical justification.

There are other substances, mostly occupational, like mustard gas, chlorine, cotton and coal dust, fumes from rubber polymers, chromium, nickel and several others (with which the great majority of us are not likely to come in contact), that are carcinogenic to the lung. Those exposed to them are well protected if the adequacy of the ventilation at the work site continues to be monitored, and if attention is paid to the safety measures posted by law.

I used to think that air pollution played an important role in the genesis of lung cancer. That's apparently not the case. Such air pollution, though unpleasant, is said to be responsible for only one lung cancer out of every hundred. Still it behooves all of us to lobby for clean air.

Cancer of the Colon and the Rectum—Hope Even When Prevention Fails

Although cancers of the colon and the rectum have been surpassed by cancer of the lung, they are a very close second, with 130,000 new cases each year. Unlike cancer of the lung, in which the five-year survival rate is only 13 percent, your chances of being alive at the end of that period if you've had a cancer of the colon or the rectum are 52 percent. The main reason for these happier statistics, in my opinion, is earlier diagnosis.

In order to understand the critical roles of prevention and detection in these cancers, you must know something of the anatomy of this area of the body. The intestinal tract starts at the mouth and continues as the food pipe, or *esophagus*. This widens to become the *stomach*, which is followed by the gut, many feet of twisting, winding loops of bowel called the *small intestine*. This terminates where the appendix is situated at the beginning of the large bowel *(the cecum)*, which then courses up the right side of the abdominal cavity *(ascending colon)*, across the top to the left side *(transverse colon)*, and then down the left side of the abdominal cavity *(descending colon*, which leads to the S-shaped *sigmoid colon)* and out.

Any unexplained change in bowel habits, such as alternating periods of constipation and diarrhea, abdominal pain, or the presence of blood in or on the stool, should be considered early signs of cancer of the lower intestinal tract until *proved* otherwise. Proper diagnosis at this time makes a cure possible. What's more, the routine checkup, when it includes a rectal exam, may detect early evidence of rectal cancer if it is within reach of the examining finger even before the onset of any symptoms.

Screening Techniques for Early Detection: Another reason for the generally better outlook for colorectal cancer is the fact that such tumors grow relatively slowly. When diagnosed early enough, there is a greater than 75 percent survival. The best way to make sure you are not harboring such a tumor is to follow the recommendations of the American Cancer Society. Every year, after the age of forty, you should have a digital rectal exam. I was taught long ago, by an old professor of surgery, that "if you don't put your finger in, you put your foot into it." If such proper screening were widely followed, it is estimated that twenty thousand to twenty-five thousand lives would be saved each year.

In addition to the digital exam, you should have a chemical examination of your stool at least once a year after the age of fifty. This is very easy to do and inexpensive. You can buy your own test card in any drugstore. (More about this on pages 410–411.) Follow the simple instructions, and if the specimen applied to the card changes to the appropriate color when the chemical reagent that comes with the kit is added to it, notify your doctor immediately. Most physicians provide their patients with these cards, which are sent back to the office for analysis.

Other tools in the early detection of colorectal cancer are proctosigmoidoscopy and/or colonoscopy, in which the rectum and lower colon are inspected by means of a hollow lighted instrument. This should be done at ages fifty and fifty-one, even if there are no symptoms. If the results are negative on both occasions, then repeat studies are not usually necessary more often than every three to five years. Neither examination is what you might call enjoyable, but the colonoscope is less unpleasant than the sigmoidoscope. The former is thinner and flexible, and can be introduced much higher up into the intestinal tract than can the larger, rigid proctoscope. Opt for the colonoscope or the flexible sigmoidoscope if you have the chance. The barium enema is also a useful screening technique for the early detection of colorectal cancer. You should discuss with your doctor which among these various procedures is best for you.

Some of the epidemiologic data (information derived from populations rather than from individuals) concerning colorectal cancers are very revealing. For example, they occur more frequently in industrialized countries like the United States than they do in underdeveloped areas like Africa. The major exception is Japan, which is probably the only developed nation with a very low incidence of colorectal cancer. We will discuss the reasons for that in a moment. Within the United States, the greatest case load is found in the urban Great Lakes area. The lowest incidence in this country is in the South and Southwest. Other statistics tell us that those in the highest socioeconomic stratum are at greatest risk for colorectal cancer. So are the most sedentary among us. Both sexes become vulnerable over the age of forty, much more so after fifty, and women slightly more than men.

There are certain personal and familial characteristics that significantly increase the risk of colorectal cancer. One of these is a previous history of benign polyps. If you've had even only one at any time in the past, you must be rechecked very carefully and at regular intervals for the rest of your life. Polyps may be precursors by ten to fifteen years of colon cancer, and removing them as soon as they are found is the best way to prevent malignancy. If you personally have never had any, but there is history of colon polyps among your close relatives, you are at increased risk. A recent example of such familial incidence is the identical type of bowel cancer suffered by President Reagan and his older brother. There is an uncommon disease called familial polyposis in which the entire bowel is studded with polyps. Since such patients almost always develop intestinal cancer, the entire large bowel should be removed prophylactically. Chronic bowel disorders like ulcerative colitis and Crohn's disease also constitute a risk for cancer. If you've had ulcerative colitis for ten or more years, you are at twenty times the normal risk of developing colon cancer. Here too removal of the affected portion of the bowel *before* the cancer appears is often recommended.

The Anti-Cancer Diet: In addition to all those cases of colorectal cancer with known geographic, socioeconomic, familial and personal risk factors, many individuals develop the malignancy for no apparent reason. How can they reduce their risk? The answer appears to be mainly dietary. In general, a high intake of fats, both saturated and unsaturated—meat, milk, milk products, salad oils—is associated with an increased incidence of colorectal cancer. Maybe it's because the fat in the intestinal tract triggers the release of bile acids, which then promote the action of other cancer-causing agents. We're not sure. But the fact that individuals who have had their gallbladder removed for whatever reason are at slightly increased risk suggests that this bile-acid theory may have validity. It is significant that the Japanese, who consume much less fat—only 20 percent of their total calories, as compared to more than 40 percent in the American diet —have a far lower incidence of colorectal cancer than we do. In general, populations whose consumption of meat is high have more colon cancer than do those who eat large amounts of "seed foods," like maize, beans and rice. This may be due to some potentially harmful substance in the meat itself, or the presence of a protective anti-cancer enzyme in the seeds. One such enzyme called protease inhibitor has actually been isolated. There is considerable research now in progress to determine whether it does in fact prevent or retard the development of cancer.

Japanese who have moved from their homeland to the United States usually abandon their native diet for the typical American fare. Within one generation they then "enjoy" a cancer rate no different from that of native Americans. In other words, the Japanese do not have a low incidence of colon cancer because of any special genetic protection. It appears to be a matter of what they eat.

While the evidence is not always consistent, many doctors believe not only that fat of any kind promotes colorectal cancer but that the dietary fiber in fruits, vegetables, legumes and whole-grain products protects against it. The reasons are complex. Perhaps it's because high-fiber foods, which speed the transit time of the fecal material through the bowel, decrease the duration of contact of any carcinogens with the bowel wall. Or some constituent of the fiber itself may inhibit the formation of cancer-producing substances. Here's an interesting question. What happens to people who eat a lot of fat but who also have a high-fiber intake? The Finns and the Danes provide the answer. Finns who live in rural areas and Danes who live in the city of Copenhagen have a similar fat intake, but the incidence of colon cancer is much lower among the Finns. That's presumably because, unlike the Danes, they also eat large amounts of high-fiber foods.

Not only is the evidence for a protective effect of a diet high in fruits and vegetables very convincing, but the cruciferous vegetables, in particular—cabbage, broccoli, Brussels sprouts and cauliflower— also seem to be protective. This may be due to their high content of vitamins A, C, fiber and other micronutrients.

It has been suggested that vitamins C and E, both antioxidants, possibly have a protective effect against cancer of the bowel by preventing the conversion of fat to nitrosamines, which are potent carcinogenic agents. Although the evidence is intellectually appealing at this time, it is still inconclusive.

What other factors appear to be associated with increased risk for developing this type of colon cancer? Excessive intake of sweets, overweight and certain agricultural chemicals have all been implicated. So have environmental pollutants, since there is a higher incidence among machinists working with cutting oil and firemen exposed to smoke.

Given all these diverse observations, the National Cancer Institute now recommends that in order to reduce the risk of colorectal cancer our diet should be rich in fiber, obtained from whole-grain breads, cereals, fresh fruits and vegetables, and contain no more than 30 percent fat. They make no specific recommendations vis-à-vis vitamin supplements.

What about *selenium?* This is a trace mineral that has recently received a great deal of publicity and for very interesting reasons. The facts are these. In those areas where the selenium level of the soil is low, there is a higher incidence of cancer, especially of the intestinal tract and the prostate. Furthermore, in persons with a low blood selenium, and who also have decreased vitamin A and E blood concentrations, the malignancy rate is even higher. Experimentally, if selenium in moderate doses is added to the diet of animals, it's more difficult to induce cancer in them by chemical means.

Another interesting report seems further to support the belief that *small* amounts of selenium may be protective. (Remember, however, that high doses of selenium may be toxic.) Back in the early 1970s, a large study was started to determine what happens to individuals with high blood pressure who are treated in various ways. At the very beginning of the study, blood was drawn and analyzed for virtually every constituent you can think of. After ten years, when the number of deaths was calculated, an interesting association was observed. Among those individuals who died of cancer in this group (remember, this isn't what the researchers were originally looking for), it was found that the selenium level measured *at the beginning of the study,* before there was any evidence of cancer, was low. Previously recorded decreased selenium levels in patients with cancer had been attributed to the fact that the cancer itself reduces the concentration of calcium and that the diminished values were not the cause, but the *result,* of cancer. However, since in this particular study, bloods were drawn long before the cancer ever appeared, it would seem that decreased selenium levels may in fact contribute to the development of malignancy.

When the End Justifies the Means: What then is the bottom line for your "conquering" colorectal cancer? First, there is early detection. You must know the warning signs. Abdominal discomfort, a change in bowel habits and the appearance of blood in the stool are all important danger signals. Anyone over age fifty is at risk, especially if there is a family history of cancer or polyps. Follow the screening advice given by the American Cancer Society with respect to the frequency and type of bowel examinations (notice that X rays are not required). Then there is prevention itself. Dietary advice boils down to two basic recommendations: reduce consumption of all fats, saturated and polyunsaturated, and eat lots of fiber, in the form of fresh fruits, vegetables and whole grains. Whether you choose to go beyond that and add small amounts of selenium, vitamin C or vitamin E to your diet is at this moment optional. Vitamin C in amounts less than 1,000 mgs. a day and 400 units of vitamin E are, in my judgment, safe and may conceivably confer some protection. Additional vitamin A in capsule form is not recommended.

Finally, there is an exciting development with regard to the prevention of *recurrences* of colon cancer. A nationwide study is now in progress to test the efficacy of a vaccine that may do just that. Cancerous tissue that has been removed at operation is frozen and kept alive in the laboratory. When the patient from whom the cancer was taken has recovered sufficiently from the surgery, the malignant tissue is thawed out, radiated to render it biologically inert and an extract prepared. An "adjuvant" substance is added to it that stimulates the immune system. The resulting vaccine is then injected into the patient, in whom it apparently seeks out and destroys any cancer cells that may have been left behind. This pilot study was undertaken because of the observation that a few patients so treated had a significantly lower incidence of cancer recurrence and death. This may herald a new approach to cancer prevention generally.

Breast Cancer—Not for Women Only

This past year two of my patients consulted me because they had found a lump in a breast, which I confirmed in my own examination. Mammography strongly suggested that both growths were malignant, a fact confirmed by biopsy. The two patients underwent modified radical mastectomies. There is nothing unusual about this scenario given the fact that there were about 116,000 new cases of breast cancer in the United States in 1984. What does make these two particular patients somewhat special is the fact that they were men—in their sixties. So although breast cancer is overwhelmingly a disease of women, men are by no means immune. If you're male and your doctor examines your breasts, he's not odd, he's just being careful.

Until 1984, cancer of the breast was the leading cancer killer of women in this country. It is now second, having been replaced by cancer of the lung. It is number three in overall (nonskin) cancer incidence. Statistics tell us that one in every eleven women, more commonly white than black, and more frequently Jewish than any other ethnic group, will develop breast cancer in this country. The highest incidence of this disease is in the United States and other Western and industrialized countries; the lowest, in Asia, Africa and Latin America.

The Rewards of Eternal Vigilance: What can you do to reduce your chances of developing cancer of the breast? First, let me emphasize, as I did with cancer of the bowel, that early detection is crucial. Persistent breast changes, like a lump, a thickening, swelling, dimpling or irritation of the skin, distortion of the shape of the breast, nipple scaliness, retraction or discharge, pain or tenderness, are all fairly late manifestations. You must *look* for the cancer before any of these signs are manifest. Maintain a high index of suspicion and adhere to the following recommendations of the American Cancer Society: Every woman over twenty years of age should learn how to examine her own breasts and do so every month. This is best done in the shower or bath when the skin is wet. In addition to your own self-exam, you should have your doctor check your breasts every three years between the ages of twenty and forty and annually after age forty. At age thirty-five, have a base-line mammogram, so it can be compared with those you will be taking later in life. Between the ages of forty and forty-nine, you should have a mammogram every two years, depending on your risk profile, which I will discuss in a moment. Beginning at age fifty, have a mammogram annually. Newer X-ray techniques now give off much less radiation than formerly, and permit the detection of tiny malignancies too small to be felt by you *or your doctor*.

Who's Vulnerable? Although genetics are obviously important, most cases of breast cancer are probably due to a combination of environmental and hormonal factors. Here are some statistics that may help you define your own vulnerability. In countries such as ours, where the incidence is high, the breast-cancer rate begins to rise after age thirty. By fifty, age is a definite risk factor. So the older you are, the more likely you are to develop breast cancer. Your chances of developing it are increased by two or three times if your mother or sister suffered from this disorder. The risk is greater if their cancer occurred before the menopause, involved both breasts and was present in two close female relatives in one generation. Also, if you yourself have had cancer of one breast, a second one is more likely than if you hadn't had any prior cancer.

There is a condition called *benign fibrocystic disease* in which the breasts are chronically lumpy and painful. Women with this disorder are terrified that one of these lumps may be or become cancerous. They often request multiple biopsies for reassurance. The results of a recent large-scale study should be comforting to them. Some three-thousand women, all of whom had had breast biopsies because of fibrocystic breast disease, were followed for periods of up to seventeen years. Seventy percent of them had no higher incidence of breast cancer than the general population despite their lumpy breasts. Another 26 percent had a moderate increase in the number of cancers, but only 4 percent were at substantially higher risk. What's more, the latter could be identified by biopsy, which revealed the presence of "atypical" cells. This finding was especially significant if there was also a bad family history.

The bottom line of this study is: fibrocystic disease of the breast is a normal condition that really shouldn't be called a disease at all. If you have such breasts, all you need do is follow the usual anti-breast-cancer precautions. However, if you have a bad family history *and* fibrocystic disease, you should have a biopsy to make sure you don't have any "atypical" cells. If you do, subsequent monitoring should be more frequent.

If you started menstruating before the age of twelve and did not have your menopause until after fifty-five, you are probably at some increased risk for developing breast cancer, possibly because of the longer exposure of your breast tissue to the hormonal stimulus that started earlier and ended later in life. By the same token, if your ovaries were surgically removed for any reason before the ages of forty or forty-five, your risk is decreased, presumably because of a shorter exposure to this hormonal stimulation.

What about childbirth? The older you were when you gave birth to your first child, the higher the risk of breast cancer. For example, the chances of having breast cancer are three or four times higher in women whose first child was born after age thirty than in those who became mothers before the age of eighteen. Women who have never had children are also at high risk. Thus, nuns have a disproportionately high rate of breast cancer.

Will breast-feeding your child have any impact on your vulnerability, one way or another? Apparently not.

Women with large, heavy breasts are at several times the risk of developing cancer, presumably because early malignancies are difficult to feel. So mammography is especially important for them.

Regardless of the probabilities listed above, every woman is vulnerable to breast cancer, and should know what she can do to protect herself. As with colon cancer, diet appears to play an important role. For example, Japanese women not only have fewer colon cancers than we, they also have less breast cancer. But when they move to the United States, they lose that advantage for both colon and breast. If, on the other hand, they settle in Hawaii, rather than in the mainland United States, their incidence of breast cancer is somewhere between that in Japan and the United States. The reasons given for these fascinating statistics are that the Japanese consume very little fat. Their diet is rich in vegetables, fiber, and fish, and low in meats and saturated fats. When they adopt the high-fat Western diet, they develop more breast cancer (and colorectal malignancies as well). So if you're seriously concerned about breast cancer, reduce your fat intake.

There is some statistical evidence too that overweight, if you're postmenopausal and also relatively tall, increases your breast-cancer risk (presumably because excess weight can alter hormonal status). Greater body weight may, of course, simply reflect an increased fat intake. This apparent adverse influence of height and weight may explain, at least in part, why women of higher socioeconomic status have a greater incidence of breast cancer. They eat more and burn off fewer calories. So the second step in prevention, after reducing the fat content of your diet, is to try to keep your weight optimal, especially if you are postmenopausal. Women who have had cancer of the endometrium (lining of the uterus), ovary or colon (remember, the latter is also linked to a high-fat diet) are at twice the risk for breast cancer. Similarly, women with breast cancer are more likely to develop endometrial and ovarian malignancy.

Known or Suspected Causes: As it is with so many other cancers, there appears to be a link between radiation and cancer of the breast. For example, women who had frequent chest films years earlier because of tuberculosis, or who were treated with radiation for postpartum mastitis (breast irritation and inflammation after delivery), something that's no longer done, have a higher-than-usual frequency of breast cancer. But remember, *do not allow the hazards of excessive or unnecessary radiation deter you from following the recommended schedule of mammography.*

The burning question asked by most women is whether or not estrogen-replacement therapy will enhance their risk of breast cancer. My interpretation of the literature suggests that it may, over the long term when the doses are large and cumulative. But some studies report no association whatsoever, while others even suggest a reduced risk when progestin is given along with the estrogen. However, virtually all doctors agree that prolonged estrogen use in high doses should be avoided. The bottom line is this: If you *need* the hormone to prevent or treat osteoporosis, to relieve menopausal symptoms, or because your vaginal lining is dry and sex is uncomfortable, take it. But be sure to monitor the status of your breasts, by yourself, with your physician and by mammography.

Another hotly debated issue is the association of birth-control pills and breast cancer. Despite the fact that the Centers for Disease Control has concluded that oral contraceptives do not raise the risk over an eleven-year period, the FDA nevertheless requires that oral-contraceptive packages carry a label stating that the matter is still not settled.

DES (diethylstilbestrol), the "anti-sterility" hormone, was found to be associated with an increased risk of breast cancer. As you probably know, offspring of mothers who took this medication in order to prevent spontaneous abortion also have a higher incidence of vaginal cancer.

Recent research indicates that high-fiber intake may lower the risk of cancer of the breast as well as that of the bowel.

Again, geographic areas whose soil is low in selenium also have a high breast-cancer rate. Women at special risk by virtue of a bad family history should probably take selenium supplements in small doses.

Methylxanthines, the chemicals found in coffee, tea, cola drinks containing caffeine, and chocolate, as well as in some pain and cold remedies, have been implicated as carcinogens. Because their status is still in flux, I recommend moderation in their use—until all the evidence is in. For example, no one should drink more than three cups of coffee a day for this and other reasons.

Although some studies suggest that vitamins E, B and C may all relieve the symptoms of cystic breasts, there is no evidence that they prevent breast cancer.

To sum up: First, establish whether you are at high risk for breast cancer (but remember that every woman really is). Follow the guidelines of the American Cancer Society with respect to the kind of examination you should have, and how often. Reduce your total intake of fat. Avoid overweight, especially after the menopause. Take estrogen-replacement therapy if you need it, but for no longer than is necessary, in the lowest effective dose and in combination with progestin.

Prostate Cancer—The Rewards of Early Detection

There were 76,000 new cases of prostate cancer in 1984, making it the fourth most common malignancy overall. It is mainly a disease of older men, and its incidence increases with age. Blacks are more likely to have it than whites, and married men more so than bachelors. Although I have seen several men with cancer of the breast, I must admit I've never come across a woman with cancer of the prostate!

By the time most cases of prostate cancer are detected they have already spread—and by then it's usually too late to effect a cure. That's the bad news. But the good news is that when found early enough, cure is possible. And such early detection requires nothing more than the physician's examining finger. No X rays. No invasive testing. I believe that if every man over the age of forty were to have a careful rectal examination every year, the death rate from prostate cancer would be substantially less than it is now. The five-year survival rate for cancer of the prostate is a hefty 75 percent when detected early enough and treated promptly. It is estimated that the cost to society of finding each curable prostate cancer is about $6,500 —a real bargain!

The causes of prostatic malignancy are unclear, but this malignancy seems to be statistically associated with cancers of the colon, rectum and breast. The role of diet and workplace carcinogens is being actively explored. Several population studies now tie high fat consumption (and possibly even increased protein intake) to prostate cancer. A high-fat diet may possibly predispose to this malignancy by affecting the production of sex hormones. The prostate depends on testosterone (male hormone) for its growth and development.

Workers exposed to cadmium during welding, electroplating and the production of alkaline batteries, as well as those in the rubber industry, also have an unusually high incidence of this tumor.

I'm frequently asked by men with waning sexual potency for injections of testosterone. When in the course of their evaluation, I find a decreased level of male hormone, I accede. Such shots sometimes help. But in most cases, decreased sexual performance usually has little to do with how much male hormone is circulating in the blood. The problem is more frequently psychological, or due to some disease like diabetes, hypertension, arteriosclerosis, neurological disorders or medications.

I don't like to administer testosterone supplements because they may activate a small cancer hidden in the prostate. Such malignancies are often found at autopsy in men who died of other causes. The tumors were never any trouble because they remained dormant deep inside the prostate gland. Such tiny tumors are also frequently discovered during the course of an operation for simple enlargement of the prostate. Testosterone given for whatever reason may activate these otherwise quiescent cancers.

Incidentally, the selenium link, which keeps cropping up in various malignancies, appears to pertain to the prostate gland too.

From a practical point of view, there is nothing the average man can really do to prevent cancer of the prostate except reduce his intake of fat. The key to survival is early detection by the doctor's examining finger. Symptoms of prostate enlargement—difficulty in initiating the stream or controlling it, the need to urinate frequently, or pain on voiding—are not necessarily indicators of prostate cancer.

Urinary Cancers

Cancer of the urinary bladder and the kidney, which together rank number five in frequency, are grouped under the heading of urinary cancer. There were about 57,000 such malignancies in 1984, of which 39,000 were bladder cancers.

Cancer of the Bladder: This is primarily a disease of white men. It strikes women in less than one-third of the cases. It is two to three times more common in smokers than in nonsmokers, and it is estimated that about 40 percent of the cases in men and 29 percent in women are due to cigarettes. How tobacco smoke affects the urinary bladder is not clear, but it must be via some blood-borne substance, as is also presumably the case with cancer of the cervix (see below).

Remember all the trouble you've had in the last fifteen years getting the artificial sweetener you preferred for your morning coffee? All the fuss was due to the fact that various of these products supposedly caused bladder cancer in laboratory animals. So, first the cyclamates were removed from the market in 1969 and we were left with saccharin. Then it was reported that saccharin also induced cancer in laboratory animals, and attempts were made to ban it as well. But, responding to public pressure, the FDA relaxed its position somewhat. Although it still considers saccharin a weak carcinogen, it has permitted it to remain on the market, with a warning label on the bottle. Yet ironically, the evidence for carcinogenicity of the banned cyclamates is much weaker than that for saccharin.

Every now and then coffee gets blamed for something or other— cancer of the pancreas, an increase in fetal abnormalities, or heart trouble. It has in the past been implicated by some in cancer of the bladder. Here again, be reassured that there is little or no increase in bladder cancer among coffee drinkers as compared to those who don't drink coffee.

Treatment with several anti-cancer drugs, long-term use of painkillers containing phenacetin (no longer permitted to be sold in the United States), and infection by certain parasites have all been shown to be associated with a high incidence of bladder cancer. There is in particular one group of chemicals used in the dyestuff industry that does raise the risk of bladder cancer substantially. These are referred to as aromatic amines—compounds used in the manufacture of dyes. Also, workers in rubber and leather industries, as well as painters, chemical workers, printers, metalworkers and hairdressers, are all at high risk because of exposure to combinations of other cancer-inducing substances.

Uterine Cancer—Cancers of the Endometrium (Lining of the Uterus) and the Cervix

Cancer of the uterus ranks fifth in the malignancy index in the United States, a total of 55,000 cases having been reported in 1984. Of these, 39,000 involved the lining of the uterus; the other 16,000 were in the cervix. For some reason, the incidence of uterine cancer in white women in the United States is among the highest in the world. It usually affects females between the ages of fifty and sixty-four. After an unexplained large increase during the 1970s, death rates from this malignancy are now beginning to drop.

Endometrial Cancer: Who is at risk for endometrial cancer and how can it be prevented? Many of the same factors that predispose to cancer of the breast are operative in cancer of the endometrium. As I indicated earlier, women at special risk for breast cancer also have a greater chance of developing endometrial cancer—probably by virtue of certain common factors. These include obesity, few or no children, early menstruation and/or late menopause, a diet and life-style that accompany a high socioeconomic status, and excessive exposure to estrogen.

Women who are twenty pounds or more over ideal weight are twice as likely to develop cancer of the endometrium, and the incidence rises even further with increasing weight. Since estrogen is produced in fatty tissue, fat women, especially after the menopause, have higher levels of this hormone than they should, and this may predispose to endometrial cancer. Obesity becomes even more important statistically in women who are taller than 5 feet 7 inches.

If you have diabetes and/or high blood pressure, the likelihood of developing endometrial cancer is also increased, probably because overweight is common in these two diseases.

If you've had multiple births (four or more children), you've dropped your risk of endometrial cancer to one-third. But if you've had no children, especially because of "infertility" (and the presumed hormonal abnormalities that accompany it), you're at high risk. When we review the medical histories of patients with endometrial cancer, we commonly find that many have had irregular periods for years, or failed to ovulate normally.

The uncertainty regarding the relationship between estrogen-replacement therapy and cancer of the breast does not apply to endometrial cancer. Any woman on estrogens is at six to seven times the general risk of developing uterine cancer. The longer she's been taking the hormone and the higher the dosage used, the worse the odds. But cancer of the uterus can be spotted early and cured. So unless you've had a hysterectomy, if you are on estrogen supplements, you must be examined by your gynecologist and have an endometrial tissue sample taken at least twice a year. A Pap test is not enough. Unlike its effectiveness in detecting malignancy of the cervix, the Pap test is less than 50 percent accurate in finding endometrial cancer. Even if you are not taking estrogens, the American Cancer Society still recommends that at menopause you have an endometrial tissue sample done every one and a half to two years. This is a simple office procedure. It is standard practice now to add some progestin, another female hormone, when prescribing estrogens. This dramatically reduces the occurrence of endometrial cancer.

You do not raise your chances of endometrial cancer with the birth-control pill. In fact, the reverse is true. Women on the pill for at least one year reduce their risk by half. This is especially true for childless women who normally would be at greater risk.

Remember that early detection is the key to dealing with endometrial cancer. Ninety percent of cases can be completely cured if the tumor is spotted in time. So let your doctor know immediately should you have any bleeding or discharge between periods.

Cancer of the Cervix: The cervix, from which the Pap smear is taken, is the lowest portion of the uterus. The 16,000 new cases of cervical cancer in 1984 do not include the very early grade I, or "suspicious," Pap test reports, since many of these never progress to become cancer. Unlike the other cancers described earlier, which appear to be related to fat consumption and are more prevalent in the higher socioeconomic groups, cancer of the cervix is found in greater numbers among blacks and the economically disadvantaged.

The combination of endometrial and cervical cancer ranks sixth in incidence in this country. Presumably because of earlier detection by the Pap test, which is done more frequently in this country than anywhere else in the world, the incidence of invasive cervical malig-

nancy has been declining while the number of very early stage abnormalities is rising. Despite these statistics, some authorities continue
to insist that the Pap test need not be performed as frequently as
many doctors recommend!

There is a host of interesting observations which suggest that if you
modify your life-style, you may be able to prevent cervical cancer.
All kinds of things can happen to the cervix during intercourse—
trauma, infection and exposure to whatever substances, including
sperm, are introduced into the vagina. Bearing all this in mind, here
is what you can do to reduce the risk of cancer of the cervix. Shun
multiple sex partners. That should come as no surprise, since you
never know what any of them brings to your cervix in terms of
infection and carcinogenic agents. Regular intercourse begun in the
pre- or early teens predisposes to cancer, presumably because the
tissue of the cervix may be more vulnerable at puberty to whatever
it is that causes cancer in the first place. That may very well be a
virus or some other infectious agent. There is a good deal of support
for the theory that cancer of the cervix is transmitted in much the same
way as are venereal diseases. For example, genital herpes increases
the risk of cervical cancer by as much as eight times. Components of
the actual herpes virus have been found in cervical tumors. Other
sexually transmitted diseases, like papilloma virus, which causes genitourinary warts, and the now seemingly ubiquitous chlamydia organism, are also believed to predispose to cervical cancer.

Given the relation between infection and cervical cancer, it is no
surprise that barrier methods of contraception, in which the cervix is
covered or protected, are associated with a lower incidence of this
malignancy as compared to oral contraceptives. So, if you're on
the pill and not using barrier methods, you should be screened by
your gynecologist more frequently for evidence of early cancer of
the cervix.

I can't for the life of me understand why the relationship exists,
but the statistics tell us that women who smoke have more cervical
cancer than do nonsmokers. Whether it is some substance in the
tobacco that is absorbed in the bloodstream and finds its way down
to the cervix or because female smokers have other habits that predispose to cancer is not clear. But if you're worried about getting
cancer of the cervix, lung, bladder, mouth or pharynx—or a heart

attack—stop smoking, right now, and never start if you haven't already.

If your mother took diethylstilbestrol (DES) during pregnancy, you are at risk for developing cervical and vaginal cancer. I suggest you have a colposcopic exam every six months. This involves introduction of an instrument into the vagina that can survey that entire area of the genital tract.

There is even more you can do to help minimize your chances of getting cervical cancer. Beta-carotene, thought to be protective against lung cancer, is also believed to reduce the incidence of cancer of the cervix. Vitamin C and folicin (one of the B-complex group) may also do so.

Early detection of cervical cancer is crucial. There is some difference of opinion between the American Cancer Society and the American College of Obstetricians and Gynecologists how best to do that. The former recommends that you have your first pelvic exam and Pap test after initial sexual contact. Another Pap test should be done a year later. If both are negative, then pelvic exams and Pap tests should be done at three-year intervals until age forty. Beyond forty years, the ACS says all women should have an annual pelvic exam and a Pap test at least every two years. The American College of Obstetricians and Gynecologists thinks these recommendations are too lax. Their specialists advise yearly pelvic and Pap tests for *all* sexually active women. Given the simplicity and relatively low cost of the Pap test, I personally favor the advice of the College of Obstetricians and Gynecologists.

Kidney Cancer: Considered alone, kidney cancer ranks number twelve in the incidence of malignancies in this country, with about 18,000 new cases in 1984. Statistically, it's twice as common in men as in women, and, in either event, usually occurs after the age of sixty.

Cigarettes seem to be the most important risk factor for cancer of the kidney. Smokers are twice as likely to develop it as are non-smokers, and it's estimated that 30 percent of these cancers in men and 24 percent in women are directly caused by tobacco. So your best chances of preventing it are to stop smoking or never to start. Overweight seems to be an additional precipitating factor in women, perhaps because of high estrogen levels associated with the conversion of other hormones into estrogens by fatty tissue. As in cancer of the bladder, the long-term use of pain-killers containing phenacetin or acetaminophen may also increase the risk of at least one form of kidney cancer, although a rare one. With respect to industrial toxins, asbestos has been implicated, as have various oils used in the petroleum industry.

Cancer of the Mouth and the Pharynx

Malignancies in the oral area rank number seven in incidence in the United States. In 1984, there were some 28,000 new cases reported. These tumors occur more than twice as often in men as they do in women, and 90 percent of them appear only after age forty-five.

Prevention means being careful about what goes into your mouth. Again, the chief offender is tobacco. Here, it's not smoking that does it, but chewing and dipping. These habits contribute most to cancers of the mouth and the throat, the risk increasing by as much as fifteen-fold depending on the amount and type of tobacco you use. Indians (from Asia, not North America) have the highest rates worldwide because they chew a mixture of betel leaves, tobacco and lime, which accounts for about 75 percent of their mouth and throat cancers. Women in the southern United States who take snuff in their cheeks have a very high rate of oral cancer too. Cigarette smoking causes throat cancer. More than a pack a day results in a six times higher incidence than among nonsmokers. Pipes, which were always considered less harmful than other forms of tobacco, cause more cancer of the lip because of heat and pressure from the stem, especially when it is curved.

Heavy alcohol intake, defined as more than seven drinks a week, doubles the risk of cancer of the mouth and the pharynx. If you smoke *and* drink, the chances are multiplied as much as fifteenfold. No matter how modestly you drink, even if it's only one and a half ounces of alcohol a day, if you also smoke forty or more cigarettes, this increased risk exists.

So, the combination of alcohol and tobacco, by virtue of local irritation and perhaps some chemical influence, is the major cause of oral cancer. But any chronic irritation can also do it. For example, older people with ill-fitting dentures, persons who have sharp or broken teeth, and anyone with a "bad" dental history (many extractions that were poorly done, or who've needed repeated root-canal therapy) are all vulnerable to oral cancer.

One interesting link that cannot be ignored is the mouthwash phenomenon. If you smoke and drink, you increase your chances of getting cancer of the mouth and the throat. If you do neither, are of the female sex and use a mouthwash frequently, your risk is apparently increased as well. It doesn't appear to make any sense, but there it is.

As with so many other malignancies, certain occupations predispose to cancer of the mouth. Bartenders who "taste" once in a while, waiters, waitresses, outdoor workers and those working with asbestos also appear to be more vulnerable.

Nutrition in itself—the amount of fat, protein, carbohydrates and vegetables you eat—has no apparent relationship to oral and pharyngeal cancer, but vitamin deficiencies may play a role. So, if you are elderly, and not eating as well as you once did, or if you are a heavy smoker and drinker, it's a good idea to supplement your diet with extra vitamins A, B and C. The A should be derived from food, not pills, but the B and C may safely be taken in tablet or capsule form.

As with so many other cancers, early detection offers a good chance of cure. You should have a regular dental checkup if you're a smoker and drink alcohol, if your nutrition is poor or if you have chronic irritation in your mouth from whatever source. The important warning signs in this area are any sore in your mouth that doesn't heal or that bleeds easily, and any lump or thickening. A particularly important and visible piece of early evidence of oral malignancy is leukoplakia, a persistent white or reddish patch anywhere in your mouth or on your tongue.

Pancreatic Cancer—One of the Worst

The pancreas lies deep within the abdomen in the midline just above the level of the belly button. Pancreatic cancer ranks eighth in overall incidence. Twenty-five thousand persons will develop it in 1986; only 2 percent will survive five years; most will die within the year. I know of nothing that will slow the rapid progression to death. We haven't the slightest idea what causes pancreatic cancer, nor do we know how even to begin to prevent it. There are, however, certain factors that appear to be associated with an increased risk. Chief among them is the cigarette; smokers have a twofold risk over nonsmokers. Interestingly, no such association has been shown for either pipes or cigars. This suggests that the risk factor may lie in the carcinogens in inhaled smoke, since most pipe and cigar smokers inhale less deeply. Alcohol has not been implicated. There is no association with diet, although in one study there appeared to be some relationship between increased meat consumption and decreased vegetable intake and pancreatic cancer.

Two reports did cause quite a stir by suggesting that too much coffee, decaffeinated as well as regular, might contribute to cancer of the pancreas. These observations have not been confirmed. In fact, they have subsequently been refuted. Still, since where there's smoke there may be fire, I suggest you limit your coffee intake to three cups a day (for other health reasons as well).

Cancer of the pancreas occurs anytime after thirty, and the incidence increases with age.

Diabetics are said to be more prone to cancer of the pancreas than are other individuals, but since insulin is produced in the pancreas, it may be that the malignancy causes the diabetes, rather than the other way around.

Whenever a patient complains of vague persistent abdominal pain, for which there is no apparent cause, I always think of pancreatic cancer. The routine diagnostic work-up, which consists of a careful physical examination, an upper-GI series, and a barium enema, is usually normal. But we can now usually detect cancer of the pancreas by the abdominal sonogram or by CAT scan. It nevertheless remains the one killer for which neither effective prevention nor treatment is yet available.

Stomach Cancer—Number Nine, But Things Are Looking Up

Since so many people use the word "stomach" whenever they refer to the abdominal cavity ("I have a stomach ache"), you may get the impression there is an awful lot of stomach cancer around. Actually, it's less common than you think. It is, however, a serious malignancy with a five-year survival of only 16 percent. It occurs more frequently in men than in women, and in blacks and low-income groups.

The stomach itself is a discrete portion of the intestinal tract, where the digestive process is initiated. J-shaped, it begins where the food pipe ends, and ends where the small intestine begins.

What are some of the factors identified with stomach cancer? First, there is the matter of its acid content. Excessive amounts are associated with ulcers; a deficiency, with cancer. How would you know you have too little acid? Certain diseases are associated with such a lack (and all carry an increased risk of gastric malignancy). These include pernicious anemia, which results from the absence of "intrinsic factor" and a resultant inability to absorb the vitamin B-12 you eat; atrophic gastritis, where the lining of the stomach wall is unable to secrete acid; and achlorhydria, the absence of hydrochloric acid in the stomach secretion. If you have any of these conditions, you should be very carefully and frequently monitored for early evidence of gastric cancer.

There is some confusion among lay persons about the relationship of stomach ulcers to stomach cancer. An ulcer is neither a forerunner nor a cause of cancer. But what is diagnosed as a stomach "ulcer" may actually *be* an early cancer. The distinction between the two cannot always be made on an X ray, and requires a biopsy. This is performed by means of a thin flexible tube inserted into the mouth and swallowed. There is a light at the end of it and a small forceps. The doctor looks into the stomach, identifies the site of the "ulcer," snips a few tiny pieces from various locations and has them analyzed. It's especially important to biopsy any gastric "ulcer" that doesn't heal after a few weeks of vigorous anti-ulcer treatment.

If you've had radiation therapy for any reason, you must consider yourself at somewhat increased risk for stomach cancer. For example, atomic-bomb survivors in Japan have a higher incidence of this malignancy than does the rest of the population in that country. Cigarette smoking has been implicated too. Also, if any of your blood relatives had stomach cancer, you are at two to three times the risk yourself. And here's a fascinating piece of information that relates to your blood type. There are four major blood groups—A, B, AB and O. Persons with type A have more stomach cancer than do the other three categories. No one knows why.

What you eat has a lot to do with whether or not you'll develop stomach cancer. The relatively low incidence and continuing decline in this country probably reflect our increasing consumption of fresh fruits and vegetables. In Japan, stomach cancer causes more deaths than all malignancies combined, and is five to six times more frequent than it is here in the United States. This is presumably because of the large amounts of pickled, salted and smoked foods eaten in that country. The latest nutritional guidelines from the American Cancer Society would have us cut down on these particular items. Retrospective dietary studies on patients with stomach cancer also reveal them to have eaten less food rich in vitamins C and A. These vitamins prevent the formation of nitrosamines, potent cancer-producing substances that form in the stomach when nitrates (chemicals found in some water supplies, green vegetables, cheeses and cured meats) combine with the normal bacteria in the intestinal tract. The higher incidence of stomach cancer among persons with lower socioeconomic status may be due to the fact that their diets are higher in starch and lower in fresh fruits and vegetables laden with vitamin C.

The best way, therefore, to reduce the chance of getting stomach cancer is to cut down on your intake of those foods suspected of increasing the risk—namely smoked, barbecued, pickled, salted, and cured meat and fish, and to eat plenty of food rich in vitamin C and vitamin A.

The Leukemias—Cancers of the Blood and Bone-Marrow Cells

Although this group of malignancies ranks roughly tenth in incidence in this country, with some 25,000 new cases reported in 1984, it accounts for about 45 percent of children's cancers. There is slightly more leukemia among whites than blacks, among Jews than other whites, and among women than men.

There are several different types of leukemia. Some reflect genetic traits (there is not much you can do about those, since we cannot choose our ancestors); others are due to an impaired immune system, previous exposure to radiation and ongoing contamination by certain chemicals.

Individuals with certain genetic traits, for example, mongolism (Down's syndrome), have as much as twenty times the usual chance of developing leukemia. This appears to be due to specific and abnormal chromosome patterns.

Does leukemia run in families? Although a number of such "clusters" have been investigated, there is no definite evidence of any familial predisposition (such as is observed in malignancies of the breast or the bowel, for example).

Almost everyone knows about the relationship between radiation and leukemia. Atomic-bomb survivors, patients who have received X-ray therapy and excessive diagnostic irradiation in the past, military personnel who participated in nuclear tests and residents in areas receiving fallout from those tests, all have a higher-than-normal incidence. Years ago, I used to fluoroscope all my cardiac patients routinely to obtain additional information concerning heart size and cardiac contraction, as well as to look at the lungs. These days, however, the availability of such sophisticated nonradiologic diagnostic techniques as echocardiography, which do not expose the patient to radiation, has rendered the fluoroscope obsolete. If your own doctor has not removed this equipment from his office, I suggest you think twice before permitting him to use it on you.

Industrial solvents like benzene, as well as some anti-cancer drugs, are also linked with the increased risk of leukemia. And I needn't tell you of the concern regarding leukemia in those communities adjacent to toxic-waste dumps.

The most exciting research area in leukemia, and one that promises effective prevention—hopefully in the not-too-distant future—is related to viruses. We have for years been able to induce leukemia in animals by infecting them with certain viruses. But it is only recently that we have proved that the T-cell leukemia or lymphoma virus (HTLV) causes an unusual form of leukemia in humans. The hope is that variations of this and other viruses will in the future permit the manufacture of vaccines to prevent more common types of leukemia.

In the meantime, the best we can do is keep our environment clean, avoid contamination from harmful waste chemicals and reduce exposure to any form of radiation to the absolute minimum.

Lymphomas (Non-Hodgkin's Type)

Lymphocytes are the white blood cells that are the immune system's indispensable frontline fighter against infection. Ironically, they can themselves become malignant, and when they do, the resulting blood cancer is called *lymphoma*. There were 24,000 new cases in 1984, many of which responded to treatment. It is thus the eleventh most common malignancy in this country.

Lymphomas may run in families. They also occur in patients who have some problem with their immune system. Such disorders of resistance may be congenital or develop later in life. The "bubble boy" who lived twelve years in his sealed environment in a Houston hospital before he died was born with an immune system that was, for all practical purposes, nonfunctioning. However, when patients are deliberately "immunosuppressed" in order to prevent rejection of transplanted organs, the risk of lymphoma increases anywhere from forty-one to one hundred times.

Ovarian Cancer

With more than 18,000 new cases in 1984, and 11,000 deaths annually, ovarian cancer is the twelfth most common malignancy overall in the United States. But among American women, it is the fourth leading cause of cancer mortality.

White women, aged forty to fifty, living in highly industrialized countries (except Japan) are most likely to develop ovarian cancer. Females who've had children are at only half the risk. The greater the number of pregnancies, the smaller the chance of ovarian cancer. The pill, which creates a hormonal environment similar to that of pregnancy, reduces the likelihood of ovarian cancer by as much as 50 percent. Females at highest risks are those who have not had any children, whose periods have usually been irregular and in whom there is a strong family history of ovarian cancer. Since the ovaries are the major source of estrogen production, these observations suggest that this cancer is hormone-related. There are other endocrine-related risk factors as well—overweight, the presence of cervical polyps and gallbladder disease, all of which are in some way involved with estrogens. In fact, women who take this hormone after the menopause are at two to three times the risk for developing ovarian cancer. If you've had cancer of the breast, you have twice the chance of coming down with an ovarian cancer too (and conversely, if you have an ovarian cancer, you're three to four times more likely to suffer breast malignancy later on). So there is without doubt a key hormonal role in the causation of ovarian cancer. With the exception of one theory suggesting that the mumps virus is implicated in this malignancy, a viral role has not been postulated.

Particles of asbestos and talc have been found in normal as well as cancerous ovaries. There were two studies—both fascinating—that reached diametrically opposite conclusions with respect to their risk in the causation of ovarian cancer. One reported an increase among talc users; the other did not. Even though talc itself has not been shown to cause cancer in animals, and despite the fact that tighter regulation and testing by government and industry have resulted in less asbestos in talc, I suggest you put something other than talcum powder on your diaphragm and your baby's genital area.

Ovarian cancer is such a wicked one that postmenopausal women who are undergoing a hysterectomy are usually advised to have their ovaries removed at the same time, to avoid any possibility of ovarian cancer later on.

Unfortunately, cancer of the ovary results in very few early symptoms. Every woman should therefore report any vague, persistent discomfort in the lower abdomen. In the absence of such symptoms, the tumor is usually first detected by a doctor during a routine pelvic exam.

So if you are white, American, female, between the ages of forty and fifty, and have had no children, keep your weight down, avoid unnecessary estrogen supplements, and if you must take them, do so in the lowest dose possible, for the shortest possible time, and be sure to have regular gynecological examinations at least once a year.

Malignant Melanoma—The Worst Skin Cancer

The major exception to the usually excellent prognosis of most skin cancers is the malignant melanoma, which ranks number thirteen in cancer incidence. There were some 18,000 cases reported in 1984 in the United States, and the worldwide attack rate is rising sharply. Despite the fact that this cancer involves a specific skin cell called the melanocyte, which synthesizes the dark pigment called melanin, it is uncommon in blacks. The highest incidence of melanoma is in Australia, which is near the Equator and closest to the strong rays of the sun. Persons with fair complexions and red hair, or of Irish descent, are at greatest risk.

Malignant melanoma is a bad cancer. Unless it is detected early and removed completely, it spreads like wildfire throughout the body. But as serious as it is, the cure rate is close to 90 percent when it is treated in time. So be melanoma conscious, especially if you've been a sun worshiper all your life or have the high-risk physical characteristics mentioned above. However, no matter who you are, give your skin a good going over—frequently. Look for lesions on your head, neck and arms, but especially on the trunk if you're a man and on the lower legs if you're a woman. Be suspicious of any mole whose borders have become less regular or more poorly defined, or that has changed color or assumed new shades, especially red, white and blue. Be very leery too if it has changed in feel (for example, from smooth to rough), in size (larger or even smaller), in sensation (because it begins to itch, tingle or hurt), and when it becomes inflamed, bleeds or oozes. Melanoma recognition is so tricky that when I have even the slightest suspicion I send the patient to an expert dermatologist. It's better to be safe than sorry.

The course of this cancer is unpredictable. It often remains silent somewhere in the body for years, then suddenly and for no apparent reason spreads widely. A case involving one of my patients is a good example of such variability. He was a man in his sixties who "loved the sun" and spent most of his winters in Florida. During a routine examination, he asked me about a mole on his forehead that had recently become darker and larger. I referred him to a dermatologist, who biopsied it and found it to be a malignant melanoma. He was then sent to a surgeon who completely removed the tumor. Everyone believed we had effected a cure. My patient resumed his normal activities, except that he now avoided the sun. For the next four years, he felt well and maintained his weight, appetite and vigor. One day, he asked to see me because "I think I'm having a gallbladder attack." He complained of pain in the right upper part of his abdomen, and he had a little fever. When I examined him, he was tender in the gallbladder area. I agreed with the diagnosis he had made and, to confirm it, sent him for a sonogram of his abdomen. To my horror, in addition to the expected gallstones, his entire liver was virtually replaced by cancerous tissue! A needle biopsy showed it to consist of typical melanoma cells—this after a symptom-free period of four years! Why the cancer had spread now, after four years of hibernation, is a mystery we have not yet solved.

This man has responded to a combination of radiation to his bones, also invaded by the cancer, and chemotherapy. Almost two years later he is again symptom-free. I have no idea what to expect next—or when.

There is no question that melanomas are related to ultraviolet radiation—from any source, but especially from the sun. However, the association seems to be more complicated. While other forms of skin cancer are almost always due to long-term cumulative solar exposure, melanoma is also apt to occur in persons who have had intense overdoses of sun over short periods—repeated crash tanning with little or no time for the skin to adjust. An example is the tourist who bakes for a week or two on some tropical isle, gets burned, then tanned, returns home and repeats the cycle the following year. Patients with melanoma also tell of frequent blistering and slow-healing sunburns during childhood (a good reason to protect your children from excessive exposure of the sun). However, the high and increasing incidence of this malignancy in southern Arizona suggests that chronic exposure to sun, in addition to the short, intense solar experience, is also dangerous.

Aside from avoiding excessive exposure to sun, there are other ways to prevent malignant melanoma. For example, oral contraceptives may increase the risk. It has been observed that moles frequently change their appearance during periods of high hormonal activity. In one study, women who used oral contraceptives for five or more years, as well as those who'd had their first child after the age of thirty, were found to have a higher incidence of melanoma. So if you happen to have had a melanoma, and been "cured," I suggest you avoid the pill for contraception and keep away from estrogen replacement.

You should be aware of the *dysplastic nevus syndrome,* a forerunner, or precursor, of melanoma. These are moles that may be either flat or bumpy, with irregular borders and a variety of colors. They are anywhere from one-quarter inch to one-half inch or more in diameter, and there may be a hundred or more in areas *not* normally exposed to the sun—breasts, buttocks, genitals, scalp and back. Dysplastic nevi precede a third of all melanomas. Anyone with such nevi who also has a family history of malignant melanoma is at ten times the usual risk for developing this particular cancer. These lesions require careful monitoring, both by you and a dermatologist. In most cases, I recommend their immediate removal. If you are prone to dysplastic nevi, keep out of the sun at all costs. Even the apparently harmless large congenital black birthmarks appear to carry a high risk of melanoma, and some surgeons recommend their early excision as well.

Cancer of the Liver

Primary liver cancers, that is, those that originate in that organ, are fourteenth in incidence of malignancies in this country, with 13,500 new cases in 1984. They occur mostly in elderly black males and, although fairly rare in the United States, are a leading cause of death elsewhere in the world, especially in Africa.

Sixty to 90 percent of liver cancers occur in persons with cirrhosis, a late consequence of either hepatitis B or alcoholism. But the most important risk factor worldwide is hepatitis B, which can now be prevented by a vaccine. Everyone at high risk for developing this infection—homosexuals, those receiving multiple transfusions, drug abusers, persons in contact with hepatitis B patients, and infants born of mothers who are hepatitis B carriers—should be vaccinated.

There is a rare type of liver cancer associated with exposure to vinyl chloride used in the production of plastics. Liver tumors caused by the pill are almost always benign.

Liver malignancy is almost always fatal because it is usually discovered late in the game. The recent availability of a rapid, sensitive screening test using monoclonal antibodies may enable earlier detection of liver cancer. Attacking such malignancies with radioactive monoclonal antibodies has reportedly resulted in some cures.

The most practical fact for you to remember with respect to preventing liver cancer now is that if you are at any risk for developing hepatitis B infection, you should have the vaccine as soon as possible. If you're an alcoholic on the road to cirrhosis, your best bet is to get on the wagon—fast.

Cancer of the Brain and the Central Nervous System

Nervous-system malignancies rank fifteenth in incidence in this country with some 12,000 cases per year. In children they are second in frequency only to leukemia. They are more often found in men than in women, in whites than in blacks. In adult life, they are most common after age fifty-five.

If someone you know has developed cancer of the brain and you're wondering what on earth might have caused it, you will not find the answer in these pages. Very little is known about how and why these particular malignancies come about. Various studies have, however, linked them with occupational, environmental, viral and genetic factors. For example, there seems to be a higher proportion of such cancers among workers in the oil refineries on the Texas Gulf Coast, chemists, pharmaceutical workers, embalmers, those exposed to vinyl chloride, cattle and sheep ranchers, dairy farmers and grain millers. These widely different occupations do not appear to have a common factor. A history of long-term exposure to pesticides has also been noted. A viral cause has also been invoked, because some younger patients report exposure to sick animals sometime in the past.

Certain nervous-system cancers—for example, retinoblastoma, a rare eye malignancy—often run in families. Curiously, too, if one of your children has epilepsy, his or her brothers or sisters appear to be at higher risk for developing brain cancer.

Despite these leads, there is very little you can do to prevent this form of cancer. For the moment, you must simply keep your fingers crossed and hope you and your loved ones are spared.

Cancer of the Thyroid

This malignancy has a fairly low incidence—only 10,000 new cases in 1984. It is usually so slow-growing that the five-year survival rate is about 93 percent. It affects twice as many women as men, any time between twenty-five and sixty-five years of age. The major avoidable risk factor is radiation.

Before 1950, infants and children were frequently treated with X rays for benign conditions of the head and neck, like enlargement of the thymus gland, inflamed tonsils and adenoids, and acne. Now, years later, many of these individuals are developing thyroid cancer. The younger the age at which the radiation was received, the greater the dose and the closer the intervals of radiation, the higher is the risk of thyroid cancer.

Although you might expect goiter (a benign thyroid condition that sometimes looks like a bicycle tire around the neck) to predispose to cancer, there is, in fact, little relationship between goiters and malignancy.

Here, then, is the bottom line with respect to thyroid cancer. If you keep away from excessive radiation, your chances of developing one are pretty small.

Multiple Myeloma

We know very little about this cancer, which had an incidence of approximately 10,000 new cases in 1984. It involves the plasma cells in the blood, whose function it is to produce immunoglobulins or antibodies. I have had several patients of both sexes with multiple myeloma, all adult. It occurs particularly frequently among older black men, and for some reason, the highest incidence is among those living in the San Francisco Bay area.

The most widely accepted theory holds that multiple myeloma results from some change in the immune system associated with age. However, there may also be an inborn susceptibility, and a hormonal tie as well. Certain other connections, mostly occupational, have been made too. For example, male compositors in printing offices, exposed to lead vapors, workers in the plastics manufacturing industries, farmers, and those in rubber and petrochemical jobs have a higher incidence of multiple myeloma than does the general population. Atomic-bomb survivors and radiologists who have been exposed to long-term, low-dose ionizing radiation are also at greater risk, as are siblings of patients with this disease.

Unfortunately, there is no known way to prevent this cancer at the present time. It presents typically as diffuse bone pain not caused by injury.

Cancer of the Esophagus

Fortunately there were only 9,000 new cases of cancer of the esophagus, or food pipe, in this country in 1984. It occurs most frequently in black males over the age of fifty-five, and, in the United States, more among city dwellers than rural inhabitants. There is strong evidence that this terrible cancer is caused by environmental and life-style factors over which most of us do have some control. The major risk factors are excessive consumption of tobacco (cigarettes *and* cigars *and* pipes) and alcohol, especially in combination. In one study of black males with this disease in Washington, D.C., heavy drinking accounted for 80 percent of the cancers, although poor nutrition was also implicated. In Bombay, India, the local alcohol brew coupled with cigarette smoking constituted the high risk there; while in northern Iran and northern Afghanistan, eating opium-pipe residue has been implicated. In one area of the People's Republic of China, a pickled vegetable mix is the prime suspect. Low socioeconomic status and poor nutrition, especially diets deficient in riboflavin, vitamin C and vitamin A, appear to predispose to cancer of the esophagus. Zinc deficiency may also be a factor, as is iron deprivation, which causes the esophagus first to become inflamed and later cancerous.

The earliest symptom of esophageal cancer is trouble swallowing. Unfortunately, by the time that happens, it's usually too late for a cure. Surgery is performed only to relieve symptoms of obstruction.

Your best bet, then, is prevention, and that means modifying your life-style. If you're a heavy user of tobacco and alcohol, quit fast. Until you do, and it can't be too soon, take extra vitamins A and C in your diet.

Hodgkin's Disease—Almost "Conquered"

Earlier I discussed non-Hodgkin's lymphomas. Hodgkin's disease itself is a specific form of cancer of the lymph system which accounts for about 7,000 new cases a year. It is one of the most common malignancies found in young adults.

We don't really know how to prevent this particular lymphoma any more than we do the others, but happily, its treatment is very satisfactory and the cure rate is high. I am not aware of any significant environmental risk factors. We used to think that children who'd had their tonsils out were vulnerable, the theory being that since the tonsils play a part in the disease-fighting capability of the lymph system, their removal increases susceptibility. This association has not been confirmed. Although most physicians these days discourage the routine tonsillectomy, it's not for that reason. Other links between Hodgkin's, polio and multiple sclerosis have been explored, but all without success. I expect that the causative agent will probably turn out to be one of the lymphoma viruses.

Testicular Cancer

There are about 5,600 new cases of cancer of the testicle each year in the United States. This particular malignancy is one of the most common cancers in a well-defined population—males between the ages of fifteen and thirty-four. Its incidence is four times higher among whites than among blacks.

The good things about testicular cancer are that (a) it is easily diagnosed; (b) it is frequently curable even after it has spread (the five-year survival rate is greater than 75 percent); and (c) it can, under certain circumstances, be prevented.

There is actually very little known about the causes of this malignancy. However, men with an undescended or partially descended testicle, or one that comes down into the scrotal sac from the abdominal cavity after the age of six (the testicles normally descend completely shortly after birth), are at much higher risk. In fact, this particular cancer occurs in 11 to 15 percent of men whose testicles are undescended. So every male infant should be carefully examined at birth to make sure both testes are where they ought to be. If your child is found to have one of his "missing," it should be brought down by means of a simple surgical procedure before age six, ideally between one and two years.

Exposure to synthetic estrogens before birth, as for example in sons of mothers who took DES (diethylstilbestrol), has been implicated in testicular abnormalities. There are some other rare genetic disorders that appear to be associated with an increased incidence of testicular cancer—hermaphroditism, hypospadias (in which the urethra opens on the underside of the penis instead of up front), and the failure of the testis to develop. None of these is preventable.

Trauma to a testis, such as might occur in certain sports, may increase the chances of testicular cancer. For example, in one recent study, teen-agers who did a lot of bicycling and horseback riding seemed to be more vulnerable. This observation needs confirmation. Another report suggested that viral diseases involving the testicles—mumps, for example—might cause cancer later on, but this too is unconfirmed.

It is extremely important that young men be taught how to examine their testicles just as young women are encouraged to check their breasts. The American Cancer Society recommends that all males between the ages of twenty and thirty-five do this every month. It's really quite simple: after taking a warm shower or bath, which relaxes the scrotal sac, gently roll each testicle between the thumb and fingers. Feel for and report immediately the presence of any hard lumps, nodules or evidence of enlargement. It goes without saying that the testes should be regularly examined by your doctor as well, as part of your general checkup.

Cancer of the Gallbladder—Fairly Uncommon

Gallbladder cancer occurs more frequently in women than in men, and there is a very high incidence of both gallstones and gallbladder cancer among American Indians. Here, the major cause of the cancer is the presence of the stones, which irritate and inflame the lining of that organ. Certain other risk factors, however, may also predispose to this form of cancer. These include being female, over age forty-five, overweight, receiving estrogen therapy or the birth-control pill, and with an elevated cholesterol. Although most doctors no longer recommend the removal of gallstones unless they cause symptoms, it has been shown that the presence of larger stones (those greater than one and a half inches in length) may increase the risk of cancer. But that chance is so small, 0.5 percent, that the presumed benefit of preventing the cancer by removing the stones surgically must be weighed against the operative risk. In some patients, especially cardiacs, the real dangers of any operation are much greater than the theoretical prospects of developing gallbladder cancer.

However, all it takes is one case to make you think very seriously about prophylactic operations. One of my patients recently died of gallbladder cancer after being treated medically for her gallstones for fifteen years.

Summing It All Up

So there you have it, the list of the most common kinds of cancer. You can see that in many cases heredity and environment both play important roles. But as I look at the data, it seems to me that lifestyle and the environment probably account for between 60 and 90 percent of all cancers. One cannot help but be struck by the fact that tobacco and diet, especially one high in fat and low in fiber, are the two major risk factors. Some oncologists believe that as many as half of all cancers in women and about one-third in men are in some way related to nutrition. Here and there I've made reference to viruses. They probably are responsible for up to 10 percent of cases. Hormonal influences, including childbirth and pregnancy, rank as high as 7 percent. I would have thought that industrial occupations would play a more important role than the mere 4 percent assigned to them, but that may be because so few of us, relatively speaking, are involved in these occupations. Those who are, however, are at considerable risk. Alcohol alone accounts for 3 percent, but it also acts as an enhancer to other toxins. Geography—where you live and the amount of radiation to which you are exposed from space, the sun and local background sources—accounts for 3 percent. The kinds of things we doctors do to and for people, our treatments and the medications we prescribe, including X rays, account for one cancer in every hundred. Food additives, which have had so much publicity in recent years, are responsible for only 1 percent or less of malignancies, as are industrial by-products. Urban air pollution surprisingly causes as little as 1 percent of all cancer deaths. If you credit 2 percent to heredity and 5 percent to the unknown, you have the entire picture.

As I see it, there are six cancers—lung, colorectal, breast, uterine, oral and skin—that account for most cases of cancer and for more than half the deaths. These offer the greatest chance for prevention or cure.

Preventing the Big Six

Specific dietary recommendations for preventing cancer vary somewhat, depending on who's offering them. For example, the National Cancer Institute suggests you (1) cut down on foods high both in saturated *and* unsaturated fats; (2) eat generous amounts of fruits, vegetables and whole-grain cereal products; (3) have lots of dietary fiber; (4) make sure your diet is well balanced; and (5) avoid both overweight and underweight.

These recommendations are very general, so let's see what the American Cancer Society (ACS) says. It offers seven major nutritional guidelines. (1) Avoid obesity. (This conclusion is based on its own twelve-year study that found a significant increase of cancers of the uterus, gallbladder, kidney, stomach, colon and breast in overweight persons, especially those 40 percent or more in excess of ideal figures.) (2) Cut down on total fat intake. Like the National Cancer Institute, the ACS believes that excessive intake of any fat increases the likelihood of breast, colon and prostate cancer. Specifically, it would have you decrease fat intake by 10 percent by reducing consumption of fatty meats, whole milk, dairy products, butter, and cooking oils and fats. (3) The ACS encourages intake of more high-fiber foods, such as whole-grain cereals, fruits and vegetables, both for their possible anti-cancer effect and as a wholesome substitute for fatty foods. (4) It advises the addition of foods rich in vitamins A and C in the daily diet. These would include green and deep-yellow vegetables and certain fruits, so that each day you would be eating carrots, tomatoes, spinach, apricots, peaches and cantaloupe—all rich in beta-carotene, a precursor of vitamin A. This substance appears to reduce the incidence of cancer in animals, and in humans it may lower the risk of cancer of the larynx, the esophagus and the lungs. But excessive vitamin A, in capsule form, is not recommended because of possible toxicity. Epidemiologic studies indicate that people who consume diets rich in vitamin C—heavy, for example, on fruits and vegetables—are less likely to develop cancer, especially of the stomach and esophagus. As mentioned in the discussion of stomach cancer, vitamin C seems to inhibit formation of carcinogenic nitrosamines in that organ. (5) The ACS believes that cruciferous vegetables —cabbage, broccoli, Brussels sprouts and cauliflower—may reduce the risk of cancer, especially of the gastrointestinal and respiratory tracts. These vegetables have also been shown to contain several types of natural cancer inhibitors, which in animal tests prevent chemically induced cancers. (6) You are encouraged to be moderate in the consumption of alcohol. Heavy drinkers, especially those who also smoke, are at an unusually high risk for cancer of the oral cavity, larynx and esophagus. Alcohol abuse can also give cirrhosis, which occasionally progresses to liver cancer. (7) The ACS warns about eating too much salt-cured, smoked and nitrite-cured foods. The United States Department of Agriculture and the meat industry have already substantially reduced the amount of nitrite in prepared meats. The food-processing industry is now using a liquid smoke thought to be less hazardous than traditional methods. Hams, fish and some kinds of sausage smoked in the usual manner absorb cancer-causing tars similar to those in tobacco smoke. There is also evidence linking salt-cured or pickled foods to cancer of the stomach and the esophagus.

The American Cancer Society has called attention to seven additional dietary factors for which it makes no specific recommendations at this time. Let's see what they are and what one should do about them.

(1) *Food additives*. The ACS felt that there were insufficient data regarding the benefits versus the risks of food additives to warrant any recommendations for or against their use. It indicates that those *known* to cause cancer are already banned, and that others may actually protect against cancer.

My own feeling is that whenever a food can be safely eaten without an additive, none should be used. But remember that these additives help preserve not only the appearance of the food but its quality as well, and delay its deterioration.

(2) *Vitamin E*. Although antioxidants such as vitamin E have been shown to prevent some cancers in animal research, the ACS says there is no evidence that this vitamin does so in humans. The National Cancer Institute, on the other hand, takes the position that both vitamin E and an enzyme dependent on selenium act as antioxidants and are able to block damage to cellular DNA from some carcinogens. It points out that cell cultures can also be prevented from becoming cancerous. But it agrees with the American Cancer Society that there is no evidence that *megadoses* of this vitamin help protect against cancer. If, like most people, you're getting enough in your diet, they don't believe you need to supplement it.

(3) *Selenium*. The ACS says that the evidence cited earlier that selenium, a trace element, offers protection against some cancers is still insufficient for it to recommend that selenium be added to the diet. It is also concerned that selenium supplements may be harmful, especially if unsupervised. The Council on Diet, Nutrition and Cancer of the National Research Council shares this position on selenium.

(4) *Saccharin* is currently found in tabletop sweeteners, diet food and drink mixes, sodas, mouthwashes, toothpastes and cosmetics. It is widely used among diabetics as a sugar substitute. The ACS states that although high doses have been shown to cause bladder

cancer in rats, there is no clear evidence for increased risk among people who are moderate users. It is, however, concerned about saccharin consumption by children and pregnant women since it is probably a weak carcinogen. Nor has it accepted the recently approved sweetener *aspartame* because of concern regarding the manner in which tests of its safety were performed. (There has been a great deal of conflicting evidence on this subject. I personally avoid aspartame because I cannot tolerate it, although I believe that the product is probably safe.)

(5) *Coffee.* Some epidemiologic studies implicate high intake of coffee in malignancy of the bladder and pancreas; others do not. The ACS considers the evidence linking them inconclusive. My own suggestion is that intake of beverages containing caffeine should be limited to three cups a day.

(6) *Cooking meat and fish at high temperatures* gives rise to a number of potent mutagens in the food (agents that cause genetic changes), some of which have induced cancer in animal tests. Although the ACS makes no recommendations in this regard, other experts emphasize that cancer-causing polycyclic aromatic hydrocarbons (PAHS) are formed when fat drips into flames over charcoal. Therefore, do your poaching, baking, sautéeing or broiling carefully over aluminum foil, remove fat and char before eating, avoid nitrite-containing foods, and include vitamin-C-rich drinks and foods with your meals.

(7) *Cholesterol.* Although at least one study has linked low cholesterol levels with colon cancer, the ACS states that the evidence is inconclusive.

I believe that a composite of the positions from the American Cancer Society and the National Cancer Institute gives you the total state of the art with respect to the dietary prevention of cancer. If you follow either one of them faithfully over the long term, you will substantially reduce your risk.

The Cardinal Warning Signs

I have emphasized time and again in these pages how important it is to be aware of the warning signs of cancer and how their recognition can lead to earlier diagnosis and cure. What follows is a list of the important ones.

(1) Unintended *weight loss* of ten pounds or more if you're otherwise healthy may be a sign of malignancy, especially of the pancreas, stomach, esophagus or lung.

(2) *Persistent unexplained fever* is a common manifestation of cancer and may be the first sign in Hodgkin's disease, non-Hodgkin's lymphoma and certain kidney cancers.

(3) *Fatigue* may be an early sign of colon cancer and tumors of the bone marrow, as well as of Hodgkin's disease.

(4) *Pain* usually occurs in advanced disease, but may reflect a curable cancer if it is muscular (sarcoma), in the bone (primary bone cancer), in the scrotum (testis), in the arm, shoulder, scapula or upper chest (certain lung tumors), in the mouth (cancers of the oropharynx) or if it occurs before voiding (bladder).

(5) *A change in bowel habits* may be an important clue to colorectal cancer.

(6) *Change in bladder function* may indicate cancer of the prostate or bladder.

(7) *Sores that do not heal*—(a) in the skin (usually basal-cell or squamous-cell cancers); (b) oral lesions (especially in smokers, tobacco chewers, and drinkers); and (c) leukoplakia, the white or pink patches in the mouth, a premalignant condition that should be biopsied and then treated.

(8) *Unusual bleeding or discharge from any source* may be early evidence of colorectal cancer, but is usually a late sign of lung cancer. Bloody discharge from a nipple may be the sign of beginning breast cancer. Bloody urine may constitute early evidence of bladder cancer, but is usually a late sign of kidney cancer.

(9) *Thickening or lumps* in the breast or anywhere else may reflect early or late disease.

(10) *Indigestion or difficulty in swallowing* is often a late sign in cancer of the esophagus, stomach or pharynx.

(11) A recent *change in the appearance of a wart or a mole,* if detected early, may result in the cure of a malignant melanoma.

(12) *Cough or hoarseness* is often a late sign of laryngeal cancer and should always be investigated promptly.

CHAPTER **24**

Abnormal Babies—Not from Genes Alone

The numbers are frightening. In the United States alone, almost 600,000 babies are stillborn each year. Among the 3.25 million born live, more than 250,000 have obvious physical and mental defects. They are retarded, crippled, blind, or deaf, or have hearts and brains so deformed as to preclude a life of normal quality or duration.

When a Little Knowledge Isn't Better Than None

Twenty-five years ago we were blissfully unaware of all the things that could go wrong during a pregnancy. In those days before thalidomide (the sleeping pill "without side effects" that caused deformities in many infants whose mothers took it during pregnancy), we didn't know or think too much about the effect of drugs on the fetus. As a matter of fact, at that time we had identified only four or five teratogens (substances that can produce structural abnormalities in the offspring—"*terat*" being the Greek word for "monster").

We did know that some diseases seemed to run in families, but the genetic mechanisms were not as well understood as they are today, and we were not really able to predict the chances of an infant being born with an important defect. Amniocentesis and fetal ultrasonography had not yet been developed. Nor were the importance of maternal infections during pregnancy or of smoking, drinking and diet

349

then fully appreciated. We were simply aware that a whole lot of babies either died at birth or, if they lived, were seriously impaired—and for no apparent reason. Today, however, it is appreciated that there are many defects we *can* anticipate and prevent, and that's what this chapter is about.

Despite the long list of documented drugs and other substances that we now know must not be taken by pregnant women, birth defects still account for more than 20 percent of all deaths in the first year of life and are the third leading cause of infant mortality. What's more, in about two-thirds of all such cases, we are unable to fathom the mix of genetic and environmental factors responsible for "nature's error." In other words, two times out of three, when a child is born with some defect, the family history on both sides is perfectly normal, the mother was not at all sick during the pregnancy, she took no drugs that could in any way be implicated, her nutrition was adequate, and there was no abnormal bleeding. When a patient with such an adverse experience asks me what she can do to insure a normal baby next time around, I advise an amniocentesis and/or ultrasound. These procedures can at least forewarn of the presence of a serious defect in time to have an abortion, if one is inclined to do so.

Amniocentesis is a procedure performed during pregnancy in which a small amount of fluid from the sac surrounding the baby is withdrawn with a needle inserted through the abdomen (not the vagina). It is usually done in the fifteenth or sixteenth week. Cells from this aspirate are examined under the microscope, and the chromosomes, which carry the genetic material, are counted and analyzed. Certain congenital abnormalities are associated with variations in the number and shape of these chromosomes. Amniocentesis, when properly performed, carries with it only a minimal risk, mostly of infection. But always make sure that whoever interprets the results is qualified to do so. I know of several patients who were given the "green light" to proceed with their pregnancy and who subsequently gave birth to abnormal infants. In each case, review of the evidence obtained at amniocentesis indicated that the original interpretation was incorrect.

If you suspect that you or your spouse may be transmitting a genetic defect, you should have an amniocentesis. If, however, the pregnancy is not progressing normally (for example, your weight and size are not commensurate with the fetal age), you should have an *ultrasound* examination. In this test, sound waves are directed at the uterus through the abdominal wall. Analysis of the echoes that bounce back reveals how far along the baby really is, and whether any gross defects are present. Although ultrasound is a safe procedure that may be done anytime during pregnancy and as often as necessary, it should not be abused. Don't ask for it merely to get the first picture of your baby to put in its photograph album, or to determine its sex. Some theoretical questions have been raised about the long-term effects of these sound waves, since sonography does involve energy, which has an impact on the cells of the living fetus. What it may do to tissues when administered repeatedly or in high dosage is not yet established. And although I am not aware of any case of proved adverse effects of ultrasound in humans, there is evidence in animal experiments that it can alter some cells. So it's fine when needed, but ultrasound is not for fun.

Sometime after the fourteenth week, I advise every expectant mother to have a blood test that measures how much *alpha-fetoprotein* (AFP) is present in her blood—regardless of her family history or past obstetrical record. AFP is a protein produced by the fetus. Some of it enters the mother's circulation. Its level can be measured in her blood or from an amniocentesis sample. Too much AFP is a predictor of a number of abnormalities, the most important of which involve the brain and spinal cord. These are called neural-tube defects and occur in two of every thousand pregnancies. Affected children are born with deformed heads, or with structural disorders in the brain, the nerve tissue running within the bony spinal column or the backbone itself. The child may also have water on the brain (hydrocephalus), which may cause mental retardation. Excessive AFP may also reflect a multiple pregnancy, a dead fetus or one with a low birth weight. What makes this test so useful is that none of these abnormalities is necessarily associated with any previous family or genetic history. If this simple test reveals too much AFP in the maternal blood, sonography and/or amniocentesis can further clarify its meaning.

It's one thing to predict such nervous-tissue abnormalities, and quite another to prevent them. Can it be done? A very interesting report from England suggests that it may be possible. For some reason this abnormality occurs more frequently there than it does in the

United States. British obstetricians say that a single multivitamin tablet or capsule a day (you don't need a megavitamin) significantly lowers the incidence of neural-tube defects. American doctors have raised some questions about the validity of these statistics, and they would like to confirm them here using their own methods. But they are having trouble getting a double-blind study going. After all, what woman in her right mind would volunteer for an experiment in which she is deprived of a daily multivitamin just to see if she will end up giving birth to a deformed baby?

One of the possible explanations for the greater incidence of neural-tube defects in England may be the fact that Americans, particularly pregnant women, already take more vitamins than do their English counterparts. In any event, if you are pregnant, I advise you to have one multivitamin a day. If the British study turns out to have been statistically flawed, and vitamins do not in fact prevent neural-tube defects, what have you lost?

There are at least two thousand different genetic diseases that can affect a fetus. Living testimony to that statement are twelve million Americans among us who were born with at least one! Certain of these disorders are well known and easily recognizable, like Cooley's anemia, hemophilia, Tay-Sachs disease, sickle-cell anemia, or diabetes. Eighty percent of all cases of retardation are probably due to a genetic fault. If you know of any such disorder either in your own family or that of your spouse, you should obtain genetic counseling before planning a family. By analyzing your family tree as far back as possible, a good geneticist can calculate the risk of your child's being born with a specific inherited disorder. Depending on the odds, you may prefer adoption. If, however, you decide to take your chances with a natural birth, sonography and amniocentesis will often indicate in advance whether your gamble paid off.

Women in their middle to late thirties and forties are at high risk for giving birth to a mongoloid (Down's syndrome), or offspring with other genetic defects. So if you're pregnant and over thirty-five, have an amniocentesis to determine whether or not your fetus is normal.

Infections During Pregnancy—Potential Bad News

After we screen all pregnant women for AFP, identify those with a strong family history of genetic abnormalities or who have previously given birth to abnormal infants, and carefully monitor the pregnancies of women in their middle and late thirties or forties, what more can be done to insure a healthy baby? Several things. First, we must prevent those maternal infections that constitute a special hazard to the fetus. The most important ones are represented by the acronym TORCH. "T" stands for toxoplasmosis (a serious disease caused by a parasitic organism), "R" for rubella (German measles), "C" for cytomegalus virus (which we've been hearing so much about these days and which causes chronic low-grade illness), and "H" for the various herpes viruses. "O" is for "other," the most important of which is syphilis. If a pregnant woman develops any one of these infections, the unborn fetus is seriously threatened. Syphilis, of course, should be treated immediately it is recognized, whether or not you're pregnant. Of particular interest is German measles, which can now be prevented by a vaccine. Approximately 90 percent of females have had German measles by the time they reach childbearing age. That still leaves a very substantial 10 percent. Because records may be difficult to obtain, and memories of childhood diseases are so unreliable, I suggest that every young woman planning to become pregnant should have a blood test to measure the level of her antibodies to the rubella virus. If these antibodies are absent or very low in number, she should receive the rubella vaccine before she becomes pregnant.

I remember one patient who was sure she had been vaccinated when she was very young, so her obstetrician didn't think it necessary to check her antibody level. She became pregnant and in her third or fourth month ran a fever for a few days. There was no rash, and she didn't feel sick. The illness cleared up, and the rest of her pregnancy was uneventful. Tragically, she gave birth to a child with severe cardiac abnormalities. Her illness had been a rubella "viremia." That means she had enough of the virus to affect the fetus, but insufficient to give her a rash. Sometimes when a vaccine is administered very early in life, immunity wanes with the years, and a mild, unrecognized reinfection occurs years later. That's why I believe that, regardless of your German-measles history, it's a good idea to be checked before you're pregnant and to get a booster vaccine if you need it. In fact, check your entire childhood immunization schedule to see what, if any, shot you missed. Except for polio, it's not a good idea to receive a live vaccine during pregnancy.

Herpes deserves special mention. Tests are now available that indicate whether or not you have been infected with herpes. If you know you have it, be sure to tell your obstetrician. He will then watch you very carefully throughout your pregnancy. If your herpes sores become reactivated near the time of delivery, you will need a Cesarean section. This avoids the infant's passing through the infected vaginal canal. When that happens, the consequences are serious and include stillbirth and blindness.

I've already referred in Chapter 3 to the importance of screening for the maternal carrier state of hepatitis B. Any pregnant female at risk for this disease and who may have unknowingly contracted it should have a simple blood test to identify hepatitis B antibodies. Those most likely to have such hidden infection include anyone whose work puts him or her in contact with infected patients, as well as certain ethnic groups—notably émigrés from Africa, Latin America, Asia, various Caribbean islands, and American Indians and Eskimos. When the antibody test for hepatitis B is positive, administration of specific hepatitis B immune globulin together with the vaccine at birth prevents the disease from occurring in about 85 to 90 percent of newborn infants.

Everyone is aware of the ever-increasing incidence of AIDS among individuals not previously thought to be at risk. Infants can contract this dreaded disease from their mother during the birth process. Pregnant women known to have had bisexual lovers, a previous history of prostitution or drug abuse, or who received multiple blood transfusions for whatever reason are most likely to transmit AIDS to their offspring. Since there is as yet no effective treatment or prevention of this disease, the desirability of such individuals deliberately becoming pregnant is open to question. Any woman who has AIDS or is known to be a carrier should certainly avoid becoming pregnant and should have an abortion if she already is.

Other Prenatal Precautions

Supposing your genetics are fine, and your AFP level is low. You're under thirty years of age. You've never had any trouble with previous pregnancies, and you have not been infected with a virus or anything else. What more can you do to prevent an abnormal birth?

Avoid *all* X rays whenever possible: no chest films, no GI series and no dental radiography—especially in the first three months. That's when the fetus is most vulnerable to radiation. If, for some reason, your doctor tells you it's absolutely necessary for a radiologic study to be done, make sure the most modern equipment and the fastest film are used, so that your exposure is minimal. However, such studies are sometimes mandatory. For example, I saw a young pregnant woman who had developed severe headaches, raising the possibility of bleeding within the brain. She needed a CAT scan of the head. It was abnormal and she required surgery. Such circumstances are serious and unusual. Remember, however, that if a sonogram will give the same information (as, for example, in studies of the gallbladder or clarification of structural changes in the kidney), have that done instead of the X rays.

Pregnant women should avoid *all unnecessary medication*. Whether it's a prescription drug or an over-the-counter preparation available in the supermarket, remember that *any* product other than a natural food is suspect, be it a diet pill, a pain-killer (even an aspirin), a sleeping pill or a tranquilizer. Although you may seem to tolerate a given medication, you have no way of predicting its impact on the fetus, your inevitable and nonconsenting partner in everything you consume. I cannot understand why doctors in this country prescribe an average of four prescription drugs (other than vitamins and minerals) for almost 90 percent of pregnant women. I am sure these are all considered "safe," but so was thalidomide at one time. What's equally bad is that 65 percent of pregnant women take over-the-counter medications without their doctors' knowledge or consent on the false assumption that because these agents are available without prescription they must be safe. I'll detail some of the more obviously hazardous substances a little farther along.

Now a word about the effect on the fetus of some hormones and the pill. Briefly stated, estrogens are dangerous to the pregnant woman and should be avoided at all costs. Remember DES (diethylstilbestrol), a synthetic estrogen used to prevent spontaneous abortion? It has resulted in increased vaginal and cervical cancer in daughters born of mothers who took it, as well as some testicular and prostatic abnormalities in their male offspring.

Male hormones (androgens) are sometimes prescribed for the treatment of anemia, fatigue and lassitude. Avoid them if you're pregnant. They may adversely affect the fetus much the same way as do estrogens. Finally, if you've been on the pill for years, and you now decide you want to have a baby, wait for at least four months before becoming pregnant. That doesn't mean you should abstain from sex during all that time. Simply use some other contraceptive technique, preferably a condom, while your body rids itself of the last vestiges of the oral contraceptives you were previously consuming. I'm often asked whether spermicidal jellies are safe during this waiting period. I'm not sure they are. The evidence is conflicting, and "probably OK" is not good enough. So don't take a chance. Stay with the condom.

Hippocrates, the father of medicine, said many hundreds of years ago that "in every medicine, there is a little poison." Don't take any drug you do not absolutely need. But from time to time, it may become necessary for you to have a specific medication. Let me run down a list of some of the more commonly used agents and see how safe they are during pregnancy.

Although a given drug may act adversely at any time during the nine months, the period of greatest risk is usually the first trimester. That's when many of the fetus' organs are being formed. As a matter of fact, the first week of pregnancy, before most women even know they have conceived, is critical. So if you are working at getting pregnant, assume at all times that you have just succeeded, as far as drugs, radiation, infection and diet are concerned.

- Suppose you're a *diabetic* and have been taking oral agents to keep your blood sugar down because diet alone wasn't enough. Now you become pregnant. Should you continue the medication or switch to insulin? In my opinion, you're best off stopping the oral drug, especially during the first three months. Although these medications are not teratogenic (injurious to the fetus), they can lower not only your blood sugar but that of the embryo as well. An abnormally low blood sugar is harmful to the embryo, and is difficult to correct. Insulin, on the other hand, does not seem to have this effect. So if your diabetes requires something other than mere attention to what you eat, you're better off with insulin for the "duration."

  Also, if you're a diabetic, your risk of having a malformed baby is about three times that of the normal population. But you can reduce that likelihood by really focusing on your diabetic control. My last five or six diabetic patients who did so gave birth to babies who were perhaps slightly overweight but otherwise perfectly normal. According to experts at the famous Joslin Clinic, when diabetic mothers are carefully monitored throughout their pregnancy, and their blood sugars are controlled by diet and insulin, 96 percent of the babies born are normal.

• Which *antibiotics* are safe during pregnancy? I don't normally advise their use by anyone for trivial upper-respiratory infections unless there is a compelling reason to do so, for example, when the patient is old, fragile and vulnerable to pneumonia, or is diabetic, or has chronic lung, heart or kidney disease. A healthy pregnant woman doesn't fall into any of those categories, as far as I'm concerned. But if you're pregnant and running a respectable fever—one in excess of 101°—for two or three days, you should take an antibiotic. Penicillin is safe (unless you're allergic to it), but avoid tetracycline, because it can interfere with the bone growth of the infant, may discolor its teeth later in life and may cause other bodily deformities. Avoid streptomycin, not often prescribed anymore. There is a whole group of antibiotics called aminoglycosides (these include kanamycin, gentamicin and vancomycin) that are very powerful and usually are used only in life-threatening situations. If no other drug will do the job, you may have to take one of them, but I'm not entirely convinced of their safety.

• *Sulfa drugs* are frequently used for urinary and upper-respiratory-tract infections. They are considered safe but, from time to time, have been observed to cause bleeding abnormalities in the fetus. So take them if you must, but never casually or capriciously. Septra and Bactrim, excellent agents in the treatment of urinary infections, have been shown to cause cleft palate in animals. I'd avoid them during pregnancy.

• *Thyroid disorders* are common in young women. The gland may be overactive, underactive, enlarged or have some nodules in it. If you are hypothyroid and require thyroid replacement, there is no reason not to supplement it when you're pregnant. After all, you're just replacing something that's missing—thyroid hormone. In fact, if you fail to take it, you may give birth to a cretin—a fetus that has been deprived of enough thyroid hormone during the critical weeks and months of its development in the uterus. But treatment of an *overactive* gland is another matter. The usual options include: (a) radioactive iodine to "wipe out" the toxic gland, (b) antithyroid drugs like propylthiouracil to "suppress" it, or (c) surgical removal. *The pregnant female has only one choice—surgery*. Radiation in any form is obviously out of the question. The various antithyroid drugs, which have an iodine base, cause the gland of the fetus to enlarge so much that it can compress the airway and interfere with respiration when the fetus's lungs begin to function. There have also been reports of mental retardation in the offspring following their use. Indeed, all pregnant women, even those with normal thyroid activity, should avoid iodine in any form, because it may interfere with the function of that gland. For example, if you're asthmatic or have a chronic cough, make sure your cough syrup or decongestant isn't loaded with iodine.

• One of my patients called me a few weeks ago. She had just learned she was pregnant, and her husband was so delighted with the news he offered her a trip to Egypt, sailing down the Nile. She called me, not merely to say goodbye, but to check on the safety of the various drugs she was taking along, "just in case I need them." We had a lengthy discussion about each one, and I told her much of what I have written in this chapter. As I was about to hang up, I remembered malaria prophylaxis, a must for anyone going anywhere in Africa. "Oh, that's easy. We're old hands with malaria. We just take one chloroquine tablet a week for two weeks before we leave, then every week while we're there and for six weeks after we come back. That's all right, isn't it? I mean, it's only one pill a week."

Well, the fact is, chloroquine is great for preventing malaria but can cause deafness of the newborn—at least when it's used in the larger doses required to *treat* malaria. Whether the lesser concentration used for prophylaxis is dangerous, I'm not sure. It makes sense to avoid it during the first three months anyway. Do you know what I advised this young lady? To postpone her trip until the second trimester, or better still, to celebrate the happy event in a malaria-free environment. However, if you're pregnant and must go to a malaria zone, or if you actually come down with the disease and require treatment, your doctor may prescribe Primaquine or Penta-quine—alternatives to chloroquine—which may be less harmful to the fetus.

While we're on the subject of toxicity of quinine (of which chloro-quine and related drugs are derivatives), don't forget some other common products in which this substance is found. Do you love cold, sparkling tonic water with or without gin or vodka? Avoid it during pregnancy. There is reason to believe that even in this pleasant form, quinine may cause congenital problems, mostly related to hearing and vision. Do you have leg cramps at night? Tried everything, and nothing works? Chances are your doctor will prescribe quinine at bedtime. It may help, but it too should be avoided during pregnancy.

- Here's a practical problem that may confront a young woman with *epilepsy* who needs medication to control or prevent seizures. Most of the anticonvulsants like Dilantin, trimethadione and paramethadione are very likely to cause serious birth defects, everything ranging from growth deficiency and cardiac abnormalities to deformed genitals and mental retardation—the works. Even a drug as benign as phenobarbital, which is often used in conjunction with other antiepileptic agents, is not without significant risk. The likelihood of trouble is so great that I advise epileptic women not to become pregnant if they require any of these drugs. What's more, if they unknowingly do conceive and have taken any of these agents in the first trimester, the risk is so great I offer them the option of abortion. Some patients, however, can have their minor, or petit mal, seizures controlled by a less toxic agent called Zarontin. Check with your neurologist.
- *Anticoagulants,* or blood thinners, can pose a problem to women of childbearing age. The most common circumstances in which such therapy is necessary are phlebitis (in which a leg vein becomes inflamed) and valvular heart disease, when the heart rhythm is very irregular (atrial fibrillation). These disorders can lead to embolism (a small blood clot travels to the lungs from the veins, or to some other part of the body, from the heart). Or a pregnant woman may have undergone valve replacement, and needs to have her blood thinned because clots may form on the prosthetic valve and become dislodged, or embolize. (The only artificial-valve patients who do not need anticoagulation are those with porcine valves. That's why I recommend the insertion of such a valve in young women who may become pregnant later on.) The best preventive against catastrophe in any of these circumstances is anticoagulation, using warfarin. However, warfarin carries with it a 20 to 50 percent risk of severe congenital abnormalities and *must not* be used during pregnancy, either in its early or late stages. Unfortunately, I don't know of a safe, practical substitute that's as effective.
- One of the most common problems a doctor sees in daily practice is *high blood pressure*. There is a host of agents available, singly and in combination, to normalize elevated readings. And it is important to do so, even during pregnancy. These drugs include the beta blockers (like Inderal), diuretics, Aldomet, clonidine, calcium channel blockers, Ismelin, rauwolfia derivatives (reserpine), captopril, and on and on. The only proved safe one of the lot during pregnancy, as far as I know, is hydralazine (Apresoline).

A special word about beta blockers, the prototype of which is propranolol (Inderal). As you have read elsewhere in this volume, it is effective not only in the treatment of hypertension but also for angina pectoris, migraine headaches, overactive thyroid and certain irregularities of cardiac rhythm. The list of its indications is an ever-growing one. And there is one special condition for which a young woman in her childbearing years might well be taking propranolol— mitral valve prolapse. (See Chapter 9.) In the great majority of cases, this condition is only a nuisance. However, it frequently results in "palpitations," the best treatment for which is propranolol. I've seen several young women with mitral valve prolapse who have become pregnant and wondered about continuing with this medication. As always during pregnancy, I tell them that if they can live comfortably without it, they should do so. But if they feel they must have the drug, their obstetrician should be alerted to that fact. Every attempt should be made to stop its use at least forty-eight hours before labor, because propranolol can slow the fetal heart just as it does the heart of an adult, prolong the delivery and depress the fetus.

- *Aspirin* is the most commonly used drug in our society, but it is unsafe during pregnancy, both at the beginning and at the very end. Recent studies have shown that infants born of mothers who treated their cold or flu symptoms with aspirin during the first trimester have twice the incidence of congenital heart defects. Aspirin also interferes with blood clotting. That's why it's used for the prevention of heart attacks and strokes. But this mechanism can cause bleeding in the infant, so avoid its use during the last week or two of pregnancy. If you don't, the baby may be born with internal hemorrhages.

- *Ergot* is a drug widely prescribed in the treatment of migraine headaches. It is most effective when taken at the very first indication that a headache is about to strike (during the "aura" of flashing lights that the migraine patient experiences just before the onset of the headache itself). Taking an ergot preparation (the one I prescribe most is called Cafergot) at that time will often abort the headache. But ergot is an abortifacient, that is, it induces abortion. So if you have migraines and become pregnant, you'll have to stop the ergot if you want to have the baby.

- There are various other drugs that, although they may not cause deformities in the newborn, do interfere with its adaptation to life outside the uterus. Some sleeping pills you've grown to depend on may not give your baby a hole in the heart, but it may make him or her awfully sleepy, with depressed respirations at birth. If you're hooked on any narcotic, your baby will be too. So don't take what you don't need.

What Is Safe?

And now the good news. What drugs *may* you take in moderation if you need them throughout pregnancy? Those generally considered "safe" include various anti-asthmatic preparations like theophyllin; terbutaline; isoproterenol; penicillin (unless you're allergic to it); and antihistamines.

What about such commonly used "social" substances as coffee, alcohol and tobacco? We've been kept on a Yo-Yo with respect to *coffee* during pregnancy over these last few years. Conflicting reports have had us constantly changing our minds and our drinking habits. As of 1985, coffee is all right, but limit it to three cups a day. There is some evidence that more may result in decreased infant birth weight.

Alcohol is a very big no-no for the pregnant woman. Most cocktail lounges post signs stating that alcohol should not be taken by pregnant women. And that is absolutely true. When the mother is frankly an alcoholic, the risk of giving birth to a severely impaired child is anywhere from 30 to 50 percent. Such infants have tiny heads and jaws, little eyes and are riddled with cardiac defects (fetal alcohol syndrome). But even an occasional drink may be hazardous. *There is no minimal safe dose of alcohol during pregnancy.*

By this time, you know how I feel about *tobacco* in any form and under any circumstances. It's bad for everyone, including pregnant women. Most scientists agree that mothers who smoke are more apt to have spontaneous abortions or to give birth to infants who are smaller and weigh less than normal. In fact, the term "fetal tobacco syndrome" has been coined to describe such babies. Whether or not the incidence of congenital defects is also greater is not certain.

Temperature affects pregnancy significantly. Stay in an air-conditioned environment in very hot weather, and for goodness' sake, don't spend your time in a sauna. Very high temperatures have been shown to result in an increased number of fetal abnormalities, at least in studies coming out of Japan. However, the Finns, who originated the sauna, vigorously deny that allegation.

What else can you do to help assure a healthy infant? Keep away from any fad diets, like the high-fat, high-protein, low-carbohydrate regimen proposed some years ago, or the macrobiotic diet, or the mostly pineapple diet. You require three "balanced" meals a day.

Some researchers have even speculated that the cravings and dis-
tastes for certain foods that many women have during pregnancy may
reflect the body trying to tell us something. I understand that for the
most part such women prefer dairy products (rich in calcium and
good for both mother and child), and sweets and fruits (sources of
rapidly available energy). These same women don't usually seem to
want as much coffee as they normally did, or alcohol, or protein.
Perhaps we ought to let the pregnant patient, with nature's guidance,
eat what she desires—provided, of course, that she can afford to do
so, and adds a good vitamin-and-mineral supplement.

Don't worry that your fetus will be deprived because you're a
vegetarian—as long as you eat eggs and dairy products. And forget
your lifelong commitment to "thin is beautiful." These nine months
are no time to lose weight. If you fail to gain the usual twenty or
twenty-five pounds, you're likely to give birth to an underweight
infant whose resistance, health and even survival may be in jeopardy.
If you become constipated, as many pregnant women do, drink more
water, eat more fiber and avoid all but the natural laxatives.

An abnormal baby is neither the will nor the wrath of God. It is
often a preventable disaster if you watch what you eat, are careful about the medications you take or are given, protect yourself
against infection, radiation and pollution—and pick your ancestors
carefully.

CHAPTER **25**

Chelation, Arthritis "Cures" and Other False Hopes

I could write volumes about all the quick health fixes we are offered these days. I have alluded to some of them elsewhere in this text. Any disease that is chronic, and for which we do not yet have a cure, from which people still suffer, lends itself to deceptive claims. In the last century it was Lydia Pinkham's Pills. Today it is vitamin B-15. Government supervision has done away with much of the quackery of the nineteenth-century patent medicines, but fraudulent remedies are still with us. Heart disease and arthritis are particularly good hunting grounds for the health speculators, so let me discuss some of the more popular but unproved remedies with which we are tempted.

Chelation—Good Medicine or Good Business?

A few months ago, I advised one of my patients, a fifty-four-year-old man with severe angina pectoris, to undergo coronary bypass surgery. He was experiencing chest pressure and shortness of breath upon the least exertion. He had recently begun to be awakened at night by chest discomfort. I had tried every available medication at maximum dosage to give him relief—nitroglycerin topically applied to the chest, supplemented by the long-acting nitrates in oral form; a succession of beta blockers, starting with Inderal and ending with Tenormin; all three of the calcium channel blockers (verapamil, nifedipine and diltiazem), supplemented by an aspirin a day. He was extremely cooperative, and followed all my instructions to a T. He had lost weight as directed, hadn't smoked for years and had even tried the Pritikin diet. However, his symptoms persisted without abatement.

He was terrified of hospitals, needles, tubes and, most of all, operations. (He insisted he wouldn't have permitted his ritual circumcision at birth if he'd had any say in the matter!) When I finally advised a coronary angiogram to see whether or not he might benefit from bypass surgery, he became so anxious just discussing it he had to slip a nitroglycerin tablet under his tongue. Finally, after a great deal of psychological support, together with liberal doses of sedatives, we were able to get this gentleman to and through the angiography. The results did not surprise me, given the severity of his symptoms. All three of his major coronary arteries were severely narrowed. Happily, the heart muscle itself was still good. (I had feared that it might already be so damaged that the bypass operation would be of no real benefit. There is no point bringing a new blood supply to a "dead" muscle.) If the obstructed vessels were bypassed with new veins from a leg or an internal mammary artery from his chest wall, his symptoms would almost surely disappear. I thought it was important to do so before one of the narrowed arteries closed, an event that would damage his currently intact cardiac muscle.

When I brought him this good news, he reacted very negatively. "Doctor, why should I undergo a serious, painful and maybe even life-threatening operation when I can have my blocked arteries opened medically?"

I was puzzled. I knew of no Roto-Rooter for the arteries. Was there something in this week's *Time* magazine I had missed? Or was it in the morning's *New York Times?* On the other hand, perhaps he was thinking of balloon angioplasty, in which the plaques blocking the arteries can be compressed by inflating the balloon inside each artery, thus avoiding surgery. His case wasn't suitable for that procedure because all three arteries were involved, and in locations the balloon couldn't reach. Had he been reading about the experimental laser-beam approach, which promises to vaporize the plaques with but a brief burst of energy? That procedure is still some years away from use in humans. "All right, I give up. What do you have in mind to open your arteries?" I asked.

"Why, chelation, of course."

And thereby hangs a tale, because there are thousands of Americans receiving this treatment in the belief that it will cure or prevent almost anything, especially hardening of the arteries.

Chelation involves the injection into the bloodstream of a substance called edetate disodium (EDTA), which is supposed to unite with or bind some other chemical that shouldn't be in the body (or which is present in excess quantities). The EDTA and the offending material are then excreted together in the urine. Chelation is a recognized form of treatment for overdosage, poisoning or overload with certain metals, such as iron, lead and copper. The chelating agent does indeed remove the offending substance from the body and can be lifesaving. But that's not what the proponents of the chelation my patient was talking about have in mind. They have seized upon a principle that is valid for one kind of problem and are using it for a very different one—arteriosclerosis. Their logic goes something like this. Patients with arteriosclerosis have calcium in the plaques that narrow their blood vessels, so why not inject EDTA to bind and remove the calcium? This should reduce the obstruction, widen the channel and improve blood flow within the arteries. According to them, it's as simple as that, and they claim miraculous results. They say that patients with obstructed leg arteries can walk much farther than before, some even without limitation. Individuals with angina pectoris have allegedly become pain-free, and emancipated from the fear and necessity of bypass surgery. Some with narrowed arteries in the brain, who were also suffering from senility, have apparently improved too. In short, they have come upon a panacea.

On the basis of these reports, the number of doctors practicing chelation therapy has increased throughout the United States and in certain European countries as well, including the Soviet Union. There are now chelation centers and clinics throughout the country. The nearly one thousand physicians who offer this treatment have formed a medical society of their own. They hold conferences, publish magazines, proselytize the rest of the profession and have a very high visibility for their relatively small number. (There are some 300,000 M.D.s in the United States.) They flood the media with reports of the wonders of chelation and how much it benefits their patients.

On the surface, this all seems logical and reasonable. There are, however, several important doubts concerning chelation therapy when used for the treatment and prevention of arteriosclerosis. First, and perhaps most important, is the basic fallacy of the theory on which such treatment is based. The fact is that the arteriosclerotic plaque does not contain any appreciable amount of calcium until very late in the disease. Most such plaques are composed of a sac containing cholesterol, covered over by tissue that has no calcium in it. When calcium does form, it constitutes only a small and inconsequential portion of the plaque. Even if chelation did in fact suck out whatever calcium there is in such an obstruction, blood flow within the artery would only be minimally increased, if at all. When the chelation enthusiasts were confronted with this observation, they formulated other theories to justify its use. They said in effect, "Well, maybe the injection of EDTA works by giving increased collateral blood flow, or decreasing the thickness of the blood [viscosity]; perhaps it improved the 'function' of the heart cells or reduces spasm." Others suggested that EDTA corrected some undefined abnormality of calcium metabolism caused by nutritional factors, like too much fat or too many refined carbohydrates, lack of magnesium, lack of selenium, lack of exercise, lack of fiber, or aluminum pollution. You name it, chelation corrects it! To the best of my knowledge, not a single one of these supplementary theories has been proved to the satisfaction of the medical scientific community.

Another problem with chelation is that the claims for its success are for the most part anecdotal. By this I mean that most reports do not follow the usual standard scientific technique for drawing conclusions about a particular therapy. You can't treat one, two, ten or even fifty people and, simply because they tell you that they are feeling better, conclude that you have a "winner" on your hands. That is not to say the patient is lying, or even unreliable. But the natural desire to feel better, to report success to the doctor, and the equally human hope of the doctor to effect a cure, plus the fact that the course of so many diseases fluctuates over the short term, all add up to what we might call the "placebo effect." If a patient can be sufficiently motivated by an enthusiastic and caring doctor, even a few drops of water served twice a day will improve almost any symptom at least 50 percent of the time. In order really to justify or document a result, one must have "controlled studies" in which some patients are given the treatment and others a "blank." Ideally, neither the patient nor the doctor knows who is getting what. After the trial is finished, the number of persons responding favorably in each group is determined. One also looks for some objective evidence of improvement. This is what the medical scientific community requires before any claims are considered valid. And so it has, for the most part, rejected the use of chelation treatment for arteriosclerosis and considers it at best controversial, unproved and still experimental. Those organizations that have come to this conclusion based on the available evidence include the National Heart, Lung and Blood Institute (a section of the National Institutes of Health), the American Heart Association, the American College of Physicians and the American Medical Association.

My personal feelings in the matter lie with the Establishment. I do not recommend or indeed permit any of my patients to undergo this form of therapy for fear it may divert them from more effective, proved treatment. I also worry about such complications as kidney failure, although I personally have not witnessed any.

However, I have enough confidence in most doctors to acknowledge that where there is smoke, there may be fire. I am sure that among some of the practitioners of chelation therapy, there is an earnest conviction that what they are doing is helping their patients. That being the case, I think it is incumbent on "organized medicine," be it at the university or government level, to launch additional impartial controlled studies to settle the matter once and for all. Until such time, I think anybody submitting to chelation therapy should do so bearing in mind all the reservations I have described.

In my zeal to tell you about chelation, I left you hanging with respect to my patient who wanted that therapy instead of the operation for his coronary disease. There was no stopping him. He signed up for a course of chelation, which involved about fifty injections, given two to four times a week, at a cost of $60 per injection. (They can range up to $100.) His total bill was about $3,000. After the first ten days, he felt really wonderful. He had less pain, and I learned that he told his family he would never come back to see me. He was through with "conservative Establishment" doctors. Two weeks later he had a massive heart attack, for which he called *me* in the middle of the night. He was admitted to our hospital and was tided over his acute coronary. One month later, because his original symptoms recurred, he finally consented to undergo bypass surgery, which was performed without any problems whatsoever. At the time of writing, one year later, he is leading a virtually normal life.

This single case history is not meant to document or prove that chelation is bad and that bypass surgery is good. What I said about anecdotal medicine applies to me as much as it does to the chelation enthusiasts. But still, that's the way it happened in this one case.

How (Not) to Prevent Arthritis

One American in seven, or about thirty-six million people in this country, have some form of "arthritis." You see some of them in public places, in their wheelchairs, with their canes and crutches, limping, bent over, fingers gnarled and distorted. They represent only the more visible aspects of the problem—the tip of the "arthritis" iceberg. The larger picture is the chronic pain and suffering that is an integral part of the lives of countless millions of people who spend billions of dollars on doctors, hospitals, analgesics and steroids to help make life bearable.

Arthritis is not a single disease entity. There are at least one hundred different conditions that can hurt the joints, leaving one or more of them painful, swollen, stiff, red, warm or deformed, and all of which represent some kind of arthritis.

Many of these can, in fact, be prevented. When you strike your knee, you may develop *traumatic* arthritis. If you're careful at work or play, you can, at least, theoretically avoid such arthritis. When a joint is involved by infection elsewhere in the body, such as occurs, for example, in Lyme disease, rheumatic fever or gonorrhea, the resulting *infectious* arthritis can be prevented by administration of the appropriate antibiotic.

Gout is a form of arthritis that is a result of chemical changes occurring within the body. Uric-acid crystals are deposited in a joint, most commonly the big toe, and you wake up one morning in agony with *gouty* arthritis. Such attacks reoccur either unpredictably or in response to some dietary indiscretion (eating red meat, animal organs and alcohol excess), stress or infection. Regardless of the provocation, acute gout can almost always be prevented by maintenance medication such as allopurinol (Zyloprim), probenecid (Benemid) and/or colchicine.

But in the real world of arthritis, we narrow our focus on two conditions—osteoarthritis and rheumatoid arthritis—that plague and cripple millions.

Osteoarthritis is the one that leaves you with stiff joints when you wake up in the morning; it's usually the cause of your bad back, sore shoulder or the painful hip that needs replacing. We used to believe that osteoarthritis was basically a mechanical problem—local malfunction of a joint resulting from years of wear and tear. Today, however, most rheumatologists feel the process involves the whole body, and is simply most visible in the joints. Whatever the mechanism responsible for osteoarthritis, its cause or causes have not yet been established. The incidence seems to be declining in the Western world, perhaps because of the growing availability of automation and the many labor-saving devices that spare some of our joints from trauma.

Rheumatoid arthritis (RA), whose cause is also as yet undetermined, is more disabling and crippling than osteoarthritis. It affects about seven million people in this country to some degree or other and strikes many organs in the body (lungs, heart, skin), in addition to the joints. During the active phase of rheumatoid arthritis, patients have fever, anemia, fatigue, weight loss, lack of appetite and generally feel really lousy. The joints themselves are painful, warm, stiff, swollen and, ultimately, usually deformed. However, severe crippling happens much less frequently than is popularly supposed.

There is a great deal that can be done to manage patients with both rheumatoid arthritis and osteoarthritis—medication, physiotherapy and corrective surgery. Pain can be reduced or controlled by a wide variety of drugs, starting with aspirin and moving up to the "nonsteroidal anti-inflammatory" agents like Motrin, Clinoril, Naprosyn, Dolobid and several others. In resistant cases of RA, patients may respond to gold, penicillamine, antimalarial agents like chloroquine, certain anti-cancer drugs that interfere with the immune system of the body, or steroid hormones.

But osteoarthritis and rheumatoid arthritis can neither be cured nor prevented, and the marketplace is full of quackery, oddball concepts and unproved remedies that exploit arthritis patients emotionally and cost them, nationwide, more than $1 billion a year. The cure peddlers are so persuasive that some 90 percent of patients with rheumatoid arthritis who are actually under the care of a physician have experimented with one or more of these unorthodox measures. While many are harmless, some are hazardous. Here is the real low-down on the more popular of these "alternative" therapies.

The Copper Bracelet: I am not sure exactly when it was that I met the Duke of Windsor. It must have been at least twenty years ago. The occasion was an annual fund-raising dinner of the New York Heart Association, held at the elegant Waldorf Astoria. His Royal Highness had graciously agreed to present an award to some deserving volunteer worker or scientist—I can't remember which. But for me, this was a very special event. I had recently moved to the United States from Canada, where I was born, and Edward, Duke of Windsor, had been, albeit briefly, my king—Edward VIII. I had not yet become an American citizen. You can imagine the thrill of sitting down to dinner (with several hundred other people, of course) a mere stone's throw away from my former king!

Aside from the royal presence, the event itself was a rather humdrum affair until, at one point, the duke found it necessary to leave the festivities for a few moments. What a great opportunity this presented for me! For some reason, I suddenly got the urge too. As we stood side by side in the room that is the great equalizer, I summoned enough courage to introduce myself. The duke seemed pleased to meet a former subject, and we shook hands! As we did so, I saw on his wrist, under the crisp white cuff of his dress shirt, a copper bracelet! Beneath that, I saw the telltale blue-green discoloration of the skin.

A later experience with a copper bracelet is in some ways more pertinent and even more surprising. A few years ago, my wife and I were invited to a cookout and swim at the home of one of our doctor friends. There were about twenty guests in all, mostly physicians. It was a beautiful summer day, and we sat around the pool discussing doctors' favorite subjects—disease, government intervention and the stock market. One of the guests, a medical-school professor engaged full-time in research and teaching, seemed very knowledgeable in a wide range of subjects—immunology, arteriosclerosis, infertility, hypertension . . . and arthritis. We were deeply engrossed in conversation when our host came around, listened for a moment or two, and then said, "Gentleman, no shop talk. You'd better have your swim now because the hamburgers and frankfurters will be ready in a few minutes." So we got up and went to the dressing room where my professor friend got into his bathing suit. And there, to my astonishment, on the ankle of this august medical personality was—a copper bracelet!

Now, don't get me wrong. I have no objection to anyone wearing copper bracelets. They're very much like any other amulet and don't do any harm. Some are even decorative, with silver or gold plating on the outside.

I can understand the duke expecting his to prevent arthritis. Royalty, after all, is not always medically sophisticated. But why would a senior academician at an Ivy League medical school have one on his ankle?

I'm not sure how the copper bracelet fad started. I think it was because, many years ago, somebody observed that workers in copper-processing industries were relatively free of arthritis. Since so many people the world over wear these bracelets, several studies have been done to determine whether there is any scientific justification for their use. The results are interesting, and, for me, surprising: it seems that some patients with rheumatoid arthritis really are copper-deficient and do absorb tiny amounts of copper from the bracelet. But despite that, there has never been a single objective study showing that this piece of jewelry benefits any form of arthritis.

Acupuncture: After relations with the People's Republic of China were established a few years ago, visitors to that country returned with incredible accounts of the miracle of acupuncture. The Chinese were apparently using it for the treatment of everything from infertility to diabetes, and as an anesthetic too. "For arthritis, it's a godsend," one of my friends told me. "I saw this crippled man in Hangchow just get up and walk after only three treatments"—shades of Lourdes.

I am constantly asked by my patients to refer them for acupuncture therapy for their arthritis, and for relief from various chronic aches and pains. I almost always do so, especially if they're enthusiastic, because, although it is much more expensive than wearing a copper bracelet, like the latter, it can really do no harm. But I must frankly tell you (as I do these patients) that I have *never* seen acupuncture benefit the arthritis patient. From time to time, patients have told me that their pain "seemed" less severe after therapy, but I have attributed this to the placebo response, the effect of "laying on of the hands" by a physician or other "healer." Please don't think that, being a member of the Establishment, I have a negative attitude toward "alternative" forms of medicine. Actually, I do not. I went to China and saw with my own eyes—and photographed—a young woman undergoing repair of one of her heart valves. She was wide-awake through the entire procedure, from the moment the surgeon first incised her skin, sawed open and spread her rib cage, and worked in her exposed chest for about an hour. All this time, she was sipping water and smiling without anesthesia, hypnosis—or pain. So acupuncture does result in analgesia. The Chinese, who have used the technique for years, have never really understood its mechanism. Research done in this country, however, indicates that acupuncture releases certain natural opiates, predominantly meta-encephalins from the brain, and hence in some cases does control pain. However, it does nothing to or for the disease causing the pain. That being the case, if you have arthritis, you're probably better off, in terms of predictability of pain relief, using one of the many new and effective analgesics or anti-inflammatory agents that, when taken over the long term, probably do slow down the underlying process.

Diet: A great deal has been written about how you can prevent arthritis (and cure the disease if you have it) simply by changing your diet in some way—eliminating caffeine, alcohol, tomatoes, red meat, saturated fats, spices, sugar or tobacco; or adding megavitamins—enormous doses of vitamins A, D, C, B-6 and E. (High doses of the fat-soluble vitamins, like A, D and E, can have serious consequences, while excessive B-6 may cause neurological problems in doses exceeding 2 grams a day.) Most scientific studies to date have not confirmed any objective benefit from any of these dietary interventions.

However, if you have rheumatoid arthritis, it may be worth checking with an allergist to see whether you have any unsuspected food allergies. In a few cases, an appropriate elimination diet has been of some help.

The Pill: According to a report from England in 1978, later substantiated by Dutch researchers, women who have taken estrogen either as an oral contraceptive or as replacement therapy after the menopause have less rheumatoid arthritis than women who don't. Unfortunately, a more recent analysis failed to confirm these earlier observations. If you believe that where there's smoke, there's fire, and if you have early rheumatoid arthritis, use the pill for contraception—it's still probably the safest and best technique of all anyway. If your periods are just over and done with, hot flushes have begun to appear, and your gynecologist tells you you are hormone-deficient and have a "touch" of arthritis, try the estrogens for two or three years. You'll feel better, reduce your chances of developing osteoporosis, and, who knows, you may even be protected against rheumatoid arthritis.

DMSO: DMSO (dimethyl sulfoxide) is an ointment that is absorbed through the skin into the body. Although it is said to be a pain-killer, it has only limited legal approval—for the treatment of inflammation of the urinary bladder—for use in humans. It may, however, be given to animals, and finds its greatest legal application in horses with injured joints. Whatever analgesic properties it has are probably due to counterirritation. (It's the kind of thing you may do when you hurt somewhere. You push, press or pinch yourself at a nearby site to "distract" you from the more serious pain. This sometime helps, on the principle that nerve fibers can carry only a certain number of pain messages at any given time, and it's better to have them preoccupied with some lesser stimulus than with a major one.)

In any event, whatever the mechanism, it was only a matter of time before someone would come up with the suggestion that if DSMO is good for horses, why not try it on people? Before its efficacy and safety could be evaluated to satisfy the requirements of the FDA, "black-market" DMSO found its way onto and into human knees, shoulders, elbows, hands, backs—in fact, wherever arthritis of any kind was present. The preparations people employ in this illicit manner are usually industrial solvents, or the formula approved for use in humans (available in pharmacies as a 50 percent solution), or the veterinary product (a 90 percent solution not approved by the FDA for human use). At first, any doctor publicly criticizing its use as premature and unproved received a barrage of testimonials from satisfied patients. But then reports began to appear of DMSO toxicity, due mostly to the absorption of impurities in the drug and bacteria on the surface of the unwashed skin, and the initial enthusiasm cooled somewhat.

DMSO may relieve the pain of arthritis in some cases, but then again, so does aspirin. If you're determined to try it, stay with the preparation available in pharmacies and make sure the surface to which you are applying it is clean. Also, remember it has an awesome garlicky stench. Personally, I don't think the benefit nearly equals the stink.

Venoms: Remember the scare a few years back when we were threatened by an invasion of "killer" bees from South America? They were supposedly advancing relentlessly at X miles an hour, and would soon overrun every part of North America. Apparently, that might not be all bad if you had arthritis, because if you survived the sting, there were those who said your arthritis might improve from the venom. An entire book has been written on the subject, claiming that bee venom is effective in the management of arthritis. I am not aware of any scientific research supporting this therapy, and I would not advise anyone to provoke a bee in search of a cure. Ant venom, on the other hand, may be a different story. A preparation made from the Bolivian ant is currently being tested at the University of Miami in patients with rheumatoid arthritis. Although preliminary results are said to be encouraging, it's still too early to tell.

Here's a list of some other "remedies" promoted to patients suffering from arthritis, none of which, in my opinion, are worth your time, trouble or hope.

Cobra venom used to be sold in Florida by a snake handler who claimed it had curative powers. His little enterprise was closed down when analysis of the product he peddled revealed that its contents differed from batch to batch and often contained no cobra venom, but the potentially more toxic moccasin venom.

A doctor in California reported that *cocaine,* when applied topically in the nose, was effective against arthritis. He is no longer practicing, and his original claims for cure have not been validated. Other practitioners, including some in the New York area, insert a cocaine-soaked pledget into the nose for relief of disabling back pain. I'm not aware of any scientific evidence to justify such therapy, yet I know many sober people, including doctors with bad backs, who swear that it works. Attempts by local medical authorities to have this treatment halted on the grounds that it has no scientific merit have not been successful, at least in New York. Every time the matter is raised, the authorities are deluged by testimonials from those patients who claim to have benefited from this therapy.

Then there is *procaine,* best known as a local anesthetic, marketed throughout Europe as Gerovital H-3. Some of the most down-to-earth people I know take this substance regularly by mouth or injection, usually after a stint in a Romanian health clinic run by a Dr. Ana Aslan. Gerovital is supposed to be good not only against arthritis, but—like chelation—for whatever else ails you: impotence, aging skin, graying hair, senility—you name it, procaine will fix it. It has been extensively evaluated in the United States and has been found to have little, if any, effect. It does mildly dilate the arteries of the skin, producing a flushed feeling, which some interpret as reflecting its potency. Although the FDA has not approved it, procaine is available in Nevada. If you're determined to use it for whatever reason (and I see none), make sure you don't have myasthenia gravis. Procaine will aggravate the symptoms of that disease.

If you thumb through some of the popular "health" magazines or browse in health-food stores, you will come across *SOD (superoxide dismutase)*. One brand is marketed as Orgotein. It's supposed to prevent arthritis by some chemical action or other. The only problem is that the pill you swallow is digested by the stomach and never gets into the bloodstream at all. So in my opinion, taking SOD by mouth is just an expensive way of slightly increasing your protein intake.

There are several other products "guaranteed" to help your arthritis. For example, you may be advised to take the extract of the *green-lipped mussel*, a rare New England mollusk. Forget it. Or maybe you prefer *chuifong toukuwan*, a Chinese herb containing some agents that do reduce inflammation, but with so much toxicity that some of the ingredients are illegal in this country. There are practitioners who will offer you vaccines of different kinds (bacterial or flu). None of them work. *Flagyl*, a medicine used for the treatment of infections by worms and other parasites, is recommended here and there in the belief that arthritis is due to amoebic infection (one doctor proposed this theory, another wrote a book about it, but no one has yet confirmed it to be so).

Antibiotics are also espoused by some. The latest one is tetracycline, which will ostensibly rid your body of Mycoplasma organisms, allegedly the cause of arthritis. Well-meaning friends may send you south of the border to Mexico, or north to Canada, to get miracle potions whose ingredients are rarely revealed, but which when analyzed almost always contain steroids (not without risk) or sex hormones. There are "authorities" who will advise you to have your tonsils removed, your teeth extracted, your appendix extirpated, your blood purified by plasmapheresis—and other cures, preventives and remedies that are costly, wasteful, often dangerous and never effective. If you have arthritis and come across a promising "new approach," check it out with your doctor or the local chapter of your Arthritis Foundation.

CHAPTER **26**

Raising the Question of Impotence

An estimated ten million men in this country are impotent. I have no idea how that statistic was obtained, because, unlike syphilis or AIDS, this condition is not one your doctor is legally obliged to report. Nor is it the kind of information solicited by or freely given to a census taker. Very few men will admit to being impotent—to their best friend or even to their doctor.

It seems like only yesterday that if you were impotent you usually consulted a psychiatrist, since everybody was sure the trouble was "all in the head." More often than not, the impotent male still accepts his lot as inevitable, or denies it, or rationalizes it, or keeps hoping that things will be better "next time." However, since we are now more comfortable airing the matter of sexual inadequacy, there appears to be a better understanding of the problem—and more hope.

Although the normal male erection seems simple and straightforward, it is, in fact, a very complicated event, starting with a stimulating thought process in the brain and ending in the penis. In between, all kinds of things need to happen. Your hormone level must be high enough for you to be stimulated in the first place. That depends on a normal glandular system. Some psychological hang-up or other can cancel out the whole train of events, leaving you limp. But if your psyche does give your brain the green light, nerves must then carry the good news south, and the arteries that supply the penis must be unobstructed so as to permit enough blood (about seven times the usual flow) to enter and stiffen it. There is a multitude of diseases, disorders, medications and emotional problems that can cut the pathway at any point and result in impotence.

Many cases of impotence *are* psychogenic, and have their roots in childhood and cultural taboos. One hopes that new mores and social values will reduce their number. But there are countless men who, after years of normal sexual activity, suddenly or gradually lose their ability to obtain or maintain an erection as a result of anxiety or depression. The problem is usually attributed to aging, working too hard or just plain fatigue. Discuss it with your doctor. If he is able to rule out the physical bases discussed below, his reassurance, psychological support and appropriate medication may be all that's necessary.

Heart trouble of any kind is frequently a source of anxiety, which may result in preventable sexual problems. It affects women as well as men. The latter become impotent; the former, "frigid," or disinterested in sex. Fear is the culprit among such patients. No matter what your heart condition happens to be, if you can manage two flights of stairs, you may safely enjoy a normal sex life. I try to give patients with heart trouble the necessary self-confidence early in the course of their illness. For example, soon after a heart attack or bypass surgery, long before the patient leaves the hospital, I put him or her through a series of exercise tests just to prove how well physical exertion is tolerated. I also have many of them join some supervised cardiac rehabilitation program. A wife who knows her "cardiac" husband is working out at a gym three or four times a week, and thriving on it, will not worry about killing him with sex.

As I was giving discharge instructions to one of my patients, a sixty-two-year-old man who had recovered from a run-of-the-mill heart attack, I suggested to him that he refrain from sexual activity for about six weeks. He took this prohibition very graciously and left for home. Two weeks later, he came to my office for a follow-up examination, which was entirely satisfactory. After a total of four weeks, he returned to my office again and did a low-level stress test, which indicated good healing of the damaged heart. That night he became very amorous after his long period of enforced abstinence. But his wife remained adamant. "John, the doctor said six weeks, and I'm not going to jeopardize your life for a few minutes of pleasure." His pleading and cajoling were to no avail. She was a devoted, strong-willed woman. So the next day, he came to see me at the office to discuss his predicament. "Doctor, you've got to give me a note permitting me to have intercourse. After all, I'm feeling just great."

I agreed and penned the following letter: "Dear Mrs. Smith: I have today examined Mr. Smith and found him in excellent physical condition. His recovery from his heart attack has been much better than expected. His electrocardiogram is stable. His blood pressure is normal; his heart sounds are strong; his lungs are clear. In short, I am permitting, and indeed encouraging, him to resume normal sexual activities. Yours truly." I had my secretary type up the letter, and I gave it to him for his perusal. After reading it carefully, he looked up and said, "That's exactly what I need. It's excellent. But may I ask you to make one small change? Instead of 'Dear Mrs. Smith,' would you start it with 'To Whom It May Concern'?" Instilling that kind of confidence is a sure way of preventing the psychogenic impotence that so often develops after a heart attack.

Newer diagnostic techniques now make it possible to distinguish impotence arising from purely psychological causes from those that have an organic basis. An important diagnostic test tells us to what extent erections occur during sleep. If they do, that usually means that the impotence is psychogenic, since all the mechanisms necessary to effect erection are intact. We don't need fancy machines to get that information either: you could just take five or six stamps from a roll, moisten the end of one, form the stamps into a ring and fasten them around the flaccid penis when you go to bed. If the ring is broken in the morning, you must have had an erection during the night.

Those causes of impotence that *are* purely organic, or physical—and preventable—fall into several categories. Most men, especially as they get older, tend to blame all their sexual problems on a waning hormone supply. They look for a quick and simplistic solution in the form of testosterone supplements, by shot or tablet. These are sometimes effective, usually for psychological reasons (the placebo effect). The fact is, hormone levels rarely drop until the seventies or eighties. When they do, however, testosterone supplements may be useful.

Hypothyroidism is another glandular disorder associated with impotence. Prevention here simply involves replacing the missing thyroid hormone.

Any man over fifty who becomes impotent for no apparent cause should also have his prolactin level measured. Too much of it interferes with erection. This hormone is produced by the pituitary gland in the brain and an excess can be treated with medication or surgery.

When Your Doctor Makes You Impotent!

In reviewing the subject of drug-induced impotence, I recently counted the number of different drugs reported to interfere with normal sexual function of both men and women. There were at least seventy-five! If you suspect that any medication you are taking may be doing you in, ask your doctor to check into it. Refer him to the August 5, 1983, issue of *The Medical Letter*.

There are some twenty-five million people in this country receiving treatment for high blood pressure. The most commonly used agents for this purpose are:

(1) *Diuretics* (water pills), of which there are many different brands on the market (Diuril, Hydrodiuril, Lasix, Dyazide, Moduretic, Esidrix, Enduron and several others). They are said to cause impotence in about one-third of cases.

(2) The *beta-blocker drugs* (Inderal, Lopressor, Corgard, Visken, Tenormin, Blocadren and Sectral are the ones currently available in the United States, but more are on the way). These medications, in addition to lowering elevated pressure, are also effective and widely used in the management of angina pectoris, certain disorders of heart rhythm, migraine headaches, tremor, "performers' anxiety" and symptoms of overactive thyroid function. They may result in a number of unwanted symptoms—fatigue, cold hands and feet, bad dreams, low blood pressure, slow heart rate, asthmatic attacks in vulnerable patients and heart failure in some cardiacs. But the complaints I hear most (from men) are fatigue and impotence. These are often serious enough to force discontinuation of the beta blocker, especially in young patients. An alternative category of drugs is the calcium channel blockers, which do not appear to have any adverse effects on libido or performance. These are effective in the management of angina, hypertension, migraine headaches and

certain heart-rhythm irregularities, but not for tremor, anxiety or an overactive thyroid.

(3) Aldomet, a drug used in the treatment of hypertension, has a strong negative effect on sexual potential in men. In addition to reducing the sex drive, it may enlarge the breasts, prevent adequate erection and result in retrograde ejaculation (the sperm, instead of coming out the penis in the usual way, back up into the bladder and are later excreted in the urine). If you are taking Aldomet and have recently become impotent, that may well be what's doing it. Women, on the other hand, seem to tolerate Aldomet quite well, although generally speaking, any drug that renders men impotent also decreases sexual desire in women. (Its prolonged use may cause temporary liver damage in both sexes.)

(4) Ismelin is another antihypertension drug that may be responsible for impotence. It may not affect the erection, but can prevent ejaculation. (The same is true for Dibenzyline, a drug many urologists now prescribe for men with large prostates who have to get up frequently during the night to empty their bladder.)

Despite the above, you don't have to choose between a normal blood pressure and sexual potency. There are three drugs, Minipress, Apresoline and Capoten, that rarely have any adverse sexual effects. However, if one medication leaves you impotent, another may not. Your doctor will usually be able to work out some combination that will effectively control your pressure, yet leave your sexual capacity intact. But he'll never know you have the problem if you suffer silently and don't tell him about it.

The most widely prescribed drug in the United States is Tagamet (cimetidine), used in the treatment of peptic ulcer. It's great for that purpose. But it also has an anti-androgen effect. (Androgens are male hormones—the stuff of which erections are made.) So if you've got an ulcer, are taking Tagamet and have become impotent, try switching to Zantac (ranitidine) or Carafate. Zantac works on the ulcer in much the same way as does Tagamet but does not appear to have the same anti-androgen effect. Carafate is not absorbed by the body, and so has no hormonal effects.

Drugs used in the treatment of depression, anxiety and other psychiatric disorders are notorious for reducing the sex drive in both men and women. They do so by various mechanisms, some of which are hormonal. Use of these agents is sometimes necessary, at least temporarily. But there is no reason for anyone to take marijuana, excessive alcohol and "recreational" narcotics.

Impotence: When It's Not All in Your Head

Among the various *diseases* that can interfere with the body's communication and delivery systems that make erection possible, perhaps the most important is diabetes mellitus. About half of all diabetic men become impotent because of a double whammy: (a) the nerves in the penis are damaged by the disease (diabetic neuropathy); and (b) arteries to that organ become blocked and narrowed due to arteriosclerosis induced by diabetes, so that the increased blood flow necessary to enlarge it cannot be delivered. Can any of this be prevented? There is growing evidence that if blood sugar levels are well controlled over the years, damage to nerves and blood vessels can be reduced. It seems reasonable, then, for any diabetic to try to maintain readings as close to normal as possible, by a combination of diet and drugs (insulin or the oral anti-diabetic agents).

Long-standing high blood pressure can also leave a man impotent by accelerating arteriosclerosis of the arteries that supply blood to the penis—very much like what happens in diabetes. The key to prevention is effective blood-pressure control over the years. Many hypertensive men feel that their sexual problems arise not from the hypertension but from the drugs that are prescribed to lower it. That, as you have seen above, is entirely possible. But about a third of male hypertensives receiving no therapy become impotent anyway. In them, it's the disease, not the treatment, that does it.

Alcoholics as a group are prone to impotence. Prevention involves going on the wagon—early on, because 50 percent of alcoholics remain impotent after they've stopped drinking. Alcohol leaves you impotent by depressing brain function. It also damages the nerves that carry the impulses to the penis (alcoholic neuropathy—similar to the neuropathy of diabetes). Finally, enough alcohol taken over a prolonged period of time affects the liver, which has a great deal to do with sex. Men and women alike produce both male and female hormone. Women make more female hormone, and very little male hormone. The reverse is true in men. One of the liver's many functions is to break down these hormones as new quantities are constantly made. This prevents too much from accumulating in the body. The ability of the liver to metabolize or detoxify these sex hormones is impaired by excessive alcohol. What happens in alcoholic males is that the female hormone, normally present in small amounts, accumulates. As it does so, the man needs to shave less often, his breasts become larger and his testes smaller. His sex drive and performance also suffer. So, despite the machismo about holding your liquor like a "real man," if you drink enough for long enough, the one thing you won't be is a "real man."

Men who drink usually also smoke. The nicotine in tobacco constricts the blood vessels, and when those supplying the penis have already been narrowed by other mechanisms, cigarettes may tip the balance and result in impotence.

Earlier, I mentioned that many men and women who develop heart trouble have psychological problems adjusting sexually. The same is true after prostate surgery. About 20 percent of men over the age of sixty need to have their prostate removed, not because of cancer, but because the enlarged gland interferes with normal emptying of the bladder. Such surgery need not interfere with normal sexual function. The prostate gland does not make male hormone, the testes do, and they are not involved in prostate surgery, except when there is a cancer. Also, most surgical procedures of the prostate do not interfere with the nerves or the blood supply to the penis. Therefore, impotence occurring after surgery for benign (noncancerous) enlargement of the prostate gland is largely psychological. To prevent postoperative psychogenic impotence, it is critical that the male patient understand that "maleness" is in no way reduced as a result of such surgery just as femininity is unimpaired when the uterus is removed and the ovaries are left intact.

Cancer of the prostate is another matter. Most forms of therapy will result in impotence, and there's no way that can be prevented. If the entire gland is removed, impotence may be due to the trauma to nerves and blood vessels during the surgery. When the malignancy has spread to bone or lung, the testes, which are the main source of testosterone, are usually excised. An alternative approach to such surgery is the administration of female hormone to neutralize the action of testosterone. Here, the end result is the same as if the testes had been removed. However, when the doctor and the patient choose radiation rather than surgery to treat the cancer, only 50 percent of men become impotent if the external beam form is used, and only 7 percent when the radiation is delivered by implanting radioactive gold seeds directly into the cancerous prostate gland.

There are several forms of impotence that cannot be reversed. These include injury to the penis or its partial removal due to a malignancy; multiple sclerosis and other neurological diseases affecting the nerve supply to the penis; brain injuries and strokes; and occasionally surgery of the large bowel (when large portions of that organ are removed because of extensive disease).

So, what's the bottom line? If you're impotent, first determine the cause. I mentioned the simple technique using stamps wrapped around the penis during the night. There are, obviously, more sophisticated ways to evaluate penile blood flow. Neurological testing can be done to see whether the nerve supply is intact. If your impotence is drug-related or physical, try to identify and eliminate the cause(s). If the problem is psychological, seek appropriate counseling.

Whether it's psychological or physical in origin, if your impotence does not respond to treatment, there are satisfactory surgical alternatives. These consist of two different approaches. In one, rods are inserted into the penis, leaving it semirigid at all times. This makes penetration and intercourse possible. The drawback, of course, is the unrelenting turgidity. When you wear a bathing suit, people think you're boasting. The second approach, preferred by most patients, consists of an inflatable penile prosthesis. Hollow rods are inserted in both sides of the penis, a small pump is placed into one of the testicles, and a reservoir containing fluid is implanted under the skin of the abdomen. When the situation requires it, the patient squeezes the pump, which causes fluid from the reservoir to enter the rods in the penis, making it erect. The whole system can be quite subtle. One man I know has now been married for two years and his wife has no inkling as to the secret of his prowess! Neither does his mistress!

CHAPTER **27**

Classic Prevention—The Checkup, Immunization and Home Testing

What—No Checkup?

A couple of years ago, a young man, recently arrived in this country from Italy and speaking virtually no English, applied for a messenger's job at my office. My receptionist mistook him for a patient, and directed him to an empty examining room, where she instructed him to remove his clothes and wait for me. I found the bewildered lad sitting there in his birthday suit. He didn't think it unusual to be examined in these circumstances, since he had heard that almost everyone in America goes for regular checkups. He assumed that a job applicant had to have one too!

For at least fifty years, the routine physical was considered as American as apple pie, as traditional as Thanksgiving or Mother's Day. But that's no longer true. Lots of people now wonder whether the annual exam of healthy individuals is really necessary, and whether it in fact helps prevent disease.

Statisticians, economists, politicians and even some "academic" doctors—all of whom deal more with computers, numbers and the theories of disease than with real, sick people—have concluded that, with few exceptions, the health-maintenance exam is not cost-effective. Most practicing doctors disagree. Each and every one of us knows from personal experience that disease is often unexpectedly detected. The "naysayers" respond by saying that these routine evaluations are not worth all the time, expense and effort. They agree that a life may be saved here and there, but they'd rather use the money spent on checkups of healthy people to care for the elderly, the poor, the malnourished and the ill.

Although I understand the rationale behind most of these arguments, I don't happen to agree with the conclusion, which in my opinion is unsafe, unwise, undesirable and unprofitable. In the final analysis, prevention really *is* cheaper than treatment, and *properly* targeted exams *are* cost-effective. You'll read about some convincing examples in a moment.

People are not, after all, inert, inanimate machines. The human body is a dynamic organism in a constant state of flux. Changes occur in every one of our organs from moment to moment, from day to day and certainly from year to year. Much can and does happen quite unpredictably in a twelve-month period—a dangerous rise in blood pressure; the onset of diabetes, glaucoma, arthritis or gout; the appearance of a cancer somewhere; or the insidious clogging of a major artery supplying a critical organ—the heart, brain or kidneys. What's more, there is often, early on, an "incubation period," during which a problem, not yet apparent to the patient, may be detected during a checkup. And it is at this time that the trouble can usually be nipped in the bud most effectively.

Most patients, in the course of giving a routine history, have told me, for example, that they had "gas"—a symptom "not worth complaining about." Their problem often turned out to be angina pectoris. Doctors frequently detect a small lump in the rectum, breast or testicle of which the patient was unaware, and which proves to be a malignancy—detected early enough to cure. At other times, we hit "pay dirt" in some routine procedure, like a chest X ray, electrocardiogram, a battery of blood examinations, the Pap smear, and stool or urine analysis.

So most practicing doctors continue to recommend periodic exams for most "healthy" adults, looking for disease that has not yet caused symptoms, or to which certain vulnerable patients are prone.

Why then do the statisticians and their computers come up with negative conclusions? I believe it's because some of the data they're analyzing are incomplete. Computer programming is insensitive and "inhuman." Here is one example.

Jack Smith was forty-eight years old, a successful executive, married, with two children. He'd been coming to my office for his annual physical examination every year for sixteen years. At his most recent visit, I gave him an excellent report, as usual. His weight was practically ideal, his heart was normal, lung function was perfect and there was no evidence of malignancy anywhere. His personal habits were good too. He wasn't smoking, he "worked out" at least twice a week, walked three miles a day, and generally ate and drank in moderation. When he was given his card for next year's appointment, he surprised me with "Doctor, do you think it's really necessary? Why don't I just call you if something goes wrong? I hear that the routine checkup is really a waste of your time and my money. And, anyway, I am in pretty good shape. You've never found anything really wrong with me in sixteen years. My insurance agent tells me I could almost have paid up a handsome life-insurance policy with the money I've spent on these checkups."

Everything Jack said was true—as far as he went. But there is more to the story than meets the eye. He was correct when he said I had not found much wrong with him over the years. However, at his very first office visit, the detailed questionnaire he completed was very revealing. His father had suffered a heart attack at age fifty and died four years later; an older brother had developed high blood pressure at age forty; three paternal uncles had died of coronary disease before the age of sixty; and a maternal aunt was diabetic. Nor did Jack remember that sixteen years ago, when he first came to see me, he was thirty pounds overweight, smoked twenty to thirty cigarettes a day, was totally dedicated to physical inertia and had a borderline blood pressure of 146/92. In short, he was a perfect setup for big trouble. For that reason, at each "routine" annual visit, we sat and talked prevention. I explained to him again and again and again how and why his family history and personal habits made him vulnerable to heart disease. After two or three such sessions, he got the message. He stopped smoking, began to exercise regularly, and attained and maintained ideal weight. As a result, his blood pressure dropped to a normal reading of 136/86 without his having to take any drugs. Because his cholesterol, triglycerides and HDL levels were borderline, he avoided excessive amounts of saturated fats. He even began taking one baby aspirin every day in an attempt to head off a heart attack or stroke. I believe that by simply having been convinced to quit cigarettes and stay off them, he reduced the risk of a heart attack and cancer by about 30 percent. Losing weight, exercising and watching his diet probably added a few more years to his life expectancy. In short, as far as I was concerned, his "unnecessary" visits all these years had resulted in a life-style that gave him a better chance to live longer. Yes, it's true that Jack could have spent all that money to pay for life-insurance premiums over the years, but his insurance agent would probably have benefitted most.

Now, how would a programmer looking into the "cost-effectiveness" of Jack's routine exams have dealt with this case? He would have "told" the computer that the patient had come to see me each year for sixteen years, spent X number of dollars and during all that time nothing had "happened." I had found no cancer, no heart disease and no other hidden disorders. The inevitable conclusion? It was all a waste.

I think that at least some of the data from which the negative reaction to the checkup is derived contain many "Jack-like" stories. There is no way that a computer, no matter how sophisticated, can evaluate the important benefits of successful long-term risk-factor control. Yet it is computer statistics on which health policies are largely based.

As a result of Jack's history and scores of similar experiences, I advise any "healthy" person who is especially vulnerable, for whatever reasons and to whatever diseases, to have periodic (if not annual) re-evaluation.

But what about a healthy individual who is not at special or obvious risk? Should he or she have a routine electrocardiogram at regular intervals if there is no chest pain, no shortness of breath and no palpitations? Some doctors say it's pointless. According to them, the ECG will almost certainly be normal, especially in view of the fact that 60 percent or more of all patients *with established heart disease and angina pectoris* have normal tracings anyway. So why spend the money? And supposing you're healthy, and the tracing turns out to be abnormal. If there are no supporting symptoms and nothing unusual in the physical exam, the ECG abnormality either represents a false alarm or reflects "silent" disease. In order to determine which it is, a certain amount of additional testing becomes necessary. If, thousands of dollars and much anxiety later, the changes turn out to reflect some mild coronary disease, what can be done about it anyway? What medication would we give a patient who has no symptoms? On the other hand, if the ECG abnormality was a false alarm, all we've accomplished is to scare a perfectly healthy individual out of his wits, put him to great expense and probably left him with permanent anxiety about his state of health.

Well, it's not as simple as that, at least not in my experience. When I am asked what is to be gained by having a healthy person take an electrocardiogram, I recall this next case. Saul was a friend of mine, a confirmed bachelor, fit in every way except that he was overweight. At the age of forty-six, he fell in love with a beautiful young woman whom he very much wanted to marry. But he hated the thought of being a fat, old bridegroom. So before proposing, he decided to "get into shape," and signed up for a strenuous exercise program. Fortunately, he had the old-fashioned common sense to go for a checkup first. Now remember, he was totally without symptoms and his physical examination was unremarkable except for the overweight. Blood pressure was satisfactory, heart sounds were good, there were no murmurs, lungs were clear and even the electrocardiogram *at rest* was normal. But then, because he planned to exercise so vigorously, his doctor advised a stress test. It was dramatically abnormal! Since such changes do occasionally occur in healthy people (we call them "false-positive" responses), Saul was put through several additional diagnostic procedures. The last of these, the coronary angiogram, indicated severe disease in all three coronary arteries, including the critical left main stem vessel. The decision was made to operate, and he successfully received five coronary bypass grafts (two of his arteries required two grafts each, the third needed only one). Within three months his ECG stress test, previously so bad, had returned to normal. He married, and was soon exercising with great gusto and loving every moment of it. Now, if this man had failed to have that routine ECG and treadmill test before embarking on this fitness program, he might well have become an adverse statistic.

There are two messages in this case history. The first is that a normal electrocardiogram taken at rest is not conclusive evidence of normal coronary arteries. The second is that for any man over age forty, an ECG stress test is a must before signing up for a vigorous exercise program.

Given the negative statistical data on the one hand, and the supportive anecdotal account on the other, what's the bottom line with respect to the annual exam? I believe that it is a good thing for most persons. Simply stated, it can't hurt. The worst that can possibly be said about the routine physical is that our national standard of living has fallen to the level that we are less able to afford it. That, of course, is a very real consideration. So, despite my enthusiasm, I regretfully concede that the facts of life necessitate some compromise. The following is the least my principles and conscience permit me to accept.

A periodic health evaluation should consist of specific tests at regular intervals based on age, sex, genetics, occupation and particular vulnerability. Clearly, someone at risk because of a bad family history (e.g., a woman whose mother and/or sisters have all developed breast cancer, or a man whose parents both died at an early age of hypertension and coronary-artery disease, or someone with significant risk factors—cigarette smoking, high cholesterol and high blood pressure) should be checked at specific intervals in the appropriate way. For the rest of us, healthy, without complaints and not especially vulnerable, I suggest the following schedule. Remember, however, that no two doctors or "committees" agree on this question and that these are my personal views based on my own experience.

A complete physical should be done as indicated in the following table.

FREQUENCY OF COMPLETE CHECKUPS IN HEALTHY PERSONS

Ages	Frequency
15–19	once
19–35	every 5 years
35–45	every 3 years
45–55	every 2 years
55 plus	annually

A complete checkup means a careful history and a thorough physical exam. It should take at least one hour and include a battery of routine blood tests, urine and stool analysis, and at intervals specified below, chest X ray, electrocardiogram and stress test.

One complete exam during adolescence (ages fifteen to nineteen) is necessary as a base line to make certain that no important abnormalities were missed during childhood, e.g., a heart murmur, hearing loss, lactose intolerance, learning disabilities, visual problems and the like. It also gives the doctor an opportunity to discuss and advise the youngster about life-style (diet; exercise; use of alcohol, drugs, tobacco; contraception; and sexually transmitted diseases).

Between ages nineteen and thirty-five, major degenerative diseases (cardiac, arthritis, pulmonary, kidney) are not yet common, so a complete exam need not really be done during that period more often than every five years in the absence of symptoms. However, there are special tests that should be performed more frequently. For example, cancer of a testicle is important in young men during these years. They should be taught how to examine themselves, just as we teach young women to examine their breasts, and they should do so at least twice a year. In this age group, blood pressure should be checked annually in both sexes, but especially in women receiving oral contraceptives. At age thirty, both sexes should begin to submit stool specimens once a year (done easily on a "hemoccult" card) for chemical evidence of blood (not apparent to the naked eye). You can test it at home with a new over-the-counter kit. If it shows blood, you contact your doctor.

Of all the "routine" tests that are done in one's lifetime, the two with the greatest yield of treatable or curable disease are the blood-pressure reading, and the stool exam for blood, which may reflect hidden bowel malignancies. Women, as soon as they have become sexually active, should have Pap tests annually for the rest of their lives. Daughters born of mothers who took DES for fertility problems should have Pap tests twice a year. The American Cancer Society recommends them only every three years in women without symptoms because cervical cancer usually grows so slowly that there is time to cure it if you test within a three-year period. However, I understand from some of my gynecologist colleagues that they are now seeing types of cervical cancer that develop more rapidly than was previously supposed. Since the test is so simple and inexpensive, I see no reason to compromise in this area. Finally, a yearly pelvic exam should be done in those women who have an intrauterine device, which renders them more vulnerable to pelvic infection.

The breasts should be checked carefully by a doctor every year, and by the patient herself at least once a month, between menstrual periods, usually in the shower with her breasts well soaped. You can be taught to do this by your own doctor, by branches of your local cancer society and by community clinics. There is a teaching program called Mammacare, available in several breast clinics throughout the country, where a more sophisticated technique using specially constructed breast models is available. I believe every woman should have a mammogram done as a base line at age thirty-five. If there is no family history to indicate special vulnerability, she may wait until age forty for her next one and then repeat the test every two years thereafter until age fifty, when it should become an annual affair. Make sure the equipment used in performing the mammogram is the modern type, which generates less radiation than older machines.

Between ages thirty-five and forty-five, a complete exam should be done every three years. An electrocardiogram should first be recorded at that age—as a base line. Stress tests, in the absence of chest symptoms, need only be obtained if you are planning to start a vigorous exercise program, but annually after age fifty-five.

When you have reached age forty-five, for the next ten years you begin to be more vulnerable to the major killers—heart and vascular disease, cancer and stroke. You should now see your doctor for a complete exam every two years (but remember that blood pressure, stool, breast and Pap tests are done annually).

By the time you've made it to fifty-five, you've earned the right to a yearly checkup.

I used to do a chest X ray every year on all my adult patients. However, an expert panel of consultants for the FDA's National Center for Devices and Radiologic Health recently issued the following statement: "The yield of unsuspected disease (such as lung cancer, heart disease and tuberculosis) found by routine screening chest X-ray examinations of unselected populations not based on history, physical examination or specific diagnostic testing has been shown to be of insufficient clinical value to justify the monetary cost (two billion dollars per year), added radiation exposure and subject inconvenience of the examination." This panel urged, among other things, the discontinuance of all routine chest X rays of "unselected populations": in other words, they don't recommend it even at five-year intervals. That, I think, is going a bit far. My own patients with heart or lung disease, who smoke cigarettes or work in a polluted air environment, have a routine chest X ray annually. I insist on one every four or five years for everyone else. This provides useful information about the size and shape of the heart as the individual gets older, and whether or not areas of calcification are developing in the heart and major arteries. There is another reason. Every now and then, one will serendipitously stumble across a finding that, if unrecognized, would have been fatal. This next example illustrates such a case.

Cynthia was forty-eight years old, without a complaint or worry in the world. I never suggested that she come to the office every year for a checkup, but she did anyway because that was the only way she could get her husband to do so too. He worked very hard, was tense, had a strong family history of heart disease and she felt he was at risk for "trouble." So they visited me together every September. About eight years ago, I found a suspicious shadow in her chest X ray that turned out to be a malignant tumor. (Incidentally, Cynthia was not a smoker.) Lung cancer is about the worst kind of malignancy you can have. Once detected, it is almost always rapidly fatal. But in this particular case, when the surgeon carefully searched the chest cavity after removing the tumor, he found all the surrounding glands free of disease. Nor was there evidence of malignant spread anywhere else —not to her brain, her liver or her bones.

Today, eight years later, Cynthia is alive and well. She was cured of the tumor that had been diagnosed serendipitously. But statistics and computers tell us that lung cancers are almost always fatal by the time you detect them on a chest film. So the question is asked, why bother taking an X ray in the first place? According to statisticians, it is obviously a waste of money, not to mention the unnecessary radiation. To the money manager, and in the larger scheme of things, Cynthia is only a statistic—one case who happened to "make it" among thousands who didn't. From a dollars-and-cents point of view, to save one Cynthia, it is not worth the cost of the X rays and exams on all the other people who are either free of disease or have cancer too late to cure. But try telling that to her!

The important point of this story is that the minimal amount of radiation involved in a single chest X ray in my judgment justifies taking one every few years. Who knows how many Cynthias we may pick up just doing that?

Interestingly enough, most people don't think about routine dental X rays when considering the matter of avoidable radiation. Although

I am no expert in the field, it seems to me that altogether too many dental films are taken without sufficient cause. Personally, unless I have a toothache or a dentist finds some other problem in my mouth that mandates it, I refuse to undergo the ritual routine dental X ray every year. Obviously, your dentist needs one complete set as a base line from which to work, but after that, question her closely about the necessity for X rays.

Although a checkup at the intervals I have suggested requires the skill and training of a doctor, a substantial number of the special procedures that I recommend be done at yearly intervals can and should be done by specially trained nurse practitioners, physician assistants or other paramedical personnel. Blood tests, stool and urine analyses, blood pressure determinations, even Pap tests and breast examinations are good examples. This can go a long way toward reducing the cost of medical care, yet make detection in key areas available to the American public.

I think most caring doctors, concerned patients and enlightened politicians will find the recommendations I have listed above responsible and reasonable. We ought to resist their further erosion by economic and political pressures. If you think prevention is expensive, try disease.

Shots: Not for Kids Only

There is no more pertinent subject to be covered in a book on prevention, nor any more dramatic example of how disease can be prevented, than immunization. (Immunization is the term used to denote that immunity to a disease has been conferred. Vaccination, the introduction of a living or dead organism, is the most common form of artificially induced immunity. Such immunity is frequently a natural occurrence, resulting from the body's reaction to infection.)

In 1953, when I was a medical resident, there was a whole wing full of polio patients at my hospital. Their survival was possible only as long as they remained in their iron lungs. In some respects, their lives were not unlike those of patients with artificial hearts tethered to their pneumatic pump consoles.

Then came Jonas Salk and his injectable polio vaccine, made from killed viruses, followed by Sabin's oral live vaccine. As a result, in the past twenty years, I have not seen a single new case of polio either in my own practice or in my hospital. Although several out-breaks did occur in this country in the 1970s among nonimmunized individuals, there are few if any functioning iron lungs in America anymore.

Remember when we used to need smallpox shots every time we left for a trip abroad? Smallpox is now extinct everywhere in the world, thanks to immunization.

Are you old enough to remember the whoops of a child with per-tussis (whooping cough)? I am. They were paroxysms of unrelenting, fatiguing, successive dry coughs followed by the agonized inspiratory breath with its characteristic whoop. I haven't heard that sound in thirty years.

We call tetanus "lockjaw" because it affects the muscles that open and close the mouth. When is the last time you heard of anyone getting it? Actually, a few people do—those who have not had their tetanus booster shots as required.

Most adults associate vaccination with memories of childhood, and think that shots are for kids only. But recently, more and more grown-ups of all ages have been asking whether or not they need any follow-up vaccinations of their childhood shots. Some of them don't really remember what immunization they received as infants and chil-dren, or their childhood diseases that might have conferred immu-nity. Parents, if still alive, are little help if they didn't keep this information on record—and very few do. Pediatricians or family doc-tors are often dead or retired, or have moved away. In any event, the health file is no longer available. So what do you do if you're planning a trip to the Third World, where there is still some polio around, and don't know for sure whether or not you were immunized, or when? Or suppose you wish to become pregnant and have read about the dangers of rubella (German measles)? You think you were vacci-nated, but are not sure. Or perhaps you are a thirty-five-year-old man whose baby has come down with the mumps. You just don't remem-ber whether or not you were vaccinated—should you take a shot to be safe? Also, are there new vaccines that were not available when you were a child? Should you have any of them now? Is late, in fact, better than never at your age? There isn't a week goes by but that a patient of mine will call up with some news that he or she "stepped on a nail," "cut my finger on a tin can" or "didn't quite make it over a barbed-wire fence." And, "Should I have a tetanus shot?"

If you have wondered about any of these questions and don't have the answers, let me review for you the current thinking about immunization at all ages, including adult life. Also, it's useful for parents to know the immunization schedule their children will have to follow.

There are eight diseases against which one should be protected—starting in childhood. These are measles, mumps, rubella (German measles), polio, diphtheria, tetanus, pertussis (whooping cough) and *Hemophilus influenzae* meningitis (Hib).

First, let's get smallpox out of the way. Not only do you *not* need it, you should steadfastly refuse to accept a shot in the unlikely event it is requested by an obstinate health official somewhere or other. Except for a sporadic case in some remote area, smallpox has disappeared from the face of the earth as a result of worldwide vaccination over the years. Receiving the vaccine does carry with it a small risk, which was unavoidable at the time when the vaccine was necessary, but is no longer justified.

I'll bet you haven't seen or heard of a case of diphtheria in years. I've only come across one patient with this disease in the past decade. But it *is* still around and associated with a 10 percent death rate. Diphtheria itself is best known for its attack on the throat, but it may involve other organs, especially the heart. In the classic case, the throat becomes sore and is covered by a grayish dirty-looking membrane, which, if it dislodges, may cause death by suffocation. The reason we see so little diphtheria anymore (at the turn of the century it claimed the lives of 15 of every 100,000 persons in this country) is because of immunization. My one patient with diphtheria was a woman in her thirties. She "thought" she had gotten the vaccine as a child, but couldn't remember how many doses. She certainly never received a booster shot. Diphtheria vaccine is combined with tetanus and pertussis, and is usually first given at the age of two months (the infant is protected for the first few weeks of life by its mother's antibodies) and again four to eight weeks later. A third injection is usually administered at six months, another at eighteen months and a booster is given at the start of school—ages four to six years. Now here is an important fact not sufficiently appreciated by most persons or acted upon by enough doctors: *you maintain your immunity to diphtheria throughout adult life only if you receive booster shots every ten years*. Most of us know that we should have tetanus boosters at ten-year intervals. But I've yet to come across a patient who's asked me for a diphtheria booster. If you haven't received yours, get it—now, or whenever you go for your next tetanus shot. The amount of diphtheria vaccine given adults is usually less than what children get in their primary vaccinations. Tetanus and diphtheria are not live vaccines, like rubella, oral polio, mumps and measles, and therefore not subject to the same precautions which are discussed below.

Tetanus boosters are very important. They protect against unforeseen infection by the tetanus bug. If you do develop the disease, the risk of death is about 50 percent, despite modern treatment. The tetanus organism is found in earth, in human and animal excrement, and in dust. It gains entry to the body through a break in the skin. Once in, the organism produces a poison that causes spasm and stiffness of various muscle groups. Despite all our educational efforts, there are still more than fifty cases of tetanus reported in the United States each year, almost always in unvaccinated adults.

As far as pertussis, or whooping cough, vaccination is concerned, the last dose you will ever need is the one combined with the tetanus and diphtheria shot you were given at the time you started school— between ages four and six. Children with neurological abnormalities such as recurrent epileptic attacks should not receive the vaccine. When a side effect is observed after the administration of this combined diphtheria, tetanus and pertussis vaccine, it is most likely due to the pertussis component. Sometimes, the reaction is severe and the child may develop convulsions. If that occurs, most doctors will not include pertussis in the next shot of the multiple vaccine. Adults never need a booster shot of whooping-cough vaccine. But, in the unlikely event that you never received diphtheria, tetanus and pertussis in childhood, it goes without saying that you should receive at least the diphtheria-tetanus shot as soon as possible.

Some doctors have recently recommended against whooping-cough vaccination because of its side effects. In my own view, that's a mistake. (I understand that one of the major national pharmaceutical houses has discontinued manufacture of this vaccine because so many people were suing for compensation for adverse reactions.) If this vaccination is stopped, it is estimated that there will be about 350,000 cases of whooping cough annually in the United States. I advise that your child not be among them. Whooping cough can and still does cause serious bronchial infections, especially from May through July, in this country. Every now and then there are outbreaks in isolated areas. The disease itself, although usually self-limiting and curable, can produce brain damage and seizures, as well as pneumonia, emphysema and other serious lung problems.

The first available polio vaccine was the preparation containing the killed or inactivated virus introduced by Dr. Jonas Salk. Millions of people received it as soon as it became widely available in the rush to be protected against the dread polio virus. And it did its job well. However, the immunity conferred by the killed injectable vaccine is not lifelong. The oral live Sabin vaccine developed later does afford permanent protection, and it is the one now used almost exclusively. The immunization schedule for this vaccine (it can be given in a sugar cube) is as follows: age two months, four months (some doctors also recommend it at six months to be absolutely safe), eighteen months and the final booster dose at the start of school. That's it—no more is ever necessary.

If you are an adult and suspect you were never immunized against polio, the Centers for Disease Control does not feel you need to do so now, except if you are going to an area where polio is prevalent— for example, parts of Africa, Asia and Latin America. But unvaccinated children should be immunized. As recently as 1972, there was an outbreak at a school in the northeastern United States where 11 of 128 students came down with the disease. To everyone's surprise, it was found that the stricken youngsters had never been vaccinated in the first place with either the Salk or the Sabin preparations.

The remaining four diseases against which you need protection in childhood are: mumps, measles, German measles (Rubella) and *H. influenzae* meningitis. One shot containing vaccines against the first three is normally given at age fifteen months and confers lifelong immunity. If you don't know whether you've had that vaccination, here is what to do. If you were born before 1956 you probably have enough protection against measles and mumps so as not to require any immunization. If, however, you were born after that time, you should receive the triple vaccine.

Rubella deserves special attention. Although the disease itself is mild, it frequently causes serious birth defects in the offspring when contracted by a pregnant woman, so much so that it is grounds for abortion when religious and personal beliefs permit. Rubella vaccine was licensed in 1969, but it is estimated that about 20 percent of Americans have not been immunized against it, either naturally by contracting the disease, or by the vaccine. Any female in the child-bearing age who even suspects she may be unprotected should be vaccinated immediately, provided of course she is not already pregnant. And if she is vaccinated, she should wait for a full three months before becoming pregnant, because this is a live vaccine, which can be transmitted to and harm the unborn child. Recent studies claim that the vaccine is *not* dangerous during pregnancy. I suggest you be very conservative about this finding. Any health professionals likely to come in contact with German measles should also be vaccinated, since they can transmit the disease as carriers.

If you are pregnant and have definitely been exposed to polio, and have not been immunized, it is wise to get the Salk vaccine. Check that with your own doctor.

The latest vaccine to be developed for children is that against the *Hemophilus influenzae* organism. Despite its name, this bacterium does not cause the flu. It is responsible for a deadly form of meningitis that strikes one child in two hundred in this country, and carries with it a 5 percent mortality rate. This new vaccine was approved for use in the U.S. in April 1984, and, in my opinion, every child should receive the one-shot immunization at the age of twenty-four months. As far as I am aware, this vaccine carries no risk and very few side effects. Vulnerability to Hib meningitis increases when numbers of children are in close contact over prolonged periods. In the preschool age group, this is most apt to happen in day-care centers. So if your child happens to be enrolled in one, you may want him or her to be vaccinated before twenty-four months, even though the vaccine is less effective when given earlier in life.

So much for the vaccines given during childhood. What shots should adults take?

I've already indicated in Chapter 2 that, in my opinion, influenza vaccine should be given to high-risk persons or anyone who wants it, provided there is no history of allergy to hens' eggs and chicken. It's a killed virus, so it can be taken during pregnancy, if necessary. Annual booster shots are required.

The pneumonia vaccine, protective against twenty-three bacterial forms, should be administered to all persons over fifty years of age, or to anyone with a chronic illness such as diabetes, lung trouble, heart disorders, or who has had his or her spleen removed. (The latter group are particularly vulnerable to the ravages of pneumonia.)

We are now able to make hepatitis B vaccine by using recombinant DNA techniques, and can identify blood containing evidence of previous infection with the AIDS virus, so the fear of contracting AIDS from this vaccination is no longer justified. Anyone at high risk for contracting hepatitis B should be immunized against it. That includes doctors, dentists, other exposed health workers, homosexuals, drug abusers, and those requiring frequent blood transfusions.

Travelers going abroad often ask whether to take shots against cholera and typhoid fever. Quite frankly, I don't recommend these for my own patients. The injections often make you sick. Cholera is a treatable disease, and I don't personally know of any Westerner who, even if he or she contracted it, wasn't cured by lots of intravenous fluids and the appropriate antibiotic. So in my judgment, the cholera vaccine is not worth taking, although certain countries require it for entrance. I feel the same way about typhoid vaccine. I'm not convinced it's protective. But don't take my word for it; ask your own doctor. Chances are he will agree with me. If he doesn't, remember, he's the boss.

Yellow fever is another matter. If you are going to any area where the disease is endemic, you must be immunized. Also, many countries are very fussy about this particular vaccination, and you won't be admitted unless you have documented evidence that you have been protected. If you are pregnant, do not take the vaccine, since it is a live preparation, unless you absolutely must go to some area where yellow fever is prevalent.

Adults going to areas, such as India, where *H. influenzae* is endemic should receive the *H. influenzae* vaccine discussed on page 399.

There is nothing more important you can do than see to it that your immunization requirements and those of your children are fulfilled and kept up to date. Once you have done so, it is important to keep proper records. If you are a parent, don't depend entirely on the pediatrician's office to do it for you. Keep your own file and give it to your children when they leave home.

When Prevention Begins at Home—Home Testing

Patients are now also able to perform, in the privacy of their own home, many of the procedures that were formerly done only by a doctor, a hospital or a laboratory.

The following pages deal with several of the do-it-yourself kits now available. While none of them actually prevents disease, the results they provide directly to you can result in its earlier detection and more effective control—and that's almost as important as prevention itself.

The following discussion is limited to those tests I consider most practical and useful. If you really want to explore virtually *every* self-diagnosing possibility, there is a book you can buy that describes more than 160 tests. It is called *Do-It-Yourself Medical Testing* and was written by Dr. and Mrs. Pinckney. If you're a frustrated would-be doctor, performing these procedures at home will keep you happy and busy for many hours. (Incidentally, if you have a bona fide reason for buying a particular medical kit, have your doctor write you a letter confirming its need. Your insurance company may pay for it, and even if it doesn't, you will be able to deduct the kit as a medical expense.)

However, before you rush out to buy any gadget, learn how to do the simple things first. The other day, one of my patients asked whether I thought it was a good idea for him to use a pulmonary-function machine at home. He had chronic bronchitis and emphysema, and was interested in monitoring his progress, as well as determining the efficacy of his medication. The unit he had in mind cost several hundred dollars. I found his query quite amusing. You see, he also had an irregular heart rhythm that required treatment, yet he had never bothered to learn how to take his own pulse! That costs nothing, is very easy to do and in his case would be helpful to us both. Indeed, the very first thing most doctors do in *their* examination is to take your pulse. You'll find this new skill invaluable, especially if you have any kind of heart condition, or want to know the impact on your heart rate of any exercise you're doing.

Taking Your Pulse

The most convenient place to feel for your own (or anyone else's) pulse is in the wrist. With your palm facing up, you will easily find the beat if you draw an imaginary line running from your index finger to your wrist, just above your thumb. However, its location varies somewhat from person to person so you may have to roam a little before you find it. Although most doctors apply the pads of their index and middle fingers when counting your pulse, you should use whatever digits you like.

After you've located the pulsation, determine whether or not its rhythm is regular and then count it. To do that, you'll need a watch with a second hand. Multiply the number of beats in twenty seconds by three; that's the rate per minute. Don't you concern yourself with the *quality* of your pulse—leave that to your doctor. It may seem weak even when your heart is strong because of something as innocent as fat overlying the artery, a variation in the location of the blood vessel itself or the fact that you are pressing too hard on it— and you may panic unnecessarily. So just learn to count it.

If you have trouble finding your pulse at your wrist, try your neck on either side of your Adam's apple. But be careful not to push too hard, because sustained pressure on a carotid artery (whose pulsations it is you're feeling) can slow your heart rate to dangerously low levels and make you faint. There is also a pulse in your groin. You may look for it at home, but doing so in public may be embarrassing!

Anyone can—and should—learn how to examine his or her pulse. But it's one thing to take it sitting down, when you have time to feel for and count your heart rate in a leisurely fashion; it's quite another matter when you're jogging, running, or working out in some other vigorous way. Finding your pulse, counting it, watching the second hand *and* continuing to exercise becomes quite a challenge—yet the information may be important. If you've had a heart attack or have angina, your doctor may have prescribed an exercise program for you—walking, bicycling, jogging or perhaps even running. In order to provide you with a goal, or safe upper limit of exercise, she will first have you perform some kind of standardized stress test, usually a treadmill or bicycle ergometer. This makes it possible to determine the heart rate you should attain. If you do your workout at a cardiac rehabilitation center where you are constantly monitored (something

I recommend for most cardiac patients, at least for three to six months), they will let you know when you've reached your target rate. But when you're doing it on your own you may have difficulty. So I recommend you buy your own pulse indicator, which can be worn during exercise. These devices come in various forms—usually finger cuffs, or cuffs worn on a wrist. Whatever style you choose, it's a very valuable addition to your home-testing armamentarium. You can purchase one at any medical supply house. Before paying for it, ask to borrow it for a few days to make sure it's working right. Some of them are very temperamental.

Finally, a Thermometer You Can Read

Before investing in any other equipment for home diagnosis, get yourself a good thermometer. The traditional glass rod containing mercury has long been the bane of many patients (and doctors), especially those with impaired vision. Another disadvantage of this type of thermometer is that one is never sure about the site of its last insertion!

There is good news about thermometers. You can now buy thin sheaths with which to cover the part that goes under your tongue. These do not interfere with the reading. After you've taken your temperature, you discard the cover and put on a new one. No more washing the thermometer with alcohol and no more wondering where it's been. More important is the availability, at very reasonable cost, of electronic or battery-operated thermometers with a clearly visible digital readout. Goodbye to all that endless jiggling to make the mercury column visible, and no more panic because the 104° reading from your last illness stayed up there despite your most vigorous shaking of the thermometer. There is a variety of brands available that cost anywhere between $10 and $20 and can be purchased at most drugstores or medical supply houses.

Home Blood-Pressure Readings

One of the most important and useful "procedures" you can perform at home is measuring your own blood pressure. I encourage all my hypertensive patients to do so. It's an important screening test that can never be done too often, as far as I am concerned. There was a time, mind you, when the desirability of having patients take their own pressure was seriously questioned. Doctors worried that faulty technique would cause panic if the numbers were too high, and a false sense of security if they were normal. Furthermore, an incorrect reading might also result in an inappropriate change in the dosage of any drug being taken.

When the only blood-pressure machine you could buy was a manual one like your doctor's, some of these concerns were justified. Obtaining an accurate blood-pressure reading is not as easy as it looks. There are many pitfalls of which one must be aware. For example, the cuff must be the right size. If your arm is too fat and the cuff too small, you will get a false high result; it must be snugly applied at the proper level on your arm—not too loose and not too tight. Putting the stethoscope over the right spot on your arm is important too; you must also know how to interpret changes in the quality and intensity of the sounds you hear as you inflate and deflate the cuff. Other variables include the position you assume when taking your pressure (sitting, lying down, standing); what happens when you change that position (does the pressure rise or fall?); the difference, if any, between a reading on your right arm and your left—and a worn cuff, a leak in the bulb, or a defect in a machine with a circular gauge (the old units with the mercury column are still the most accurate and reliable) can distort the results you obtain. So, for all these reasons, many doctors did have reservations about patients taking their own pressure even though they were theoretically in favor of them doing so.

Today, however, much of the guesswork and potential for error in recording blood pressure have been removed by the advent of new machines. At first, if you wanted to check your blood pressure, you could do so only in drugstores, supermarkets, airports, parking lots and shopping malls. Some of the numbers spewed out by these earlier "public models" were frightening. A life-threatening reading of 260/140 often turned out to be 140/80 a few hysterical moments later in a doctor's office. But now, most of these machines have dropped so much in price, size and complexity that home use is quite feasible. Which unit should you buy? One of the earliest manufacturers of this product, Marshall Electronics, started turning machines out in 1973, and now has fourteen different models on the market, ranging in price from about $20 to $250. Their top-of-the-line machine is called Astropulse and is fully automatic. You put the cuff on your arm and push a button. The sphygmomanometer (a mouthful of a word meaning "blood-pressure machine") does the rest. It automatically inflates, deflates, displays the blood pressure and heart rate, and then prints them out. Other well-known electronics firms like Timex and Norelco have also entered the market, in addition to scores of Japanese, Korean, Swiss, German and American manufacturers.

Don't buy the first unit the dealer shows you. Have him demonstrate several. Take your pressure on all of them and see whether you get identical readings. Discard any that are awry. Why not test only one for accuracy against your doctor's unit? Because in a recent survey of doctors' blood-pressure equipment, one out of three was found to be faulty. So if there were to be a discrepancy between your newly purchased cuff and your doctor's, you'd never know whose was right. In any event, having selected and bought a unit, take it back to the dealer at least once a year to have it serviced, just as you would your car. Every one of these machines has parts that can wear out and compromise the accuracy.

If you have hypertension, there are many good reasons why you should buy a sphygmomanometer. The ability to record your own levels at various times during the day is extremely important in determining ideal dosage of pressure-lowering drugs. A single reading in your doctor's office, either in the morning after a restful night's sleep, when you are raring to go, or late in the afternoon after a stressful day at work, when you're exhausted and keyed up, makes decisions about how much medication you need a hit-and-miss affair. Recent research with automated blood-pressure devices that record continuously indicates that there are wide and often unpredictable swings of pressure throughout the day. Self-recording at frequent intervals documents these patterns in every individual. If you take your own pressure several times a day and keep a diary of what you were doing at the time, and with whom you were interacting, it makes for smoother and more effective pressure control. Another reason for monitoring your own levels is the prevalence of "the white-coat syndrome." There are many individuals whose pressure goes sky-high the moment they approach a cuff in a doctor's office. I have close friends who have been coming to me as patients for years. There is almost nothing I can do to them medically that fazes them: they will let me look way back in their throat without gagging; they don't mind my pushing hard on their belly; they even tolerate the more personal gloved aspects of the examination without a murmur—yet the moment they see me with cuff in hand, they look grim and their pressure rises. When they go home, relax and slip a cuff on themselves, their pressure is virtually normal. This response is probably worse when the doctor is a stranger, as occurs in the setting of insurance examinations. I wonder how many premiums are rated for hypertension when the diagnosis should really read "white-coat syndrome." Your doctor has no choice but to treat you, and the insurance company will rate you on the basis of the numbers it finds. You can't really expect the insurance people to accept the results *you've* obtained at home, but your doctor surely will.

Are You Sweet?—Monitoring Diabetes

Another home kit measures blood sugar levels and is extremely important for diabetics requiring insulin. Before these units were available, patients with diabetes were forced to rely on urine tests in order to regulate their diet and insulin dosage. Back in 1941, when home urine testing became possible for the first time, one dropped a tablet (Clinitest) into the urine and looked for the color change. Fifteen years later, the test-strip technique, in which a chemically treated strip was dipped into the urine and the color change matched against a chart, became available; it still is. Each plastic strip costs about ten cents. This is still far and away how most diabetics monitor their sugar.

Urinalysis is useful, but is not nearly as helpful as actual blood sugar determinations. The reason is that the amount of glucose in one's urine reflects, but does not actually measure, its concentration in the blood. Excess blood sugar is filtered through the kidneys and ends up in the urine. In some persons, the kidneys excrete sugar into the urine even when blood levels are normal. Also, after urine reaches the bladder, it remains there until enough has been accumulated for you to get the signal to void it. By the time your urine sees the light of day for you to test it for sugar, you don't really know what's taking place at that moment in your blood.

The ability to check your true and actual sugar level in your blood any time of the day or night is a real advance, especially since there is growing evidence that maintaining blood sugar at normal levels and

on an even keel throughout the day and night is the best way to
prevent the complications of diabetes—arteriosclerosis, blindness,
kidney trouble, etc. You can decide within five minutes whether
you'll need more insulin because you ate that extra piece of apple
pie, and whether you feel faint because you took too much insulin or
need more. The first step is to obtain a drop of blood from your
fingertip. No need to find a vein in your forearm like your doctor
does when he draws blood. But sticking one's own finger is not
always pleasant, especially if you're going to do it several times a
day. To make it easier there is a finger-puncture aid. Don't get involved in home blood sugar testing without one. These units are
automatic, quick and painless, and several good ones are available.
Most of my patients like the models made by Ames (Autolet), Bio-
Dynamics (Autoclix) and Monoject (Monojector). The newest entry
on the market is called Autolance, made by Becton Dickinson. There
are, however, at least ten others on the market.

Once you've got the blood, there are two routes you can go. Both
are accurate, and superior to urine testing. The first involves placing
the drop of blood on a plastic strip for about one minute. Then you
either blot it dry or wash it off and match the color reaction on the
strip against a color chart that is provided. Each of these strips costs
about fifty cents—that is, five times more than the urine dipstick.
But it's far more accurate. For most diabetics that's all that's necessary. For optimal control, you should check your blood in this manner ten minutes before each meal and at bedtime.

But you can go one step farther with blood sugar testing. You can
buy a meter that will give you a digital readout of your blood sugar.
This electronic device is probably a little more accurate than the
strip. It costs anywhere from $150 to $300 (and most insurance companies will reimburse you for it). One unit, which sells for about
$1,000, contains a computer that not only reads your sugar level but
also calculates your next insulin dose! The most popular makes in my
practice are the Ames Glucometer and the Accuchek II by Bio-Dy-
namics. However, there are at least a dozen others available, all
probably equally good.

None of these devices is foolproof. A microchip in the computer
may go haywire or become defective. So always double-check the
instrument with your doctor's lab before you buy it and at regular
intervals thereafter. Most important, if you're getting results that

don't seem right, before making any drastic changes in your insulin dosage, let your doctor know immediately. The problem may be in the unit and not your diabetes.

Testing urine for sugar is only one of more than twenty different bits of information you can obtain from its analysis. Most of the additional information is available by dipping a test strip or stick into the urine and reading the color reaction obtained on as many as ten different areas on each strip. Each of these detects a different constituent—blood, protein, bacteria, bile (for liver damage), ketones (acids that appear when diabetes is badly out of control or when you've been fasting for several days), acidity (when you're monitoring the effects of diet meant to prevent kidney stones), phenylketonuria (PKU—for the presence of an inherited metabolic disorder that causes mental retardation in infants) and pregnancy. It's perfectly reasonable to use as many of these urine tests as are necessary to monitor a particular problem, but remember to take advantage of your own five senses as well. And don't ignore your sixth one, common sense. For example, if your urine has a persistently bad odor, report it to your doctor. In an infant, for example, it may reflect the presence of some genetic disease; in an adult, infection. The frequency with which you void may be significant; and in men the force of the stream and the volume each time the bladder is emptied are often indicators of enlargement of the prostate gland.

Your Private Pregnancy Test

Another widely used home test is that which detects pregnancy. By measuring the presence of a certain hormone (human chorionic gonadotropin) in your urine, you can tell whether or not you are pregnant as early as three days after your last missed period. Many women, both married and single, spent a total of more than $50 million last year buying these tests. So it obviously appeals to them. They want to be the first to know whether their last missed period is the harbinger of motherhood or merely a false alarm. According to the manufacturers of these kits, as well as the American College of Obstetricians and Gynecologists, the kits are 98 percent accurate when used properly. Several such home pregnancy tests are currently available. The one with which I am familiar is called EPT-plus, made by Warner-Lambert. It costs about $10, as do most of the other kits. They all take anywhere from thirty minutes to two hours to read. Some manufacturers maintain a hot line monitored by experts to answer any question you may have about the result of your test. But remember, certain drugs may cause false-positive results, which also may occur in women approaching the menopause. So here, perhaps more than in any other do-it-yourself test, consultation with your doctor is extremely important, regardless of whether or not the test indicates you are pregnant. He will not only check your urine, but examine you as well. That can be critical.

I know a career woman of thirty-nine who did not want to have a baby. After she missed her period (she had previously been perfectly regular), she was sure she was pregnant and bought a home kit to confirm it. It read "positive." She repeated the test a few days later and again it was positive. She then contacted an abortion clinic, told her story and was all set to have the pregnancy terminated—something the clinic was quite prepared to do on the basis of her submitted evidence and a cursory examination. I suggested she consult her own gynecologist. He examined her carefully and concluded that the tests she had done were in error. She had missed her period because her ovaries had begun to work less well, not because she was pregnant. In other words, she was becoming menopausal prematurely.

While on the subject of ovarian function, you should know that there will soon be a test available that will permit women to determine their peak fertility time. This kit, to be manufactured by Personal Diagnostics, will consist of a computer that measures certain enzymes in your saliva that change in their composition about five days before the ovum, or egg, is released from an ovary. It will be useful for couples who have had trouble conceiving to know exactly when to concentrate their reproductive efforts.

The Dangers of False Modesty

Taking your pulse is not the only "gadget-free" test you can perform. Always pay attention to what you excrete. Anything leaving the body carries with it important information. Recently, a patient came to see me because of increasing constipation and abdominal cramping. My first question to her, quite naturally, was whether she had noted any blood or other change in the appearance of her stool. She looked at me aghast, incredulous. "Look in the toilet bowl? Me? Why on earth would I ever do *that?*" Another woman (it seems men are more relaxed about these things) never paid attention to her urine, and could only comment about it after eating asparagus. (Even that can provide important information. The length of time it takes for the odor of the asparagus to appear is a rough measure of kidney function. The longer the interval, the less efficient it is.)

Make it a habit to look not only at your feces and your urine, but at what you cough up, spit up or vomit. This provides you with early and more sensitive clues to trouble than any other test you can perform at home.

Detecting Colorectal Bleeding

One of the best ways to detect cancer of your bowel while it is still curable is to check your stool yourself for the presence of occult blood (not visible to the naked eye) at regular intervals, at least once or twice a year. Of course, when there is obvious bleeding, such as occurs from hemorrhoids or ulcerative colitis or a polyp in your gut or even cancer in your bowel, you don't need to test for blood. (Although, believe it or not, one of my patients, a doctor, no less, erroneously attributed the red blood in his stool to the beet soup he had been eating!) Early in the development of cancer anywhere along the intestinal tract, tiny amounts of blood, which can only be detected chemically, appear in the stool. The home kit involves spreading with a wooden applicator a thin film of your stool on a small piece of specially treated paper. Or the paper may be provided as a wipe. But whichever way the specimen is obtained, a few drops of a chemical are added to it, so that it turns a distinctive color when blood is present. These cards are available at any drugstore. The one I give my patients routinely at virtually every visit is made by Smith-Kline & Beckman. Learn how to use them. Test yourself frequently, especially if there is a strong family history of cancer of the intestines or if you've had a polyp or malignancy yourself sometime in the past. Also, if you take aspirin regularly, whether it's for the control of arthritic pain or to help prevent a stroke or a heart attack, erosion of the lining of your stomach may produce insidious blood loss. This is an important cause of anemia in older individuals and can be diagnosed by stool tests for occult blood.

But be careful about interpreting a positive test. There are several conditions that can mimic one. For example, if you eat a lot of rare meat or certain vegetables like radishes, artichokes, raw mushrooms, broccoli, turnips, if you take vitamin tonics or large doses of vitamin C, or even if you brush your teeth overvigorously, you may show a falsely positive test. However, if your specimen indicates the presence of blood, it's better not to attribute the result to any of these spurious causes. Consult your doctor and let him take it from there. Some ominous diseases cause bleeding that is intermittent, and you may thus be lulled into a false sense of security if after one positive test your next two or three are negative. Even if you have a single abnormal test, tell your doctor about it.

I believe that looking regularly for blood in your stool reduces the need for frequent routine screening exams for cancer by other means, such as barium enema, proctoscopy or colonoscopy. However, it does not replace them, particularly in persons who have symptoms suggestive of bowel trouble (sudden constipation, diarrhea or other change in bowel habits), a family history of cancer of the bowel, or some condition (like ulcerative colitis) that renders them vulnerable to cancer.

As with urine testing, do not depend on the occult-blood analysis alone. It does not provide all the answers. *Look at every stool you pass*. You'll be surprised at what you can learn from it. Should its caliber become narrowed and stringlike on several occasions, suspect the presence of a tumor that is narrowing the passage through which the stool descends. If you are a devotee of steak tartare, or sashimi and other raw fish, you may even discover a worm responsible for some of your undiagnosed abdominal symptoms. The color of your stool is important too. One that looks like clay may indicate obstruction of the bile ducts, usually by a gallstone or occasionally by a tumor in that area.

Will You Report Yourself?

There are about one million new cases of gonorrhea reported every year in the United States, and I suspect that that's only the tip of the iceberg. You can now determine at home whether you have this disease. The company that makes the gonorrhea detection kit guarantees anonymity. You call them a couple of days after you've sent in a specimen and give them a code number. They then tell you whether your specimen is positive or negative. But this test is the subject of some controversy. You see, when a doctor diagnoses gonorrhea, he is obliged by law to notify the local health authorities. This law was not meant to punish or embarrass the patient but to find all potential contacts who may either have infected or been infected by him or her. Frankly, do you think many people are likely to report themselves, provided they're able to get adequate treatment without doing so? This leaves their contacts free to keep infecting anyone else with whom they are intimate. Also, one of my patients didn't even bother going for treatment after he discovered, using this test, that he'd been infected. In his words, "If this is the kind of disease they let you test for at home, it can't be very serious."

Whatever your personal ethical position with regard to reporting, if you have any concern about gonorrhea, it's better to perform this test than to do nothing about it. If the result is positive, get yourself treated as soon as possible.

Culture Can Begin at Home

Most run-of-the-mill sore throats are usually caused by a virus, and clear up without any treatment after a few days. Strep throats, however, are bacterial infections that can lead to rheumatic fever and serious heart disease. To separate one from the other, your doctor will usually obtain a throat culture. While you are both waiting for the results, which take a couple of days, he usually begins treatment with an antibiotic just to be safe. Now, for $10, you can buy a disposable kit that will read your throat sample within four hours and indicate whether or not you have a strep throat. This can save you not only the cost of an office visit but may also spare you taking antibiotics unnecessarily for several days. Of course, if the symptoms persist, regardless of what the test reads, and especially if there is an accompanying fever, you'll need to be examined. These kits are also available to doctors, but unless they have a small laboratory on the premises, most prefer to send the specimen to an outside facility.

Identify the " 'Pause" That Depresses

Are you developing hot flushes? Are your periods becoming irregular and unpredictable as you approach the fifties? You can now detect the menopause with a dipstick in your urine. Take two samples one week apart and mail them to a laboratory. They'll tell you whether or not you are menopausal. Ask your doctor or pharmacist about this test.

Telling When You're Tense

Whether or not you respond to biofeedback and other relaxation techniques is a very individual affair. It's much like hypnotism. Some people can be put into a "suggestion trance" very easily; others can't. If you're among those who respond to these techniques, and suffer from migraines, hypertension, an irritable bowel or stress situation, you can now purchase home biofeedback equipment, which, by measuring the wide variety of physiological parameters—muscle spasm, heart rate, skin temperature—can tell you whether you are under tension and how effectively you are handling it. Inquire at a medical supply house in your own area about buying or renting such equipment.

Wrapping Up the Breast Cancer

Perhaps the most exciting new test in the wings, one which women everywhere will welcome, is the Senocrom. This is a breast-cancer detection kit that is already in use in Europe and other foreign countries. It is expected to be marketed very soon in the United States by Thermascan, Inc. The test consists of a thin, flexible foil containing liquid crystals that change color in response to temperature variation. It is wrapped around a breast for several hours and then removed. Tumor tissue produces a change in the color pattern by virtue of the increased heat it generates (presumably because the cancer cells are growing more quickly than normal tissue). I don't know how reliable this kit will turn out to be, but if it succeeds in alerting you to the possibility of underlying disease, which can then be evaluated by more conventional techniques, like the mammogram, it is still a big plus.

These are but a few of the more important ways you can now, or will in the near future be able to, test yourself at home. Other procedures available to you include lung-function tests, checking your vision for the presence of color blindness, hearing evaluations, mental and intelligence determinations, various skin patches for determining allergy and so on. Using those you need intelligently will not only save you time and money, but will also give you a better handle on whatever ails you. But remember, these aids should help you and your doctor decide *together* whether or not you have a particular disorder and how best to treat it. Test yourself by all means, but be sure to communicate the results to him—whether you like them or not.

Where Do We Go from Here?

Since I conceived the idea for this book and began writing it, several of the more exciting theories and concepts I have discussed have become the subject of big multinational studies to prove or disprove the benefits claimed. For example, with respect to diet and cancer alone, our government's National Cancer Institute is currently supporting twenty-six major studies here and abroad. Thus, thousands of vulnerables will be followed for years to see whether receiving beta-carotenes, vitamins C and E and the trace minerals, all of which I have recommended in moderation, can in fact reduce the incidence of cancer of the breast, lung, bowel and esophagus. In some projects, a low-fat diet is being given to 6,000 women who are at risk of breast cancer, to see if it is protective. The retinoids, derivatives of vitamin A, are being administered to women who have had mastectomies, to determine if these substances prevent recurrence of the cancer. There are 950,000 women now alive in the United States who have had breast cancer who will be anxiously awaiting the results of that particular trial. In Linxian province of China, whose population numbers 700,000, one new case of cancer of the esophagus is diagnosed every day. A trial of multivitamins and minerals—much higher than anything prescribed in this country—is being conducted to learn whether the incidence of this malignancy can be reduced. Some 30,000 men and women are enrolled in that study and questions about the potential of selenium as an anti-cancer substance may finally be resolved. Even wheat bran, concerning which I am so enthusiastic, is being evaluated for its impact on bowel polyps.

Some of you will be frustrated by being unable to find mention of some disease or other in which you have a particular interest or a special vulnerability. If it is missing from these pages, it is because (a) I didn't think of it (to err is human) or, more likely, (b) because it is not preventable. Common and important disorders like diabetes, for example, cannot now be prevented. Neither can Lou Gehrig's Disease, multiple sclerosis and several other major afflictions. They can be managed, even treated, but not *prevented*—and so I have not dealt with them in this volume.

Nature is the great healer. During the course of a lifetime, every one of us has brief illnesses or symptoms which clear up despite, not because of, what we do for them. Doctors refer to these attacks as "self-limiting." In most cases, we never discover what caused them in the first place. That being the case, it is very easy to attribute magical powers to any treatment upon which we have stumbled or about which we have read, which apparently "cured" the problem or prevented its recurrence—as, for example, the herbs, the mega-vitamins, the coffee enemas, the rays allegedly emitted from a variety of metal boxes and a host of other nonsensical approaches. If you are into any of them, and are convinced they are working *for you,* don't argue with success. Continue with them, by all means, but first check with your doctor to make sure it is safe for you to do so. In fact, double-check with her too about any advice I've offered in these pages. No two patients are the same and it is conceivable that what benefits the great majority of individuals may not be good for you.

As you reflect on the contents of this book, I hope you will reach, and act upon, certain inescapable conclusions. The first is that effec-tive prevention basically involves modifying your lifestyle—your habits, what you eat, drink, the work you do and where you do it, and your attitude toward life. All these things have a measurable impact not only on the major killers like arteriosclerosis and cancer, but on a host of so-called "minor" illnesses as well—illnesses which, though not immediately life-threatening, can nevertheless result in pain and suffering. It should also be clear that *you* are the major protagonist in the drama of prevention. As I stated in the opening chapter, your doctor can guide you, answer your questions, even occasionally inspire you to do the right thing while you are still well. But most physicians will not keep after you or monitor your adher-ence to a health maintenance regimen which will only be effective if it is practiced continuously over a lifetime. *The drive, the interest and the initiative must come from you.* The underlying purpose of this book is to give you that motivation, to show you not only that prevention does work, but how and why it does so. Now that you know, the rest is up to you.

Index

ABOUT THE AUTHOR

ISADORE ROSENFELD, M.D., a cardiologist, is Clinical Professor of Medicine at the New York Hospital–Cornell Medical Center. In addition to his private practice, teaching and research activities, he also appears weekly as medical consultant and commentator on the long-running, nationally syndicated television series "Hour Magazine" with Gary Collins. He is President of the New York County Medical Society, an Overseer of Cornell University Medical College and a member of the Board of Visitors of the University of California School of Medicine at Davis. He is the author of *The Complete Medical Exam* and *Second Opinion,* as well as a prolific contributor to the scientific literature. Dr. Rosenfeld practices in Manhattan and lives in nearby Westchester County, New York, with his wife, Camilla.